ATM Networks

OTHMAR KYAS

GREGAN CRAWFORD

Prentice Hall PTR
Upper Saddle River, NJ 07458
www.phptr.com

ISBN 0-1

D1504892

90000

936010

Library of Congress Cataloging-in-Publication Data

Kyas, Othmar.
    ATM networks / Othmar Kyas, Gregan Crawford.
        p. cm.
Includes index.
    ISBN 0-13-093601-4
    1. Asynchronous transfer mode. 2. Computer networks. I. Crawford,
Gregan. II. Title.
    TK5105.35 .K93 2002
    004.6'6--dc21   2002005841

Editorial/production supervision: *Jessica Balch (Pine Tree Composition, Inc.)*
Production coordinator: *Anne R. Garcia*
Composition: *Pine Tree Composition, Inc.*
Cover design director: *Jerry Votta*
Cover designer: *Talar Agasyan-Boorujy*
Art director: *Gail Cocker-Bogusz*
Interior design: *Meg Van Arsdale*
Manufacturing buyer: *Maura Zaldivar*
Executive editor: *Jill Harry*
Editorial assistant: *Sarah Hand*
Marketing manager: *Dan DePasquale*

© 2002 by Prentice Hall PTR
A Division of Pearson Education, Inc.
Upper Saddle River, NJ 07458

Prentice Hall books are widely used by corporations and government agencies
for training, marketing, and resale.

For information regarding corporate and government bulk discounts please contact:

Corporate and Government Sales (800) 382-3419 or corpsales@pearsontechgroup.com

All products or services mentioned in this book are the trademarks or service marks of their
respective companies or organizations.

Printed in the United States of America

10 9 8 7 6 5 4 3 2 1

ISBN 0-13-093601-4

Pearson Education Ltd., *London*
Pearson Education Australia Pty, Limited, *Sydney*
Pearson Education Singapore, Pte. Ltd.
Pearson Education North Asia Ltd., *Hong Kong*
Pearson Education Canada, Ltd., *Toronto*
Pearson Educación de Mexico, S.A. de C.V.
Pearson Education—Japan, *Tokyo*
Pearson Education Malaysia, Pte. Ltd.

CONTENTS

Part III ATM Networks: Design and Planning   379

Part IV　ATM Networks: Analysis and Operation　427

PREFACE

Over the past decade ATM has become one of the most widely deployed transport technologies for communication networks. With its flexible architecture it is capable of providing the broad variety of transmission properties that modern multiservice networks require. New, advanced service offerings such as third generation (3G) telephony or DSL are built on ATM, expanding its reach from communication backbones out to millions of users. ATM is the most powerful communication transport mechanism, and it is the most complex one at the same time.

This book was written to provide an in-depth understanding of all aspects of ATM, while serving as a single complete reference source. With this in mind, the reader should not expect an easy-to-read book. However, the reward for working through it will be an in-depth understanding of one of the most important and fascinating communication technologies today.

Gregan Crawford, Edinburgh
Othmar Kyas, Colorado Springs
April 2002

ATM: An Introduction

Chapter 1

DEMANDS ON TODAY'S DATA COMMUNICATIONS TECHNOLOGIES

1.1 The Evolution of Data Transmission Technologies

For decades the development of data transmission technologies has not kept pace with the explosive increase in the capabilities of individual computer systems. Processor performance and data storage capacity in PCs, for example, increased a hundredfold in the 1980s, while data speeds in wide area networks increased only tenfold over the same period. Data speeds in local area networks even remained unchanged for long intervals, mainly due to the lengthy standardization processes involved in introducing new technologies. In the mid-1990s, however, this situation began to change, as high-speed technologies such as Asynchronous Transfer Mode (ATM) and Gigabit Ethernet were finally standardized and a wide range of affordable products for use with these technologies became available.

1.1.1 Local Area Networks

The majority of the local area networks (LANs) in use today are still based on transmission principles developed in the early to mid-1980s: 10/100 Mbit/s Ethernet (IEEE 802.3), and 4 or 16 Mbit/s Token Ring (IEEE 802.5). Since a substantial increase in network bandwidth was not feasible for many years, the number of network nodes per segment had to be reduced in order to accommodate the increasing use of multimedia and network-oriented applications made possible by faster processors. In the 1980s, for example, 802.3 Ethernet networks with more than 300 stations were not unusual, whereas today the average number of stations per segment is between 10 and 20 and falling.

A new LAN standard, called Fiber Distributed Digital Interface (FDDI), was introduced at the end of the 1980s. Based on fiber optic media, FDDI technology provided a data speed of 100 Mbit/s. FDDI was the first technology that made it possible to build high-performance backbone structures, but it gained acceptance only slowly because it required expensive hardware components, such as lasers on network cards and optical fiber cabling. Furthermore, it was soon apparent that even its bandwidth of 100 Mbit/s, shared by all nodes, would not be sufficient for emerging multimedia applications; in other words, FDDI was a medium-term solution at best. Nonetheless, for lack of alternative network technologies, many backbones were converted to FDDI in the years following its introduction. This all changed once again when LAN switching, 100 Mbit/s Ethernet, and 155 Mbit/s ATM technologies became marketable, providing more flexible and economical backbone solutions than those based on FDDI. Since then, the use of FDDI has been declining, and it is rarely considered as an option when new networks are designed. At the beginning of the first decade of the third millennium, further improvements in speed with technologies such as Gigabit Ethernet and 10 Gigabit Ethernet are starting to become widely deployed.

Although ATM is often mentioned in the same context as other high-speed technologies such as Fast Ethernet, Gigabit Ethernet, and LAN switching, there is a significant difference between ATM and all other communication technologies used in local area networks. Unlike the connectionless transmission mechanisms used by other LAN topologies, ATM uses connection-oriented data communication. Before transmission starts, a signaling process sets up a channel with the required bandwidth, delay, and other characteristics. User data is sent over this channel until a command on the signaling channel ends the connection. Insufficient bandwidth is not the only limitation that makes traditional network topologies unable to handle today's multimedia applications, since the effective bandwidth can be increased by limiting the network to one station per segment, as seen in segment-switching topologies. In addition to bandwidth, the transmission of multimedia applications over networks also requires real-time behavior that simply cannot be provided by the connectionless LAN data transmission technologies of the 1980s. ATM permits unrestricted use of multimedia applications in LANs. A connection between two ATM stations is not affected by the number of other stations in the network, since each station is supplied with transmission paths of fixed bandwidth and guaranteed communication characteristics, which are set for each connection in a "traffic contract."

Similar quality of service (QoS) mechanisms have been implemented in the IP protocol family over the past years. They enable the transmission of real-time IP services such as audio and video over broadband connectionless infrastructures such as Gigabit Ethernet. This has lead to the situation that today in local area networks ATM is primarily implemented for demanding, high performance backbones with specific needs, whereas the majority of LANs are migrating toward Gigabit Ethernet as a backbone infrastructure.

1.1.2   Wide Area Networks

While the transmission capabilities of LANs have been evolving in few step functions over the past decades, the available data speeds in wide area networks (WANs) have increased steadily over the years. X.25 connections, for example, widely used in the 1970s with data speeds of 2.4 kbit/s and 4.8 kbit/s, were replaced by Frame Relay links with speeds of 1.5 Mbit/s and 45 Mbit/s in North America, and 2 Mbit/s and 34 Mbit/s elsewhere (Figure 1.1). The Integrated Services Digital Network (ISDN), introduced in the mid-1980s, permitted more efficient use of communication lines by bundling analog and digital services. Especially in Europe, ISDN became an important medium for telephony and data transmission, until in 2000 xDSL technologies started to provide even higher data rates over the same telephony infrastructure. While ISDN provides transmission capacities of between 56 kbit/s (Basic Rate ISDN, or BRI) to 2 Mbit/s (Primary Rate ISDN, or PRI), the various xDSL services deliver data speeds from 128 bit/s to 8Mbit/s.

When the ISDN specifications were developed in the early 1980s, it was assumed that bandwidths of 128 kbit/s (BRI) and 2 Mbit/s (PRI) would be sufficient for years to come. Soon after the protracted standardization process for ISDN was concluded, however, it was already apparent that the payload bandwidth of $n \times 64$ kbit/s on which ISDN is based would not meet the rapidly increasing demands placed on data communications technology. The next step had to be the development of what were termed "broadband transmission systems," with bandwidths far beyond 2 Mbit/s. In the second half of the 1980s, standardization work was begun on a broadband ISDN (B-ISDN) specification, intended to be the future universal wide area network technology. The Asynchronous Transfer Mode, or ATM, was selected by the ITU in 1988 as the

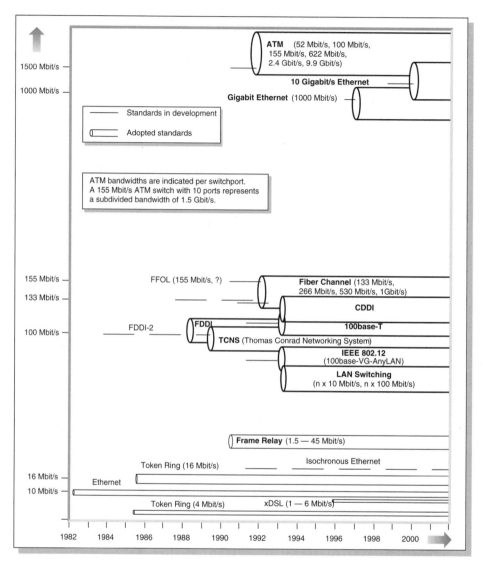

Figure 1.1
The evolution of data transmission technologies, 1980–2000.

transport mechanism for B-ISDN. Since then, major telecommunications providers around the world have been setting up and operating B-ISDN (mostly referred to as ATM) communication networks.

1.2 Contemporary Bandwidth Requirements

For decades, only alphanumeric information was stored on computers. Since the early 1990s, however, a rapid drop in the cost of mass storage media and high-speed processors has opened the door to widespread use of multimedia applications in computer systems. Today, information is increasingly stored in the form of image, video, or audio files, which take up many times the amount of space required by text files. A parallel development in the field of data communications has been the shift from text-oriented user interfaces, such as FTP or Telnet, to more advanced multimedia communications infrastructures, including the World Wide Web, video conferencing, IP telephony, and multimedia email, to name just a few examples. This has meant an increase both in the amounts of data transmitted and in the sensitivity of that data to transmission delay. To meet today's requirements, networks must have extensive bandwidth available, and use the latest transport mechanisms. Figure 1.2 shows the real-time processing capabilities required by various applications, as well as the volume of data transmitted. Classic applications such as file transfer, backups, and LAN-to-LAN connections have the lowest real-time requirements. At the high end of the scale, with regard to both the real-time capabilities required and data volume, are supercomputer networks and virtual reality applications. The four main types of user data—text, image, audio, and video files—and the demands that each of these place on networks are discussed individually below.

1.2.1 Voice Communication

When voice signals are restricted to the 4 kHz frequency bandwidth used in telephony, a data rate of 64 kbit/s is required for digital transmission. This is corroborated by Nyquist's equation, which holds that a sampling rate of 8 kHz is required to digitize all the information in a 4 kHz voice channel. Every sampled value is coded in 8 bits for a resolution of 256 signal levels. This yields a bit stream of 8000 × 8 bits per second, or 64 kbit/s. In North America this bandwidth is often reduced to 56 kbit/s, as 4 kbit/s is used to carry signaling;

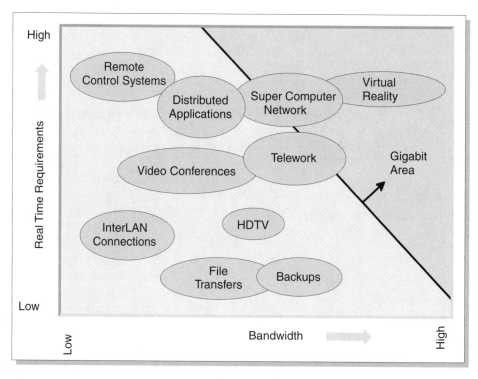

Figure 1.2
Network services: Bandwidth and real-time processing requirements.

this data rate reduction is known as "bit stealing." If compression mechanisms are used, however, the same information can be transmitted over a fraction of this bandwidth.

1.2.2 Alphanumeric Data Communication

A typical text-based application uses a 40-line screen page at 80 characters per line. As a rule, each character is coded in 8 bits, so that a screen page equals 25.6 kilobits of data. Thus it takes 2.6 seconds to transmit the content of one screen page over a 9.6 kbit/s line. Transmission of an entire page, however, is only occasionally necessary—when a new dialog mask is displayed, for example. When only screen input and output are updated, the average data speed required drops significantly, so that a rate of 2.4 to 4.8 kbit/s can be entirely adequate for interactive alphanumerical applications. Again, bandwidth requirements can be significantly reduced by using data compression.

1.2.3   LAN-to-LAN Communication

With the integration of WANs into enterprise data communication infrastructures, LAN-to-LAN communication has gained steadily in importance ("enterprise" networks are networks confined to handling the private data of a corporation or other large organization where data may have to be moved between sites often separated by long distances). The bandwidth required for a connection between two LANs can vary widely, depending both on the network load within individual segments and on intersegment traffic levels. Measurements performed on LAN-to-LAN connections have shown that network levels at peak use times can be as much as 25 times higher than during low-use periods. In most cases, however, less than 10% of LAN data traffic actually travels over LAN-to-LAN links (see Figure 1.3). Depending on the LAN topology used (100/1000 Mbit/s Ethernet, Token Ring, or FDDI), bandwidths between 1 and 10 Mbit/s are usually sufficient.

1.2.4   Bandwidth Requirements for Video Applications

The bandwidth required by today's video applications ranges from 10 Mbit/s for video to 900 Mbit/s for uncompressed, broadcast-quality high-definition television, or HDTV. Again, the volume of data actually transmitted can vary greatly depending on the optimization and compression techniques used.

Graphic Data Communication

A single screen page contains around 1 million pixels. On a color monitor, each pixel is defined by 24 bits. Thus, sending a single screen page in color entails transmitting some 24 megabits. If the data is not compressed, it takes 6 minutes to render the image over a 64 kbit/s line, or 0.15 seconds over a 155 Mbit/s line (See Figure 1.4 and Table 1.1).

Video Data Communication

Of the four kinds of data examined here, video sequences place the heaviest load on network infrastructures. Thanks to the advanced data compression techniques developed over the past few years, however, data speed requirements for transmitting video data have dropped significantly. The first international standard for transmission of compressed video data, MPEG-1, was introduced in 1992. MPEG-1 processes 25 images per second at a resolution

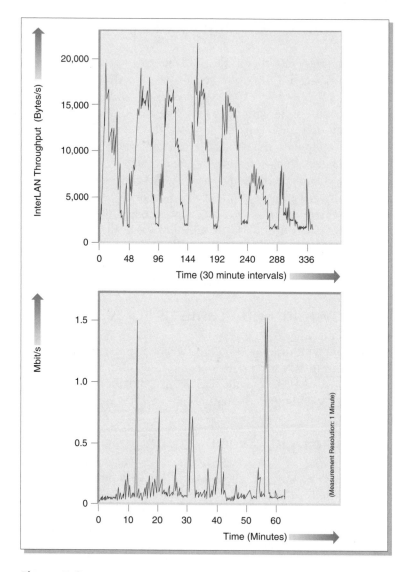

Figure 1.3
Profile of LAN-to-LAN traffic.

of 352×288 pixels. The MPEG-1 compression ratio is 26:1, resulting in a bit stream of 1.15 Mbit/s. As for audio communication, however, the bandwidth required for video conferencing increases with the number of conference participants.

At the end of 1993, the MPEG-2 standard was introduced for broadcast-quality video transmission. MPEG-2 processes 25 video images per second at

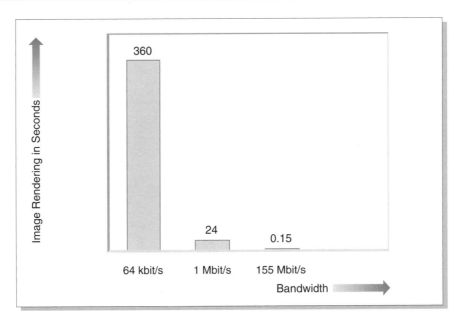

Figure 1.4
Image rendering and bandwidth.

a resolution of 720×576 pixels, which yields a level of quality equal to that of broadcast television. Transmission of MPEG-2 data requires over 4 Mbit/s, however. The high-resolution HDTV format (1000–1200 screen lines) requires 30 Mbit/s—after compression! Table 1.3 shows the average bandwidth requirements for various video applications. Depending on the screen content, however, the amount of bandwidth required can vary significantly. Video sequences that contain only slow or very little movement generate far less data than fast-changing images (Figure 1.5).

To deploy multimedia applications to new types of networks, including those employing relatively low bit rates such as wireless telephony and wireless LAN networks, the MPEG-4 standard was developed. It became an

Table 1.1   Bandwidth Requirements for Image Data

Information Service	Bandwidth	Typical Application
Image transmission	<1 Mbit/s	Monochrome images
	1–10 Mbit/s	Color images
	10–100 Mbit/s	High-resolution color images

Table 1.2   Comparison of Bandwidths

User Interface	Resolution	Bandwidth (1 channel, half duplex)	Bandwidth (Video Conference 4 users)
Video (MPEG-1 compressed	352 x 288	1.15 Mbit/s	13.8 Mbit/s
Video (MPEG-2 compressed)	720 x 576	4 Mbit/s	48 Mbit/s
Video (MPEG-3 compressed) (HDTV)	1920 x 1080	20 Mbit/s	240 Mbit/s
Video (MPEG-4 compressed) (Videophone)	176 x 144	0.064 Mbit/s	0.768 Mbit/s
ASCII-based interfaces	40 x 80 characters	0.0096–0.0144 Mbit/s	--------
Graphical user interfaces in LAN environments	800 x 600	* Peak traffic: up to 4 Mbit/s Average traffic: 5–50 kbit/s	
* Loading of office applications such as Word or Excel; duration of traffic peak: app. 5 seconds			

international standard in the year 2000 and for the first time represents the various aural, visual, and audiovisual components of multimedia applications as separate units, called media objects. The data streams associated with these media objects can be multiplexed and transported over network channels providing QoS (Quality of Service) appropriate for the nature of the specific media object. This allows, for example, the transportation of the same MPEG-4 file as video and audio objects across high bandwidth networks, as still image and audio objects across low bandwidth networks.

Table 1.3   Bandwidth Requirements for Video Conferencing

Service	Bandwidth	Application
Video/Multimedia conferences	< 1 Mbit/s	Talking heads
	1–10 Mbit/s	Small screen, high quality
	10–100 Mbit/s	Large screen, high quality

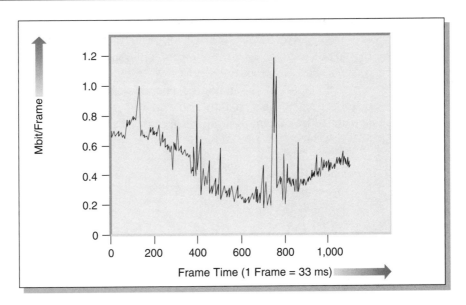

Figure 1.5
Profile of data traffic generated by moving images.

1.2.5   End-to-End Delay

Another important communication parameter for multimedia applications is the end-to-end delay. ITU studies have shown that, for transmission of lower-quality conversational voice services, the maximum acceptable network delay is 150 ms. For real-time graphic visualization systems, the upper limit is 30 ms.

Table 1.4   Transfer Delay and Audio Transmission Quality

Delay per Direction	Impact on Communication
> 600 ms	No communication possible.
600 ms	No continous communication possible.
250 ms	Delay perceptible— communciation style needs to be adapted.
100 ms	No delay perceptible if listener occurs via the network only, and not in parallel direct.
50 ms	No delay perceptible.

In general, for high-quality multimedia services the delay should not exceed 100 ms in WANs, or 30 ms in LANs. In LAN workgroups, propagation delay should be limited to 10 ms to allow for additional latency in intersegment components such as routers and bridges.

As discussed in the following chapters, ATM is a technology that can provide both the high bandwidth and the real-time processing capabilities demanded by current multimedia applications.

Chapter 2

COMMUNICATION TECHNOLOGIES
FOR HIGH-SPEED NETWORKS

This chapter contains a brief summary of the technologies available for building local and wide area high-speed networks. It will help to understand ATM as it relates to the various technologies it interfaces with in today's complex heterogenous networking environments. Most of these technologies complement rather than compete with ATM, since they serve as local backbones to bundle the data traffic of departmental networks (100/1000 Mbit/s Ethernet, switched LANs) or as tributaries connecting applications with lower bandwidth requirements to ATM (Frame Relay, ISDN, xDSL). The various communication techniques are described here with their basic communication mechanisms and typical applications.

2.1 Broadband Communication Systems and High-Speed Networks

Due to the historically separate development and architecture of WANs and LANs, high-speed networks are defined differently in the two contexts. In local area networking, "high speed" generally refers to network topologies with data

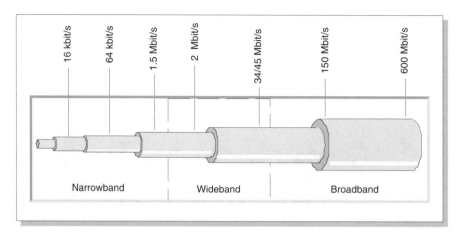

Figure 2.1
Definitions: narrowband, wideband, broadband.

throughput exceeding the Token Ring rate of 16 Mbit/s. Thus typical high-speed LAN technologies include 100 Mbit/s Ethernet, Gigabit Ethernet, ATM, and FDDI. In wide area networking, the term "broadband network" is generally preferred to "high speed network." Furthermore, because communication bandwidth has always been lower in WAN media than in LANs, the WAN term "broadband" is applied at significantly lower data rates than the LAN term "high-speed." According to an ITU definition, the term "broadband applications" should be used to refer to all applications that require data communication speeds higher than the primary rate. The primary rate is the first level of a multiplexing hierarchy devised in the early 1970s for the efficient transport of 64 kbit/s voice channels. After the analog voice signals have been converted into digital 64-kbit/s data streams, these are bundled into a primary multiplex frame of 24 channels in North America or 32 channels in Europe. This yields a total data rate of 1.544 or 2.048 Mbit/s, called the "primary rate." Conversely, systems with data rates below the primary rate are called narrowband systems. The lower end of the broadband range, between 2 Mbit/s and 45 Mbit/s, is sometimes referred to as wideband. Figure 2.1 illustrates these bandwidth ranges.

2.2 Leased Lines

Traditionally, data communication structures make use of dedicated data lines, or "leased lines." The network operator provides the subscriber with a data line that guarantees a given continuous bandwidth (such as 384 kbit/s,

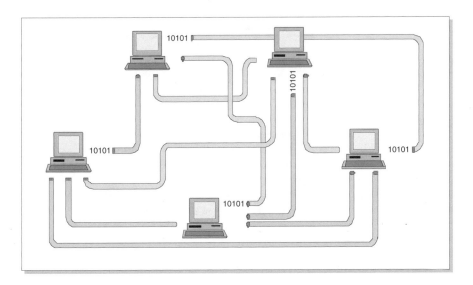

Figure 2.2
Network based on leased lines.

2 Mbit/s, or 34 Mbit/s) between two points (see Figure 2.2). Originally, leased lines were used only for point-to-point communication. Nowadays, however, routers are often used to connect several sites with one another over a network of leased lines. Even so, the fundamental drawback of leased lines is that data routing is restricted and expensive. For example, 10 leased lines are necessary to connect just five sites to one another. Furthermore, it is often impossible to distribute the data load over the various lines automatically, or even manually. Rapid bandwidth adjustments, as performed in Frame Relay, are not possible.

2.3 ISDN: The Integrated Services Digital Network

The Integrated Services Digital Network, or ISDN, was the first communications infrastructure designed to carry both voice and data. The transmission technique is based on 64-kbit/s user channels (B channels) and separate signaling channels (D channels). There are two types of network access in ISDN, each with different bandwidth capacities: basic rate access provides a total data rate of 144 kbit/s over two 64 kbit/s B channels and one 16 kbit/s D channel, that is, a maximum user data rate of 128 kbit/s; primary rate access

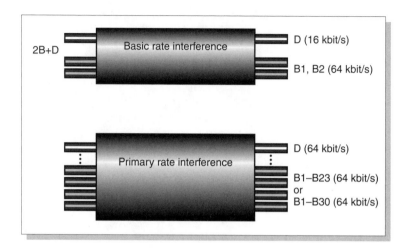

Figure 2.3
Basic rate and primary rate ISDN access.

provides total data speeds of 1536 kbit/s in North America (23 B channels and one 64 kbit/s D channel) or 1984 kbit/s in Europe (30 B channels and one 64 kbit/s D channel), that is, a maximum user data rate of 1472 kbit/s or 1920 kbit/s, respectively (see Figure 2.3).

The major drawbacks of ISDN from today's standpoint are the limitation of the data speed to a maximum of 1536 or 1984 kbit/s, which cannot be incrementally expanded, and the synchronous structure of the transmission channels, which does not permit dynamic allocation of bandwidth within the network. The latter characteristic was one of the reasons for the development of Frame Relay, a dedicated data transmission service that dynamically adjusts the bandwidth in use for more efficient data transfer. On the other hand, however, ISDN has the advantage of being an established international standard, providing a uniform digital interface for voice and data transmission worldwide.

2.4   Frame Relay

Frame Relay is a communication technique for WAN links that was originally developed in the early 1990s as a tributary service for ISDN. Frame Relay multiplexes data packets from a number of sources to a number of destinations over one line, allocating bandwidth on a statistical basis (see Figure 2.4). The throughput of Frame Relay is commonly between 56 kbit/s and 45 Mbit/s, though 155 Mbit/s has also been specified. Like X.25 and ISDN, Frame Relay is a connection-oriented communication technique. This means that a virtual connection must be defined before data communication can take place. The signaling necessary to set up the connection is usually transported over the user data channel itself, which is known as in-band signaling. The alternative to in-band signaling is to provide dedicated channels for signaling, like the ISDN D channel.

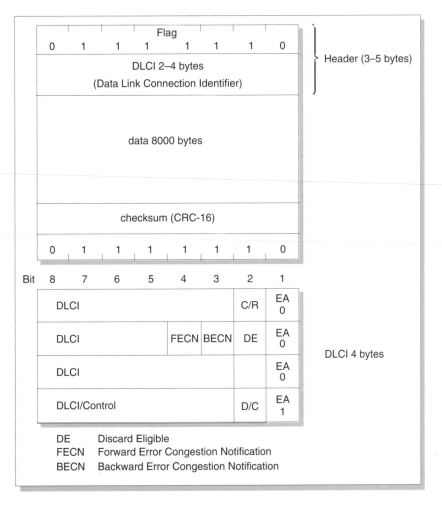

Figure 2.4
Structure of the Frame Relay data packet.

The essential difference between Frame Relay and the older X.25 consists in the error correction mechanisms. X.25 was developed many years ago to transport data over analog telephone lines of relatively poor quality. For this reason, extensive error correction mechanisms and algorithms for retransmitting lost data packets had to be implemented. With the low error rates of today's WAN links, this is no longer necessary. Frame Relay therefore provides no retransmission of lost or damaged data packets. The correction of communication errors is left to the higher-layer application protocols. The Frame Relay protocol only tests for the validity of the addresses and the occurrence of bit errors.

The structure of a Frame Relay data packet is simple: between the beginning and ending flags of the frame are a header field of 2 to 4 bytes—the Data Link Connection Identifier, or DLCI, field—and the Information field, followed by a checksum for bit error detection. Up to 8 kilobytes of user data can be transported in the Information field. The DLCI is a unique numerical value assigned to each virtual channel for identification.

Due to the lower protocol overhead, Frame Relay links can transport up to 30% more user data than X.25 connections with the same bandwidth. In the past few years, Frame Relay has therefore become the preferred communication protocol in wide area networking. The only weakness of Frame Relay is that it is not suitable for multimedia applications. When data and voice connections are sent by Frame Relay simultaneously, for example, the voice signal is received with noticeable jitter. This is because both short and very long data packets can occur, and thus the probability of transfer delay variation is quite high. However, Frame Relay is extraordinarily well suited as a transport service for data applications with bandwidth from 64 kbit/s to 45 Mbit/s due to the high payload of up to 8000 bytes per data packet.

2.5 xDSL: Digital Subscriber Lines

In order to achieve adequate digital data rates for today's application requirements over the existing telephone cabling infrastructure, a number of standards were developed in the 1990s that are known collectively as xDSL. Until then, modem data communications over telephone lines used only the 3 kHz analog telephony band, although most of the telephone lines in place today are able to carry frequencies of up to one MHz. The xDSL technologies take advantage of this fact, and obtain throughput of up to 50 Mbit/s (see Figure 2.5).

DSL technology originated after ISDN had first produced digital data communication over the analog telephone network's cable plant. The 144 kbit/s

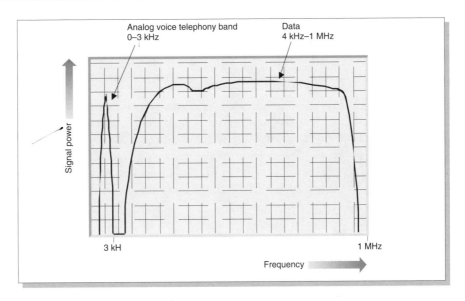

Figure 2.5
Frequency bands used by analog telephony and ADSL.

data rates obtained (two B channels and one D channel) are no longer sufficient today, however, to transport modern multimedia applications. Five new communications standards have been developed for different application scenarios: ADSL, HDSL, RADSL, SDSL, and VDSL. These are defined below and in Table 2.1.

- ADSL (Asymmetric Digital Subscriber Line) provides an interface with unequal transmitting and receiving bandwidths. The uplink bandwidth can be from 64 kbit/s to 384 kbit/s, and the downlink bandwidth from 1.544 Mbit/s to 6 Mbit/s. ADSL is mainly used for high-speed access to the Internet, since Web surfing calls for high-downlink but low-uplink bandwidth.

- HDSL (High-Speed Digital Subscriber Line) is a symmetrical interface with throughput of 128 kbit/s to 1.544 Mbit/s in both directions. Potential applications include video conferencing or Web server connections.

- RADSL (Rate-Adaptive Digital Subscriber Line) is a variation on ADSL that is able to vary the available bandwidth depending on the line quality. The uplink rates are up to 1.544 Mbit/s, downlink bandwidth can be as high as 6.1 Mbit/s.

- SDSL (Symmetrical Digital Subscriber Line) is a single-pair version of HDSL.

Table 2.1   xDSL Technologies and Standards

	ADSL	HDSL	RADSL	VDSL	SDSL	ISDN (S_0)
Download Bitrate	1.544 Mbit/s– 6 Mbit/s	128 kbit/s– 1.544 Mbit/s	< 6.1 Mbit/s	< 51 Mbit/s	128 kbit/s– 1.544 Mbit/s	160 kbit/s
Upload Bitrate	64 kbit/s– 384 kbit/s	128 kbit/s– 1.544 Mbit/s	< 1.544 Mbit/s	1.6 Mbit/s– 2.3 Mbit/s	128 kbit/s– 1.544 Mbit/s	160 kbit/s
Encoding	CAP, DMT	CAP, 2B1Q	DMT	CAP	CAP	2B1Q
Standard	ANSI T1.413					ITU I.120 – I.451

- VDSL (Very High-Speed Digital Subscriber Line) provides uplink rates from 1.6 Mbit/s to 2.3 Mbit/s and downlink rates of up to 51 Mbit/s.

The xDSL technologies achieve their high data rates by using the full physical transmission bandwidth of 1 MHz in conjunction with efficient encoding schemes such as CAP and DMT. ISDN, an older standard, uses the simpler multi-level code 2B1Q (two binary, one quaternary), in which each pair of bits is encoded as one of the four signal levels: −3, −1, +1, +3. By contrast, xDSL uses the two encoding techniques that come closest to the theoretical maximum line capacity determined by the Shannon limit: carrierless amplitude/phase (CAP) modulation and discrete multitone (DMT) modulation. CAP is based on the same principle as QAM, but generates the phase/amplitude-modulated signals not by means of mixed sine and cosine carriers, but by using two digital band pass filters whose frequency response differs by $\pi/2$. DMT, however, divides the available frequency band into n subcarriers, and transmits bits over each channel in the form of phase/amplitude-modulated signal tones. In this way it works as n parallel QAM systems, with each QAM system using the carrier frequency of one of the DMT subchannels.

The transport mechanism used for transmitting user applications across xDSL lines is ATM. With the explosive growth of xDSL services, ATM has become a key technology in access networks as well.

2.6   SONET/SDH: The Synchronous Digital Hierarchy

Back in the late 1970s, Bellcore (now Telecordia) saw the need to replace the Plesiochronous (near-synchronous) Digital Hierarchy (PDH) in the North American Bell System (as it was then known) with a new synchronous network, so it started work on what we now know as SONET, the Synchronous Optical NETwork. PDH networks had evolved in a rather ad hoc manner and it was time to improve on this. What was needed was a transmission standard that allowed higher rate transmission, properly planned network management facilities and, most importantly, a means to time lock the digital channels being carried so that individual lower rate channels could be accessed directly without the need to break down the PDH signal by hierarchy level, taking into account the justification (stuffing) that had occurred at each level during signal construction; SONET would be able to provide all this. SONET technologies were adopted by the ITU in 1988 as an international standard for wide area data communications under the name Synchronous Digital Hierarchy (SDH). When ATM was chosen as the transfer mechanism for the ITU-T's Broadband ISDN project, SDH/SONET frames became the transmission vehicle of choice for ATM cell streams. This coupling of ATM and SDH/SONET was still widespread when, some years later, ATM began to be used in local area networks. This is how SDH/SONET, originally developed for wide area networks, also came to be used in LANs as well.

2.7 DQDB-Based MANs (Metropolitan Area Networks): CBDS/SMDS

To supply high-density business areas with a network infrastructure that combines high communication bandwidth with low cost, a standard for metropolitan area networks (MANs) was defined in the late 1980s. After a number of MANs were successfully built and operated during the 1990s, however, the rapid spread of ATM in both wide area and local area networking is putting an end to the MAN era.

Metropolitan area networks are usually based on the Distributed Queue Dual Bus (DQDB) communication technique, specified for data rates of 34 Mbit/s and 45 Mbit/s. The European implementation of DQDB is known as CBDS (Connectionless Broadband Data Service), while the North American variant is called SMDS (Switched Multimegabit Data Service). The differences between the two variants are only minor, however. Table 2.2 compares the corresponding functional elements of SMDS and CBDS.

The DQDB technique used in CBDS and SMDS MANs is the same. The data is transported in a 125-μs frame containing multiple slots for data cells of 53 bytes (48 bytes of user information and a 5-byte header). Each frame

Table 2.2 Metropolitan Area Networks: SMDS and CBDS

Bellcore-TA-TSV-001061, 001062, 000773, 001060	ETSI-300 211 Metropolitan Area Network Principles and Architecture
SMDS (Swiched Multimegabit Data Service)	CBDS (Connectionless Broadband Data Service)
SIP_L3 (SMDS Interface Protocol Layer 3)	IMPDU
SIP_L2	SM-PDU
SIP_L1	DQDB PHY

consists of a header, n cells, and padding bits if necessary; Figure 2.6 shows the arrangement. The number of slots contained in such a frame depends on the bit rate of the MAN. At a data rate of 34.368 Mbit/s, a 125-μs frame is 4296 bits (or 537 octets) long, and can thus transport ten 53-byte cells.

The data format used in DQDB MANs has the same length and general structure as that used in ATM. All cells are 53 bytes long and consist of a 5-byte header and a 48-byte information field. Figure 2.7 shows a comparison of the DQDB and ATM cell headers.

With the deployment of new technologies suited for metropolitan area networks such as ATM, PoS (Packet over SONET/SDH), and 10 Gigabit Ethernet, DQDB based MANs lost importance and are about to disappear from the fast-changing landscape of data and telecommunications.

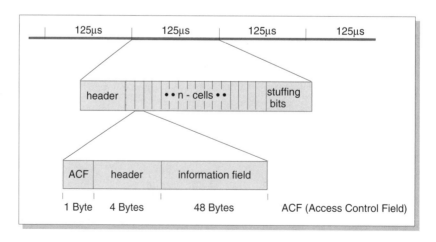

Figure 2.6
Frame and cell format in SMDS/CBDS MANs.

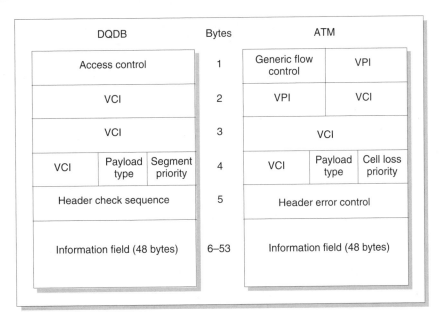

DQDB			Bytes	ATM		
Access control			1	Generic flow control		VPI
VCI			2	VPI		VCI
VCI			3	VCI		
VCI	Payload type	Segment priority	4	VCI	Payload type	Cell loss priority
Header check sequence			5	Header error control		
Information field (48 bytes)			6–53	Information field (48 bytes)		

Figure 2.7
DQDB and ATM cells in comparison.

2.8   Fiber Channel

Fiber Channel was originally developed as a technology for high-speed communication between computer systems and peripheral devices, as the enormous data volumes that need to be transported between servers and disk arrays began to exceed the capacity of conventional I/O interfaces such as SCSI. Fiber Channel eliminates this bottleneck, attaining throughput rates from 133 Mbit/s to 1 Gbit/s. Since the development of Fiber Channel switches, Fiber Channel technology can also be used to set up whole networks. Due to its 2-kilobyte frame length, Fiber Channel is especially suitable for transporting high data volumes without real-time sensitivity. As a universal transport system that can also carry multimedia applications, however, Fiber Channel is not appropriate. Today Fiber Channel is mainly used for connecting mass storage systems to server clusters forming so-called storage area networks (SANs), and for networking computer systems that carry out bandwidth-intensive applications such as telemedicine or 3D CAD.

2.9 High-Speed LANs

In local area networks, all technologies that exceed the throughput rates of the traditional network topologies of 10Mbit/s Ethernet and 4/16Mbit/s Token Ring are considered high-speed LANs. Today these include 100 Mbit/s Ethernet, Gigabit Ethernet, FDDI, and ATM.

2.9.1 FDDI

FDDI (Fiber Distributed Digital Interface) was developed in the late 1980s, and is based on a dual ring topology and a token-passing mechanism. FDDI was the first topology to permit data speeds of 100 Mbit/s in local area networks. At first restricted to fiber optic media, FDDI was primarily used as a LAN backbone structure to connect several Ethernet or Token Ring networks to one another. In 1994, the FDDI standard was extended to define communication over shielded twisted pair (STP) and Cat. 5 unshielded twisted-pair (UTP-5) copper cable (CDDI). In order to support the operation of at least some multimedia applications over FDDI networks, FDDI Version 2 included some limited real-time capabilities. In addition to the shared bandwidth available to all stations, 64-kbit/s data channels were defined, which are reserved for isochronous applications such as video or audio. The transfer delay over these dedicated data channels is a constant 125 µs. The FDDI-2 specification never reached widespread use, however. With the ongoing deployment of Gigabit Ethernet and ATM, FDDI networks are increasingly being phased out and replaced by these higher performance, scalable network infrastructures.

2.9.2 Ethernet

Ethernet, the classic LAN topology, is still the most popular in local area networks. Originally designed for data speeds of only 10 Mbit/s, Ethernet exists today in three widely used versions: the original 10 Mbit/s Ethernet (IEEE 802.3); Fast Ethernet, transmitting at 100 Mbit/s (IEEE 802.3u); and Gigabit Ethernet, with a throughput of 1000 Mbit/s (IEEE 802.3z).

Ethernet's half-duplex transmission technique uses the nondeterministic CSMA/CD algorithm to control access to the LAN medium. In half-duplex transmission technologies, it is not possible to transmit and receive data at the same time. When one network node is transmitting, all other nodes in the segment must be in "receive" mode. Before attempting to transmit, a station must "listen" to see if any other station is transmitting. If two Ethernet stations start to transmit simultaneously, their data packets collide and are destroyed—this is detected by each station, as what they "hear" is not what they transmitted. After a collision, each node involved must pause for a random delay period before starting the next transmission attempt. The probability of collisions increases with the number of active nodes in a segment. Another important factor determining the likelihood of collisions is the length of the network segment: the greater the distance between two nodes in a network segment, the greater the so-called slot time, which is the critical parameter of the CSMA/CD algorithm. Slot time is defined as twice the time it takes a signal to travel between the two nodes that are farthest apart in an Ethernet segment, and is therefore the longest time it can take for a transmitting node to detect the occurrence of a collision.

In 10 Mbit/s Ethernet networks, a choice must be made between linear bus topologies using coaxial cables and star-shaped topologies using twisted-pair cabling with multiport repeaters (also known as hubs). In the high-speed Fast Ethernet and Gigabit Ethernet variants, however, linear bus topologies are no longer an option. High-speed Ethernet networks require star topologies of high-performance twisted-pair cabling. To further increase the efficiency of Ethernet networks, segments that carry high data loads are increasingly designed using LAN switches instead of hubs. These Ethernet switches route all incoming packets directly to their destination ports, rather than broadcasting them to all ports as passive hubs do. This means that adjacent segments are not unnecessarily burdened with traffic addressed to stations not present. Aside from the frame format, however, this method of packet transmission has little in common with the original Ethernet transmission mechanisms. Both the broadcast and the CSMA/CD transmission algorithms have been abandoned in favor of the more efficient switching method.

The third variant, alongside hub and switch-based Ethernet topologies, is full-duplex Ethernet. It is specifically designed for high-speed point-to-point server connections. Each full-duplex node is equipped with a full-duplex Ethernet interface, so that transmission and reception can take place at the same time. This doubles the effective transmission bandwidth to 20 Mbit/s, 200 Mbit/s, or 2 Gbit/s. When full-duplex nodes are connected by full-duplex switches, complete full-duplex Ethernet segments can be built.

2.9.3   LAN Switching

LAN switches connect network segments or nodes and use a direct forwarding technique for data transmission. The LAN switch forwards each incoming frame directly to the switch port that is connected to the destination device. This can help ease congestion in network traffic, since multiple ports on a given LAN switch can operate simultaneously (as long as the transmission paths involved do not overlap). The high-performance forwarding hardware that makes this multiple parallel forwarding possible comprises the main difference between a LAN switch and a router or multiport bridge. The way in which frames are forwarded by the LAN switch can be configured individually for each switch port. Thus any port on a given LAN switch may act as a repeater, a bridge, or a router.

LAN switches can be deployed in all traditional LAN topologies, including 10/100/1000 Mbit/s Ethernet, 4/16 Mbit/s Token Ring, and FDDI. LAN switches generally use one of two techniques for forwarding data packets: "cut-through" or "store-and-forward." When the cut-through technique is employed, the switch makes the forwarding decision for each incoming frame as soon as it has received the first 6 bytes (which contain the destination address). The benefit of this technique is that the switch can forward frames at a high rate; latency is reduced to around 40 μs. The drawback is that the switch begins forwarding the data packet before it can determine whether there are errors in the frame, which could result in the propagation of defective frames.

With the store-and-forward technique, which is increasingly used in state-of-the-art switches, the switch does not make the forwarding decision until it has received the entire frame. This has the advantage that defective frames are not propagated. The drawback is greater latency that is dependent on the frame size. The latency of a 1000-byte data packet in a 10base-T network, for example, is over 800 μs. If the transmission path leads through multiple store-and-forward switch ports, the transmission delays could be significant, and higher-layer timers might time out. The search for a solution to this problem has led to the development of "fragment-free" cut-through forwarding. In this method, the forwarding decision is not made until the first 64 bytes of a packet have been received. This has the advantage of eliminating the majority of defective packets, because the most common errors (including runts) can be detected within the first 64 bytes. At the same time, the latency involved is not as long as in store-and-forward switching. Many of the LAN switches available today also offer an "adaptive forwarding" feature, which enables each switch port to change between the store-and-forward and cut-through techniques based primarily on the numbers of runts and defective packets received at that port (see Figure 2.8).

2.10   B-ISDN and ATM

B-ISDN is the architecture developed in the late 1980s for a modern, international, high-speed wide area network that is able not only to take on the functions of currently existing voice, data, and television networks, but also to

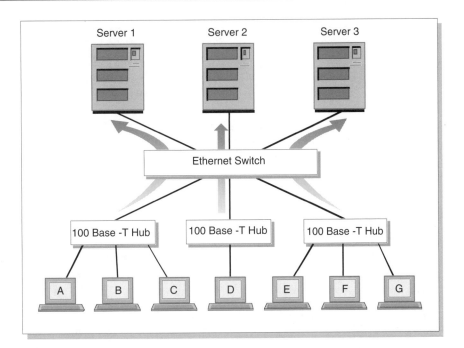

Figure 2.8
The principle of LAN switching systems.

provide sufficient capacity for the implementation of future communication technologies. The standardization process for this universal network, named by the ITU as B-ISDN (for Broadband Integrated Services Digital Network), was begun by the ITU in 1990. The data transport mechanism for the various services consists of ATM cells embedded in SDH/SONET frames. Following a great number of large-scale pilot tests, wide area networks on the B-ISDN model have been available as public data services since the mid-1990s.

2.10.1 ATM: Asynchronous Transfer Mode

ATM belongs to the cell relay family of data communications systems. Unlike packet-switched systems such as X.25, in which frames of variable length are multiplexed over a line interface, cell relay uses frames of fixed length, that is, cells. ATM is the specific implementation of cell relay that was selected for the B-ISDN standard. Thus ATM is, among other things, part of the ITU specification for B-ISDN.

ATM has since progressed from its use in the B-ISDN architecture to become a key technology in local area networking. In the B-ISDN model for wide area networks, the Synchronous Digital Hierarchy forms the physical layer for ATM, controlling the highly complex wide area switching. Because the full features of SDH/SONET are not required in local area networks, the use of the complex transmission frame is actually unnecessary. Consequently, specifications for "pure" frameless ATM have also been developed. In this variant, ATM cells are transported directly, without being embedded in a larger frame. The ITU-T has specified frameless interfaces for 155 Mbit/s and 622 Mbit/s in I.432, but these have not been adopted by the market. Another frameless interface, developed by the ATM Forum and known as ATM25, has had a little more success (discussed later in the book). ATM today is transported in SDH frames in both WANs and sometimes in LANs, although ATM is gradually being pushed out of LANs by the arrival of Gigabit Ethernet. Differences between local and wide area networks arise in operation due to the different ATM protocols for connection setup and clear-down, and to the integration of different LAN or WAN services.

2.10.2   The ATM Principle

Since the early 1980s, the field of data communications has been divided into two separate topics with little in common: local area and wide area networking. For technical reasons, data transport methods have been fundamentally different in these two areas. In wide area networks, data communication has been connection oriented: before the first bit of user data is transmitted, a signaling process takes place in which a dedicated connection to a given remote station is set up. Local area networks, on the other hand, use "connectionless" broadcast transmissions: every data packet is sent out over a medium shared among all stations without waiting for acknowledgment. It is the receiver's job to detect packets in the data stream that have its address as the destination, and process them.

Asynchronous Transfer Mode (ATM) was originally conceived for wide area data communication, but was soon adapted for local area networks because it offered, at that time, the highest data transfer rate (remember, even 100 Mbit/s Ethernet was not yet around back then). ATM creates a unified system that does away with the historical distinction between local and wide area data communication techniques (see Figure 2.9). In both ATM LANs and ATM WANs, data is transported by means of switches, according to principles that had been customary only in wide area communications, such as telephony. Every ATM end system is connected to a dedicated switch port. Every data

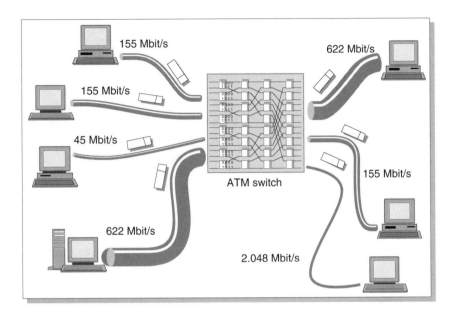

Figure 2.9
The ATM principle.

packet, or "cell," that is addressed to a given station is delivered by the ATM switch to the corresponding switch port. This means that all nodes' data packets no longer travel over the same shared broadcast medium. Pick-up and delivery of cells (data packets) is managed entirely by the ATM switch. The key advantage that results from this technique is that every station connected to an ATM switch is guaranteed a certain bandwidth on its port, regardless of how many other nodes are connected. This is possible because the switch's internal data throughput is many times higher than the bandwidth of any switch port. In conventional LANs, the average bandwidth available to any node is inversely proportional to the total number of nodes that are active. Furthermore, the switching principle is combined in ATM networks with connection-oriented data transmission. The traffic parameters necessary for a given service can be negotiated during the signaling or provisioning procedure required for every connection. For example, an end system may request a transmission path to a destination with a certain bandwidth and a certain maximum transmission delay. If the switches along the transmission route have the capacity necessary to grant the requested connection, then these communication parameters are guaranteed for the duration of the connection and appropriate network resources are reserved.

To transport the actual data, ATM uses fixed-length data packets—cells—of 53 bytes. Cells can be processed by switching equipment much more efficiently than variable-length data packets. Most important, the fixed length permits the use of large-scale parallelism in ATM switch architecture. Because all cells have the same length, all cells arriving at the input ports of an ATM switch at a given time can be forwarded simultaneously to the appropriate output ports. Due to its particular architecture and the resulting communication characteristics, ATM is the only standardized communications technology that is able to transport both multimedia applications and conventional LAN and WAN services on a large scale, efficiently and without restrictions.

Chapter 3

ATM: TECHNOLOGY FOR CONVERGED, QoS-BASED NETWORKS

Before entering upon a detailed discussion of the various aspects of ATM, this chapter describes why ATM technology is fundamentally different compared to traditional LAN and WAN data communication techniques.

3.1   In Search of New Technologies

The rapid spread of high-speed networks is due, as mentioned above, to the continuously increasing bandwidth demands of a steadily growing number of networked users. In the 1970s, networks were dominated by terminal–host topologies. Each terminal was connected to a central host computer by its own data cable, and was used only for the ASCII-based input and output of applications running on the host. The resulting bandwidth demand over the data cables was accordingly low.

Bandwidth requirements jumped with the introduction of LANs to interconnect personal computers beginning in the early 1980s. CPU performance and data storage, which until then had been concentrated in powerful mainframe hosts, were now distributed over the local area network. Moreover, the introduction of graphical user interfaces such as Microsoft Windows and the X Window system in 1985 also increased network loads dramatically. In the latter half of the 1990s, the demand for communication bandwidth jumped once again due to three parallel trends: the explosive spread of the World Wide Web in corporate networks, commercial use of the Internet, and continually increasing computer performance (Figure 3.1).

Because for more than a decade the throughput of the traditional network technologies, Ethernet and Token Ring, did not increase (remaining at 16 Mb/s, and 4 Mb/s, respectively), higher network loads required successive reductions in the only variable parameter—the number of users per network segment. However, when the bandwidth demand of a single station is on the order of several Mbit/s, then even this strategy was bound to fail, since the number of nodes per segment cannot be reduced to less than one (see Figure 3.2).

High-speed LAN technologies such as LAN switching, 100 Mbit/s Ethernet, and Gigabit Ethernet can meet such growing bandwidth demands to a certain extent. The current explosion in IP telephony and multimedia applications, however, drive the capabilities of these technologies to their limits.

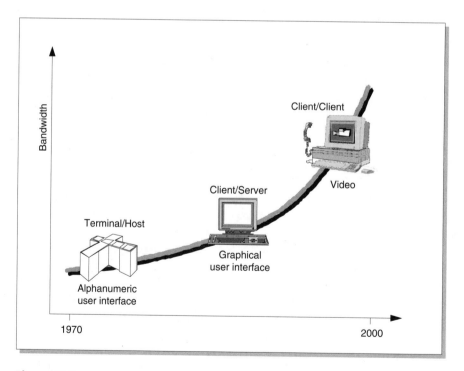

Figure 3.1
The growth of bandwidth demands.

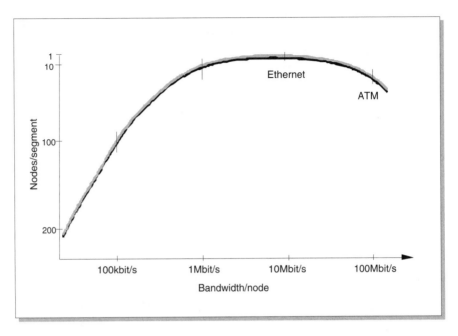

Figure 3.2
Segment size and bandwidth per network node.

As we shall see in the following section, they are unable to guarantee the necessary real-time characteristics.

3.2 The Limitations of Ethernet Networks

We discuss now in more detail what we outlined about Ethernet in the last chapter. The communication technique used in Ethernet networks, as with the token-passing technique of Token Ring, is what is known as a half-duplex technique. The individual stations are granted permission to transmit based on the nondeterministic CSMA/CD technique. Half-duplex means that a station cannot transmit and receive data simultaneously. When one station is transmitting, all other stations must be in receive mode. If two or more stations transmit simultaneously, the transmitted packets collide and are destroyed. After a collision, each station involved must wait for a certain time, determined randomly, before attempting to transmit again.

The probability of collisions increases with the number of users. In addition to the number of users, however, the length of the network segment concerned is also of critical importance. As length increases, the key parameter of the CSMA/CD algorithm—the slot time—also increases. The slot time is twice the signal delay between the two stations farthest apart, and represents the time a station requires in the worst case to detect that the current transmission has suffered a collision (see Figure 3.3).

The number of active network nodes and the segment length are thus the essential parameters that limit the capacity of Ethernet networks. When network loads are low, the CSMA/CD algorithm works extraordinarily well. When the network load reaches 40%–50% with more than 10 users, however, the effective utilization of the available 10/100 Mbit/s bandwidth decreases rapidly. This can also be demonstrated theoretically. Figure 3.4 illustrates the calculated efficiency of Ethernet for various packet lengths, assuming that the probability of a station transmitting is $1/k$ for k network nodes. A detailed mathematical analysis of the CSMA/CD algorithm can be found in O'Reilly's *Performance Analysis of Local Computer Networks*.

Finally, the chart in Figure 3.4 illustrates the third key parameter for the efficiency of networks based on CSMA/CD access control mechanisms: the frame length. The shorter the frames transmitted, the lower the performance of Ethernet, and the poorer the utilization of the theoretical communication bandwidth of 10 Mbit/s. It becomes clear that Ethernet could hardly be less appropriate for the transportation of multimedia applications. To transport analog signals, many short frames are better than few long ones. A common

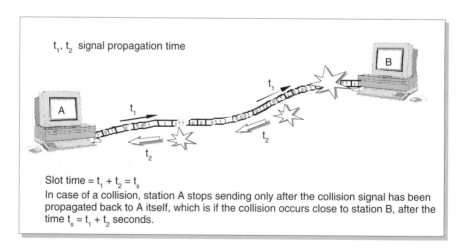

t_1, t_2 signal propagation time

B

t_1

A

t_1

t_2

t_2

Slot time = $t_1 + t_2 = t_s$
In case of a collision, station A stops sending only after the collision signal has been propagated back to A itself, which is if the collision occurs close to station B, after the time $t_s = t_1 + t_2$ seconds.

Figure 3.3
The limitations of Ethernet: slottime and collisions.

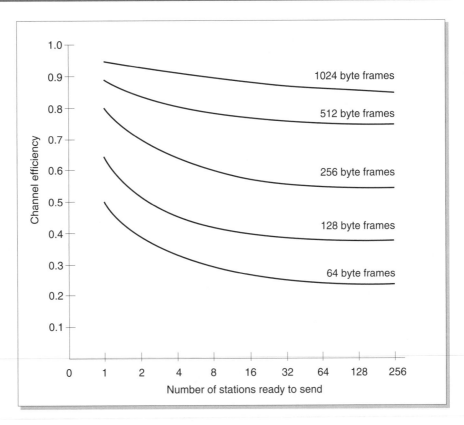

Figure 3.4
Efficiency of 802.3 Ethernet networks.

example is the communication of analog voice information sampled at a rate of 8 kHz. Every sampled value is coded in 8 bits, yielding a bit stream of 64 kbit/s; one sample is generated every 125 μs. If 8-bit samples generated at this rate were assembled into 64-byte frames, it would take 8 ms to fill each frame before it could be launched. As frames get bigger to improve efficiency, the assembly time gets longer, adding undesirable (and unavoidable) delay to the process; this delay is exacerbated if voice data compression is used—for example, 8-fold compression to 8 kb/s would mean an assembly time, and therefore delay, of 64 ms. The frame must therefore be transmitted before it can be filled up with sample values if the maximum permissible transfer delay is to be observed, so that only a fraction of each frame can be used to carry voice data (Figure 3.5). Note that assembly delay occurs regardless of the Ethernet rate used to transfer the frame and obviously does not include any other delays introduced by Ethernet switches and Internet routers.

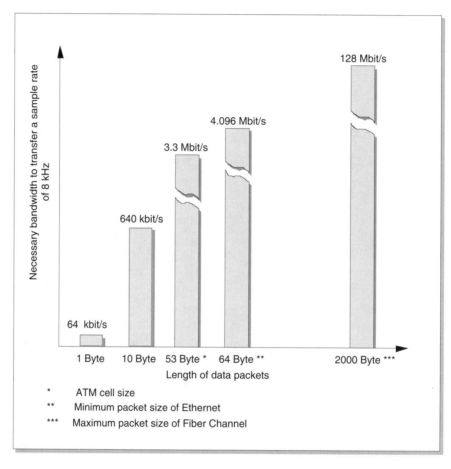

Figure 3.5
Packet size and the transmission of real-time sensitive data.

Ethernet networks thus do not fulfill the following requirements of multimedia applications:

- minimal and deterministic transfer delay,
- high efficiency especially with small frame sizes,
- high bandwidth, preferably assigned according to variable priorities.

On the contrary, the typical operating characteristics of Ethernet are:

- nondeterministic, highly variable transfer delay,
- lower efficiency with small frame sizes,
- lower bandwidth utilization when more stations are active.

Therefore in high traffic backbone environments, where transmission delay–sensitive applications such as voice over IP (VoIP) are being transported, Ethernet technologies can only be used with significant bandwidth reserve, in order to compensate for its lack of QoS characteristics.

3.3 The Limitations of Token Ring and FDDI Networks

Unlike Ethernet networks, Token Ring and FDDI are based on a deterministic media access technique. Each station in the ring is guaranteed the opportunity to transmit data at regular intervals. The method by which stations are granted permission to transmit is known as token passing. A token is a special symbol, a unique bit sequence, which authorizes the station that receives it to transmit data. After a defined maximum delay—the token holding time—the token must be relinquished to the next station, which then has its turn to send data. When no station needs to transmit, the token is passed around the ring unused. When a station has data queued for transmission, it waits until the token arrives, then it holds the token and begins transmitting data in its place. When a station recognizes its own address as the destination for a data packet, it not only copies the packet to its receive buffer, but also sets the Address Recognized and Frame Copied bits in the frame header to 1, and sends the modified frame as a receipt confirmation around the ring back to the original sender. When the modified frame is received by the station that originally sent it, this station examines the frame status bits (Address Recognized, Frame Copied) and removes the frame from the ring (see Figure 3.6).

Data packets cannot collide in Token Ring and FDDI networks since only the one station that has the token can transmit data. This means that the utilization of the theoretical total bandwidth is more efficient in Token Ring than in Ethernet networks. Only when capacity use rises above 80% does network performance decrease noticeably due to the increased time each station waits for the token.

Token Ring and FDDI thus come closer than Ethernet to fulfilling the demands placed on networks today, at least with regard to optimum utilization of the available bandwidth. Nonetheless, the communication technique of these two network topologies has its own weakness. As mentioned above, the token-holding time—the maximum time that a station can transmit before passing the token along—is limited. The default value of this timer is 10 ms in Token Ring and at least 4 ms in FDDI. This means that, if there are 30 network

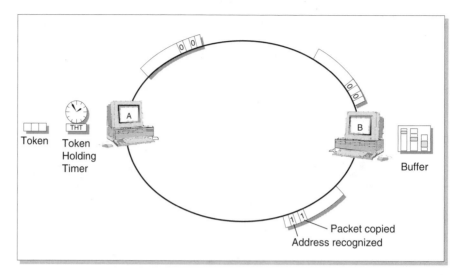

Figure 3.6
The token-passing principle in Token Ring and FDDI networks.

nodes in the ring, for example, the maximum time a station must wait before sending a queued data packet is 300 ms in Token Ring and 120 ms in the FDDI ring—many times the delay of about 10 ms that would be tolerable for multimedia applications. A limited use of real-time applications is only possible using the synchronous mode defined in the FDDI standard, in which certain stations are assigned a fixed synchronous bandwidth. This mode is rarely used in actual practice, however.

3.4   ATM: Technology for Converged, QoS-Based Networks

The question that arises is how the increasing demands on today's data network infrastructures can be met. The reasons for the limited performance of Ethernet, Token Ring, and FDDI lie not only in their access management mechanisms (CSMA/CD and token passing), but primarily in their topologies. The traditional ring topologies of FDDI and Token Ring and the star topology of 100Mbit/s Ethernet are shared-media technologies, meaning that all stations communicate over one and the same physical medium (see Figure 3.7).

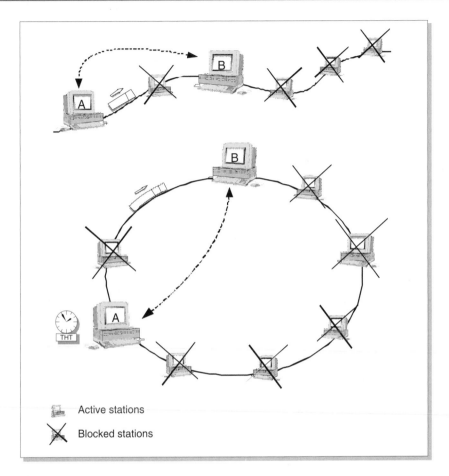

Active stations

Blocked stations

Figure 3.7
The shared-media communication principle.

As a result, transmission by a single station simultaneously blocks all other stations. All users must take turns accessing the entire communication bandwidth. Inefficient media access algorithms such as CSMA/CD exacerbate this situation, wasting a large part of this common bandwidth for the sake of simplicity. But even the apparently more efficient token-passing principle is too simple, since the division of the communication bandwidth among the users is coarse and inflexible. Each station in turn is granted a relatively large block of transmission time (4 ms in FDDI networks, which is long enough to send 10 FDDI frames of maximum length). The resulting communication characteristics are too rigid for real-time applications.

The recent adoption of the switching principle by LAN technologies such as Gigabit Ethernet and 10 Gigabit Ethernet could resolve a number of these limitations. The addition of QoS mechanisms to existing network protocols such RSVP and the definition of new protocols such as RTP have enabled the deployment of limited amounts of multimedia applications in enterprise networks.

Complementing the capabilities of state-of-the-art LANs, ATM provides a large-scale solution for IP telephony and multimedia networks. Rather than utilizing one common bandwidth pool, ATM networks supply each user with a certain guaranteed throughput and transmission characteristic on request. This bandwidth is then available to that user alone. The performance limitations of traditional LAN topologies are thus solved in ATM by means of the two principles (see Figure 3.8):

- centralized media access control instead of CSMA/CD or token passing, and
- dedicated, guaranteed throughput and transmission characteristics.

3.5   The Limitations of ISDN

The primary performance limitation of ISDN, the only communication technology originally designed for combined voice and data transport in wide area networks, is the available bandwidth, which is only available in fixed size increments of 64 kbit/s, and the inefficiencies of using it with services requiring variable bandwidth. Developed for the transmission of voice and data, ISDN provides connection-oriented communication paths with a constant, controlled transfer delay, but the bandwidth attained is not sufficient for true multimedia applications. Furthermore, the overall system architecture of today's WAN lines is designed for services with constant bit rates. If applications with widely varying data rates, such as LAN-to-LAN and video connections, are to be transported over fixed-bandwidth lines, then the capacity must be sufficient for peak loads. ATM, by contrast, is able to transport even highly variable traffic profiles efficiently, thanks to connection modes such as ABR (Available Bit Rate).

3.6   The Limitations of Packet over SONET/SDH

Packet over SONET/SDH (PoS) is a relatively new technology that provides transportation of data packets across SONET/SDH networks. It is to be found mainly in the WAN core network and is liked because it provides a more

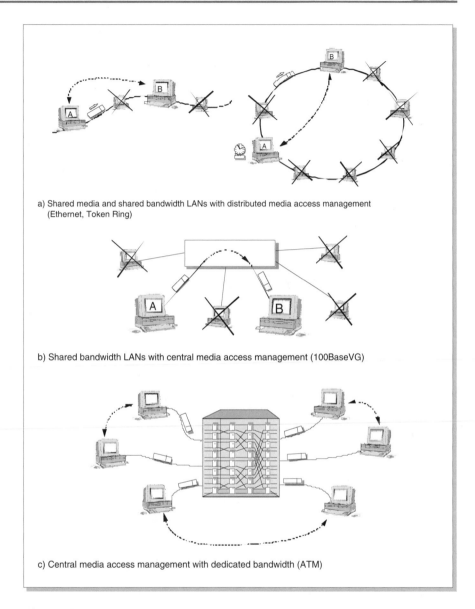

a) Shared media and shared bandwidth LANs with distributed media access management (Ethernet, Token Ring)

b) Shared bandwidth LANs with central media access management (100BaseVG)

c) Central media access management with dedicated bandwidth (ATM)

Figure 3.8
The ATM communication principle: centralized media access control and guaranteed transmission characteristic.

efficient use of network resources than ATM for the transfer of data traffic (there is no "cell tax"); data packets are directly mapped into the SONET/SDH payload, avoiding the AAL-5 segmentation process necessary in ATM. Currently PoS is gaining acceptance as an alternative to ATM because data is overtaking voice as the dominant service in WANs. For pure data, there is little doubt that PoS is the right answer; however, for conversational voice it has, in principal, some of the same limitations as Ethernet, since the same packetization (assembly) delay is involved at the edge of the network before PoS can be used to move the resulting packets efficiently to the destination. As VoIP gains favor (mainly because of the economics rather than the quality of service delivered), PoS may challenge ATM to become the dominant WAN technology; this will be a little further out in the future than some would have us believe, however.

3.7 ATM: Foundation for Large-Scale Converged Networks

The four main advantages of ATM can be summarized as follows:

- ATM is an international standard for data communication to permit universal exchange of information—whether asynchronous data, voice, audio, or video—between end systems of any type.
- ATM technologies are applicable for local area and wide area data communication networks. Thus ATM can be used to create a communication infrastructure with smooth boundaries between local enterprise and global access networks.
- With the trend to converged networks, ATM represents an intelligent, scalable technology with integrated QoS mechanisms that is capable of transporting all communication services (data, voice, video, audio) efficiently and simultaneously.
- Because ATM is scalable and therefore available in throughput classes from a few megabits up to several gigabits per second, this technology will be able to meet data communication demands for some time to come.

With the multimedia revolution finally happening, ATM networks are playing a key role in providing the necessary transport network infrastructure for the new voice, fax, video, and data services in both enterprise and access networks.

3.8   ATM in Local and Wide Area Networks

Due to rapidly advancing technology, both LANs and WANs have been changing constantly over the past few years. In local area networks, low-throughput,
shared-media technologies on the lower protocol layers (OSI layers 1 and 2)
such as traditional Ethernet and Token Ring technologies are increasingly
being replaced by high-speed topologies based on 100 Mbit/s Ethernet,
Gigabit Ethernet, Fiber Channel-based SANs (Storage Area Networks), or
ATM. In wide area networks, the more powerful and scalable Synchronous
Digital Hierarchy (SDH/SONET) is replacing the Plesiochronous Digital
Hierarchy (PDH) that has been in use since the 1970s. The X.25-based technique, which has long been customary in wide area data transport, has been
almost completely supplanted by more efficient technologies such as Frame
Relay, xDSL, ISDN, and ATM. In addition, wireless data communication
technologies such as wireless Ethernet (802.11a/b) in LANs and 3G wireless
telephony networks in WANs start to become deployed in large quantities.

With the migration of LANs and WANs toward the common and universal
IP family of network protocols, the traditional distinction between WAN and
LAN networking is disappearing. The convergence of WAN and LAN continues up through the application layers, with the World Wide Web and email
providing the platform for a growing number of applications. Conventional
WAN applications such as telephony or video conferencing are making inroads
in corporate LANs, while at the same time LAN applications such as group-
ware or workflow systems are being operated over WANs.

Nonetheless, a number of mechanisms and protocols are necessary in order
to operate the evolved LAN and WAN infrastructures jointly, and to integrate
old and new structures smoothly with the various transport mechanisms.
Figure 3.9 shows how ATM fits in the increasingly complex LAN and WAN
environments.

3.8.1   ATM in Homogeneous Private Networks

If a network is built using only ATM components, then data communication can
take place using classic ATM transmission techniques. Because ATM is connection oriented, the data virtual channel used to transport actual user data must be
defined before the data transmission by means of a signaling or provisioned
connection. With signaling, special communication protocols govern the

45

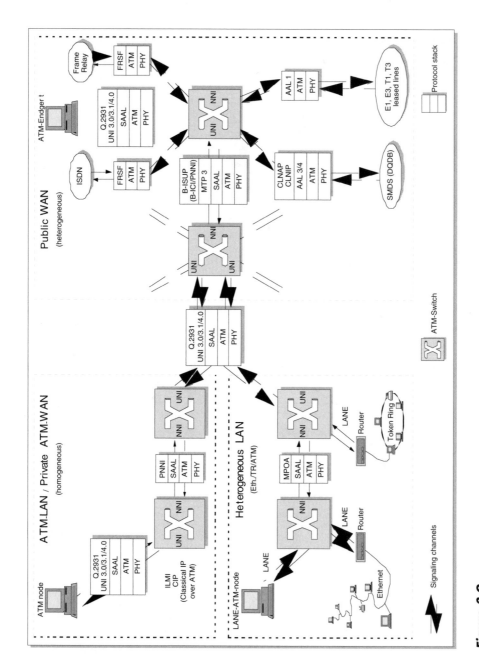

Figure 3.9
ATM in LANs and WANs: Overall view.

46

negotiation of the user data connection parameters (bandwidth, delay, routing, etc.). Data transmission takes place until the connection is terminated by an appropriate command on the signaling virtual channel. Different signaling protocols are used at the interface between the end system and the ATM switch (the user-to-network interface, or UNI) and at the interfaces between ATM switches (network-to-network interfaces/network node interface, or NNI).

In a private network, NNIs (i.e., interfaces between two ATM switches) use the Private Network-to-Network Interface (PNNI) protocol. It makes no difference whether the private network is a LAN or a WAN. In public ATM WANs, however, the NNI protocol usually used is the Broadband ISDN User Part (B-ISUP) protocol. The reason for the use of different protocols in the private and public spheres is that the ITU standardization body has left the internal operating aspects of public data networks in the control of national telecommunications companies. For example, B-ISUP does not specify how routing information is propagated or how topology detection mechanisms should be implemented. In private networks, however, it is desirable for all data communication mechanisms to be precisely defined so that communication works automatically without custom additions. For this reason, PNNI also specifies appropriate routing mechanisms in addition to the signaling processes. Because PNNI has the basic capabilities necessary for use in public WANs, and because some ATM system manufacturers provide an implementation of PNNI, but not B-ISUP, PNNI is sometimes also used in public networks, especially in North America. In Europe and Asia, however, almost all public networks use B-ISUP.

At the interface between an ATM switch and an ATM end system, that is, the UNI, connection setup is governed by the ITU-T Recommendation Q.2931 (and Q.2971 for point-to-multipoint connections), or by one of the ATM Forum's UNI signaling protocols, UNI 3.0, 3.1, 4.0, or 4.1.

When an ATM end system is installed or becomes active, it must first register with its assigned ATM switch. Information exchanged in this process includes the network address of the switch, the user address of the ATM end system, and the service characteristics of the ATM end system. All of this information is stored in the ATM switch in a defined format such as the Management Information Base (MIB). In order for this registration to be carried out automatically, a separate protocol for the exchange of MIB parameters was created, called the Integrated Local Management Interface (ILMI).

Because most network applications today build on the Internet Protocol (IP), and few native ATM applications are available to date, ATM is also able to serve as a fully transparent transport layer for IP. However, the Internet Protocol was originally designed for connectionless Ethernet networks, and therefore uses the broadcast principle for a number of functions. In the Classical IP and ARP over ATM protocol (RFC 2225, which replaced RFC

1577) defined for ATM networks, broadcasts cannot easily be translated to connection-oriented ATM; this is possible only with the ATM Forum's LAN Emulation (LANE) protocol. Nonetheless, IP can still be transported transparently over pure ATM networks. Address resolution is performed by specially defined ATM Address Resolution protocol (ATMARP) and Inverse ATM Address Resolution Protocol (InATMARP) functions; other broadcast types, however, are not supported.

3.8.2 ATM in Heterogeneous LAN Environments

Most of the time, ATM is used in combination with evolved existing network structures. In order to integrate ATM smoothly in such heterogeneous networks, the protocols LANE and Multiprotocol over ATM (MPOA) have been defined for ATM to permit complete, transparent interoperability between ATM networks and end systems on the one hand, and conventional LAN topologies such as Ethernet and Token Ring on the other. When the LANE protocol is used in an ATM network segment, every ATM end system in this network can communicate directly with every other Ethernet or Token Ring station connected through an ATM router. Furthermore, selected stations in the LAN can be assigned to an ATM LANE workgroup. That is, end systems can be grouped regardless of their location or network interface into "virtual LANs" (VLANs). MPOA provides transparent interconnection of several ATM LANE segments.

Note that because LANE is a layer 2 (link layer) protocol, emulated LANs (ELANs) are either Ethernet or Token Ring based, not a mixture of both. Layer 3 (network layer) routing is necessary to provide communication between Ethernet-and Token Ring-based ELANs via, for example, the MPOA protocol.

3.8.3 ATM in Public Wide Area Networks

When used for data communication in public wide area networks, ATM can be transparently connected with Frame Relay and Switched Multimegabit Data Services (SMDS) networks, the latter being obsolete. Transparent connection in this context means here that not only user data but also protocol information is extracted from the foreign network topology and interpreted. In the case of Frame Relay, for example, the ATM network interprets and understands the forward explicit congestion notification (FECN) bit and the DE (Discard Eligible) bit, and represents them using the corresponding ATM protocol parameters (EFCI and CLP). In connection with Frame Relay networks, ATM emulates the Frame Relay UNI by means of the Frame Relay Service Function (FRSF). Because Frame Relay is also connection oriented, it can be emulated relatively easily in ATM. Connecting SMDS networks to ATM is somewhat more complicated, since these networks, like conventional LANs, are based on the principle of connectionless communication. As in the case of LAN Emulation, the connectionless transmission principle of SMDS must be translated to ATM's connection-oriented structure. This is done by means of two protocols: Connectionless Network Interface Protocol (CLNIP) and Connectionless Network Access Protocol (CLNAP).

Another way to transport data over an ATM Network is to use the ATM Circuit Emulation Service (CES). With CES, the ATM network becomes a conduit for circuits such as E1, T1, E3, T3, and so on, so any service that can be transported over these circuits is, by default, also transported over ATM. Permanent virtual circuits are usually used for CES and special interface equipment is needed to implement CES; more details are given later in the section dealing with the ATM Adaptation Layer.

As mentioned previously, the B-ISUP communications protocol developed by the ITU-T is used at the NNI between two ATM switches in a public network. The Broadband Inter-Carrier Interface (B-ICI) is an enhanced network-to-network interface protocol developed by the ATM Forum for connecting the networks of different carriers (communications service providers), and is used mainly in North America. A number of telecommunications providers use PNNI between their public ATM switches, however, for the sake of greater simplicity in operation.

Part II

ATM: Technology and Standards

Chapter 4

ASYNCHRONOUS TRANSFER MODE

4.1 Communication Basics

Before we begin examining the operating principles of Asynchronous Transfer Mode (ATM) in detail, a survey of the various communication technologies used in wide area networks (WANs) will help to introduce the mechanisms on which ATM is built. These techniques differ from one another mainly in the multiplexing techniques, switching methods, and connection types that are used to transport data.

4.1.1 Multiplexing Techniques

Multiplexing makes it possible to transport several independent data streams over one and the same physical medium. This concept was first implemented by telephone companies in the 1930s, when frequency domain multiplex (FDM) techniques were used to transmit at first 12 and later 12,000 voice channels over coaxial cable. Each voice channel was modulated onto a certain carrier frequency before transmission, and demodulated again after reception of the total frequency band. This meant that each telephone connection no longer required its own physical two-wire circuit, and communication became much more economical. The many different multiplex techniques in use today can be divided into three categories: wavelength, code, and time multiplexing. Wavelength and time multiplexing techniques now play the most important role in modern optical communication networks. Time division multiplexing (TDM) is further divided into synchronous time division (STD) and asynchronous time division (ATD), illustrated in Figure 4.1.

Synchronous Time Division Multiplexing

In synchronous time division techniques, the communication signal is divided over time into frames, each of which consists of a fixed number of time slots. Each user is assigned a certain time slot in the frame to send or receive data. The individual channels are identified by the position of the time slot in the frame. For this reason synchronous time division multiplexing is sometimes

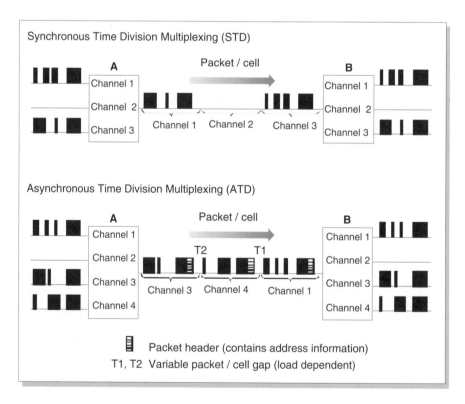

Figure 4.1
Synchronous and asynchronous time multiplexing.

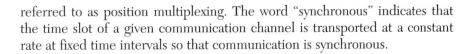
referred to as position multiplexing. The word "synchronous" indicates that the time slot of a given communication channel is transported at a constant rate at fixed time intervals so that communication is synchronous.

Asynchronous Time Division Multiplexing

In asynchronous time division multiplexing, the data streams to be transmitted are first converted into information units of fixed or variable length, then transported asynchronously. The information units, or packets, are assigned to the various communication channels by channel identification numbers (channel identifiers) attached to each packet. Asynchronous time division multiplexing is therefore sometimes referred to as address or label multiplexing. If variable-length frames are used, the technique is called frame switching. If the frame length is fixed, then the frames are called cells, and the multiplexing technique is referred to as cell switching.

4.1.2   Switching Methods in Data Communications

Switching in data communications refers to the way in which the communication path between sender and receiver is determined. The two basic methods are known as circuit switching and packet switching. In circuit switching, a physical connection between sender and receiver is established either manually or by means of a signaling process that takes place before the actual data communication. Once the signaling procedure has been completed, a continuous transmission path (usually of copper or fiber optic cable) exists between the communicating parties. This path generally crosses several switches. Thus a defined, continuous communication path must exist before data can be transported. The drawbacks of this technique are the long connection setup time, which interferes with many applications, and the fact that communication comes to a complete halt when the line continuity is interrupted. Once the connection has been established, however, the only transmission delay is due to the finite propagation speed of the electromagnetic signals—on the order of 6 ms per 1000 km. Examples of circuit-switched communication are leased data lines or early analog telephony.

In the 1960s, engineers at the U.S. Advanced Research Project Agency (ARPA) developed packet-oriented switching, in which information is converted into packets, then transported over the best available paths provided by the network. The switches may store packets temporarily, and packets belonging to the same connection may be transported over different communication paths. There is no fixed physical connection between sender and receiver.

In addition to the difference in communication delay, a key difference between circuit switching and packet switching is that circuit switching requires that a fixed bandwidth be allocated in advance, whereas in packet switching, bandwidth can be requested as needed. If a circuit-switched connection does not require all of the bandwidth allocated, the surplus is lost. Packet-switched networks can allocate unused capacity to other connections. Due to the highly variable bandwidth requirements of many data communications applications, modern computer networks are usually packet-switched. Furthermore, packet-oriented data communication is significantly more fault-tolerant than the older circuit-oriented communication. If one of the communication paths is no longer available, the frames are simply transmitted to the destination over backup routes. Because no fixed communication lines are allocated to connections in packet-switched networks, packets may be lost if the buffer capacity of a switch is exhausted. Figure 4.2 illustrates the evolution of switching and multiplexing methods since the beginning of digital communication.

4.1.3   Connection Types

Packet-switched data communication techniques permit both connection-oriented (CO) and connectionless (CL) communication. (The term "connection-oriented" here refers to logical connections on OSI layers 2 and upward. It does not imply circuit-switched connections on the physical layer, as discussed in the previous section.)

Connection-Oriented Communication Techniques

Connection-oriented communication techniques are characterized by "virtual connections" between the communicating parties. The virtual connection is set up either by provisioning or by a signaling process in which the sender and receiver negotiate an identification number for the data packets they will exchange. Once the virtual connection has been established, each data packet can be attributed to that connection by this ID. As the term "virtual connection" implies, individual packets belonging to a given connection may be transported over different paths, and be interspersed along the way with packets belonging to other virtual connections. The virtual connection is constituted not by a physical circuit or data path, but by the logical assignment of ID numbers. The data packet's virtual connection ID is usually combined with a sequence number, so that the receiving station can determine whether a received packet sequence is complete. The receiver can then request retransmission of any missing packets. Examples of connection-oriented communication techniques are X.25, Frame Relay, ISDN, and TCP.

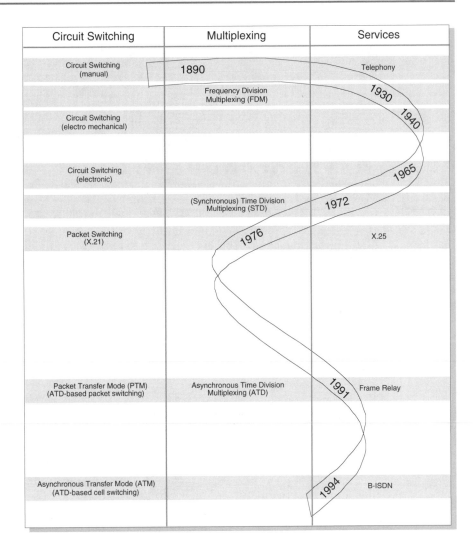

Circuit Switching	Multiplexing	Services
Circuit Switching (manual)	1890	Telephony
	Frequency Division Multiplexing (FDM)	1930
Circuit Switching (electro mechanical)		1940
Circuit Switching (electronic)		1965
	(Synchronous) Time Division Multiplexing (STD)	1972
Packet Switching (X.21)	1976	X.25
Packet Transfer Mode (PTM) (ATD-based packet switching)	Asynchronous Time Division Multiplexing (ATD)	1991 Frame Relay
Asynchronous Transfer Mode (ATM) (ATD-based cell switching)		1994 B-ISDN

Figure 4.2
Data communication techniques.

Connectionless Communication Techniques

In connectionless communication, data packets are transported without a prior handshake sequence or signaling procedure between the communicating parties. The packets are simply sent out on the assumption that they will reach the intended receiver. The transmitting station has no information as to whether the destination station receives the data or is active at all. Error correction or requests for retransmission of a packet sequence must be handled by the higher-layer application that builds on such a protocol. Examples of connectionless communication protocols are IP, UDP, and the MAC layer protocol in Ethernet LANs.

4.2 Asynchronous Transfer Mode (ATM)

Many communication techniques are based on various combinations of the transport mechanisms described above. For an understanding of ATM, the most important of these are Synchronous Transfer Mode (STM), Packet Transfer Mode (PTM), and Asynchronous Transfer Mode (ATM), illustrated in Figure 4.3.

Asynchronous Transfer Mode is a packet-switched, connection-oriented communication technique in which data is transported in fixed-length packets using asynchronous time-division multiplexing (see Figure 4.4). Because of their constant length, the data packets are called cells. ATM cells are 53 bytes long. Five of the 53 bytes are reserved for the cell header, in which the virtual connection is identified by a combination of virtual channel ID (VCI) and virtual path ID (VPI). All network nodes are connected to one another over one or more ATM switches, which forward the cells toward their respective destinations. Due to the fixed cell length, the ATM switches can forward cells very efficiently, processing several cells on parallel paths simultaneously, and thus attain very high data throughput compared with conventional routers. End systems in the network do not have to share a common communication medium, as is the case in conventional local area networks, but simply unload their outgoing cells at the nearest ATM switch without having to perform any media access algorithms. Before the actual data communication begins, the communication path for the user cells is provisioned or negotiated and set up by a signaling procedure. The traffic contract provisioned or negotiated by this procedure guarantees certain traffic parameters, such as transfer delay, bandwidth, or cell loss ratio, for the entire duration of the connection. This feature makes it possible to transmit multimedia communication services over ATM networks in high quality and quantity.

The fixed cell length of 53 bytes is the result of a necessary compromise between the requirements of analog voice and digital data communication. When analog voice signals are transported over digital networks, they are sam-

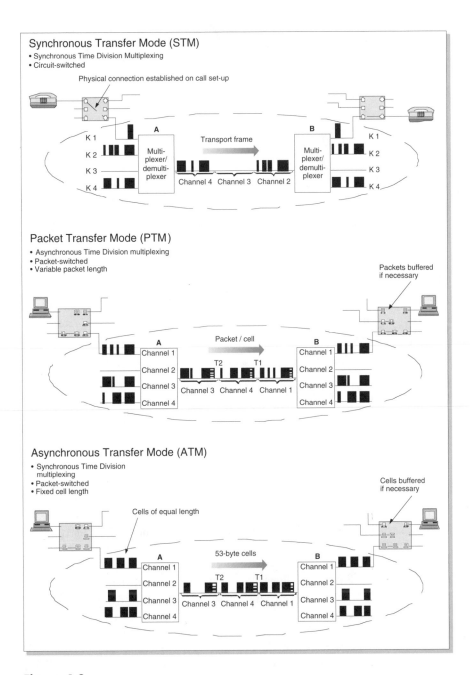

Figure 4.3
ATM, STM, and PTM.

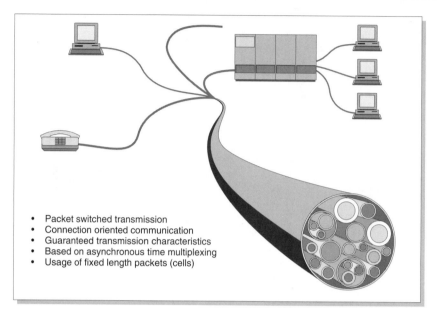

- Packet switched transmission
- Connection oriented communication
- Guaranteed transmission characteristics
- Based on asynchronous time multiplexing
- Usage of fixed length packets (cells)

Figure 4.4
Principles of ATM.

pled 8000 times per second, and each sampled value is coded in eight bits. This means that if no data compression is used, 64 kbit/s per voice channel—a one-byte sample every 125 μs—must be transported. This communication technique for analog signals is known as pulse code modulation (PCM). The 48-byte cell payload could accommodate 48 voice samples but it would take 6 ms (48 × 125 μs) to assemble enough samples to fill a cell payload before the cell could be sent. This delay, known as the cell assembly delay, is entirely dependent on the 64 kbit/s service and independent of the cell rate that will be used to transfer the cell. If compressed voice were used, the delay would be worse—voice compressed to 8 kbit/s would be delayed 8 times as long (i.e., 48 ms), which would use up too great a share of the allowable delay budget for conversational voice communications (150 ms is the preferred maximum for all delay components).

Thus for analog signals, the cell length should be as short as possible. During the ATM standardization process, European countries, which traditionally had less digital data traffic than the United States, proposed a cell length of 35 bytes (32-byte payload) for this reason. In the United States and Canada, however, data communication over wide area networks had for years been much more widespread than in Europe; also, it was common practice to fit echo cancellors to long-haul voice circuits in North America but rare in Europe. The North Americans favored a cell length of 69 bytes (payload of 64

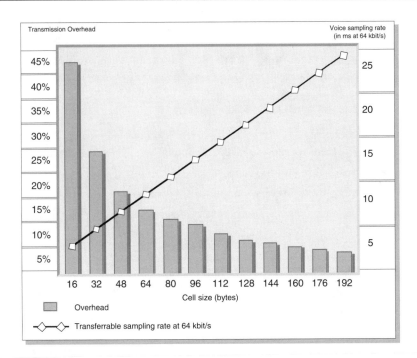

Figure 4.5
Cell size and transfer delay for analog signals.

bytes), since a larger volume of data can be transported more economically in large packets due to the lower overhead. The compromise that was eventually adopted is the ATM cell length of 53 bytes. This is short enough to be well suited to the transmission of analog signals in ATM's higher megabit/s and gigabit/s throughput ranges. The small cell size also permits quick and exact

Table 4.1   Cell Length and Bandwidth Utilization

Cell Length	Overhead Bytes	Cell Overhead %	Efficiency % (ATM over E1 link)
10	4	40	56.3
16	4	25	70.3
24	4	16.6	78.1
32	5	15.6	79.1
53	5	9.4	84.8
64	5	7.8	86.4

bandwidth allocations as well as parallel cell processing at high speeds in ATM switches.

At the same time, 53-byte cells have an overhead of 9.4%, thus containing a high enough proportion of user data to transport digital data streams efficiently. The ATM architecture therefore combines the following communication characteristics:

- Efficient utilization of the available communication bandwidth
- Scalability and modularity
- Simplified interconnection of LANs and WANs
- Definable guaranteed communication parameters for data and analog telecommunication

There are some inefficiencies attributable to ATM, as we shall see when we discuss the ATM Adaptation Layer (AAL) later in the book.

4.2.1   Efficient Utilization of the Available Communication Bandwidth

Unlike ATM networks, traditional WAN links are based on STM (Synchronous Transfer Mode) communication techniques. STM links use synchronous time division multiplexing, providing each network user a certain communication bandwidth, regardless of how much is actually required. This method is well suited for voice transmission. For data communication, however, it can be very inefficient to have a communication channel of a fixed size, since the amount of data to be transported can vary drastically. The communication profiles for video data and LAN-to-LAN traffic, for example, show great differences between peak and minimum loads.

Thanks to their use of asynchronous time division multiplexing with a fixed cell length, ATM networks are able to allocate the available communication bandwidth more flexibly. A network user can be allotted more or less bandwidth as needed. The total bandwidth is distributed among the network nodes that are active at a given moment. This means that services with very different bandwidth requirements, such as applications with dynamically varying bit rates, real-time applications, applications with fixed bit rates, and less real-time-sensitive applications, can all be implemented over ATM networks with high efficiency. ATM networks are capable of transporting all kinds of data traffic, whether video conferencing, telephone calls, or file transfers.

4.2.2 Scalability and Modularity for LANs and WANs

ATM can be implemented over a wide variety of communication media since, in contrast to traditional networking standards (Ethernet, FDDI, etc.), its specification does not define the physical layer to be used (see Figure 4.6). The ATM specifications ITU I.432 and ITU G.804 describe cell transportation over SDH networks at speeds of 155 Mbit/s and 622 Mbit/s, and over the Plesiochronous Digital Hierarchy interfaces (E1, DS1, E3, DS3, etc.). The ATM Forum has also specified other interfaces for ATM, including UTP (unsheilded twisted pair)-based ATM25 (25.6 Mbit/s) and UTP155 (155 Mbit/s) for Category 3 and Category 5 UTP cable. Thus there is no single rule prescribing the physical medium or the data rate with which ATM cells should be transported. As a result, ATM today is used in cable television networks, and even on telephone lines using ADSL technology, to transport MPEG-compressed video data.

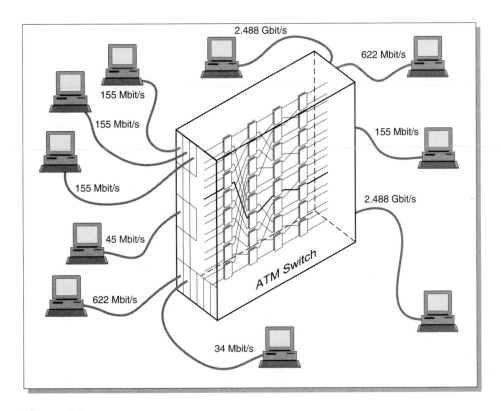

Figure 4.6
Scalability and modularity of ATM.

Another key characteristic of ATM networks is that the bandwidth available to each user does not diminish with increasing numbers of users. The bandwidth of the ATM switch is expanded by adding plug-in interface cards, which provide each new user with the full network bandwidth. The only limitation is the ATM switch's internal processing speed. Today's ATM switches, however, can process many Gbit/s, which is sufficient for actual applications. ATM can therefore be used in practically all areas of data communications, and is equally suited for local area and wide area networking, though the relatively lower costs of Fast Ethernet and Gigabit Ethernet have tended to eclipse the use of ATM in the local area network.

ATM in Wide Area Networking

ATM cells can be transported both over existing 1.5/2 Mbit/s, 34/45 Mbit/s, or 139 Mbit/s lines and over the more modern wide area SDH/SONET networks. The SDH network, strongly based on the SONET system developed in the United States, was adopted by the ITU in 1988 as a uniform international communication technology with data rates from 155.52 Mbit/s to 9,953.28 Mbit/s, and recommended for the implementation of global WAN links. Due to the flexible multiplex structure and integrated management and monitoring functions of SDH/SONET, wide area networks based on this technology are not only very powerful, but also very economical in comparison with previous communication techniques. Since the early 1990s, all major telecommunications operators have been converting their data networks to SDH/SONET. Other wide area techniques used to transport ATM cells include satellite and point-to-point wireless networks, as well as cable television infrastructures (MPEG over ATM) and telephone lines (ATM over ADSL).

ATM in Local Area Networking

Some time ago, the ATM Forum defined interfaces for LAN ATM infrastructures with data speeds of 25.6 Mbit/s, 52 Mbit/s, and 155 Mbit/s over both unshielded and shielded twisted-pair cabling (UTP Categories 3 and 5 and STP). Existing FDDI infrastructures could be converted into ATM LANs by what are known as TAXI chipsets ("TAXI" was the product name given to the first chipset of this kind by U.S. manufacturer AMD). Due to falling prices for STM-1/OC-3 components, however, TAXI solutions have essentially died out. Furthermore, the arrival of Fast Ethernet (100 Mb/s) and Gigabit Ethernet (1000 Mb/s) have limited the use of ATM for LANs.

In spite of rapidly falling prices, the use of ATM in local area networks is still mainly limited to demanding multimedia LANs and enterprise backbones that interconnect traditional LANs (Ethernet, Token Ring, FDDI, MANs). The problems of connecting existing LANs with ATM technologies are solved by using the ATM Forum-defined LAN Emulation protocol in the ATM switches. This allows ATM networks to simulate the OSI layer 2 communication mechanisms of Ethernet and Token Ring networks so that the existing network infrastructure can be linked to the ATM-based segments.

4.2.3 Simplified Interconnection of LANs and WANs

When ATM is used in the LAN as well as in the WAN, connecting the two becomes substantially simpler. Complex, resource-hungry protocol conversions, as required for conventional LAN/WAN connections, are no longer necessary. Furthermore, ATM finally makes it possible to guarantee defined communication parameters across heterogeneous LAN/WAN structures.

4.2.4 Definable, Guaranteed Communication Parameters for Data and Analog Telecommunication

One of the most important properties of ATM networks is the ability to transport data over connections with negotiable, guaranteed communication parameters and, above all, guaranteed quality of service (QoS). As described above, all important parameters of the connection are provisioned or negotiated as a "traffic contract" during the signaling procedure to define and open the user data channel. Depending on the needs of the given application, the bandwidth parameter (peak cell rate, cell delay variation tolerance, sustainable cell rate, and maximum burst size) can be specified, as well as the required maximum transfer delay or the maximum permissible cell loss ratio. These negotiable, guaranteed connection parameters make ATM a universal transport medium for all communication technologies. For the first time, all data communications applications and all telecommunications services can be transported over the same equipment.

Chapter 5

THE STRUCTURE OF ATM

The communication process commonly referred to as ATM consists of a number of protocol layers that build on one another, and that have the purpose of mapping the various network services to ATM cells, and mapping ATM cells to a wide variety of physical layers. Taken as a whole, this set of protocol layers is called the B-ISDN protocol reference model. This name is a reminder of the origins of the ATM specification, which has its roots in the ITU's Broadband-ISDN project for a universal wide area network. Since ATM technology in the data communications field has spread beyond the boundaries of conventional telecommunications, ATM has become accepted as the universal name for the B-ISDN layer model as a whole, although in a strict sense ATM refers only to cell-based data transport, that is, the ATM layer within the B-ISDN model.

5.1   The B-ISDN Reference Model

The logical B-ISDN network architecture was designed in four independent levels of communication, after the ISO OSI reference model (ITU X.200). Whereas the OSI model provides for seven layers, however, the B-ISDN protocol reference model defines the physical layer, the ATM layer, the ATM adaptation layer (AAL), and the application layer, designated in the model simply as "Higher Layer Protocols." These layers are connected to one another by information flows on three planes: the user plane, the control plane, and the management plane (see Figures 5.1 and 5.2).

5.1.1   The User Plane

The user plane represents the flow of user data between ATM network users across all protocol layers. It also includes functions such as error correction and monitoring of the data flow.

5.1.2   The Control Plane

The control plane represents the mechanisms for setting up, monitoring, and clearing down connections. Because ATM is a connection-oriented communication technique, each connection within the ATM layer must be assigned a unique connection ID number by means of the signaling process, which takes place in the control plane. Depending on the hierarchical level of the connec-

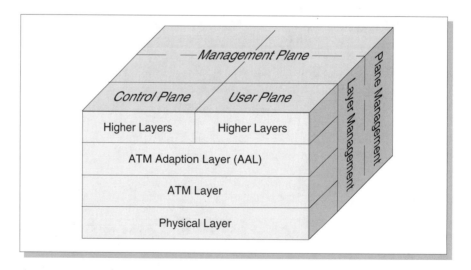

Figure 5.1
The B-ISDN Reference Model.

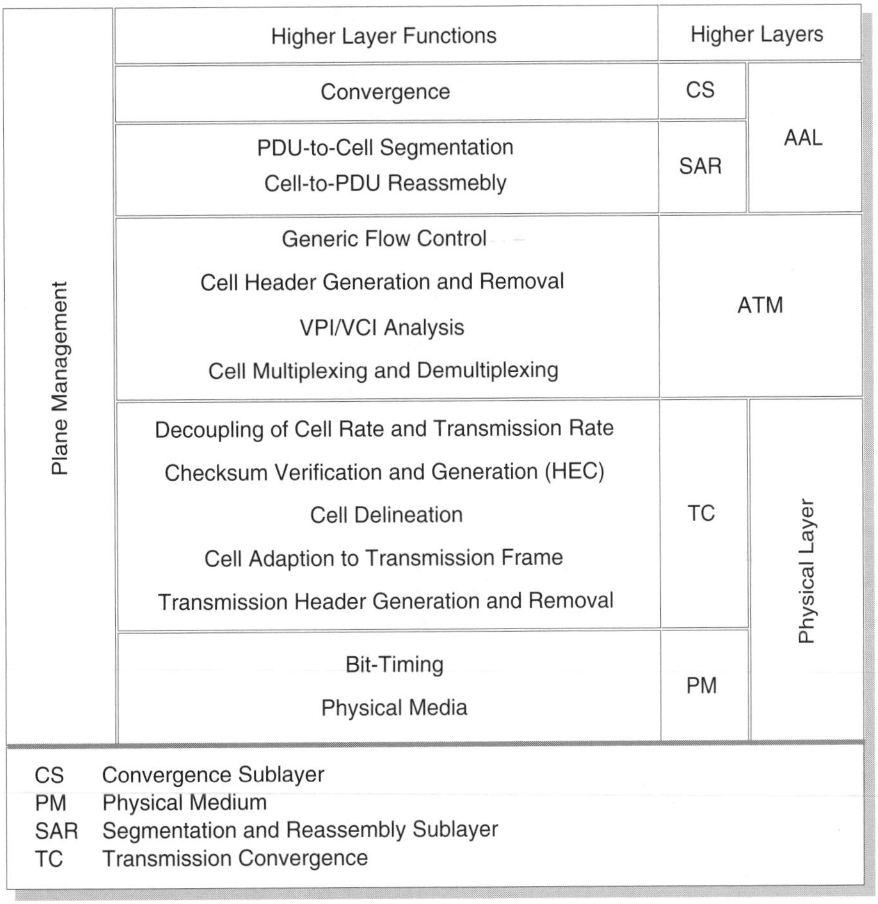

Higher Layer Functions		Higher Layers	
Convergence	CS		AAL
PDU-to-Cell Segmentation Cell-to-PDU Reassmebly	SAR		
Generic Flow Control Cell Header Generation and Removal VPI/VCI Analysis Cell Multiplexing and Demultiplexing		ATM	
Decoupling of Cell Rate and Transmission Rate Checksum Verification and Generation (HEC) Cell Delineation Cell Adaption to Transmission Frame Transmission Header Generation and Removal	TC		Physical Layer
Bit-Timing Physical Media	PM		

(Left side of table: **Plane Management**)

CS	Convergence Sublayer
PM	Physical Medium
SAR	Segmentation and Reassembly Sublayer
TC	Transmission Convergence

Figure 5.2
Functions of the protocol layers in the B-ISDN reference model.

tion, this ID number is called the virtual path identifier (VPI) or virtual channel identifier (VCI). Note that the VPI-VCI label in an ATM cell header has only local significance (i.e., for a given physical link) and, generally, the VPI-VCI is changed or "translated" at each ATM switch on the route through the network. In the case of AAL-2, an additional level of ID is present, the channel ID (CID); the AAL-2 channel is logically at a higher sublayer of the ATM reference model, that is, above the virtual channel, which is itself above the virtual path.

5.1.3 The Management Plane

The management plane has two functions: plane management and layer management. Plane management refers to the coordination of management plane functions and processes with those of the user plane and the control plane. Layer management coordinates functions such as metasignaling and the OAM information flow. Metasignaling refers to a special signaling process by which channels are selected for subsequent signaling use—that is, a signaling process to set up signaling channels. In actual practice, however, this mechanism is rarely used. OAM information (Operation and Maintenance) is used for in-service monitoring of network performance and for error management in the ATM layer. These "information flows" take the form of special cells, called OAM cells, which are inserted in the user cell stream to be evaluated at another point in the network.

5.1.4 The Physical Layer

The physical layer in ATM networks is divided into two sublayers: the Transmission Convergence (TC) sublayer and the Physical Medium Dependent (PMD) sublayer.

Transmission Convergence (TC)

Transmission Convergence is responsible for embedding the ATM layer cells in the transmission framework of the given transport medium. If ATM cells are to be transported over a 34-Mbit/s E3 link, for example, they must be fitted into the user data fields of E3 frames. The transport medium could also be an SDH/SONET or PDH frame, such as DS1, DS3, or E4. If cells are transferred over the physical medium directly, with no intermediate transport frame, this sublayer is not necessary. This form of ATM transport is known as a "cell-based physical layer." Two important functions of the transmission convergence sublayer are cell header error control and cell delineation.

Cell Header Error Control. At the TC sublayer, only the cell header is checked for errors; error control of user data, if done at all, is done at a higher layer. Cell header information is contained in 4 bytes; to this is added a fifth byte, the "HEC" (header error control) field. This HEC field is based on a cyclic redundancy check (CRC-8), which has the property that it allows a single bit error anywhere in the 5-byte header to be corrected at the receiver, even when this error is in the HEC byte itself; it also always allows a 2-bit error and sometimes a multiple-bit error to be detected (but not corrected).

Cell Delineation.   Cell delineation is the process of identifying the start and end of cells extracted from the physical layer at the ATM receiver. The mechanism used is dependant upon the particular physical layer being used. In the majority of cases, a mechanism that uses a property of all good cell headers is used: that the HEC is correct. The bit stream extracted by the TC is searched for a 40-bit (5-byte) sequence that could be a header because it "passes" the HEC check. Of course, such a sequence might be part of the user data that just happens to pass, so a further level of checking is necessary. For the header candidate sequence to be valid, there must be several similar header candidates spaced at 53-byte intervals; the number of such candidates is usually six, but is sometimes seven for a particular cell-based physical layer. Once the conditions have been met, cell delineation is declared, but an ongoing check is made to ensure that cell delineation is maintained.

In order to make the cell header more easily distinguishable from the payload (information field) of the cell, the user data in the payload is scrambled before transmission. This ensures that switching equipment can clearly and quickly identify the ATM header, regardless of the bit combinations that may occur within the information field of the ATM cell. The scrambling is performed by the TC layer immediately before the cells are actually transmitted.

The Physical Communication Medium

The physical communication media for ATM, as specified in the B-ISDN standards, are 75-ohm coaxial and 100/120-ohm twisted-pair copper cables, as used in the Plesiochronous Digital Hierarchy, and single-mode optical fiber, as used in the Synchronous Digital Hierarchy (SDH). In addition to these, the ATM Forum has specified a number of other economical transport media for local area ATM networks, such as shielded or unshielded copper twisted pair (UTP/STP) and multimode fiber, with data speeds ranging from 25 Mbit/s to 2400 Mbit/s. Yet the ATM standards are structured so that nearly any physical medium can be used, as long as a transmission convergence layer can be defined for it.

In general, the communication bandwidth attainable today for distances up to 100 meters over shielded twisted-pair copper cable (such as STP Type 1A) is about 300 to 400 MHz. Over longer distances, the maximum attainable bandwidth declines rapidly. When fiber is used, however, the length is only a minor factor in determining the maximum throughput. Bandwidths in the terahertz range are attainable in both local area and wide area fiber networks.

In LANs, the more economical electrical communication media are thus often used for ATM as well. In heavy-duty LAN backbones and in wide area networks, however, ATM networks are almost always implemented over optical media.

5.1.5   The ATM Layer

The functions of the ATM layer are completely independent of the underlying physical layer. Their chief task is to bring the data received from the higher ATM adaptation layer (AAL) to its destination. The information units of the ATM layer are the 53-byte cells. Each cell has an identification number in its header that assigns it to a certain connection. Cells belonging to various connections are multiplexed into a noncontinuous cell stream in each direction. These cell streams are hierarchically structured in virtual channels (VC) and virtual paths (VP), which correspond to one or more virtual connections. A physical transport medium (such as an optical fiber) can transport a number of virtual connections. Each cell on the medium can be unambiguously attributed to a certain connection by the virtual path identifier (VPI) and virtual channel identifier (VCI) in its header.

Cell Header Generation

When the ATM layer receives a unit of information from the higher AAL, it must generate the first 4 bytes of the ATM cell header. The 5th byte, the Header Error Control field (HEC), is generated subsequently by the transmission convergence layer (TC). The header of an ATM cell at the user-to-network interface (UNI)—that is, a cell transmitted between an end system and the ATM network—contains the following fields: a 4-bit Generic Flow Control (GFC) field; 24 bits for virtual path and channel identification (VPI, VCI); 3 bits to identify the payload type (PT); and one bit to indicate the cell loss priority (CLP) in case cells need to be dropped in transit (see Figure 5.3). Cells transported across network-to-network interfaces (NNI), however, do not contain a flow control field. Instead, they have a larger virtual path ID (VPI) field.

5.1.6   The ATM Adaptation Layer

The purpose of the ATM adaptation layer (AAL) is to disassemble the higher-layer data streams into 48-byte information fragments for transport in ATM cells. (Five of the cell's 53 bytes are used for header information, so that 48 bytes of user data are transported in each cell.) At the receiving end, the original data streams must be reassembled from the individual ATM cells. The

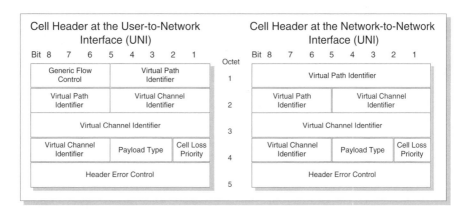

Figure 5.3
ATM cell format.

functions of the AAL are thus largely dependent on the characteristics of the higher-order applications. To provide the necessary flexibility, the AAL functions are divided into two sublayers: the Convergence sublayer (CS) and the Segmentation and Reassembly sublayer (SAR).

The AAL Types

To limit the number of different AAL implementations, four service classes have been defined: AAL1, AAL2, AAL3/4, and AAL5. Each of these AAL types is defined for a certain class of applications (see Figure 5.4). The simplest one to implement, AAL5, is by far the most widely used AAL variant today.

The Signaling ATM Adaptation Layer (SAAL)

As in narrowband ISDN, B-ISDN signaling is also handled in signaling channels that are separate from the user connections. SAAL (the Signaling AAL) is the ATM Adaptation Layer used for these signaling protocols. The purpose of the SAAL is to transport application-layer signaling protocols, such as UNI 4.0, Q.2931, PNNI, and B-ISUP, over the ATM layer. It does so using AAL3/4 or AAL5 in conjunction with the service-specific sublayer SSCOP (the Service-Specific Connection-Oriented Protocol).

5.1.7   Higher Layers

The actual network services are transported through the corresponding adaptation layers. The most common applications are:

Service Parameter	Class A	Class B	Class C	Class D
Time Compensation	Required		Not Required	
Bit-Rate	Constant	Variable		
Connection Mode	Connection-Oriented			Connectionless
Example	Circuit Emulation	Video	Connection-Oriented Data Transfer	Connectionless Data Transfer
AAL Type	Type 1	Type 2	Type 3 Type 5	Type 4

Figure 5.4
Service classes and AAL types.

- Ethernet, Token Ring, FDDI (using LAN Emulation)
- Classical IP over ATM
- MPEG (video)
- Frame relay
- Leased-line data links
- Voice (telephony)

5.2 B-ISDN Networks: Configuration and Reference Points

In order to ensure interoperability between networks and components, reference points have been specified at which clearly defined functions are available (see Figure 5.5). The definitions of the various reference points at the system interfaces were taken from the nomenclature for narrowband ISDN networks. To distinguish them from the corresponding narrowband ISDN reference points, they are written with a prefix or a subscript of "B" for broadband.

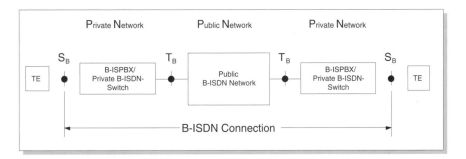

Figure 5.5
The B-ISDN reference points.

Within a B-ISDN network, a primary distinction is made between two basic functional areas. These are private terminal equipment and other end systems on the one hand, and the public B-ISDN network on the other. As a result, three reference points are defined in B-ISDN networks: T_B, S_B, and R. If both the public and the subscriber's private B-ISDN network are ATM broadband networks, and provide the same connection types, then a B-ISDN connection exists between two S_B reference points. The interface between the private and the public switches is then designated as reference point T_B. If there is no network at the subscriber end—if only a single end system is connected, for example—then the reference points T_B and S_B are located at the same point. In this case, a B-ISDN connection exists between two $T_B S_B$ reference points. The reference point R may or may not have B-ISDN functions. The reference points are located at the interfaces between functional groups (see Figure 5.6). The B-ISDN reference configuration defines the following functional groups: B-NT1, B-NT2, B-TE1, B-TE2, and B-TA.

5.2.1   Interfaces at Reference Point T_B

Only one interface is specified for reference point T_B, namely the network terminator, B-NT1. The functions of the B-NT1 include line transmission termination, transmission interface handling, and OAM functions.

5.2.2   Interfaces at Reference Point S_B

The network terminator B-NT2 is defined as the interface for reference point S_B. A B-NT2 can be an interface to one or several S_B reference points. The functions of the B-NT2 include the following:

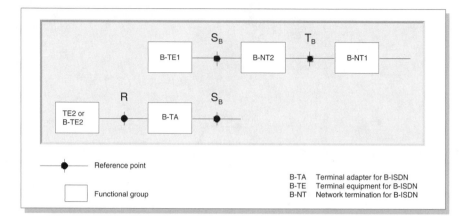

Figure 5.6
The functional groups of B-ISDN.

- Adaptation functions for various interface media and topologies
- Synchronization with individual cells
- Traffic concentration functions
- Buffering of ATM cells
- Multiplexing and demultiplexing connections
- Assigning communication paths
- Usage parameter control (UPC)
- AAL sublayer signaling
- Interface handling
- OAM functions
- Signaling protocol handling
- Switching internal connections

5.2.3   B-ISDN Terminal Equipment (B-TE)

The general functional elements of B-ISDN terminal equipment are:

- User–user and user–system interface and protocol functions
- Physical interface and Layer 1 functions
- Signaling protocol

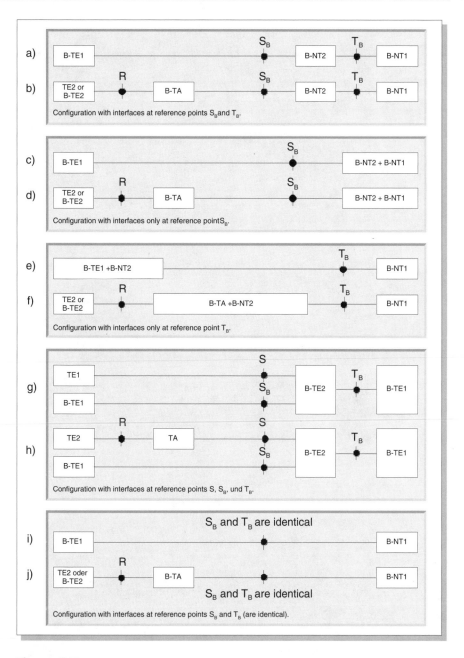

Figure 5.7
Network configuration examples.

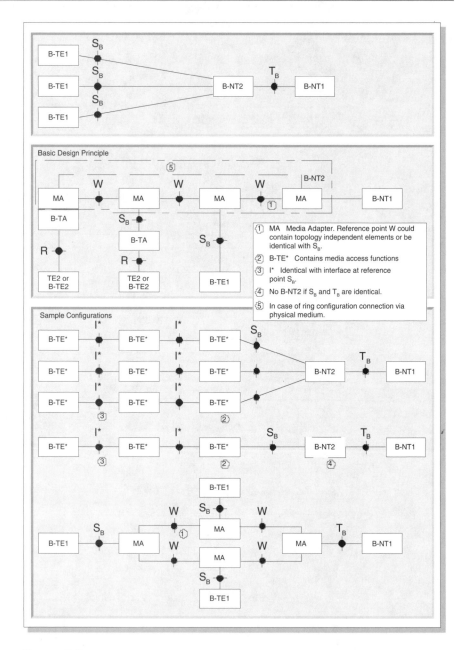

Figure 5.8
Examples of B-ISDN network configurations with resource sharing.

- Connection setup and clear-down to other end systems
- OAM functions

B-ISDN terminal equipment can be of two basic types: B-TE1 and B-TE2. B-TE1 terminal equipment has interfaces for the reference points T_B and S_B; B-TE2 terminal equipment does not.

B-ISDN Terminal Adapters (B-TA)

Terminal adapters (B-TA) connect TE-2 or B-TE2 terminal devices—that is, devices that do not have broadband capability or do not conform to the specifications for interfaces at the reference points T_B and S_B—to the B-ISDN network. Figures 5.7 and 5.8 illustrate various B-ISDN network configurations with the corresponding reference points.

Chapter 6

ATM: THE PHYSICAL LAYER

The physical layer of the B-ISDN protocol model maps the cells passed down from the ATM layer to the physical transmission medium (see Figure 6.1). This physical layer consists of two sublayers: the Transmission Convergence sublayer (TC) and the Physical Medium Dependent sublayer (PMD). The PMD defines the specific communication medium and the TC defines how ATM cells are mapped to the PMD. The higher-order ATM layer itself is completely independent of the type and data rate of the underlying physical layer.

6.1   Transmission Convergence

Three methods can be used to transport ATM cells: cell adaptation to the frame structure of the transport medium (such as PDH or SDH/SONET), transport in PLCP frames, or cell-based physical layer.

6.1.1   Cell Mapping to Existing Frame Formats

In order to prolong the useful life of existing data communications infrastructures, techniques have been developed to transport ATM cells in the container frames of the most common communications interfaces. Cell transport in

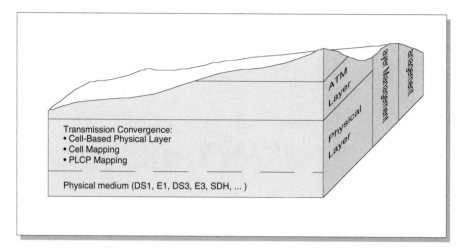

Figure 6.1
B-ISDN layer model: The physical layer.

Synchronous Digital Hierarchy (SDH) containers or in the equivalent SONET synchronous payload envelopes (SPEs) is the most widely used transport method for ATM cells today. The cell payload is scrambled before being mapped in the physical layer frames, using the Self-Synchronizing Scrambler (SSS) algorithm with the generator polynomial $x^{43} + 1$, as described in ITU-T Recommendation I.432. After the 48 user data bytes have been scrambled, the cells are inserted into the payload field of a virtual container (VC-4) and transmitted in an SDH/SONET frame.

Mapping methods have also been developed to transport ATM cells in wide area networks over the older but still widely used E1, E3, E4, T1, and T3 PDH interfaces (Figure 6.2). In this technique the cells are inserted directly in the user data field of the given transport frame, and the cell rate is adapted to the PDH bit rate by inserting "idle" cells. (In North America, "unassigned" cells are often used, which can be considered identical with idle cells for most purposes.)

Mapping to the existing PDH frames is defined in ITU-T Recommendation G.804 for the following transfer rates: 1.544 Mbit/s, 2.048 Mbit/s, 6.312 Mbit/s, 34.360 Mbit/s, 44.736 Mbit/s, 97.728 Mbit/s, and 139.264 Mbit/s. Cell transport over the T3 line type (44.736 Mbit/s), common in North America, was once defined only using the DS3 PLCP frame format (Bellcore TR-TSV-000772, TR-TSV-000773), originally developed for metropolitan area networks. In recent years, however, a more efficient, direct mapping technique has been introduced for DS3 frames and is now preferred, even though PLCP mapping is still common in older equipment.

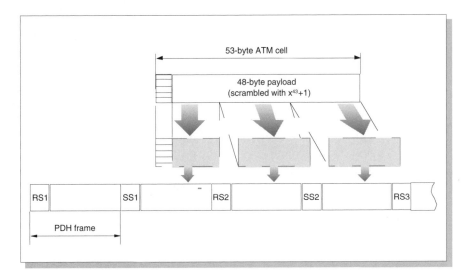

Figure 6.2
Cell mapping to PDH frames.

The transmission convergence sublayer is responsible for the following functions in frame-based physical layers (non-PLCP), shown in order of relative position within the sublayer, top to bottom:

- Cell rate decoupling (use of idle cells)
- HEC generation/verification
- Cell scrambling/descrambling (when appropriate)
- Cell delineation
- Transmission frame adaptation (cell to frame payload mapping)
- Path signal identification (C2 in SDH/SONET)
- Frequency adjustment and/or pointer processing (SDH/SONET)
- Multiplexing (when appropriate)
- Physical layer scrambling/descrambling (when appropriate)
- Transmission frame generation/recovery (frame-based interfaces)

The Header Error Control (HEC) Field of the ATM Cell Header

The HEC field is the 5th byte of the ATM cell header (the remaining bytes of the cell header are discussed in detail in Chapter 9). Although part of the ATM cell header, the functions of the Header Error Control (HEC) field are physical layer related, as can be seen from the above list. As well as providing detection of cell header errors, the HEC also plays a central role in cell delineation in frame-based interfaces, except for those using PLCP methods (see subsection 6.1.2).

Before an ATM cell is transmitted, a cyclic redundancy checksum (CRC) of the entire cell header is calculated, XORed with the "cosec" value 01010101, and placed in the 8-bit header error control field. The checksum is calculated as follows. The 32 bits of the cell header (without the HEC field) are used to form a polynomial of degree 31, which is first multiplied by x^8, then divided by the generator polynomial $x^8 + x^2 + x + 1$ modulo 2. The remainder of this division is the HEC byte. (Cyclical redundancy checks are based on the principle that any code word consisting of n bits, such as 1000000100001, can also be represented as a polynomial of degree $(n - 1)$, for example, $x^{12} + x^5 + 1$. Although the notation appears complicated, the checksum calculation can be implemented in hardware using a simple shifting register and one or more XOR (exclusive-OR) gates. Because the HEC field is used not only for bit error detection but also for cell delineation (finding the position of cells within a bit stream), the bit sequence 01010101 (with the most significant bit at the left) is also added (XORed) to the checksum before transmission. This increases the reliability of the cell delineation algorithm, described below. Before evaluating the HEC for error detection and possibly correction, of course, the receiving station subtracts (XORs) the 01010101 bit sequence again.

At the receiving end of each link, the header is checked to see if the HEC value is correct. Normally it would only be correct if there are no bit errors anywhere in the header, including the HEC itself. If a single bit error has occurred due to physical layer bit errors, for example, the HEC provides sufficient redundancy to permit correction of that error. Similarly, two bit errors in one header can always be detected, though not corrected. If three or more bit errors occur, however, they may not be detectable, because on rare occasions, multiple bit errors can result in a header whose VPI/VCI value, though corrupted, fits the corrupted HEC. If the corrupted VPI/VCI value happened to be a legal value—one that belonged to an existing virtual connection—then the errored cell would be misinserted into that virtual connection and, of course, lost to the virtual connection to which it originally belonged. If, on the other hand, the new VPI/VCI value were not supported—that is, it is an "impermissable cell," as the switch has no translation table entry for it—then the cell would be discarded. Note that some interfaces use the HEC only to detect errors, and make no attempt to correct them. This is because certain physical-layer scrambling methods can result in error multiplication, so that reliable error correction is not possible.

Cell Delineation Using the HEC Field.   The following algorithm is used to detect the beginning of an ATM cell in a bit stream (also illustrated in Figure 6.3):

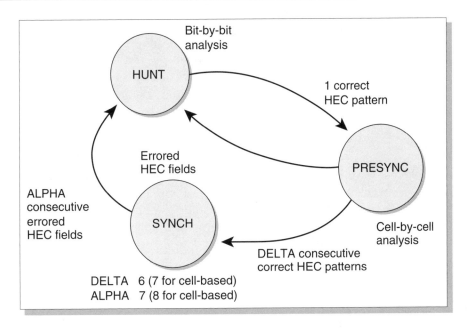

Figure 6.3
State diagram of the HEC cell delineation algorithm.

- In the HUNT state, the incoming signal is analyzed bit by bit to determine whether it could be part of an HEC pattern. As soon as a potential HEC pattern has been found, the receiver changes to the PRESYNC state.

- Under the assumption that a cell has been detected, the PRESYNC state examines subsequent "candidate cells." If the HEC fields of the next DELTA candidate cells are also possible checksums, then the receiver assumes that it has synchronized with the cell stream, and switches to the SYNC state and cell synchronization, or "delineation," is declared. If less than DELTA consecutive cells meet the HEC test, the receiving station reverts to the HUNT state.

- If ALPHA consecutive cells fail the HEC test, the receiver in state assumes it has lost cell delineation, and switches to the HUNT state.

- For frame-based physical layers such as those based on SDH/SONET and PDH, ALPHA is equal to 7 and DELTA equals 6. For cell-based physical layers, ALPHA is 7 and DELTA is 8 (see ITU-T Recommendation I.432.1).

Data Field Scrambling. The data field (payload) of the ATM cells is scrambled in order to optimize cell delineation by HEC patterns. In the HUNT state, potential HEC sequences are easier to detect when the data is scrambled. In the PRESYNC and SYNC states, an unscrambling function is activated for the 48 user data bytes of the cell, but is not applied to the cell headers. In all framing types except the cell-based physical layer, the scrambling of the data field is based on the self-synchronizing scrambler (SSS) $x^{43} + 1$. Scrambling is optional in some interface types. Due to the relatively poor overall communication characteristics of the SSS process, the cell-based physical layer uses Distributed Sample Scrambling (DSS) with the generator polynomial $x^{31} + x^{28} + 1$. Note that, because the scrambling for non-cell-based interfaces takes place in the transmission convergence sublayer of the physical layer, all cells at such an interface, including any idle, unassigned, and OAM cells, are scrambled using the SSS process, regardless of the header routing label (VPI/VCI) value.

6.1.2   PLCP-Based Cell Mapping

Before the ATM standard for DS3 was created, a metropolitan area network (MAN) service known as Switched Multi-megabit Data Service (SMDS) had been developed by Bellcore (now Telecordia), which was itself based on the DQDB (dual queue dual bus) technology defined in IEEE 802.6. In DQDB, 53 byte protocol data units (PDUs) with a very similar structure to ATM cells were used to transfer user information—indeed the choice of 53 bytes had been strongly influenced by the developing ATM standards. SMDS, which could operate at rates up to 155 Mb/s, had also been defined to operate over existing North American PDH interfaces (T1 and T3); in Europe, a similar service (CBDS) was defined for E1 and E3 rates. In SMDS, the "cells" are known as SMDS Interface Protocol level 2 (SIP L2) PDUs. SMDS is comprised of the SMDS Interface Protocol (SIP) layers 1 through 3, illustrated in Figure 6.4.

A special frame structure was invented to carry the 53-byte DQDB "cells," which allowed path management information to be transferred over the transmission path (in a Path Overhead, or POH) and which preserved the 125 μs (8 kHz) timing coming from the service; this frame structure was given the name "Physical Layer Convergence Protocol" (PLCP) and forms the SIP level 1 layer. The PLCP frame structure is carried as the payload of the underlying PDH frame structures—a kind of wheel within a wheel. As already mentioned, the PLCP frame has a frame rate of 8 kHz and a justification (or "stuffing") procedure is used to maintain this rate independently of the underlying

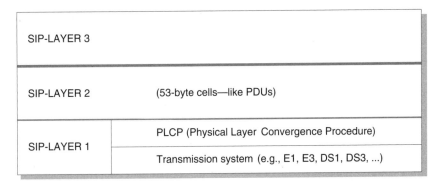

SIP-LAYER 3		
SIP-LAYER 2	(53-byte cells—like PDUs)	
SIP-LAYER 1	PLCP (Physical Layer Convergence Procedure)	
	Transmission system (e.g., E1, E3, DS1, DS3, ...)	

Figure 6.4
SMDS layers.

PDH frame, which was done to give it immunity from timing discrepancies that might occur in the physical layer. PLCP framing procedures were invented for all four of the PDH rates mentioned above (T1, E1, E3, and T3).

The ITU-T had assumed that ATM would be carried in SDH only, so the first interface developed for ATM was the STM-1 155 Mbit/s interface (and SONET OC-3 using STS-3c framing in North America). The ATM Forum, being a more pragmatic and initially a U.S.-focused organization, saw the need for a DS3 interface specification for ATM and so adapted the SMDS DS3 standard for use with ATM, replacing the SIP Level 2 PDUs of SMDS with ATM cells. This allowed existing network equipment to be adapted for use in early ATM networks. Following this, the ITU-T-defined cell mapping procedures in Recommendations G.804 and G.832 for other PDH interfaces were based not on the PLCP approach but the direct methods described earlier. The ATM Forum-adapted DS3 PLCP mapping was also adopted by the ITU-T as the only cell mapping for DS3 initially, although the more efficient direct method was later introduced, which is the preferred mapping for DS3 today. From this history, it can be seen how it was that only with DS3 was PLCP seriously used for any time. The SMDS-based PLCP mappings for other PDH interfaces were used occasionally in early ATM equipment but these never took hold.

Looking a little more closely at the PLCP procedures, the 53-byte cells are inserted before transmission into a dedicated PLCP frame, which in turn is transported in the payload field of the PDH frame. Unlike direct mapping, PLCP mapping adds another header for transmission of ATM cells. The advantage of PLCP frames is that existing facilities for PDH-based MANs can also be used for transmission of ATM cells. The price paid for this convenience, however, is that the 5-byte ATM overhead is increased not only by the

PDH frame overhead, but also by the PLCP frame header. This reduces the available user bandwidth by another 8% in comparison with direct cell mapping to existing transport frames. Figure 6.5 shows the now obsolete DS1 PLCP structure. We look at the DS3 PLCP mapping later in subsection 6.3.5.

The transmission convergence sublayer is responsible for the following functions in frame-based physical layers using PLCP, shown in order of relative position within the sublayer, top to bottom:

- HEC generation/verification
- Cell scrambling/descrambling (if enabled)
- PLCP framing and cell delineation
- Path overhead (POH) utilization
- PLCP timing (125 μs clock recovery) and nibble stuffing
- Transmission frame generation/recovery (frame-based interfaces)

HEC generation and verification is the same as that described earlier for non-PLCP frame-based physical layers but the HEC is not used here for cell delineation. This is, instead, done by establishing, PLCP frame synchroniza-

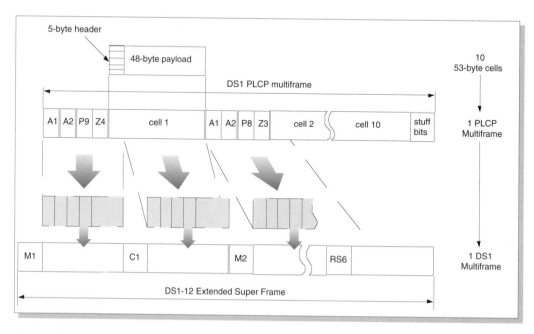

Figure 6.5
PLCP-based cell mapping: ATM cells in DS1 PLCP frames.

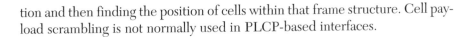

tion and then finding the position of cells within that frame structure. Cell pay-load scrambling is not normally used in PLCP-based interfaces.

6.1.3 Cell-Based Physical Layer

The cell-based physical layer (Figure 6.6) means that the ATM cells are not in-serted in any lower-layer transport frame, but simply transmitted bit for bit in the given communication medium's electrical or optical signals. The cell payload is scrambled by a different method from that used in other physical-layer inter-faces, however, since it has to ensure sufficient transitions to allow the clock tim-ing to be recovered from the incoming bit stream. The method used in the cell-based physical layer, Distributed Sample Scrambling (DSS), is described in I.432.1 and uses a 31st-order polynomial ($x^{31} + x^{28} + 1$). Because the scrambling is done by adding a pseudo random binary sequence to the payload part of the cell stream, error multiplication that sometimes occurs in scrambling is avoided.

One advantage of a cell-based physical layer is the efficient utilization of bandwidth. Because the ATM cell is not inserted in another frame, the ratio of overhead to user data remains about 1:9 (5 bytes of header, 48 bytes of data).

The disadvantage is that existing transport infrastructures can no longer be used. Many switching systems for 1.5, 2, 45, or 34 Mbit/s communication are de-signed for the corresponding DS1/E1 or DS3/E3 frame formats, and cannot process raw ATM cells. Another problem in wide area networks is the need to support monitoring and management information. In both classical PDH and modern SONET/SDH networks, the frames or containers in which data is transported also contain the monitoring and error handling information re-quired by the switching equipment. For this reason, special management cells have been defined for the cell-based physical layer, called Physical Layer Oper-ations and Maintenance, or PL-OAM, cells. These cells transport information required for the monitoring and management of the cell stream. Because many

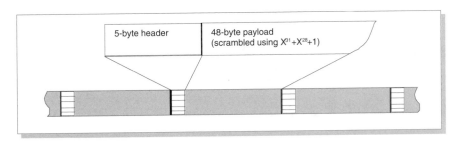

Figure 6.6
Cell-based physical layer.

of the existing infrastructures in wide area networking are unable to support the ATM cell-based physical layer, however, the use of this technique has been limited to local area networks. In practice, transportation of ATM cells in SONET/SDH frames has also gained acceptance in LANs, even though in the relatively simple LAN infrastructure—with no multiplexing hierarchy and a limited geographic range—these frames are actually superfluous as ATM transport containers. Currently, the cell-based physical layer is limited to a few ATM applications developed especially for this transport method, such as video.

The transmission convergence sublayer is responsible for the following functions in cell-based physical layers, shown in order of relative position within the sublayer, top to bottom:

- Cell rate decoupling (use of idle and/or PL-OAM cells)
- HEC generation/verification
- Cell scrambling/descrambling
- Cell delineation

6.2   ATM Data Rates

At present, a large number of transmission interfaces are defined both for LAN and WAN use, spanning a wide range of bandwidths and all kinds of transport media. Data rates range from fractional T1 (1.544 Mbit/s) to STM-64/OC-192 (9.9 Gbit/s) or even higher. The differences between the LAN and WAN specifications are primarily associated with the transport medium. Whereas single-mode fiber optic and coaxial cable are the primary media for WAN interfaces, multimode fiber, plastic optical fiber (POF), and copper unshielded twisted pair (UTP) are used in local area networking, where ATM is used. Table 6.1 lists the currently available transmission interfaces.

6.3   ATM in PDH Networks

6.3.1   The Plesiochronous Digital Hierarchy

The Plesiochronous Digital Hierarchy (PDH), specified in 1972 by the ITU-T for North America, Europe, and Japan, based on earlier national standards, is also a hierarchy of data structures at different bit rates (see Table 6.2).

Table 6.1   ATM Transmission Interfaces

Transport frame	Communication medium	Data rates (Mbit/s)
SDH/SONET	Single-mode fiber	155, 622, 2460, 9960
SDH/SONET	Multi-mode fiber	155, 622
SDH/SONET	POF, HPCF	155
SDH/SONET	75Ω coaxial cable	155
SDH/SONET	UTP3, UTP5, 150Ω STP	12.96, 25.92, 51.84, 155
PDH	75Ω coaxial cable	2.048, 34.36, 44.73, 139.26
PDH 100	Ω TP	1.544, 2.048
DXI	V.35, EIA/TIA 449, HSSI	up to 52
Cell stream	Single-mode fiber	155, 622
Cell stream	Multi-mode fiber	155, 622
Cell stream	V.35, EIA/TIA 449, HSSI	up to 52
Cell stream	UTP Cat.3, 120Ω Cat.4, 150Ω STP	25
Cell stream single	FDDI multimode/ mode (TAXI)	100

These rates are defined in ITU-T Recommendation G.702, and the physical and electrical properties of the interfaces are specified in G.703. The bit rates in the various hierarchical levels are calculated as follows:

$$T_{i+1} = m_i \left(T_i + x_i \right)$$

where m_i and x_i are specified for each hierarchical level individually; the additional bandwidth defined by x_i is necessary to accommodate the effects of frequency drift and physical layer bit jitter. ITU-T Recommendation G.702 defines a time-multiplex structure based on 64 kbit/s channels for the basic bit rates of 2.048 Mbit/s in E1 and 1.544 Mbit/s in T1. The 64 kbit/s specification dates back to the early days of digital voice signal transmission, when the conversion of voice signals into digital code was always performed at a sampling rate of 8 kHz. The analog signal is sampled at intervals of 125 μs, which, according to Nyquist, is sufficient to digitize all the information contained in a 4 kHz voice channel. Because every measured value is coded in 8 bits, the voice channel is transmitted at 64 kbit/s.

91

Table 6.2 Bit Rates (kbit/s) in the Plesiochronous Digital Hierarchy

Hierarchical Level	North America	Europe	Japan	Transatlantic
0	64	64	64	64
1	1,544	2,048	1,544	2,048
2	6,312	8,048	6,312	6,312
3	44,736	34,368	32,064	44,736
4	139,264	139,264	97,728	139,264

6.3.2   ATM over DS1: 1.544 Mbit/s

The T1 Interface (Carrying DS1 Signals)

The North American standard defines a primary rate of 1.544 Mbit/s called T1. This provides for the transmission of 24 channels at 64 kbit/s per channel or for payloads like ATM. Note that "T1" (Transmission level 1) describes the electrical signal, independent of the frame structure; "DS1" (Digital Signal level 1) defines the frame structure carried within T1; in practice, the terms tend to be used interchangeably, though, strictly, the physical interface should be called "T1." DS1 signals from T1 interfaces can be multiplexed to higher rate signals (DS2, DS3, etc.), whereas it would be wrong, strictly speaking, to talk about DS3 as being a multiplex of T1 signals.

Each DS1 frame is 193 bits long ($24 \times 8 + 1$ bits). The additional one bit is for frame alignment and yields a total of 1.544 Mbit/s (193 bits $\times$ 8 kHz). The pattern for frame alignment consists of 6 bits (101010), which are spread out over six frames since each frame carries only one alignment bit. The alignment bit is also used to identify the frames containing signaling bits, by means of another 6-bit pattern (001110). The alignment bit use alternates between framing and signal framing, so that each of the two patterns is completed once in every 12 frames. A multiframe sequence of 2316 bits (12 frames of 193 bits) containing both complete alignment patterns is also referred to as a superframe (see Figure 6.7).

Because networks have grown increasingly complex over the years, it has become necessary to include more monitoring information in data transmission frames. This has led to a new definition of Timeslot 0 in the European E1 interface (see section 6.3.3), and to the introduction of the 24-frame Extended Superframe (ESF) in the North American DS1 (see Figure 6.8). The alignment pattern in the ESF consists of 6 frame alignment bits alternating with

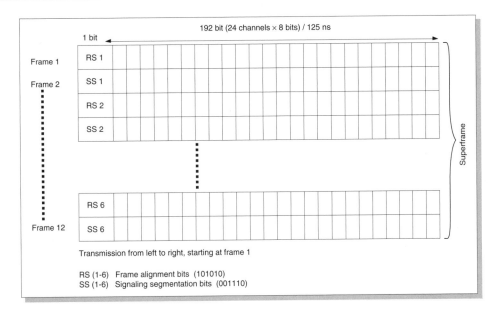

Figure 6.7
DS1 superframe.

6 CRC bits forming a CRC-6 checksum of the preceding ESF, and 12 signaling and monitoring bits. The transportation of 12 management bits per 24 frames yields a 4 kbit/s channel for signaling and error management.

At a data rate of 1.544 Mbit/s, the payload bandwidth in DS1 frames is 1.536 Mbit/s, corresponding to a capacity use of 99.5%. DS1 frames are B8ZS-encoded for ATM; another coding (AMI) is also available for voice-based DS1. The specified transport medium is 100Ω twisted-pair cable.

ATM Cell Mapping to the DS1 Frame Format

The mapping of ATM cells to DS1 line framing is specified in ITU-T Recommendation G.804 (see also the ATM Forum specification af-phy-0016.000, which references G.804). Under this standard, ATM cells can be transported in a 24-frame multiframe (Extended Superframe, or ESF) with the cells occupying bits 2 to 193. The individual ATM cells are byte-aligned with the DS1 frame, but not frame aligned. As 53 bytes is 424 bits, a single cell is spread over three or four DS1 frames, depending on alignment (see Figure 6.10). By inserting idle or unassigned cells when no valid ATM user data cells are available, the cell transfer rate is adapted to the user data bandwidth of DS1. Scrambling of the ATM cell's data field is optional, in contrast to the E1

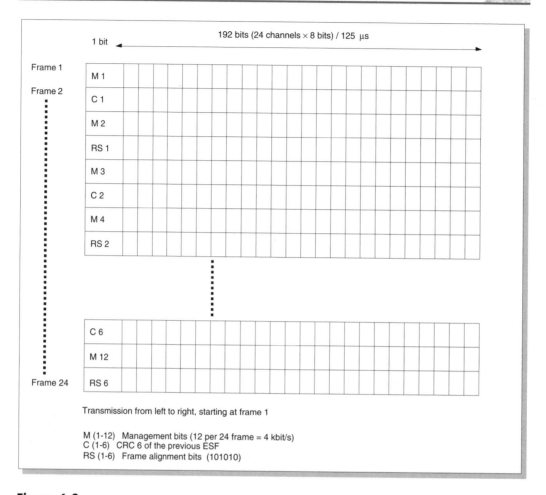

Figure 6.8
DS1 extended superframe (ESF).

ATM mapping. The self-synchronizing scrambling method is used with the generator polynomial $x^{43}+1$.

6.3.3 ATM over E1: 2.048 Mbit/s

The E1 Interface

The E1 system is based on a frame structure of 32×8 bit "timeslots" (i.e., a total of 256 bits); the timeslots are numbered 0 to 31. Like the DS1 frame, the E1 frame repeats every 125 μs; this creates a signal of 2.048 Mbit/s (256 bits

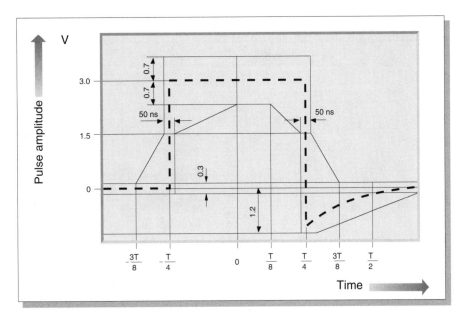

Figure 6.9
Pulse mask for the DS1 interface.

× 8 kHz). Because each 8-bit timeslot is repeated at a rate of 8 kHz, it is able to carry a 64 kbit/s channel.

Timeslot 0 alternates a frame alignment signal (FAS), containing an alignment bit pattern, with a "Not Frame Alignment" signal (NFAS), containing error management information (see Figure 6.12). Timeslot 16 was originally designed to carry signaling information, such as telephone numbers dialed. This left 30 payload timeslots (1 to 15, 17 to 31) available in the so-called PCM-30 system. In a PCM-30 system, Timeslot 16 of each frame carries signaling information for two payload channels (4 bits each). Fifteen out of 16 consecutive frames (i.e., a 16-frame multiframe) are thus required to transmit a signaling command for all 30 E1 payload channels; this method of signaling is known as Channel Associated Signaling (CAS; see Figure 6.13). CAS is very wasteful of bandwidth because, for any given payload channel, the signaling bits in Timeslot 16 are active only at the beginning of a call to set up the connection and at the end of the call to tear it down; for the duration of the call or when no call is present on the associated channel, these bits are idle. Consequently, a newer, more efficient, signaling method was invented called Common Channel Signaling (CCS), which involves the provision of a reserved 64 kbit/s channel carrying a messaging protocol that can handle the signaling for many channels from one or more E1 (or DS1) systems. Because the CCS

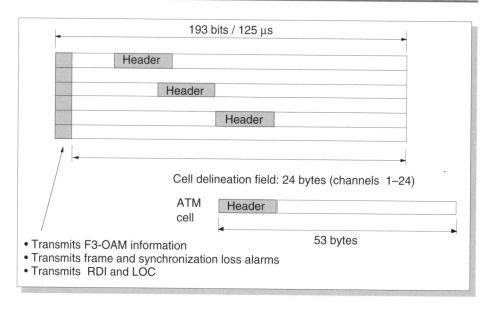

Cell delineation field: 24 bytes (channels 1–24)

• Transmits F3-OAM information
• Transmits frame and synchronization loss alarms
• Transmits RDI and LOC

Figure 6.10
Direct cell mapping to the DS1 frame format.

channel is outwardly like any other payload channel, it can be carried in any payload timeslot position and because Timeslot 16 is no longer required for carrying CAS, it can be made available for carrying a payload channel; this gives rise to the PCM-31 system; for example, one CCS channel might handle signaling for four PCM-31 systems so that three additional user payload channels are gained over the equivalent CAS PCM-30 systems. The payload bandwidth in the E1 interface is thus 1920 Mbit/s in PCM-30 systems and 1984 Mbit/s in PCM-31 systems.

The E1 bit stream is encoded using the High Density Bipolar (HDB3) technique. The specified transport medium is 75Ω coaxial cable or 120Ω twisted pair. The voltage level is ± 2.37 V.

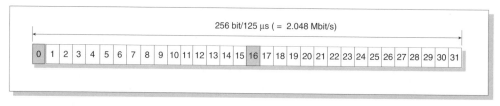

Figure 6.11
E1 frame.

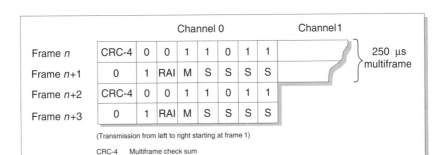

Figure 6.12
E1 Timeslot 0.

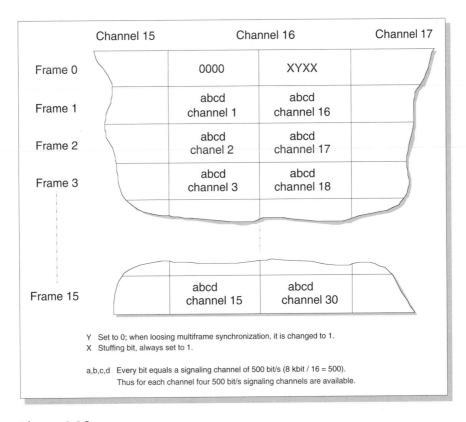

Figure 6.13
E1 Timeslot 16.

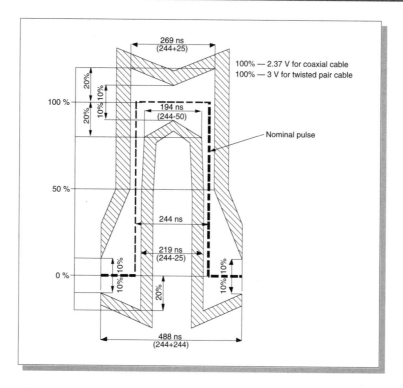

Figure 6.14
Pulse mask for the E1 interface.

ATM Cell Mapping to the E1 Frame Format

Like DS1 mapping, the mapping of ATM cells to E1 frames is also described in ITU-T Recommendation G.804 (see also the ATM Forum specification af-phy-0064.000 which references G.804). The ATM cells can be transported in bits 9–128 and 137–256, which correspond to timeslots 1–15 and 17–31. The cell rate is adapted to the E1 frame payload bandwidth of 1.920 Mbit/s by means of idle cells when no ATM cells are queued for insertion. Once again, the ATM cells are byte-aligned with the E1 frame, but not frame-aligned. Note that timeslot 16 is avoided, which is wasteful; however, by avoiding timeslot 16, this interface is compatible with both PCM-30 and PCM-31 transmission equipment (see Figure 6.15).

The 48 data bytes of each ATM cell are scrambled before transport using self-synchronizing scrambling (SSS) with the generator polynomial $x^{43}+1$. This permits fast cell delineation, allowing the receiving station to recover quickly from a loss of cell delineation due to physical layer bit errors, for example.

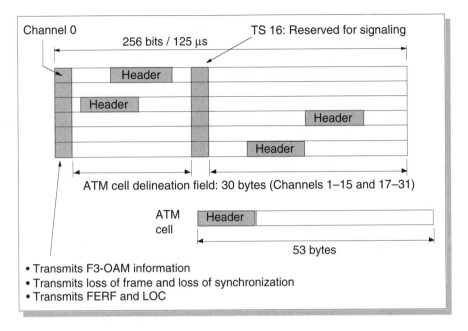

Figure 6.15
Cell mapping to the E1 frame format.

6.3.4   ATM over E3: 34.368 Mbit/s

The E3 Interface

In order to keep costs for primary-rate lines to a minimum, they are multiplexed and transported over higher bandwidth lines. Unfortunately, this cannot be accomplished by simply alternating transmission of bytes from the different primary rate signals, which would require global synchronization of all the signals being multiplexed. This is not possible, since every primary rate interface in PDH systems can derive its timing from a local clock. The differences in frequency between individual signals must be compensated by the insertion of justification ("stuffing") bits before multiplexing. When the signals are demultiplexed, removal of the justification bit restores the original signal frequency. Four multiplexed E1 signals form an 8.448 Mbit/s E2 channel, which can thus carry 120 or 124 basic rate 64 kbit/s channels (depending on whether PCM-30 or PCM-31 is in use), and four E2 signals yield a 34.368 Mbit/s E3 signal (480 or 496 basic rate 64 kbit/s channels). Note that these days the E2 rate is not used for transmission purposes, but merely as an intermediate step to E3.

34,360 Mbit/s - E3 frame ITU G.751

1	1	1	1	0	1	0	0	0	0	RAI	Res		Bits 13–384
C1	C1	C1	C1										Bits 5–384
C2	C2	C2	C2										Bits 5–384
C3	C3	C3	C3	St	St	St	St						Bits 9–384

- Frame length 1536 bits (4 x 8448 kbit/s)
- Frame alignment pattern 1111 0100 00
- RAI: Remote Alarm Indication
- Res: Reserved
- Cn: Justification Bits
- St: Stuffing bits

Figure 6.16
The E3 frame.

According to ITU-T G.751, an E3 frame is 1536 bits long and consists of four 384-bit lines, or subframes (Figure 6.16). The first 10 bits in the first subframe are reserved for frame alignment, bit 11 is used for remote alarm indication (RAI), and bit 12 is reserved for national use. In the second, third, and fourth subframes, the first 4 bits control the frequency adaptation process, or "justification," between the E2 and the E3 carrier frequencies. The first 3 bits in the first column (C1, C2, and C3) are set to the value 111 to indicate justification: in this case the first stuff bit, ST, is empty. If the first three bit values are 000, no justification is performed, in which case the stuff bit carries user data. The second, third, and fourth C-bit columns are used in the same way as the first. The sum of the bandwidths in the four E2 signals must always be lower than the bandwidth of the E3 signal, since stuffing only permits upward adjustment, or "positive justification." The bit stream is encoded using HDB3 (High Density Bipolar 3). The specified transport medium is one 75Ω coaxial cable for each direction; the voltage level is 1.0 V (Figure 6.17).

ATM over E3: 34.368 Mbit/s

The mapping of cells to the E3 frame format is described in ITU-T Recommendation G.804. The E3 frame format used is not the E3 frame format described in G.751, however, but a modified frame format described in G.832. The mapping of ATM cells to the older G.751 frame structure is difficult to accomplish: the cells would have to be "nibble-aligned," since each G.751 subframe is an integer multiple of 4 rather than 8 bits. The newer G.832 frame consists of 537 bytes, of which 7 bytes are used for overhead information (see Figure 6.18). The remain-

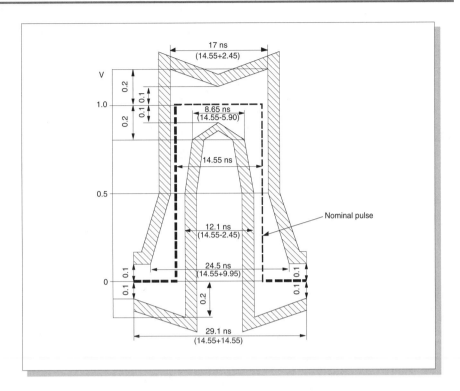

Figure 6.17
Pulse mask for the E3 interface.

ing 530 user data bytes correspond exactly to the length of 10 ATM cells, so that these can be byte- and frame-aligned (though the latter is not required—see Figure 6.19). The ATM cell rate is adapted to the E3 user data rate by the insertion of idle cells when no ATM cells are queued for transport; in North America, unassigned cells are often used for this purpose—both idle and unassigned cells are discarded at the input to switches, and so on. The 48-byte data field of the ATM cell (including idle/unassigned cells) is scrambled using self-synchronizing scrambling with the generator polynomial $x^{43}+1$.

6.3.5   ATM over DS3: 44.736 Mbit/s

The T3 Interface (Carrying DS3 Signals)

DS3 is the third multiplex level in the North American PDH hierarchy (see Figure 6.20). Four 1.544 Mbit/s DS1 signals are transported in one 6.312 Mbit/s DS2 signal; seven multiplexed DS2 signals yield a 44.736 Mbit/s DS3 signal.

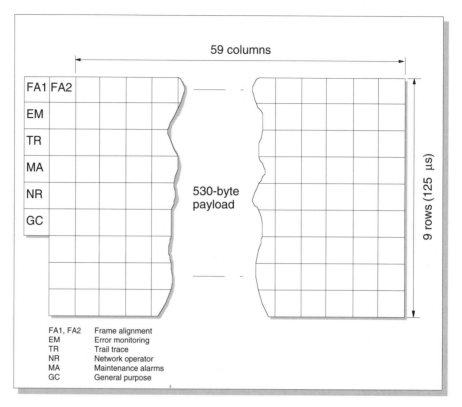

Figure 6.18
E3 frame as defined in G.832.

A 4760-bit DS3 multiframe consists of seven 680-bit frames. Each frame contains eight 84-bit payload blocks, separated by a single bit; these single bits are used for framing, stuffing, and for management purposes (e.g., alarms). Thus there are 4704 bits of user data in each DS3 multiframe, for a throughput of 44.21 Mbit/s. This corresponds to a bandwidth capacity use of 98.8%. The bit stream is B3ZS-encoded. The specified transport medium is one 75Ω coaxial cable for each direction, and the voltage level is 1.0 V (see Figure 6.21).

ATM over DS3: 44.736 Mbit/s

As discussed earlier, ATM cells can be transported over DS3 links using either the Physical Layer Convergence Protocol (PLCP) mapping found in older equipment or the direct cell mapping to the DS3 frame format preferred

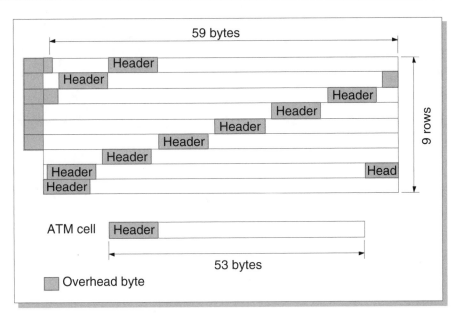

Figure 6.19
Cell mapping to the E3 frame format.

today. A DS3 PLCP frame consists of 12 rows of 57 bytes each. The last row contains an additional trailer of 12 or 13 nibbles (half-bytes) to fill out the user data field of a DS3 multiframe. The DS3 PLCP frame has a transmission time of 125 µs, corresponding to a rate of 44.21 Mbit/s, and thus fits exactly in the user data field of a DS3 multiframe (Figure 6.22).

The PLCP frame mapping of ATM cells is thus a two-stage process that is therefore complicated and also inefficient, as there is additional overhead associated with the PLCP frame structure; the cell payloads are not normally scrambled, as scrambling is only done to help isolate the cell header, which is already easily identifiable in the PLCP frame. The more efficient direct mapping of cells to the DS3 frame, sometimes referred to as "HEC" mapping, makes use of the same cell delineation process used for DS1, E1, and E3 mapping; cell payload scrambling again uses the self-synchronizing scrambling with the generator polynomial $x^{43}+1$.

The payload bandwidth for ATM cells transmitted in DS3 PLCP frames is 35.63 Mbit/s, representing a capacity use of 79%. The total overhead, including DS3, DS3 PLCP, and ATM overhead, takes up 21% of the effective bandwidth.

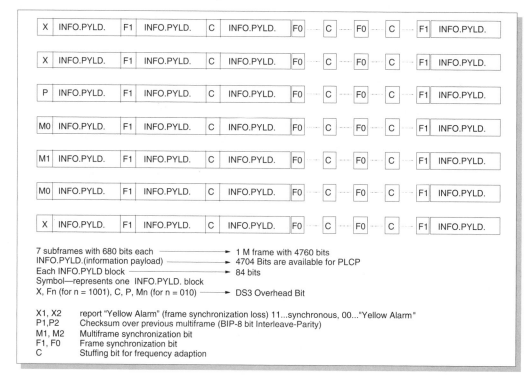

X	INFO.PYLD.	F1	INFO.PYLD.	C	INFO.PYLD.	F0	C	F0	C	F1	INFO.PYLD.
X	INFO.PYLD.	F1	INFO.PYLD.	C	INFO.PYLD.	F0	C	F0	C	F1	INFO.PYLD.
P	INFO.PYLD.	F1	INFO.PYLD.	C	INFO.PYLD.	F0	C	F0	C	F1	INFO.PYLD.
M0	INFO.PYLD.	F1	INFO.PYLD.	C	INFO.PYLD.	F0	C	F0	C	F1	INFO.PYLD.
M1	INFO.PYLD.	F1	INFO.PYLD.	C	INFO.PYLD.	F0	C	F0	C	F1	INFO.PYLD.
M0	INFO.PYLD.	F1	INFO.PYLD.	C	INFO.PYLD.	F0	C	F0	C	F1	INFO.PYLD.
X	INFO.PYLD.	F1	INFO.PYLD.	C	INFO.PYLD.	F0	C	F0	C	F1	INFO.PYLD.

7 subframes with 680 bits each ———————→ 1 M frame with 4760 bits
INFO.PYLD.(information payload) ———————→ 4704 Bits are available for PLCP
Each INFO.PYLD block ———————→ 84 bits
Symbol—represents one INFO.PYLD. block
X, Fn (for n = 1001), C, P, Mn (for n = 010) ———————→ DS3 Overhead Bit

X1, X2   report "Yellow Alarm" (frame synchronization loss) 11...synchronous, 00..."Yellow Alarm"
P1,P2   Checksum over previous multiframe (BIP-8 bit Interleave-Parity)
M1, M2   Multiframe synchronization bit
F1, F0   Frame synchronization bit
C   Stuffing bit for frequency adaption

Figure 6.20
DS3 frame format.

6.3.6   ATM over E4: 139.264 Mbit/s

The E4 Interface

E4 is the fourth multiplex level in the European PDH interface hierarchy (see Figure 6.23). Four E3 channels are multiplexed to form a single E4 channel. The E4 frame structure is also described in ITU-T G.751. Each G.751 E4 frame is 2928 bits long and consists of six 488-bit subframes; otherwise the structure is similar to G.751 E3 frames.

The bit stream is encoded using Coded Mark Inversion (CMI); the same coding method is used for the 155Mb/s SDH STM-1 electrical interface (see below). The specified transport medium is one 75Ω coaxial cable for each direction. The voltage level is ± 0.5 V (see Figure 6.24).

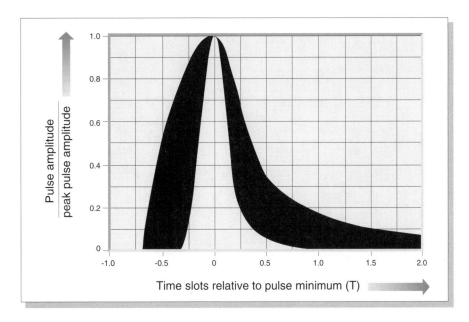

Figure 6.21
Pulse mask for the DS3 interface.

ATM Cell Mapping to the E4 Frame Format

Similar to E3, ATM cell transport in the E4 transmission frame (ITU-T Recommendation G.804) does not use the E4 frame format described in G.751, but a modified frame described in G.832. The ATM cells are inserted byte-aligned in the E4 frame payload field of the 2160-byte G.832-E4 frame (Figure 6.25). All other processing, such as the scrambling of the ATM cell payload and the cell rate adaptation, is performed as in the mapping of ATM cells to the E3 format (Figure 6.26). The E4 signal uses CMI line coding.

6.3.7 ATM over 6.312 Mbit/s and 97.728 Mbit/s

For the sake of thoroughness, we may mention at this point that ATM cell transport is also specified for the PDH bit rates 6.312 and 97.728 Mbit/s. These interfaces are only of regional importance, however, since they are almost never used outside Japan.

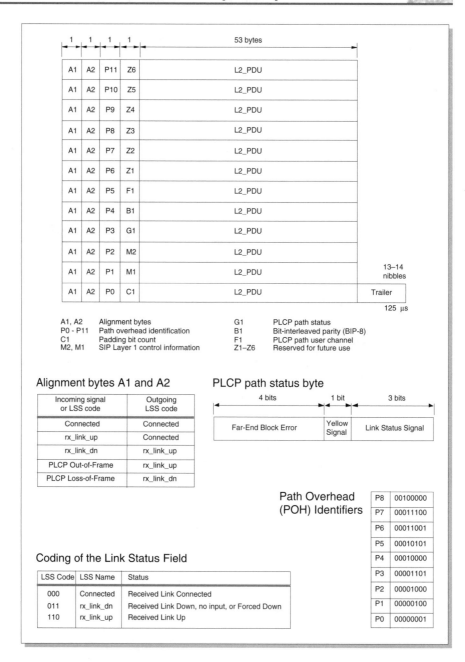

A1, A2   Alignment bytes
P0 - P11   Path overhead identification
C1   Padding bit count
M2, M1   SIP Layer 1 control information

G1   PLCP path status
B1   Bit-interleaved parity (BIP-8)
F1   PLCP path user channel
Z1–Z6   Reserved for future use

Alignment bytes A1 and A2

Incoming signal or LSS code	Outgoing LSS code
Connected	Connected
rx_link_up	Connected
rx_link_dn	rx_link_up
PLCP Out-of-Frame	rx_link_up
PLCP Loss-of-Frame	rx_link_dn

PLCP path status byte

4 bits	1 bit	3 bits
Far-End Block Error	Yellow Signal	Link Status Signal

Path Overhead (POH) Identifiers

P8	00100000
P7	00011100
P6	00011001
P5	00010101
P4	00010000
P3	00001101
P2	00001000
P1	00000100
P0	00000001

Coding of the Link Status Field

LSS Code	LSS Name	Status
000	Connected	Received Link Connected
011	rx_link_dn	Received Link Down, no input, or Forced Down
110	rx_link_up	Received Link Up

Figure 6.22
The DS3 PLCP frame.

139.264 Mbit/s E4 frame (ITU G.751)																	
1	1	1	1	0	1	0	0	0	0	RAI	Res	Res	Res		Bits 17–488		
C1	C1	C1	C1												Bits 5–488		
C2	C2	C2	C2												Bits 5–488		
C3	C3	C3	C3												Bits 5–488		
C4	C4	C4	C4												Bits 5–488		
C5	C5	C5	C5	St	St	St	St								Bits 9–488		

- Frame length 2928 Bits (4 x 34368 kbit/s)
- Frame alignment pattern 1111 1010 0000
- RAI: Remote Alarm Indication
- Res: Reserved
- Cn: Justification Bits
- St: Stuffing bits

Figure 6.23
E4 frame.

6.3.8   Inverse Multiplexing for ATM

Inverse Multiplexing for ATM (IMA) was originally specified by the ATM Forum in af-phy-0086.001 and was recently adopted essentially unchanged by the ITU-T in Recommendation I.761. IMA is the process of dividing an ATM cell stream into several component streams for transport, which are then reassembled into the original stream at the receiving end (Figure 6.27). This makes it possible to transport high bandwidths over several bundled data links of lower capacity. For example, bandwidths of 4 to 34 Mbit/s can be realized by bundling the appropriate number of E1 links, though it becomes uneconomical to consider bundles or "link groups" with more than about 6–8 links. The ATM cell are transported one at a time over each of the available lines in turn. For every M cell, a special IMA Control Protocol (ICP) cell is inserted. The ICP cell, together with the corresponding ATM user data cells, comprise an "IMA frame." Each ICP cell contains a Link Identifier (LID) indicating the individual line, an IMA frame sequence number, and various information fields used to monitor and synchronize the transmission (Figure 6.28).

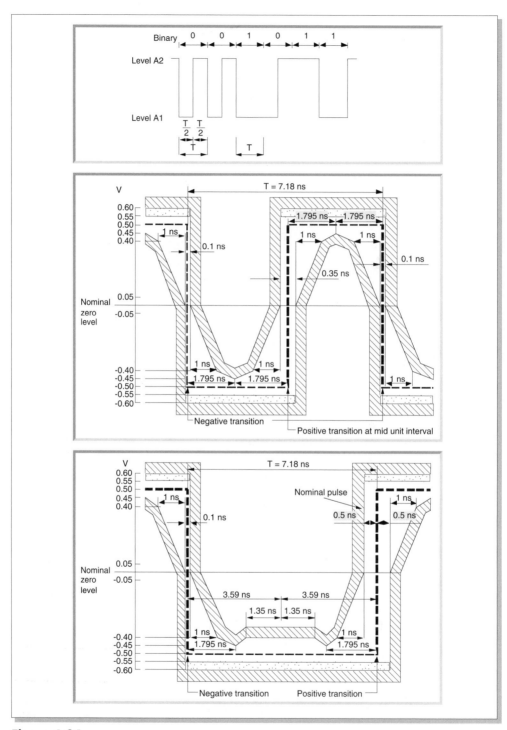

Figure 6.24
Pulse mask for the E4 interface.

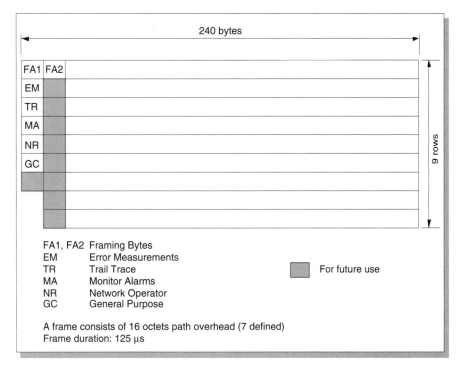

Figure 6.25
G.832-E4 frame.

6.3.9   ATM over Fractional Physical Links

IMA allows ATM transmission bandwidth to be increased through the use of multiple T1 or E1 circuits. Going in the opposite direction, ATM over fractional physical links allows ATM to be sent with bandwidths below T1 or E1 in the same way that Frame Relay can use fractional T1 or E1. As we have seen, T1 and E1 were originally used for carrying $n \times 64$ kbit/s channels. In fractional T1 and E1, multiple 64 kbit/s channels can be used together to provide sub-T1 or sub-E1 bandwidths. The ATM Forum has specified the procedure in af-phy-0130.000, which has again been adopted by the ITU-T in Recommendation I.762. In these schemes, contiguous or noncontiguous timeslots can be used in any number to create an ATM bearer channel—for example, 6×64 kbit/s provides a bearer channel of 384 kbit/s.

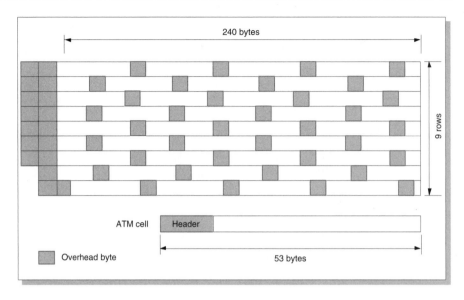

Figure 6.26
Cell mapping to the G.832 E4 frame format.

In Japan, fractional J2 is also specified, although this is not covered by ITU-T Recommendation I.762. J2 comprises 96 × 64 kbit/s (i.e., 6.312 Mbit/s) and fractional groupings are allowed as follows:

Timeslots 1–72 (4.608 Mb/s)

Timeslots 1–48, 49–96 (3.073 Mb/s)

Timeslots 1–24, 25–48, 49–72, 73–96 (1.536 Mb/s)

ATM over fractional T1, E1, or J2 is starting to be used in ATM over wireless applications.

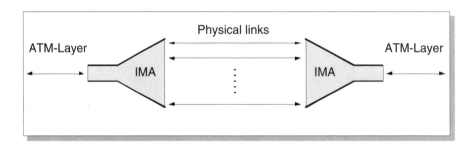

Figure 6.27
Principles of inverse multiplexing of ATM cells.

Bytes 1–5   ATM cell header: GFC=0, VPI=0, VCI=0, PTI=101, CLP=1, HEC

Byte 6   IMA label: Bits 7–0: IMA Version Value
 00000001: IMA Version 1.0
 00000011: IMA Version 1.1

Byte 7   Cell ID: Bit 7: IMA OAM Cell Types (0: idle cell, 1: ICP cell)
 Link ID: Bits 6–5: not used; set to 0
                         Bits 4–0: logical ID for IMA links 0 to 31

Byte 8   IMA frame sequence number: 0–255, cyclical

Byte 9   ICP cell offset range (0 to M–1): indicates ICP cell position in the IMA frame

Byte 10   Link stuff indication:
 Bits 7–3:   not used; set to
 Bits 2–0:   Link Stuffing Indication (LSI)
                    111 = No imminent stuff event
                    100 = Stuff event in 4 ICP cell locations (optional)
                    011 = Stuff event in 3 ICP cell locations (optional)
                    010 = Stuff event in 2 ICP cell locations (optional)
                    001 = Stuff event at the next ICP cell location (mandatory)
                    000 = This is one of the two ICP cells compromising the stuff event (mandatory)

Byte 11   Status and control change indication: Bits 7–0: Status change indication: 0 to 255
              (count to be incremented every change of octets 12–49)
Byte 12   IMA ID

Byte 13   Group status and control
 Bits 7–4: Group state
                    0000 = Start-up
                    0001 = Start-up-Ack
                    0010 = Config-Aborted - Unsupported M
                    0011 = Config-Aborted - Incompatible Group Symmetry
                    0100 = Config-Aborted - Unsupported IMA Version
                    0101 = Reserved for other Config-Aborted reasons in a future version of the IMA specification
                    0110 = Reserved for other Config-Aborted reasons in a future version of the IMA specification
                    0111 = Config-Aborted - Other reasons
                    1000 = Insufficient-Links
                    1001 = Blocked
                    1010 = Operational
                    Others: Reserved for later use in a future version of the IMA specification
 Bits 3–2: Group symmetry mode
                    00 = Symmetrical configuration and operation
                    01 = Symmetrical configuration and asymmetrical operation (optional)
                    10 = Asymmetrical configuration and asymmetrical operation (optional)
                    11 = Reserved
 Bits 1–0: IMA Frame length (00: M=32, 01: M=64, 10: M=128, 11: M=256)

Byte 14 Transmit timing information
              Bits 7–6:   not used; set to 0
              Bit 5:   Transmit clock mode (0: ITC mode; 1: CTC mode)
              Bits 4–0:   Tx LID of the timing reference (0 to 31)

Byte 15   Tx test control   Bits 7–6:   not used; set to 0
                                  Bit 5:   Test link command (0: inactive; 1: active)
                                  Bits 4–0:   Tx LID of test link (0 to 31)

Byte 16   Tx test pattern Bits 7–0: Tx test pattern (values 0–255)

Byte 17   Rx test pattern Bits 7–0: Rx test pattern (values 0–255)

Byte 18   Link 0 information   Bits 7–5: Tx status
                                  Bits 4–2: Rx status
                                  Bits 1–0: Remote Defect Indicator

Bytes 19–49 Link 1–31 info status and control

Byte 50   not used; set to 6A hex (ITU I.432)

Byte 51   End-to-end channel (proprietary channel set to 0 if not used)

Bytes 52–53 Bits 15–10: Reserved field for future use - default to all zero
              Bits 9–0: CRC–10 (as specified in ITU–T I.610)

Figure 6.28
ICP cell format.

6.4   ATM in SDH and SONET Networks

6.4.1   The Synchronous Digital Hierarchy (SDH) and Synchronous Optical Network (SONET)

Back in the late 1970s, Bellcore (now Telecordia) saw the need to replace the Plesiochronous (near synchronous) Digital Hierarchy (PDH) in the North American Bell System (as it was then known) with a new synchronous network, so started work on what we now know as SONET, the Synchronous Optical NETwork. PDH networks had evolved in a rather ad hoc manner and it was time to improve on this. What was needed was a transmission standard that allowed higher rate transmission, properly planned network management facilities, and, most importantly, a means to time lock the digital channels being carried so that individual lower rate channels could be accessed directly without the need to break down the PDH signal by hierarchy level, taking into account the justification (stuffing) that had occurred at each level during signal construction; SONET would be able to provide all this.

Initially, SONET was focused on handling PDH rates used in North America only, for example, T1 (1.5Mb/s) and T3 (45 Mb/s), and was thus based on a frame structure of 9 subframes of 60 octets (bytes) that, it turned out, precluded the more international rates of E1 (2 Mb/s), E3 (34 Mb/s), and so on. The ITU-T (then called the CCITT) also saw the need for a new synchronous network standard. It therefore worked with Bellcore to have the SONET system modified to allow a more general standard, based on a frame structure of 9 subframes of 90 octets (usually represented diagrammatically as a two-dimensional drawing of 9 rows by 90 columns), that would be compatible with North American *and* international PDH rates—after all, a new standard had to interwork with what was already in existence. The Synchronous Digital Hierarchy (SDH) was thus defined by the ITU-T in 1988 as an international recommendation (standard) for wide area data communications and is almost identical to SONET. The main differences between SONET and SDH are as follows: first, the basic rate of SONET is 51.84 Mb/s, whereas SDH has a basic rate of 155.52 Mb/s (three times 51.84 Mb/s); second, SONET defines the optical layer while SDH defines signal protocol structure above the optical layer, other ITU-T recommendations focusing on the optical layer; third, different terminology is used with each standard, a source of constant confusion and irritation. There are also some minor interoperability issues, which will be mentioned later.

SDH/SONET frames are universal transport containers for all types of digitized data, including data streams such as cell- and frame-based ATM, IP ("Packet over SONET"), Frame Relay, and leased lines, as well as the entire range of digital and analog telephony. Even in telecommunication systems that supply subscribers with analog service, voice signals have long been transmitted in digitized form over wide area backbones and reconverted to analog signals at the destination switch. Today, SDH or SONET is used by all major telecom service providers to implement high-speed backbones in wide area networks.

When ATM was chosen as the transfer mechanism for the ITU-T's Broadband ISDN project, SDH/SONET frames became the transmission vehicle of choice for ATM cell streams. This coupling of ATM and SDH/SONET was still widespread when, some years later, ATM began to be used in local area networks. This is how SDH/SONET, originally developed for wide area networks, also came to be used in LANs as well.

The main advantage of SDH/SONET over the older PDH structures lies in its use of a transparent multiplexing method that allows individual channels to be accessed directly. This means that a 64 kbit/s channel, for example, can be directly read out of, or inserted into, the highest SDH/SONET multiplex level (currently 39.81 Gbit/s). This capability is also called single-stage multiplexing.

Another advantage of SDH/SONET is its overhead structure, which is designed to support modern, highly automatic switching and network management systems. When communication errors occur, the problem domain can be quickly identified by evaluating overhead bytes. This is why the conversion of data transmission structures to SONET or SDH has been increasing steadily over the past few years. All PDH multiplex hierarchies can also be transmitted over the SDH/SONET network, so that the transition from PDH to SDH/SONET is smooth.

6.4.2   The Principles of SDH/SONET

The nodes of an SDH/SONET network, shown in Figure 6.29, are connected by different types of transport sections. The type of a given section is determined by the types of nodes at its ends. A section between two signal regenerators (repeaters), for example, is called a Regenerator Section in SDH (just "Section" in SONET), and a section between two multiplexers is a Multiplexer Section in SDH ("Line" in SONET). The end-to-end connection through the SDH/SONET network from the point at which a service (tributary signal) enters the network to the point from which it leaves the network is called a "Path" in both SDH and SONET.

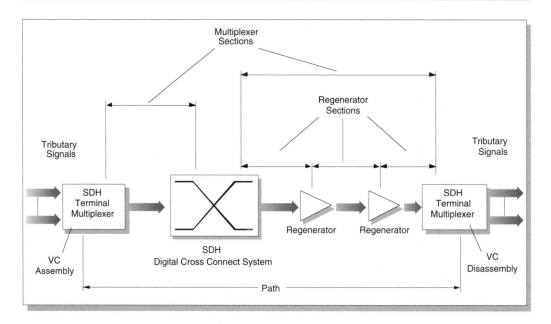

Figure 6.29
Topology of SDH/SONET networks.

In the following sections, different SONET and SDH interfaces are considered. Because SDH and SONET are so closely related, the general principals of operation for both are very similar, so a more detailed explanation of the lowest level (STS-1/OC-1) is given but can, to some extent, be generalized for higher order systems in both standards. Note that while the original first level of the ITU-T SDH system is at 155Mb/s, an SDH system corresponding to STS-1 does now exist, known as STM-0.

The SONET OC-1 and EC-1 Interfaces

The first hierarchical level in SONET is the Synchronous Transport Signal 1 (STS-1). This is an 810-byte frame that is transmitted at 51.84 Mbit/s (see Figure 6.30). When transmitted over an optical interface, the signal is known as Optical Carrier 1 (OC-1). STS-1 over an electrical interface is called Electrical Carrier 1 (EC-1), although this term is rarely used. The transmission time of an STS-1 frame corresponds to the 125-μs PCM (pulse code modulation) sampling interval. Each byte in the SONET signal thus represents a bandwidth of 64 kbit/s. The frame is divided into nine subframes of 90 bytes each. The first 3 bytes of each of the nine subframes comprise the 27-byte

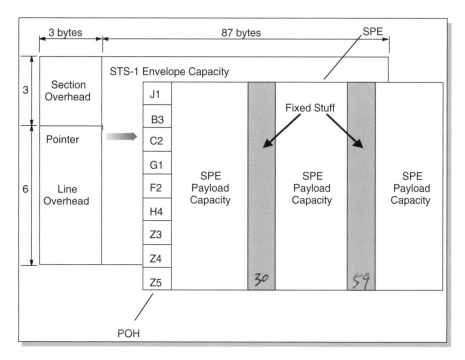

Figure 6.30
STS-1 frame.

transport overhead (TOH). The remaining 87 bytes of each subframe form the 783-byte synchronous payload envelope (SPE). SONET (and SDH) frames are conventionally represented as a two-dimensional diagram of nine rows and n columns, with each row corresponding to a subframe. Consequently, the TOH of the STS-1 frame occupies the first three columns of the frame, and the STS-1 frame payload field, or "envelope capacity," occupies 87 columns. The 27 (3×9) TOH bytes control the transport of user data between neighboring network nodes, and contain information required by the given section or line. The TOH is divided into two parts, the section overhead and the line overhead. TOH bytes A1, A2, J0/Z0, B1, E1, F1, and D1 through D3 comprise the section overhead, and bytes H1, H2, H3, B2, K1, K2, D4 through D12, S1/Z1, M0, and E2 form the line overhead.

The SPE, also a structure of 783 bytes, is located in the 9-to 87-byte envelope capacity (the frame payload area). The first column of the SPE is occupied by the POH, and columns 30 and 59 are reserved for "fixed stuffing." This leaves 84 columns of the synchronous payload envelope for carrying user traffic.

The alignment of the SPE in the SONET frame is not fixed—that is, the SPE "floats" in the envelope capacity. The beginning of the SPE is identified by a 10-bit pointer residing in the H1 and H2 bytes of the TOH. Because it is not frame-aligned, an SPE typically starts in one frame and ends in the next. The reason for this arrangement is to allow multiple SONET frames to be aligned for multiplexing into higher-order structures. (For example, three STS-1 frames can be multiplexed into one STS-3 frame.) In effect, the SPE remains fixed while the frame structure rotates to achieve alignment. Minor frequency differences between the lower-order SONET frames can also be accommodated. The SPE can drift within the envelope capacity by no more than one byte from one frame to the next, and the SONET standard even limits how frequently this can happen. When the SPE moves within the envelope capacity, the H1/H2 pointer values change, and a byte is either added to or removed from the envelope capacity, depending on the direction of the drift. This stuffing process is comparable to that described above for PDH multiplexing. If an additional byte is required—as when the tributary SONET frame rate, and hence the SPE, is running at a slightly faster rate than the higher-order SONET frame—then the H3 byte becomes part of the envelope capacity for one frame, and holds a byte of the SPE. In other words, the fourth row of the SONET frame payload area is increased from 87 to 88 bytes, and the value of the H1/H2 pointer is decreased by one. In the opposite case, that is, if one less byte is occasionally required because the lower-order SONET frame is running slightly slower, then the first byte in the fourth row of the envelope capacity (that is, the byte following the H3 byte) is omitted, so that this row shrinks from 87 to 86 bytes for one frame, and the H1/H2 pointer value is increased by one. This process occurs as multiplexing is performed at all levels of the SDH/SONET hierarchy. SDH and SONET networks are generally locked to accurate frequency standards, but certain effects cannot be avoided (such as "wander," a low-frequency variation often caused by the effects of 24-hour temperature cycles on long-haul transmission line delay), so pointer movements do occur.

For the OC-1 optical interface, the transmitter is normally a 1310-nm single-mode laser; for the EC-1 electrical interface, the same electrical coding (B3ZS) is used as for T3.

The SONET OC-3 and SDH STM-1 Interfaces

The second level of the SONET hierarchy, STS-3, is a byte-by-byte interleaving of three STS-1 frames. Consequently, the transport overhead now occupies 9 columns and the envelope capacity (payload area) occupies 261 columns. The whole frame is therefore 270 columns by nine rows (nine subframes of 270 bytes, that is, 2430 bytes in all), and has a frame rate of 125 µs, the PCM sampling interval (see Figure 6.31). The ITU-T based its first-level SDH structure on the STS-3 structure, and called it the Synchronous Transport Module (STM-1). Note that, because STM-1 is the first hierarchical level of SDH, the payload is not treated as a multiplex of three lower-level frames, as STS-3 is, but as a single entity, particularly for carrying broadband services such as ATM. In SONET there is a corresponding variant of the STS-3 structure, in which the payload, instead of comprising interleaved bytes from three unrelated payloads from the lower STS-1 multiplex level, is a single entity, renamed <u>STS-3c</u> (the "c" stands for concatenation). OC-3 (without a lowercase "c," though you will often see "OC-3c" used, incorrectly) is the corresponding optical carrier. For most purposes, STS-3c can be considered identical to STM-1. There is one important distinction, however, and this lies in the "SS" field (bits 5 and 6) of overhead byte H2: these bits hold the value 00 in SONET and the value 10 in SDH. For the sake of interoperability, receivers for either standard should ignore the value in this field.

In the SDH standard, payload data is transported in STM-1 frame payload field containers. These containers, designated C11, C12, C2, C3, C4, C4-4c, and so on, are the multiplex elements of SDH, and are defined for a variety of payload capacities (see Figure 6.32 and Table 6.3). A container together with its path overhead (POH) is called a virtual container, or VC. Path overhead information is used to monitor alarm states and transmission quality. The POH accompanies the container from the source path-terminating equipment (PTE) to the destination PTE. A distinction is made between higher-order virtual containers (<u>HVCs</u>) and lower-order virtual containers (<u>LVCs</u>), which have

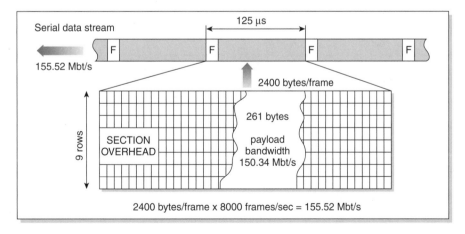

Figure 6.31
STM-1 frame.

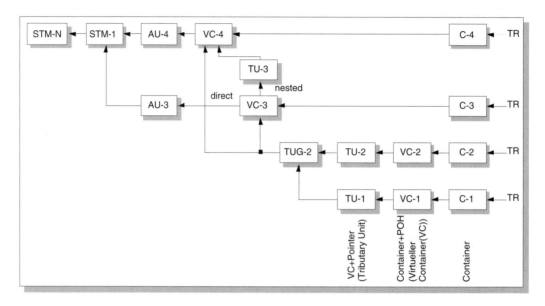

Figure 6.32
Multiplexing of lower-rate containers into SDH STM-1.

Table 6.3 SDH Container Elements

Multiplex Element (Container)	Capacity (kbit/s)
C-11	1,600
C-12	2,176
C-21	6,784
C-22	9,088
C-31	36,864
C-32	48,384
C-4	149,760

different transmission capacities. HVCs are the containers VC-4-256c, VC-4-64c, VC-4-16c, VC-4-4c, VC-4, and VC-3; LVCs are the containers VC-3 VC-2, VC-12, and VC-11. Note that VC-3 can be HVC or LVC. A similar distinction is made between the higher-order path overhead (HO-POH) and the lower-order path overhead (LO-POH).

As in PDH, the individual tributary signals in SDH networks are not in phase with one another, so that phase compensation is necessary before signals can be multiplexed. The user signal is adapted to the container bit rate by the addition of stuff bits. Like the SPE in SONET frames, the containers themselves are usually illustrated as begin aligned with the SDH transport frames. In practice, however, phase shifts occur due to alignment for multiplexing, latency, clock regeneration errors, and similar problems. As in SONET, and in contrast to PDH, the location of every virtual container in SDH is indicated by a pointer contained in the next higher multiplex layer. Phase shifts between adjacent layers are corrected by adjusting the pointer value, which means the container can be located by means of the pointer at all times. This is why any container can be accessed individually, at any hierarchical multiplexing level, without demultiplexing the entire signal stream. The combination of a virtual container and its pointer on the next higher hierarchical level (the tributary unit pointer) is called a tributary unit, designated TU-11, TU-12, TU-1, TU-2, and so on (see Figure 6.33). Several TU-1s or a single TU-2 can also be called a tributary unit group (TUG). Similarly, a tributary unit combined with its pointer on the next higher hierarchical level is called an administrative unit (AU), and the pointer is called an AU pointer.

Table 6.4 lists the various bit rates with their multiplex elements. Three VC-31 containers, for example, can be transported in one VC-4 container, which in turn is transported in an STM-1 frame. The AU-32 pointer indicates the exact position of the VC-4, whose four TU-31 pointers in turn indicate the three VC-31 containers (Figure 6.34).

In addition to the first SONET hierarchical level, STS-1 and the first SDH hierarchical level STM-1, corresponding to the second SONET level STS-3, the multiplex streams STM-4/STS-12, STM-16/STS-48, STM-64/STS-192, and STM-256/STS-768 have also been defined with data rates of 622.08 Mbit/s, 2,488.32 Mbit/s, 9.95328 Gbit/s, and 39.81312 Gbit/s. The general formulas for SDH and SONET bit rates above STS-1/STM-0 are:

$$STM - n = n \times 155.52 \text{ Mbit/s}$$

$$STS - n = n/3 \times 155.52 \text{ Mbit/s}$$

The bit rates of the higher Synchronous Transport Modules, unlike those of the plesiochronous hierarchy, are integer multiples of the basic 155.52 Mbit/s module. Higher-order SDH/SONET signals are formed from lower-order signals through byte-interleaving.

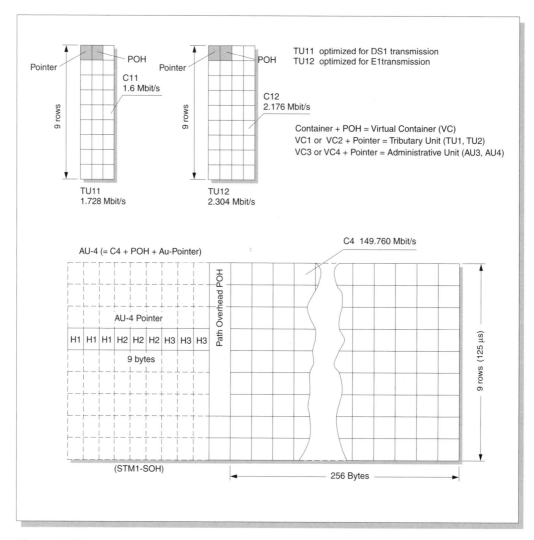

Figure 6.33
Container, virtual container, and tributary unit (TU).

Table 6.4 SDH Bit Rates and Multiplex Elements

Multiplex Element	Bitrate in kbit/s	1,544	2,048	6,312	8,448	34,368	44,736	139,264	C-11	C-12	C-21	C-22	C-31	C-32	C-4	TU-11	TU-12	TU-21	TU-22	TUG-21	TUG-22	TU-31	TU-32	AU-31	AU-32	AU-4	STM-1
		Transport / G.702 Signal							**Multiplex Element**																		
C-11	1,600	X																									
C-12	2,176		X																								
C-21	6,784			X																							
C-22	9,088				X																						
C-31	36,864					X														X	X						
C-32	48,384						X													X							
C-4	149,760							X												X	X	X	X				
TU-11	1,728								X																		
TU-12	2,304									X																	
TU-21	6,912										X																
TU-22	9,216											X															
TUG-21	6,912															X	X	X									
TUG-22	9,216															X	X		X								
TU-31	37,440												X														
TU-32	49,152													X													
AU-31	37,440												X														
AU-32	50,304													X													
AU-4	150,912														X												
STM-1	155,520																							X	X	X	
STM-4	622,080																										X
STM-16	2,488,320																										X
STM-64	9,953,280																										X

Concatenation of VC-4 Containers

As with concatenation in SONET to create STS-3c to transmit tributary signals in SDH with higher bit rates than the 149.76 Mbit/s available in a VC-4 in a single multiplex layer, a concatenated container, VC-4-4c, has been defined on the basis of the STM-4 transport module (the small "c" again stands for concatenation). This STM-4c transport module (shown in Figure 6.36) has the same size and SOH structure as an ordinary STM-4 transport frame (the SONET equivalent is STS-12c carried in OC-12). The VC-4-4c container is

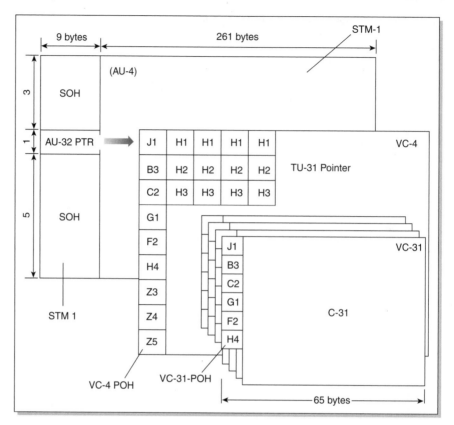

Figure 6.34
SDH multiplexing.

considered a unit, however, and is multiplexed and routed as such. The transport capacity of an STM-4c transport module is 599.04 Mbit/s. Analogous VC-4-16c, VC-4-64c, and VC-4-256c containers are also defined, with nominal capacities of 2.39616 Gbit/s, 9.58464 Gbit/s, and 38.33856 Gbit/s, respectively.

6.4.3 SDH and SONET Compared

The main difference between SDH and SONET is that SONET generally uses the VC-3 virtual container for data transmission, while ETSI SDH transports user data for the most part in VC-4 containers (see Figure 6.37). This is

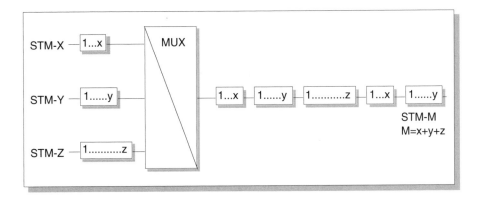

Figure 6.35
Multiplex formation of SDH transport modules.

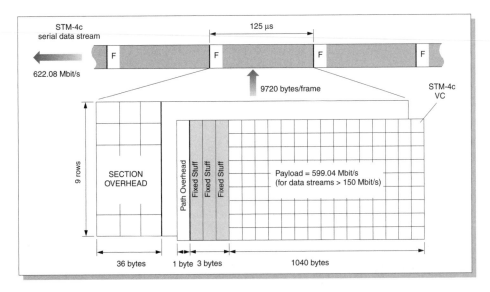

Figure 6.36
STM-4c transport module.

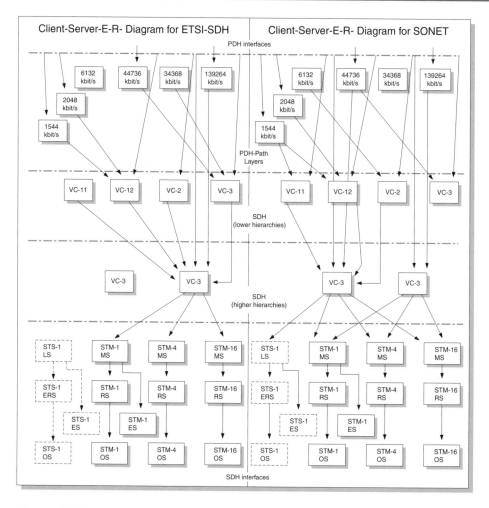

Figure 6.37
Comparison of SDH and SONET.

because the existing North American PDH hierarchy, especially the third hierarchical layer, DS3 (44.736 Mbit/s), is better suited for transport in a VC-3 than in a VC-4. Furthermore, SONET has the extra STS-1 level with a bit rate of 51.84 Mbit/s that can transport exactly one VC-3 and is thus ideal for transporting DS3 streams.

6.4.4 SOH and POH: Section Overhead and Path Overhead

As mentioned above, the section overhead of an STM-1 transport module is composed of multiplex section and regenerator section overhead bytes. These are roughly equivalent to the section and line overhead bytes that make up the transport overhead (TOH) of SONET, except that in SDH, the fourth row containing the H1, H2, and H3 bytes is not included in the multiplex section overhead, while in SONET these bytes are part of the line overhead. The following description refers to the SDH structure. For the sake of simplicity, the SONET structure, which is similar except for some terminology, is not discussed in detail here (see Figure 6.38).

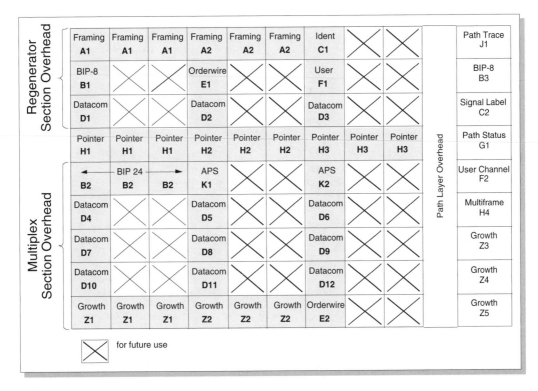

Figure 6.38
The STM-1 SOH and POH bytes.

The "multiplex section" of an SDH network designates the overall communication between two network nodes, including the intermediate regenerators and switches. Furthermore, multiplex sections are capable of independent action in the event of communication errors. For example, if a network component becomes overloaded or even fails completely, the virtual container affected can be rerouted to a backup path, called a protection channel. This procedure is called automatic protection switching (APS). A regenerator section, however, comprises only the transmission path and systems located between a network node and a regenerator, or between two regenerators. Regenerator sections do not have backup paths.

Section Overhead Bytes

The multiplexer and regenerator section overheads contain the following SOH bytes:

Multiplexer Section Overhead (MSOH)

- B2: The 24 bits in the three B2 bytes contain the bit-interleaved parity (BIP-24) code calculated from all bits of the previous STM-1 frame plus its MSOH bytes, but without its regenerator overhead bytes.
- K1, K2: Bytes K1 and K2 control backup switching functions in case of system failure, using APS messages. A distinction is made between linear APS messages (ITU-T G.783, Characteristics of Synchronous Digital Hierarchy [SDH/SONET] Equipment Functional Blocks) and Ring APS messages (ITU-T G.841, Types and Characteristics of SDH/SONET Network Protection Architectures).
- D4–D12: Bytes D4 through D12 provide a 576-kbit/s data communication channel (DCC) between multiplex systems for the exchange of network administration and monitoring information. These bytes are defined only for the first STM-1 frame in an STM-n multiplex hierarchy.
- S1: Byte S1 reports the synchronization status.
- M1: Byte M1 indicates the number of B2 errors detected downstream (MS-REI: Multiplex Section Remote Error Indication).
- E2: Byte E2 provides a 64-kbit/s voice channel between multiplex systems. Once again, this byte is defined only for the first STM-1 frame in an STM-n multiplex hierarchy.
- H1–H3: The H bytes implement the pointer functions. H1 and H2 contain the pointer itself; byte H3 is the Pointer Action byte and can contain user data in the event of negative justification.

Regenerator Section Overhead (RSOH)

- A1, A2: Bytes A1 and A2 are used for frame alignment (A1 = 1111 0110; A2 = 0010 1000).

- J0: Byte J0 is used to verify transmission between the sending and receiving ends of every regenerator section. It consists of a 16-byte sequence with a CRC-7 checksum.

- B1: Byte B1, containing a BIP-8 checksum, is used to check for transmission errors in the regenerator section. It is calculated from all bits in the previous STM-n frame before scrambling.

- E1: The E1 byte provides a 64-kbit/s voice channel between regenerator systems.

- F1: Byte F1 is reserved for network operator purposes. It is defined only for the first STM-1 frame in an STM-n multiplex hierarchy.

- D1–D3: Bytes D1 through D3 provide a 192-kbit/s data channel for administrative, service, alarm, and other functions between regenerators.

Path Overhead Bytes

A container together with its path overhead is called a virtual container. A path in SDH/SONET designates the logical connection between the point at which the tributary signal is interleaved in a virtual container and the point at which the signal is removed from the container. The information in the following list refers only to VC-4, as SDH and SONET both use this virtual container to transport ATM cells. The 9 bytes of the VC-4 POH have the following functions:

- J1: Byte J1 carries a constant 64-byte or 16-byte string. This is used to test the line between the transmitting and receiving stations, and to detect misrouted connections in cross-connect systems or multiplexers.

- B3: Byte B3 carries a checksum (BIP-8) calculated from all bits in the previous VC-4 frame before scrambling.

- C2: Byte C2, the path signal label, specifies the content mapping of the virtual container. 256 different values are possible. For ATM, this value is 0x13.

- G1: Byte G1 is used to transmit path status and monitoring information from receiver to sender, including the number of errors detected (REI).

- F2: Byte F2 is used for the network operators' communication between two SDH PTEs (path termination equipment).

- H4: Byte H4 indicates whether the payload transported in the VC-4 consists of one or several TUs.

6.4.5   Pointers in SDH

Pointers are used to align lower-order SDH/SONET tributary signals for frame multiplexing and to compensate for differences between the multiplexed SDH/SONET bit rates and the bit rates of tributary SDH/SONET signals, as described above for the SONET OC-1 interface in section 6.4.2. A pointer indicates the beginning of the frame in each virtual container (or envelope capacity) of the next lower hierarchical layer (see Figure 6.39). If the container or SPE has a different bit rate from that of its transport frame, it is shifted by positive or negative justification, and the value of the pointer is adjusted accordingly. If the tributary signal is slower than the transport frame, stuff bytes are inserted to shift the container toward the later end of its transport frame. This process is known as positive justification. Justification occurs in increments of three bytes for AU-4 (that is, VC-4 in STM-1), or one byte for AU-3 (VC-3 in STM-1).

Bytes H1 through H3 are used for pointer justification of VC-4 containers in STM-1 frames. H1 and H2 contain the pointer itself, comprising the coordinates at which the VC-4 container begins. The H3 byte is the pointer action byte: if the tributary signal is faster than the transport frame transmission rate, VC-4 user data is pulled forward into the H3 byte, so that the virtual container moves forward in its transport frame (see Figure 6.40). This is called negative justification.

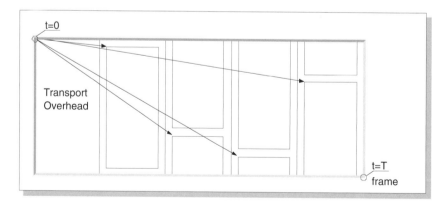

Figure 6.39
SDH pointers.

When several small containers are transported in one larger container, data rates are also justified using pointers by a procedure analogous to that described above for VC-4 and STM-1. The first byte of a tributary unit is the pointer. Because three or four TUs are combined in a group, a TUG provides three or four pointer bytes for three or four TUs. Like bytes H1 through H3 in the STM-1 SOH frame, these pointer bytes are used for positive or negative justification (see Figure 6.41).

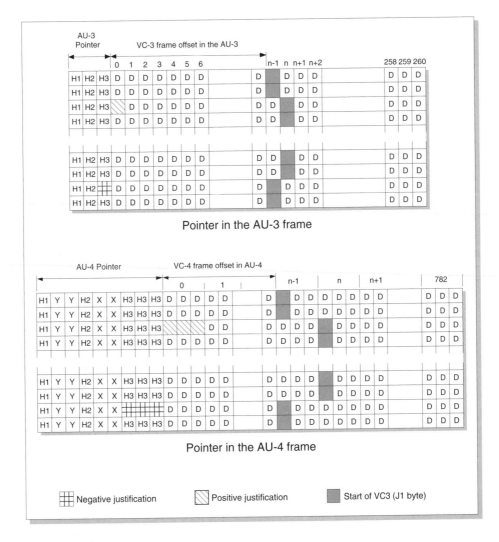

Pointer in the AU-3 frame

Pointer in the AU-4 frame

Figure 6.40
AU-4 pointer adjustment (VC-4 in STM-1).

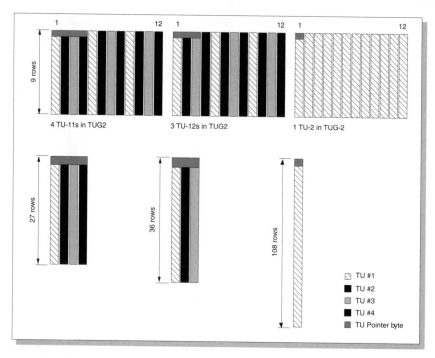

9 rows

4 TU-11s in TUG2   3 TU-12s in TUG2   1 TU-2 in TUG-2

27 rows   36 rows   108 rows

TU #1
TU #2
TU #3
TU #4
TU Pointer byte

Figure 6.41
TU pointer adjustment (VC-11, VC-12, TU-2 in TUG-2).

6.4.6   The Next Generation SDH/SONET

With traffic profiles in access and core networks changing to contain a large portion of data, SDH and SONET technologies, originally developed for time-multiplexed voice traffic, need to be adapted. The deployment of WDM (Wavelength Division Multiplexing) infrastructures calling for enhancements of the SDH/SONET network transport infrastructure adds to that as well. Current SDH/SONET implementations are ignorant of WDM topologies and have to be operated as a series of point-to-point WDM circuits.

A new SONET subprotocol, the Generic Framing Protocol (GFP), now provides the capability to efficiently encapsulate nonvoice traffic in SONET tributaries. Even more flexibility allows the Link Capacity Adjustment Scheme (LCAS) protocol. Using a technique called virtual concatenation, Ethernet traffic, for example, can be carried across a VT1.5-6 link (10.368 Mbits/s) instead of a STS-1 channel. A 100 Mbits/s Ethernet link can be transmitted over a STS-2 link (103.68 Mbit/s) instead of using STS-3. In addition, the responsible ANSI

T1 X1 committee released a proposal, which enables SONET to improve its scalability, allowing single connections to use multiple wavelengths.

6.5 ATM Transport over SDH/SONET Networks

The transportation of ATM cells over SDH networks (ATM mapping) is specified in ITU-T Recommendation G.707. ATM transport over SONET is specified in ANSI T1.105. SONET is the North American equivalent of SDH, and the two can be considered identical in most respects for equivalent interface rates. The ATM cell stream is encapsulated with byte alignment in VC-x or

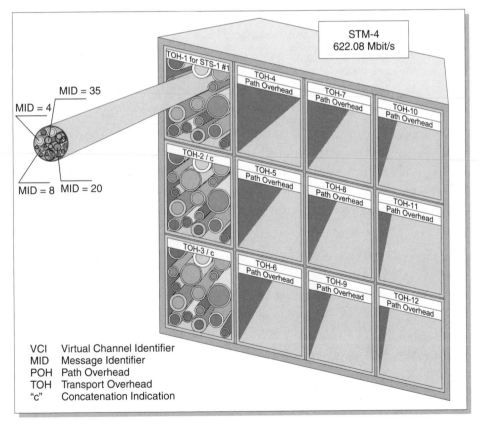

Figure 6.42
ATM and SDH.

concatenated VC-x containers (SONET in synchronous payload envelopes, or SPEs). Because the container or SPE is not an integer multiple of 53 bytes, a cell can also be split across two containers or SPEs. Before the ATM cells are inserted in the containers/SPEs for transport, the user data field of the cell is scrambled in order to facilitate delineation of the individual cells at the receiving station. The scrambling method used is self-synchronizing scrambling (SSS) with the generator polynomial $x^{43} + 1$. If the ATM data rate is lower than the user data capacity of the SDH containers or SONET SPEs, then idle or unassigned cells are inserted. If the ATM data rate is too high for the available bandwidth, then cells are discarded, beginning with low-priority cells. The resulting bit rate of the ATM cell stream is synchronous with that of the SDH container or SONET SPE. ATM cell mapping to the SDH STM-1 transport module, illustrated in Figure 6.43, is essentially identical with cell mapping to

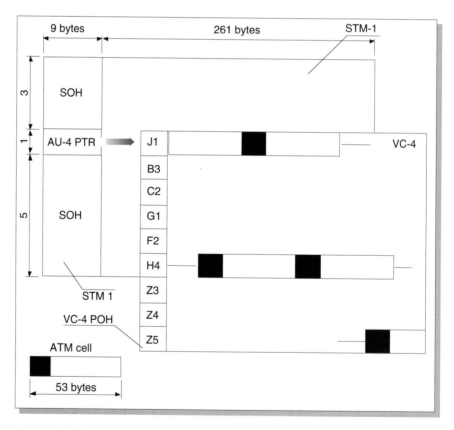

Figure 6.43
Transportation of ATM cells in the STM-1 transport module.

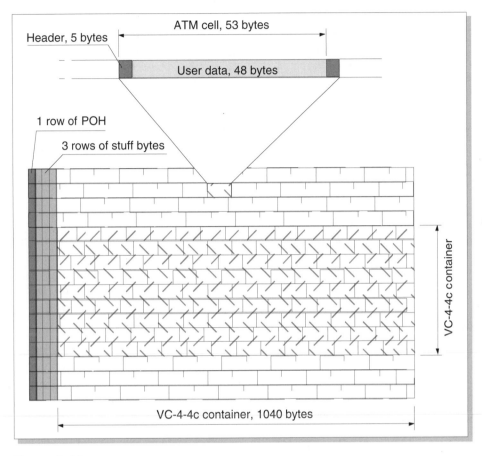

Figure 6.44
Transportation of ATM cells in the STM-4c transport module.

a SONET STS-3c transport system. Similarly, ATM mapping to a SONET STS-12c transport system is identical with mapping to the SDH STM-4c transport module shown in Figure 6.44.

Alarm and Monitoring Signals

Two types of monitoring signals are defined for ATM cell transport over SDH/SONET networks: the Alarm Indication Signal (AIS), sent downstream to report an error, and the Remote Defect Indicator (RDI) (formerly known as Far-End Receive Failure, or FERF). The RDI signal is sent upstream to report a receiving or transmission error. Both kinds of monitoring signals can be implemented using the Section/Transport Overhead (SOH/TOH) bytes of the STM-1/STS-3c frame, or using the Path Overhead (POH) of the VC4 container/SPE. Table 6.5 shows the use of the corresponding SDH overhead bytes for ATM cell transport.

Table 6.5   SDH Overhead Bytes in ATM Cell Transport

Byte	Function	Coding[1]
STM-1 Section overhead		
A1, A2	Frame alignment	
C1	STM-1 identifier	
B1	Regenerator section error monitoring [2]	BIP-8
B2	Multiplexer section error monitoring	BIP-24
H1, H2	AU-4 pointer, path AIS [3]	A11 1s
H3	Action pointer	
K2 (bits 6–8)	Multiplexer section AIS / section RDI	111/110
Z2 (bits 18–24)	Multiplexer section error reporting (REI) [4]	B2 error count
VC-4 Path overhead		
J1	Path ID/verification	
B3	Path error monitoring	BIP-8
C2	Path signal level	ATM cell [5]
G1 (bits 1–4)	Path error reporting (REI)	B3 error count
G1 (bits 5)	Path RDI	1
H4 (bits 3–8)	Not used	
FFS	Cell delineation supervision	FFS
FFS	Header error performance monitoring	FFS

1   Only the codes that are relevant for the monitoring function are listed.
2   The use of B1 for regenerator section error monitoring is optional.
3   The use of H1 and H2 for path AIS is provisional.
4   The use of Z2 for multiplexer section error monitoring is provisional.
5   The code for ATM cells is not yet defined. The value 1 (VC-3/4 path equipped) is recommended provisionally. The ATM Forum UNI specifies the C2 value 0001 0011.

134

6.5.1   Physical Interfaces for SDH

The physical interfaces for SDH are defined in ITU-T Recommendation G.957, as well as in various ATM Forum specifications. Both optical and electrical interfaces are specified for throughput rates up to the 155.52 Mbit/s of the first-level STM-1 frames. For all higher hierarchy levels, only optical interfaces are used.

6.5.2   Optical SDH Interfaces

In optical signal transmission, a logical 1 is represented by the emission of light, while 0 is represented by the absence of such emission or, at least, a substantially attenuated emission—laser performance can be improved if light is not completely extinguished. The characteristics of the transmission pulse are specified in eye diagrams (Figure 6.45). A test setup for measuring the eye diagram is described in the appendix to ITU-T Recommendation G.957.

ATM over Single-Mode Fiber

ITU-T Recommendation G.957 defines six different types of single-mode optical fiber for SDH communication, which can be installed in three different kinds of communications infrastructures: in-house links, medium-range WAN links, and long-range WAN links.

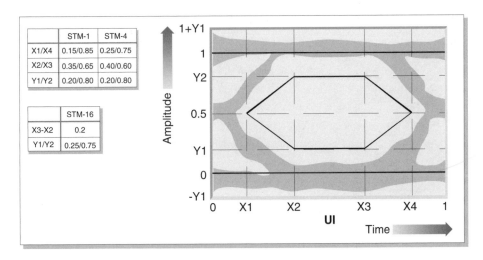

	STM-1	STM-4
X1/X4	0.15/0.85	0.25/0.75
X2/X3	0.35/0.65	0.40/0.60
Y1/Y2	0.20/0.80	0.20/0.80

	STM-16
X3-X2	0.2
Y1/Y2	0.25/0.75

Figure 6.45
Diagram of the optical transmission pulse for SDH signals.

Intra-office Links (I). Intra-office links can attain a maximum range of 2 km. The optical transmitters may be LEDs or multilongitudinal mode (MLM) lasers with a wavelength of 1310 nm. The permissible loss is between 0 and 7 dB.

Short-Haul Interoffice Links (S). Short-haul interoffice links span distances of up to 15 km. The optical transmitters may be either single longitudinal mode (SLM) or multilongitudinal mode (MLM) lasers with wavelengths of 1310 or 1550 nm (loss may be 0 to 12 dB).

Long-Haul Interoffice Links (L). Lasers with a wavelength of 1310 nm can be used for long-haul links of up to 40 km. High-powered SLM (500 μW or –3 dBm) or MLM lasers at wavelengths of 1550 nm can be used for a range of up to 80 km (the loss may be 10 to 24 dB). Table 6.6 shows the possible combinations of fiber types, wavelengths, and bit rates.

The ATM data rates attainable using single-mode fiber are 155 Mbit/s with STM-1 or OC-3, 622 Mbit/s with STM-4 or OC-12, 2.4 Gbit/s with STM-16 or OC-48, and 9.9 Gbit/s with STM-64 or OC-192. In practice, ATM is transported over single-mode fiber optic links primarily in wide area networks. Due to steadily growing demands for range and capacity, however, these media are increasingly used in LANs as well. Table 6.7 lists the single-mode fiber optic characteristics specified in ITU-T Recommendation G.957 for 622.08 Mbit/s interfaces.

Table 6.6   Cable Types, Wavelengths, and Bit Rates in SDH

Application		Intra-Office	Interoffice				
			Medium-range WAN links		Long-range WAN links		
Wavelength (nm)		1310	1310	1550	1310	1550	
Fiber type		G.652	G.652	G.652	G.652	G.652/654	G.653
Distance (km)		< 2	~ 15		~ 40	~ 60	
STM hierarchy	STM-1	I-1	S-1.1	S-1.2	L-1.1	L-1.2	L-1.3
	STM-4	I-4	S-4.1	S-4.2	L-4.1	L-4.2	L-4.3
	STM-16	I-16	S-16.1	S-16.2	L-16.1	L-16.2	L-16.3

I: Intra-office links
S: Short-haul interoffice links
L: Long-haul interoffice links
1: Wavelength 1310 nm
2: 1550 nm wavelength over G.652 fiber for S links and G.652 or G.654 fiber for L links
3: 1550 nm wavelength over G.653 fiber

Table 6.7 Single-Mode Fiber Optic Characteristics for 622.08 Mbit/s Interfaces (ITU-T G.957)

Parameter	Medium-range WAN links (15 km)	In-house links (2 km)	Units
Transmission characteristics			
Wavelength	1293–1334	1261–1360	nm
Spectral width: Mas. RMS width	4	14.5 (MLM Laser35 (LEDs))	nm
Mean signal power	–15 to –8	–15 to –8	dBm
Minimum extinction rate	8.2	8.2	dB
Eye diagram	See T1.646	See T1.646	
Reception characteristics			
Minimum sensitivity	–28	–23	dBm
Minimum overload	–8	–8	dBm
Optical path power penalty	1	1	dB

ATM over Multi-mode Fiber

In addition to the single-mode fiber specified by the ITU-T, the ATM Forum has also specified multimode fiber for ATM transmission in SDH/SONET frames in LANs at data rates of 155 Mbit/s and 622 Mbit/s. The maximum range—2 kilometers—is lower than that of single-mode fiber, but this is seldom a problem in LANs, which typically involve in indoor cabling structures with segment lengths of 100 to 1000 meters. The cost of the communication infrastructure is significantly lowered by avoiding expensive single-mode fiber and the high-quality laser sources it requires.

Multimode fiber can also be used to implement the STM-4c/OC-12 (622 Mbit/s), STM-1/OC-3 (155 Mbit/s), and STM-0/STS-1 (51.84 Mbit/s) interfaces in LANs. The STM-1/OC-3 multimode fiber optic interface uses a wavelength of 1300 nm over 62.5/125 µm multimode fiber with a modal bandwidth of 500 MHz/km. 50/125 µm can also be used. The data stream is 8B/10B-encoded for transmission, so that the physical medium's 194.4 Mbaud yields an effective data rate of 155.52 Mbit/s. Either SC or BFOC/2.5 (IEC 86B) connectors may be used. This specification, originally defined for UNI 3.0, has rarely been implemented and is described here for the sake of thoroughness, since it was retained in the UNI 3.1 specification; there has been discussion in the ATM Forum about how to obsolete such specifications, though at the time of this writing, this has not been done. Figure 6.46 lists the parameters for the multimode fiber optic interface.

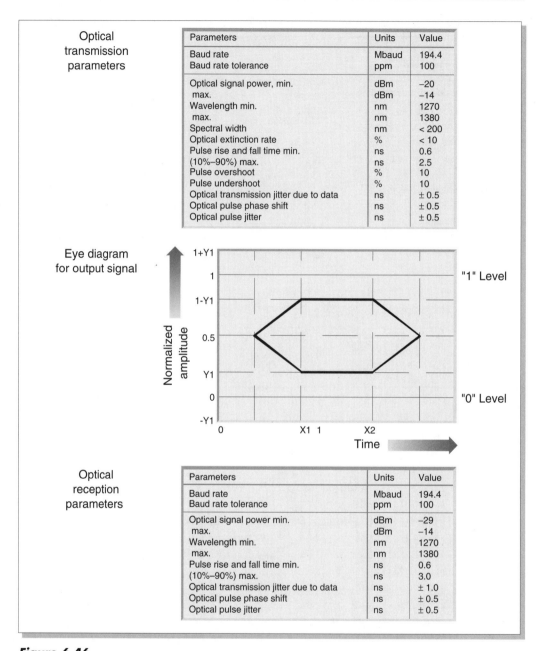

Optical transmission parameters

Parameters	Units	Value
Baud rate	Mbaud	194.4
Baud rate tolerance	ppm	100
Optical signal power, min.	dBm	−20
max.	dBm	−14
Wavelength min.	nm	1270
max.	nm	1380
Spectral width	nm	< 200
Optical extinction rate	%	< 10
Pulse rise and fall time min.	ns	0.6
(10%–90%) max.	ns	2.5
Pulse overshoot	%	10
Pulse undershoot	%	10
Optical transmission jitter due to data	ns	± 0.5
Optical pulse phase shift	ns	± 0.5
Optical pulse jitter	ns	± 0.5

Eye diagram for output signal

Optical reception parameters

Parameters	Units	Value
Baud rate	Mbaud	194.4
Baud rate tolerance	ppm	100
Optical signal power min.	dBm	−29
max.	dBm	−14
Wavelength min.	nm	1270
max.	nm	1380
Pulse rise and fall time min.	ns	0.6
(10%–90%) max.	ns	3.0
Optical transmission jitter due to data	ns	± 1.0
Optical pulse phase shift	ns	± 0.5
Optical pulse jitter	ns	± 0.5

Figure 6.46

Optical transmission and reception parameters for the 155-Mbit/s multimode fiber optic interface.

The multimode fiber (MMF) interfaces are specified for 622 Mbit/s interfaces using LEDs or short-wave (SW) lasers. Both types of MMF interfaces support the following multimode fiber types:

62.5/125 µm IEC 793-2 Type A1b
50/125 µm IEC 793-2 Type A1a

The data stream is NRZ-encoded. LED-based MMF transmitters can be used for segments of 300 to 500 meters; SW MMF transmitters have a range of about 300 meters. Table 6.8 shows the transmission and reception parameters for both MMF types at 622 Mbit/s.

ATM over Plastic Optical Fiber

As an alternative to both single-mode and multimode fiber optic media, the ATM Forum has also specified (in af-phy-0079.001) plastic optical fiber (POF) as a transport medium for ATM networks. Plastic optical fiber can be used for STM-1 or OC-3 interfaces (155 Mbit/s) with segments of up to 100 m, and hard polymer clad fiber (HPCF) with segments of up to 100 m. The POF medium used is 1000 µm multimode plastic fiber (IEC 793-2 Section 4 A4d), and the HPCF is a 225 µm multimode polymer fiber (IEC 793-2 Section 3 A3d). The maximum loss is 9.1 dB for POF media and 1.8 dB for HPCF. The minimum modal bandwidth for both fiber types must be at least 10 MHz/km at a wavelength of 650 nm. The data stream is NRZ-encoded. The specified connectors are PN or F07 in conformance with IEC 1753-BB (FFS). Table 6.9 lists the transmission and reception parameters for POF and HPCF interfaces.

6.5.3 Electrical SDH Interfaces

ATM over 75Ω Coaxial Cable—STM-1e and EC-3

SDH-based ATM transmission at 155 Mbit/s over 75Ω coaxial cable is used almost exclusively in European wide area networks. This interface is called "EC-3" (EC for Electrical Carrier) in North America, where it is rarely used, however. The physical medium and the encoding technique are the same as those specified in ITU Recommendation G.703 for the 140 Mbit/s E4 interface. The cable specified is one 75Ω coaxial cable for each direction. The bit stream is encoded using CMI (Coded Mark Inversion); the voltage level is ± 0.5 V.

Table 6.8 Optical Transmission and Reception Parameters for LED and SW-Based 622-Mbit/s ATM MM Fiber Optic Interfaces

LED-based MMF parameters			
Transmitter characteristics	62.5 µm MMF	50 µm MMF	Units
Wavelength	1270 to 1380	1270 to 1380	nm
Maximum spectral width	200	200	nm
Mean optical power	−20 to −14	−24 to −14	dBm
Minimum extinction rate	10	10	dB
Maximum rise and fall time (10%–90%)	1.25	1.25	ns
Maximum systematic interface peak-to-peak jitter	0.4	0.4	ns
Maximum random interface peak-to-peak jitter	0.15	0.15	ns
Maximum overshoot	25	25	%
Receiver characteristics			
Minimum sensitivity	−26	−26	dBm
Minimum overload	−14	−14	dBm
Maximum rise and fall time (10%–90%)	1.6	1.6	ns
Maximum systematic interface peak-to-peak jitter	0.5	0.5	ns
Maximum random interface peak-to-peak jitter	0.15	0.15	ns
Minimum eye diagram aperture at receiver	0.31	0.31	ns
Software-based MMF parameters			
Transmitter characteristics	62.5 µm MMF	50 µm MMF	Units
Wavelength	770 to 860	770 to 860	nm
Maximum spectral width	9	9	nm
Mean optical power	−10 to −4	−10 to −4	dBm
Minimum extinction rate	9	9	dB
Maximum rise and fall time (10%–90%)	0.75	0.75	ns
Maximum systematic interface peak-to-peak jitter	0.35	0.35	ns
Maximum overshoot	25	25	%
Receiver characteristics			
Minimum sensitivity	−16	−16	dBm
Minimum overload	0	0	dBm
Maximum rise and fall time (10%–90%)	1.2	1.2	ns
Maximum interface peak-to-peak jitter	0.55	0.55	ns
Minimum eye diagram aperture at receiver	0.31	0.31	ns

Table 6.9 Optical Transmission and Reception Parameters for POF and HPCF Interfaces

Transmission parameters for ATM plastic fiber interfaces	POF	HPCF	Units
Maximum spectral width (FWHM)	40	40	nm
Numerical aperture (transmitter)	0.2 to 0.3	0.2 to 0.3	
Mean optical power	−8 to −2	−20 to −14	dBm
Wavelength	640 to 660	640 to 660	nm
Minimum extinction rate	10	10	dB
Maximum rise and fall time (10%–90%)	4.5	4.5	ns
Maximum overshoot	25	25	%
Maximum systematic jitter	1.6	1.6	ns
Maximum random interface jitter	0.6	0.6	ns
Reception parameters for ATM plastic fiber interfaces	**POF**	**HPCF**	**Units**
Minimum sensitivity	−25	−26.5	dBm
Minimum overload	−2	−14	dBm
Maximum rise and fall time (10%–90%)	5.0	6.0	ns
Maximum systematic jitter	2.0	2.0	ns
Minimum eye diagram aperture (time interval reserved for clock regeneration after electrical/optical conversion)	1.23	1.23	ns
Maximum random interface jitter	0.6	0.6	ns

ATM over Copper Twisted Pair: UTP-3, UTP-5, and STP

Category 3 100Ω Unshielded Twisted-Pair Copper Cabling (UTP-3). By means of a special encoding technique called CAP-64, which obtains high data rates at low frequency bandwidths, ATM in SDH/SONET framing can be transported at a speed of 155 Mbit/s, even over low-cost Category 3 data cable, which is very common in North America. The maximum segment length is 100 meters. In addition to the STM-1/OC-3 rate of 155 Mbit/s, the ATM Forum has also specified lower bit rates for this cable type: 51.84 Mbit/s, 25.92 Mbit/s, and 12.96 Mbit/s. The encoding of the corresponding bit stream is CAP-16 for 51.84 Mbit/s, CAP-4 for 25.92 Mbit/s, and CAP-2 for 12.96 Mbit/s. CAP stands for Carrierless Amplitude/Phase-Modulation, an extremely efficient method for achieving high data rates in spite of low available frequency bandwidth. The encoding process divides the symbol stream to be transmitted into n data paths, where n is the symbol period. One of the resulting symbol streams is sent through an in-phase filter, and the others through phase-shift filters. The output signal of the in-phase filter is added to the inverted output signal of the phase-shift filter and then sent to the twisted pair through a low pass filter. In this way the information is encoded in the form of phase shifts. Each phase now contains not just one data bit, but an entire bit sequence. In CAP-16, for example, a given signal level can represent any of 16 different values, depending on its phase. The information contained in a single signal amplitude and phase state thus corresponds to four bits. If each amplitude/phase state is to represent 6 bits, 64 different phase states are necessary. Figure 6.47 illustrates the 16 phase/amplitude states of the CAP-16 encoding technique. The x-axis represents the in-phase state and the y-axis the quadrature phase, or a 90-degree shift with respect to the in-phase state.

As described in section 6.4.6 above, the ATM cells are framed in STM-1 containers in accordance with ITU-T G.707, or in SONET terms, in STS-3c SPEs per ANSI T1.646 (section 7.4). At transfer rates of 51.84 Mbit/s, the

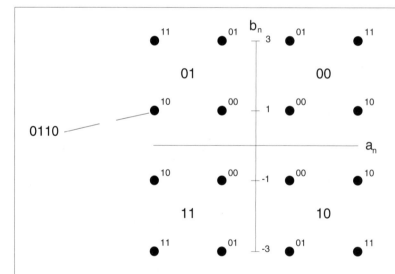

Each of the 16 phase states represents 4 bits: the two bits of its quadrant (e.g. for the upper right quadrant 00), and its own two bits. Thus the phase state of the upper right corner of the diagram represents the bit sequence »0011«. Each phase is named using the coordinates a and b and using values between ±1 and ±3.

The bit sequence 10010110 could then be coded as

$a = +1, b = -3$ as well as $a = -3, b = +1$

Figure 6.47
CAP-16 encoding.

ATM cells are transported in the payload field of the STM-0 or STS-1 frame. The entire payload field of the STM-0/STS-1 frame is filled with cells, with the exception of rows 30 and 59, for a net bandwidth of 48.384 Mbit/s. The 25.92 Mbit/s and 12.96 Mbit/s data rates are obtained by halving the frame rate:

- 51.84 Mbit/s: frame period = 125 μs
- 25.92 Mbit/s: frame period = 250 μs
- 12.96 Mbit/s: frame period = 500 μs

The maximum length of network segments at 51.84 Mbit/s is the same as for 155 Mbit/s: 90 meters, plus 10 meters of flexible patch cable. By using higher-quality Category 5 cable rather than Category 3, up to 160 meters can be spanned at 51.84 Mbit/s. The lower rates, 25.92 Mbit/s and 12.96 Mbit/s, permit segment lengths of 320 and 400 meters with Categroy 5 copper cabling. UTP-3 cabling is used with eight-pin RJ45 connectors (IEC 603-7) that conform to the electrical specification ANSI/TIA/EIA-568-A (Figure 6.48).

Category 5 100Ω Unshielded Twisted-Pair Copper Cabling (UTP-5).
When Category 5 UTP cabling is used to transmit data at up to 155 Mbit/s, the segment length must not exceed 150 meters. As for Category 3 wiring, the standard connector is the 8-pin RJ45 plug. With higher-quality receivers, segments can be up to 350 meters long. The electrical signal is NRZ-encoded.

150Ω Shielded Twisted-Pair Copper Cabling (STP)
The use of 150Ω shielded twisted pair also permits segment lengths of up to 350 meters at 155 Mbit/s. Nine-pin D-sub connectors (Figure 6.49) or IBM MIC connectors (Figure 6.50), as used in Token Ring networks, are recommended. Here once again the bit stream is NRZ-encoded.

Pin	User	Network
1	transmit +	receive +
2	transmit −	receive −
3	--	--
4	--	--
5	--	--
6	--	--
7	receive +	receive +
8	receive −	receive −

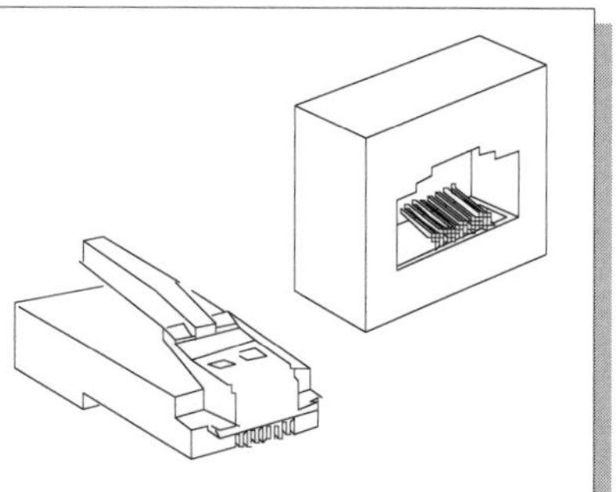

Figure 6.48
8-pin RJ45 connector for UTP-3-based ATM networks.

	Pin #	Signal		Pin #	Signal
	1	Transmit +		1	Receive +
	2	--		2	--
	3	--		3	--
	4	--		4	--
	5	Receive +		5	Transmit +
	6	Transmit –		6	Receive –
	7	--		7	--
	8	--		8	--
	9	Receive –		9	Transmit –
	Shell	ground		Shell	ground

Figure 6.49
Nine-pin D-sub connector for 155 Mbit/s over 150Ω STP cable.

6.6   Cell-Based Physical Layer

Transmission of ATM cells over data lines as a plain bit stream, using neither PDH nor SDH/SONET framing, is called a cell-based physical layer. Interface specifications exist for the cell-based physical layer at 622 Mbit/s, 155 Mbit/s, and 51.84 Mbit/s (with optional fractional rates of 25.92 Mbit/s and 12.96 Mbit/s).

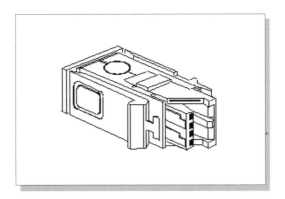

Figure 6.50
STP MIC connector.

6.6.1 ATM Cell Streams at 155 Mbit/s and 622 Mbit/s

In addition to ATM cell mapping to SDH frames, ITU-T Recommendation I.432 also defines the cell-based physical layer with throughput rates 155 Mbit/s and 622 Mbit/s. The data is transmitted in a continuous stream of ordinary ATM user cells, OAM cells, and idle cells. Every 27th cell at most may be a PL cell. These are either idle cells, which are inserted when no ATM user data cells are queued for transmission, or PL-OAM cells. The latter are used to carry out the operation monitoring functions that are otherwise accomplished by SDH headers. At least one PL-OAM cell is required for every 513 cells.

A symmetrical interface, one with identical send and receive rates, is defined for cell-based transmission at 155 Mbit/s. For 622.080 Mbit/s, either a symmetrical or an asymmetrical mode can be selected. In the asymmetrical mode, data is transported at 622.080 Mbit/s in one direction and at 155.520 Mbit/s in the other.

6.6.2 ATM Cell Streams over V35, EIA/TIA 449/530, HSSI, and E1

The ATM Forum has specified a cell-based transmission convergence sublayer based on ITU-T Recommendation I.432 for "clear channel" interfaces. This term refers to all interfaces that are capable of transparently transporting any data stream, without imposing bit stream encoding and framing restrictions. Examples of clear channel interfaces include V.35, EIA/TIA 449/530, EIA/TIA 612/613 (High Speed Serial Interface, or HSSI), and unframed E1. Any other clear channel interface can also be used, however. The cells are transferred in a continuous stream, including ordinary ATM cells, OAM cells, and idle/unassigned cells. No F1 or F2 OAM functions are specified for monitoring the network. F3 OAM functions can be optionally implemented using special physical layer OAM cells, to monitor processes at the level of transmission paths. The following parameters can be analyzed:

- The number of included cells (NIC) per OAM cell: 128
- The monitoring block size (MBS): 16
- The number of blocks monitored per OAM cell: 8
- The number of monitored blocks received by the remote station: 8

The cell rate is decoupled from an interface's data rate by inserting idle or unassigned cells. The remote station delineates the individual ATM cells using the header error control (HEC) mechanism described in Chapter 9. Cells may be transmitted either in scrambled or in unscrambled form.

6.6.3   ATM Cell Streams over FDDI Infrastructures

A special variant of cell-based ATM transmission is TAXI. The TAXI interface was developed with the purpose of using existing FDDI infrastructures to transport ATM cells. The fiber optic media and signal characteristics specified for TAXI communication are thus exactly the same as those defined in the FDDI standard ISO 9314-3. Consequently, FDDI rings could be converted into ATM networks while retaining most of the existing FDDI hardware. The name TAXI originated with the first commercially available chipset for FDDI-based ATM. The ATM cells are 4B/5B-encoded and transmitted with no further framing. In 4B/5B encoding, four bits of data are transmitted as symbols of 5 bits. This is due to the requirement that no more than three "1" bits occur in a row: the bit sequence 1111 is coded as 11101, for example. Of the 32 possible 5-bit symbols, only 16 are used to transmit data. Some of the remaining 16 are unusable because they contain too many consecutive ones or zeros; certain others are used as line states or control symbols in FDDI. The JK symbol sequence, for example, announces the beginning of an FDDI frame; and the I or Idle symbol is used as a continuous padding stream for clock synchronization. Table 6.10 illustrates the use of control symbols in ATM cell transmission.

The beginning of an ATM cell is marked by the control symbol sequence TT. In TAXI, the JK symbol sequence is used to indicate that is "idle," and is transmitted when there are no assigned cells queued for sending. Unassigned and idle cells are not used in TAXI, which is a truly asynchronous ATM interface. In case of noise, interfaces resynchronize only when the next JK idle symbol sequence is received. If higher cell losses are tolerable, fewer JK idle symbol sequences may be required, but not less than one every 0.5 seconds. The MIC connector defined in ISO 9314-3, customary in FDDI networks, is also used in TAXI (Figure 6.51).

The TAXI interface is now practically obsolete, as STM-1 or OC-3 interfaces have become commonplace in local area networks.

6.6.4   ATM Cell Streams at 25.6 Mbit/s

A further specification for a 25.6 Mbit/s ATM interface, originally intended to connect workstation computers to ATM networks economically, but more recently associated with ATM over ADSL modem interfaces, was developed in-

Table 6.10   Control Symbols for TAXI-Based ATM Transmission

Symbol	Definition
JK (Sync)	Idle
II	Reserved
TT	Start of cell
TS	Reserved
IH	Not recommended
TR	Reserved
SR	Reserved
SS	--
HH	Not recommended
HI	Not recommended
HQ	Not recommended
RR	--
RS	Reserved
QH	Not recommended
QI	Not recommended
QQ	Loss of signal

dependently of the cell-based physical layer interfaces described above. The ATM Forum specification (af-phy-0040.000, also ITU-T I.432.5) calls for Category 3 100Ω UTP (unshielded twisted pair), 120Ω Category 4 (ISO/IEC 11801), or 150Ω STP (shielded twisted pair) cabling. As in TAXI, the bit stream is 4B/5B-encoded (although the code itself is different from that used

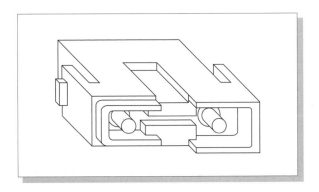

Figure 6.51
MIC plug described in ISO 9314-3.

in TAXI) and transmitted asynchronously without further framing. The transfer rate of 25.6 Mbit/s with 4B/5B encoding yields a line speed of 32 Mbaud. This interface is closely based on a specification originally developed by IBM and derived from Token Ring technology.

The specified maximum segment length for all three cable types is 100 meters (90 meters of fixed cabling plus 10 meters for patch cables). The cables must also conform to the attenuation and near-end crosstalk (NEXT) characteristics specified in EIA/TIA-568-A or ISO/IEC 11801. The connectors are RJ45 for Category 3 UTP or STP-MIC for shielded twisted pair (see Figure 6.50).

6.7 Physical Layer Monitoring in ATM Networks: OAM Flows F1–F3

A total of five information flows are defined for monitoring ATM networks, called the OAM (Operation and Maintenance) flows (see Figure 6.52). Each of these flows, numbered F1 to F5, is responsible for a certain aspect of a connection. Flows F1 to F3 are concerned with the physical layer of the B-ISDN protocol model, while F4 and F5 pertain to virtual paths (VP) and virtual channels (VC) in the ATM layer. The OAM parameters are obtained by different mechanisms, depending on the network topology used for ATM cell transport (SDH/SONET, PDH, cell-based physical layer).

A transmission path is defined as the path between the network component that inserts the user data into the transport medium and the component that extracts it again from the medium. Examples of transmission paths include the link between a B-NT2 and a switch (a VP cross-connect), or between a B-NT2 and the connection endpoint. A transmission path is composed of several digital sections, each of which may lead through one or more regenerator sections.

6.7.1 OAM F1–F3 for SDH or SONET-Based ATM Systems

In SDH or SONET-based ATM networks, the F1 and F2 OAM flows are transported in the section or transport overhead (SOH/TOH) of the transport modules, and F3 in the path overhead (POH) of the virtual container or SPE.

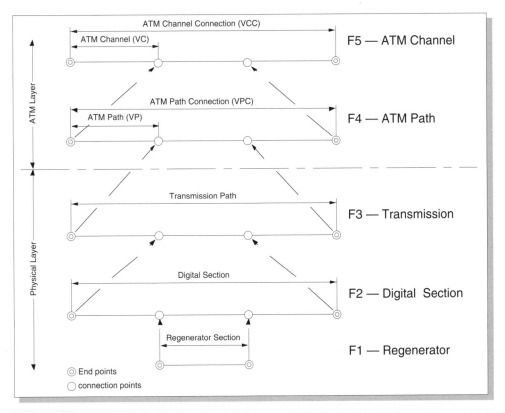

Figure 6.52
Information flows for ATM monitoring.

Part of the F3 information can also be transported in specially indicated physical layer OAM (PL-OAM) cells. Table 6.11 gives a general view of the functions of the various OAM information flows.

6.7.2   OAM F1–F3 for PDH-Based ATM Systems

In PDH networks, F1 and F3 information can be transported in the PDH header. The frame alignment byte of the header is evaluated for F1 functions, while F3 parameters are taken from the remaining header bytes. There is no provision for an F2 flow (see section 6.3).

Table 6.11 PL-OAM Cell Headers

Hierarchy	Function	Error detection	System and error reports transmitted within OAM flows		
			F2 in B-NT2 < > B-NT1-segment	B-NT1 < > LT-segment (2)	F3 betweeen B-NT2 < > path termination
Regenerator Section	Signal detection, frame synchronization	Signal loss frame loss from B-NT2 to B-NT1	MS-RDI in direction B-NT2 (3)	(1)	Path-AIS in direction of path termination, generated by B-NT1
		Signal loss frame loss of B-NT1 to B-NT2	MS-RDI in direction B-NT1 (3)		Path-RDI in direction of path termination, generated by B-NT2
Multiplex Section (MS)	Section error monitor (B2)	Signal power loss in in direction B-NT1	MS-RDI in direction B-NT2 (3, 4)	(1)	Path-AIS in direction of path termination, generated by B-NT1(4)
		Signal power loss in in direction B-NT2	MS-RDI in direction B-NT1 (3, 4)		—
Multiplex Section Adaptation (MSA)	AU Pointer operation	AU pointer loss or Path AIS in direction B-NT2	—		Path-RDI in direction path terminaton
Transmission Path Adaptation	Decoupling from cell rate	Insertion error / defective Idle cell function in B-NT2	—	(1)	(5)
	Cell synchronization	Loss of cell synchronization in direction B-NT2	—		Path RDI

(1) The ability to send operational data from reference point T_B to the Q-interface depends on the vendor implementation

(2) In coordination with the OAM-functions of the transmission system

(3) As recommended in the SDH-standard, the expression MS (Multiplex Section) is being used

(4) Can be deactivated (G.783)

(5) Does not generate an alarm

6.7.3 OAM F1–F3 for Cell-Based Physical Layer

In cell-based physical layer networks, the OAM information flows are transmitted by means of special physical layer OAM (or PL-OAM) cells. As described in I.432, values for OAM F1 and F3 parameters can be evaluated, but there is no provision for an F2 flow. The corresponding parameters are communicated as part of the F3 flow. No more than one PL-OAM cell may be inserted in the cell stream in every 27 cells, and at least one must be inserted in every 513 cells. (The 1-in-27 limit serves to facilitate interworking between cell-based interfaces running at 155 Mbit/s and 622 Mbit/s and the corresponding SDH/SONET interfaces, STM-1/OC-3 and STM-4c/OC-12. This is because the overhead in SDH/SONET [SOH/TOH + POH] constitutes exactly 1/27 of the bandwidth: 9 + 1 columns out of 270). The F1 cell contains OAM parameters for the regenerator section, while F3 cells are used to monitor the transmission path. OAM cells have a special header that makes them easily identifiable (Table 6.12).

Figure 6.53 illustrates the structure of F1 and F3 PL-OAM cells. The following fields are reserved for the F1 and F3 flows:

OAM F1 Cell Fields

PSN	PL-OAM Sequence Number (8 bits, modulo 256)
NIC	Number of Included Cells (maximum value: 512)
MBS	Monitoring Block Size (maximum value: 64)
NMB-EDC	Number of Monitored Blocks (EDC octets) (recommended value: 8)
EDC	Error Detection Code (BIP-8 value calculated over the monitoring block)
NMB-EB	Number of Monitored Blocks at the Far End (recommended value: 8)
REI	Remote Error Indication (number of bit parity errors in each block)

Table 6.12 PL-OAM Cell Headers

OAM Flow	Byte 1	Byte 2	Byte 3	Byte 4	Byte 5
F1	0000000	0000000	0000000	0000011	valid HEC = 0101110
F3	0000000	0000000	0000000	0001001	valid HEC = 0110101

Since the PL-OAM cells are not transfered to the ATM layer, they have no releveance to the ATM cells

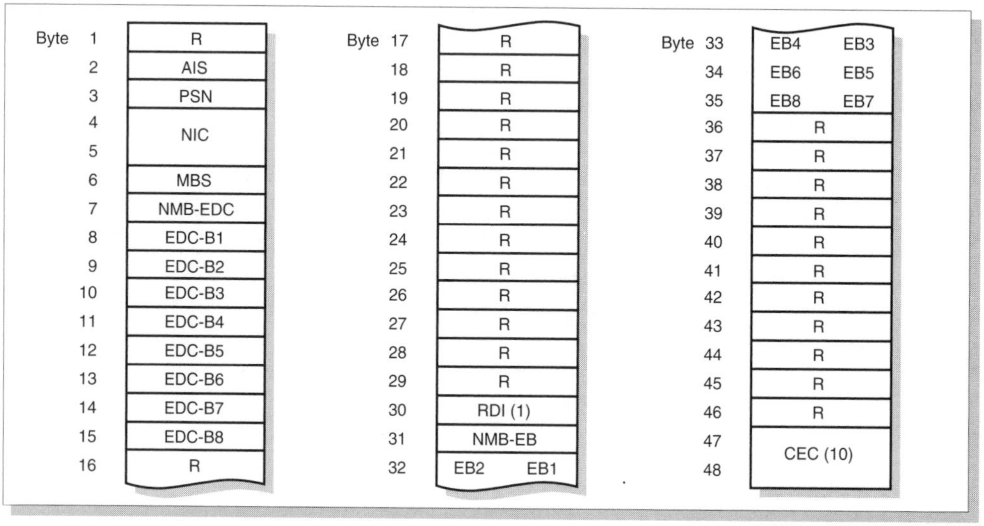

Figure 6.53
PL-OAM cell format for F1 and F3.

AIS	Section Alarm Indication Signal (sent downstream to report an upstream error; AIS-L in SONET)
RDI	Remote Defect Indicator (sent upstream to report a reception failure downstream. This occurs when frame alignment or the data signal is lost, for example.)
CRC	CRC-10 checksum
R	Reserved field (set to 0110 1010)

OAM F3 Cell Fields

PSN	PL-OAM Sequential Number (8 bits, modulo 256)
NIC	Number of Included Cells (maximum value: 512)
MBS	Monitoring Block Size (maximum value: 64)
NMB-EDC	Number of Monitored Blocks (EDC octets) (recommended value: 8)
EDC	Error Detection Code (BIP-8 value calculated over the monitoring block)
NMB-EB	Number of Monitored Blocks at the Far End (recommended value: 8)

Table 6.13 OAM F1–F3 Functions with Cell-Based Transmission for Errors Occurring in Section B-NT2 ↔ B-NT1

Hierarchy	Function	Error Detection	System and error reports transmitted within OAM flows		
			F2 in B-NT2 < > B-NT1-Section	B-NT1 < > LT-Section (2)	F3 between B-NT2 < > path termination
Regenerator Section	Signal detection, PL-OAM cell delineation	Signal loss or loss of F1-PL-OAM-cell delineation from B-NT2 to B-NT1	Section RDI in direction B-NT2	(1)	Path-AIS in direction of path termination, generated by B-NT1 (3)
		Signal loss or loss of F1-PL-OAM-cell delineation from B-NT1 to B-NT2	Section RDI in direction B-NT2		Path-RDI in direction of path termination, generated by B-NT2
	Error detection	Signal power loss in in direction B-NT1	Section RDI in direction B-NT2		Path-AIS in direction of path termination, generated by B-NT1
		Signal power loss in in direction B-NT1	Section RDI in direction B-NT1		–
Transmission Path	Decoupling from cell rate	Insertion error / defective Idle cell function in B-NT2	–	(1)	(4)
	PL-OAM-Cell delineation	Loss of F3-PL-OAM-Cell delineation in direction B-NT2	–		Path RDI
	Cell delineation	Loss of Cell delineation defect in direction B-NT2	–		Path RDI

(1) The ability to send operational data from reference point T_B to the Q-interface depends on the vendor implementation
(2) In coordination with the OAM-functions of the transmission system
(3) The B-NT1 is capable of generating a Path-AIS at layer OAM-F3
(4) Does not generate an alarm

REI	Remote Error Indication (number of bit parity errors in each block; REI-P in SONET)
AIS	Alarm Indication Signal (AIS-P in SONET)
TP-RDI	Transmission Remote Defect Indicator (RDI-P in SONET)
CRC	CRC-10 checksum
R	Reserved field (set to 0110 1010)

Chapter 7

THE ATM PROTOCOL: THE ATM LAYER

The actual transport of ATM cells takes place in the ATM layer, shown in Figure 7.1. In order to provide for the varying connection quality requirements of different applications, Quality-of-Service (QoS) parameters are first provisioned or negotiated in the signaling process. Transmission begins, after a successful connection setup, with the ATM cells of virtual channel connections (VCCs) and virtual path connections (VPCs) multiplexed in a continuous cell stream. During the connection, monitoring and control mechanisms operate to ensure that the connection parameters set during provisioning or agreed upon in the ATM switching negotiation are maintained.

7.1   The ATM Cell

An ATM cell, shown in Figure 7.2, consists of a 5-byte header and a 48-byte information or user data field. There are two basic cell types: UNI cells and NNI cells. UNI cells are transferred at user–network interfaces, NNI cells at network–node interfaces (NNI). The two cell types differ only in four header

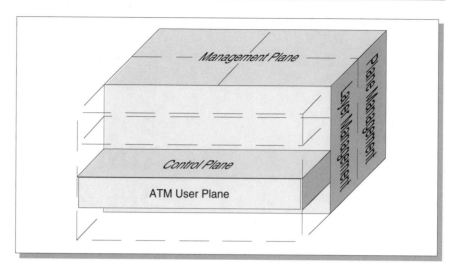

Figure 7.1
B-ISDN reference model: The ATM layer.

bits, which are used for flow control in UNI cells and to extend the virtual path identification (VPI) field to 12 bits in NNI cells.

Bit 8 is the most significant bit in all fields. The bits within each byte are therefore transmitted beginning with bit 8. The bytes in turn are transmitted in ascending order, that is, beginning with byte 1.

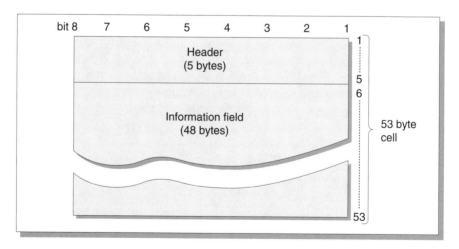

Figure 7.2
The ATM cell.

7.1.1   The UNI Header

Figure 7.3 illustrates the header structure of UNI cells. The header consists of the six fields GFC (4 bits), VPI (12 bits), VCI (16 bits), PT (3 bits), CLP (1 bit), and HEC (8 bits).

The Generic Flow Control (GFC) Field

The generic flow control field, which consists of 4 bits, is used to control local functions and to manage access and transmission rights in ATM networks. Its contents are not forwarded beyond the range of the local ATM switch, since this field is replaced with VPI data at the NNI. Its significance is thus limited to the local ATM network segment. Although specified by the ITU-T in Recommendation I.361, generic flow control has seldom or never been put into practice, and ATM Forum signaling in particular does not support this function.

The ATM Routing Label (VPI/VCI) Field

The UNI header contains a total of 24 bits for ATM layer routing purposes: 8 bits for the VPI and 16 bits for the VCI.

The combined VCI-VPI value is a label that has only local significance: that is, its meaning is specific to a single communication link between two ATM

Byte \ Bit	8	7	6	5	4	3	2	1
1	Generic Flow Control (GFC)				Virtual Path ID (VPI)			
2	Virtual Path ID (VPI)				Virtual Channel ID (VCI)			
3	Virtual Channel ID (VCI)							
4	Virtual Channel ID (VCI)				Payload Type (PT)			CLP
5	Header Error Control (HEC)							

CLP: Cell Loss Priority

Figure 7.3
UNI cell header.

interfaces. The value of the VPI-VCI field changes as cells in a given virtual connection pass through ATM switches. The meaning of the VPI-VCI field is determined by the contents of a translation table, whose contents in turn are established by the signaling process (in the case of switched virtual connections, or SVCs), or by network management (in the case of permanent or semi-permanent virtual connections, or PVCs), or by a label distribution protocol (if multiprotocol label switching, or MPLS, is used). In short, the VCI-VPI field has no end-to-end significance, which is why it is called a label, not an address. Note that there is such a thing as an ATM address, namely at the signaling level (see the section "Connection Setup at the Caller's End"); also, some publications incorrectly refer to the VPI-VCI as an address.

An ATM virtual channel (VC) refers to a two-way transmission link for ATM cells, although both directions are not always used. All cells on a given virtual channel in a given link have the same VCI value. Several ATM channels may be carried within an ATM virtual path (VP) (see Figure 7.4). In addition to the VCI, all cells transported by a given ATM virtual path are identified by a particular VPI. Note that the same value of VCI nay occur in more than one virtual path but because the VPI is different in this case, the VPI-VCI label is unique on a given link. Also, because an ATM routing label has only local significance, the same value of VPI-VCI may occur on more than one link, though the virtial circuits concerned are probably unrelated. Compared with the physical channels and paths familiar from older telecommunications techniques, the ATM concept of virtual paths permits substantially more efficient use of available bandwidths.

The Payload Type (PT) Field

Three bits of the ATM header are used to identify the type of data the cell payload contains. This makes it possible to distinguish between ordinary user data and various special payload types, such as operation and maintenance and

Figure 7.4
Virtual channels and virtual paths.

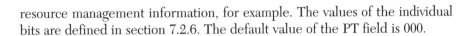

resource management information, for example. The values of the individual bits are defined in section 7.2.6. The default value of the PT field is 000.

The Cell Loss Priority (CPL) Field

The cell loss priority (CLP) bit can be used to assign cells a relative priority. If the CLP bit is set to 1, the cell has low priority; 0 indicates normal priority. If the capacity of a connection is exceeded, or if other transmission problems arise, cells with CLP = 1 are discarded first.

The Header Error Control (HEC) Field

This field and the related functions belong to the Transmission Convergence sublayer of the Physical Layer (see Chapter 8, subsection 8.1).

Reserved Header Values

Certain header values are reserved for cells with special operation, management, or signaling functions in the ATM network. Such cells include broadcasts, metasignaling, resource management cells, and, in the cell-based physical layer, PL-OAM cells and ICP (IMA Control Protocol) cells. All special cells have a VCI value in the 0 through 31 range. The ITU-T reserves for itself all VCI values below 16 and defines all values between 16 and 31 as available for proprietary purposes. The ATM Forum has used several values in this range (for example, VCI = 16 is used for ILMI, VCI = 17 is used for LANE V1.0, VCI = 18 is used for PNNI). All values above 31 can be used by the ATM layer for user traffic. Table 7.1 lists the reserved header byte values of both the ITU-T and the ATM Forum and Table 7.2 shows the full detail of of the physical layer cells identified in Table 7.1 for the UNI.

7.1.2   The NNI Header

Unlike the UNI header, the NNI header (Figure 7.5) provides 28 bits for the routing label: 12 bits for the VPI and 16 bits for the VCI. This permits the definition of a greater number of virtual paths at the network-node interface. The payload type field, the priority bit, and the HEC field correspond to the same fields in the UNI cell header.

Table 7.3 lists the reserved byte values in the NNI header.

Table 7.1 Reserved Header Bytes and VPI/VCI Values

Function	Byte 1	Byte 2	Byte 3	Byte 4	VCI value of bytes 2–4
Unassigned cells	0000 0000	0000 0000	0000 0000	0000 xxx0	VCI = 0
Physical layer cells (idle, PL-OAM, ICP*)	xxxx 0000	0000 0000	0000 0000	0000xxx1	VCI = 0
Metasignaling (default)	0000 0000	0000 0000	0000 0000	0001 0a0c	VCI = 1
Broadcast signaling (default)	0000 0000	0000 0000	0000 0000	0010 0aac	VCI = 2
OAM-F4 segment cell	0000 aaaa	aaaa 0000	0000 0000	0011 0a0a	VCI = 3
OAM-F4 end-to-end cell	0000 aaaa	aaaa 0000	0000 0000	0100 0a0a	VCI = 4
Signaling (default)	0000 0000	0000 0000	0000 0000	0101 0aac	VCI = 5
Resource management	0000 0000	0000 0000	0000 0000	0110 0a0a	VCI = 6
ILMI message*	0000 0000	0000 0000	0000 0001	0000 aaa0	VCI = 16
LANE V1.0 Configuration Direct VCC*	0000 0000	0000 0000	0000 0000	0011 0a0a	VCI = 17
PNNI routing protocol exchange*	0000 0000	0000 0000	0000 0001	0100 0a0a	VCI = 18

a   Bit available for use by the ATM layer
c   The sender shall set the CLP bit to 0.
*   ATM Forum defined (ICP - IMA Control Protocol - in coordination with the ITU-T)

7.1.3   ATM Cell Types

In addition to ordinary user ATM cells (i.e., cells with VCI > 31), there are several types of cells that are used not to transport user data, but to perform certain operational functions. These include idle cells, unassigned cells, PL-OAM cells, ICP cells, RM cells, and VP/VC-OAM cells. Note that in cells with VPI and VCI equal to zero, the least significant 4 bits in the 4th byte, normally the PT and CLP fields, are reassigned for other purposes.

Table 7.2 Physical Layer Cells at the UNI

Physical Layer Cell	Byte 1	Byte 2	Byte 3	Byte 4
Idle cell	0000 0000	0000 0000	0000 0000	0000 0001
PL-OAM (F1 flow)	0000 0000	0000 0000	0000 0000	0000 0011
PL-OAM (F3 flow)	0000 0000	0000 0000	0000 0000	0000 1001
ICP (IMA Control Protocol) cell or IMA filler cell	0000 0000	0000 0000	0000 0000	0000 1011

Byte \ Bit	8	7	6	5	4	3	2	1
1	Virtual Path ID (VPI)							
2	Virtual Path ID (VPI)				Virtual Channel ID (VCI)			
3	Virtual Channel ID (VCI)							
4	Virtual Channel ID (VCI)				PT			CLP
5	Header Error Control (HEC)							

PT   Payload Type
CLP   Cell Loss Priority

Figure 7.5
NNI cell header structure.

Idle Cells

Idle cells are physical layer cells and carry no useful information. They are used to adapt the cell rate to the bandwidth of the transmission medium. If there are not enough other cells queued to fill the allocated bandwidth, idle cells are inserted by the transmission convergence sublayer. This permits alignment of the ATM cell stream with the throughput of the physical medium (such as an SDH VC4 container or a SONET SPE). The idle cell header is

Table 7.3   Reserved Header Bytes in the NNI ATM Cell

	Byte 1	Byte 2	Byte 3	Byte
Reserved for physical layer [1, 2]	0000 0000	0000 0000	0000 0000	0000 PPP1
Physical layer F1 flow OAM cell	0000 0000	0000 0000	0000 0000	0000 0011
Physical layer F3 flow OAM cell	0000 0000	0000 0000	0000 0000	0000 1001
Idle cells	0000 0000	0000 0000	0000 0000	0000 0001
Unassigned cells	AAAA 0000	0000 0000	0000 0000	000A AAA0

A   Bit available for use by the ATM layer
P   Bit available for use by the physical layer
[1]   In cell-based physical layer and in unassigned cells, the CLP field is not used.
[2]   Cells identified by header information as physical layer cells are not passed to the ATM layer.

illustrated in Table 7.1. Unlike unassigned cells, idle cells are not passed to the ATM layer. Note that the ATM Forum, following the Bellcore definition, calls the idle cell header pattern an "invalid header" (see also "Unassigned Cells," below).

Unassigned Cells

Unassigned cells (VPI and VCI set to zero) are ATM layer cells and carry no useful payload information. They are used when no assigned cells are available to send from the ATM layer. At the receiver, they are treated similarly to idle cells and discarded. In North America (and implementations elsewhere based on certain ATM Forum specifications), unassigned cells are used where the ITU-T would specify idle cells. They are explicitly specified for rate adaptation by the ATM Forum, following Bellcore usage, which, strictly speaking, conflicts with the ITU-T standard. Despite this confusion, idle and unassigned cells can normally be considered equivalent. See Table 7.1 for the header structure.

Physical Layer OAM Cells

In the cell-based physical layer, special cells can be inserted up to once in every 27 cells to transmit operation and maintenance (OAM) information concerning the physical layer. These cells are known as PL-OAM cells. At the receiver, these cells are used by the physical layer and not passed along to the ATM layer (see Table 7.1). Their purpose is to convey some of the information (such as alarms) normally carried by the overhead of frame-based physical layers such as SONET.

VP/VC OAM Cells

VP/VC OAM cells are used to transport the F4 and F5 information flows. This information allows the network to monitor and test the capacities and availability of ATM virtual paths and virtual channels.

VP/VC RM Cells

VP/VC Resource Management (RM) cells are used to manage flow control in the Available Bit Rate (ABR) service category.

Assigned Cells

Assigned cells are cells used for communication within ATM virtual channels (VCs) and virtual paths (VPs). Assigned cells can be of the following five types:

- User data transport cells (any VPI; VCI > 31),
- Metasignaling cells (VPI = 0, VCI = 1)
- Broadcast signaling cells (VPI = 0, VCI = 2),
- Point-to-point signaling cells (VPI = 0, VCI = 5),
- ILMI cells for ATM network management (VPI = 0, VCI = 16),
- LANE v1.0 Configuration Direct VCC (VPI = 0, VCI = 17), and
- PNNI Routing Control Channels (any VPI; VCI = 18).

User cells are assigned to a specific connection by their VPI/VCI values, and transport data for higher-layer services in the 48-byte payload field. Metasignaling cells were originally conceived to select and define signaling virtual channels. Because metasignaling is not used in present-day networks, however, these cells do not occur in actual practice, though are defined in ITU recommendations. Broadcast signaling cells are defined to send signaling information to all network stations, but again, in practice, these are not used. Network nodes that do not support broadcast signaling simply ignore all cells in the broadcast virtual channel, VCI = 2. Cells with VCI = 5 are used for point-to-point signaling. For this reason the virtual channel VCI = 5 is also called the signaling channel. ILMI cells are used for local ATM network management tasks at the UNI, which include registration of new active stations with the ATM switch, querying ATM MIBs, or configuring network components.

7.2 The ATM Layer: User Plane Functions

ATM layer processes take place either in the user plane or in the management plane of the B-ISDN reference model. The user plane functions include all processes concerned with actual cell transport. Specifically, these are the multiplexing and demultiplexing of multiple virtual connections onto a common medium; cell header generation and extraction; cell VPI-VCI translation; the monitoring and control of service parameters (such as cell loss ratio and cell

Table 7.4 ATM User Plane Functions

Functions	Parameter
ATM connection multiplexing and signaling	VPI/VCI
Assignment of Quality of Service (QoS) parameters	Idle cells
Decoupling of cell rate and transmission bandwidth	Idle cells
Cell type recognition	Header byte settings
Recognition of payload types	Payload Type field (PT)
Recognition of cell loss priority	Cell Loss Priority (CLP)
Traffic shaping	Network load parameter

transfer delay); distinguishing between user cells and special cell types; evaluation of the payload type and cell loss priority; and traffic shaping (Table 7.4).

7.2.1   ATM Connections

In order to manage the wide variety of communication situations in ATM networks, the ATM layer provides for different connection types with different characteristics. Both virtual channel and virtual path connections can be structured as point-to-point or point-to-multipoint connections. The bandwidth allocated to a connection can also be asymmetric: that is, the bandwidth for transmission can be lower than for reception, or vice versa. Furthermore, a number of Quality-of-Service (QoS) parameters can be negotiated for each connection and each direction of each connection.

Virtual Channel Connections (VCCs)

ATM virtual channels represent the lowest level in the structural hierarchy of ATM data streams. (Note, however, that in terms of the protocol layer model, the VC is above the VP in the stack.) All virtual channel connections have the following four properties:

1. Quality-of-Service (QoS) parameters: The ATM switch assigns each virtual channel connection QoS parameters, which define properties such as cell loss ratio or cell delay.

2. Virtual channel connections can be either dynamically switched (SVC) or (semi-) permanent (PVC).

3. The sequential order of cells in a virtual channel connection is preserved during transportation through the ATM network.

4. For each virtual channel connection, traffic parameters are negotiated between user and network, such as the maximum bandwidth available for the connection. The result of this negotiation is the "traffic

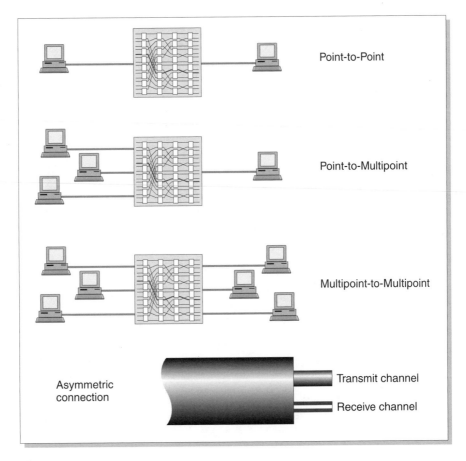

Figure 7.6
VPC and VCC connection architecture.

contract." Cells sent to the network by the user are monitored to ensure conformance with the traffic contract.

A VCC can be set up in three different ways:

1. By setting up a permanent or semi-permanent connection via network management;
2. by setting up switched virtual circuits via user-initiated signaling; or
3. by setting up Multi-Protocol Label Switching (MPLS) label switched paths (LSPs) within an ATM-based IP domain via a label distribution protocol.

Setting up permanent or semi-permanent VCCs has been the most common type of connection so far. SVCs are mainly used for PNNI- and LANE-related connections; apart from these, PVCs have dominated, particularly for providing core network connections related to Frame Relay; Frame Relay <> ATM interworking is widely used. In the future, ATM-based label switched paths for MPLS are likely to grow rapidly as demand for real-time streaming of data over IP increases.

Virtual Path Connections (VPCs)

Virtual path connections are a hierarchical level above virtual channel connections. In other words, a virtual path can contain several virtual channels. VPCs have the same properties as VCCs. Like VCCs, virtual path connections can be set up manually as permanent virtual paths via network management functions, or on demand by means of signaling or MPLS processes. One noteworthy aspect of VPCs is that, while the VPI of a VPC changes at every switching node in the network, the VCI values of all VCs within the VP are preserved end to end.

7.2.2 Multiplexing and Switching ATM Connections

As mentioned above, once the connection has been set up, the ATM cells are multiplexed into a single continuous cell stream together with those belonging to other VCCs and VPCs. Multiplexing also mixes cells belonging to connections with different QoS parameters. Virtual channel connections and virtual path connections can generally be switched in the same ATM switch (Figure

7.7). In these processes, the ATM routing labels of incoming VCCs and VPCs must be translated to the appropriate new values for the outgoing connections. Each switch contains a routing table that lists the input port with associated routing label and output port with associated label for each virtual connection (input and output are reversed for the other direction of the virtual connection). Figure 7.8 shows the routing table principle.

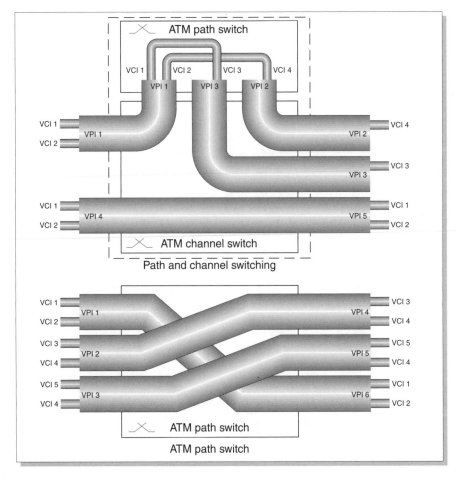

Figure 7.7
Paths and channel switching in ATM.

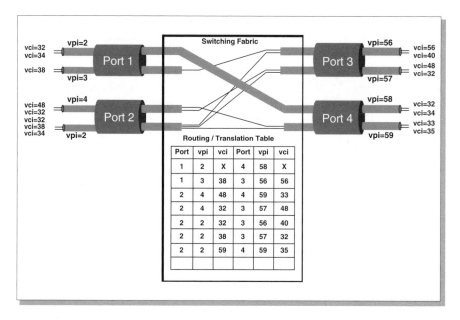

Figure 7.8
Routing table principle.

7.2.3 Quality-of-Service (QoS) Parameters

In ATM networks, services with widely differing communication requirements are transported concurrently. Real-time applications with variable bit rates are much more demanding with regard to average cell delay, for example, than simple data transfer at a constant bit rate. For this reason, the ATM layer assigns to each connection quality-of-service parameters that specify certain characteristics of the connection when the connection is set up. ITU-T Recommendation I.356 defines seven cell transfer performance parameters:

- Cell Error Ratio
- Severely Errored Cell Block Ratio
- Cell Loss Ratio
- Cell Misinsertion Rate (the proportion of cells with a valid but incorrect header)
- Cell Transfer Delay

- Mean Cell Transfer Delay
- Cell Delay Variation

On connection setup, any user can request a "traffic contract" that specifies a particular QoS class for each direction of communication, or specific traffic parameters. Once the traffic contract has been negotiated, the ATM network, or rather the ATM switches along the transfer path, guarantee the QoS parameters granted as long as the user respects the traffic contract (Figure 7.9).

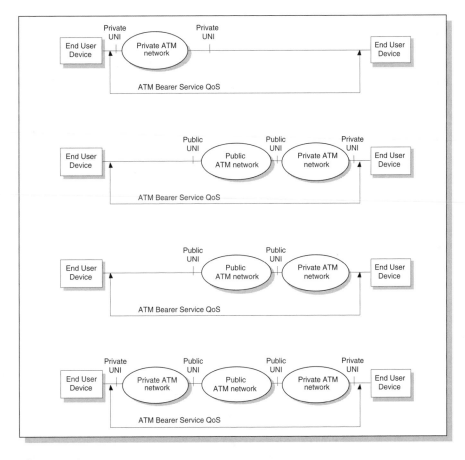

Figure 7.9
Quality of Service (QoS) parameters in ATM networks.

A basic distinction is made between service classes with defined QoS parameters and service classes without performance parameters. QoS classes with performance parameters must specify at least two such parameters. If a QoS class contains two parameters for cell loss ratio, then one value applies to cells with a Cell Loss Priority (CLP) of 1, and the other to cells with CLP = 0. Performance parameters that can be specified in a QoS class include:

- Maximum Cell Transfer Delay
- Cell Delay Variation
- Cell Loss Ratio for cells with CLP = 0
- Cell Loss Ratio for cells with CLP = 1

Quality-of-service classes are defined for each of the six service classes defined in the ATM Forum's Traffic Management specification (Table 7.5).

A service class can be requested without QoS parameters, as in a request for a connection with the "best effort network service," for example. Such a request, in which no QoS parameters are specified, may be made when no explicit network performance guarantee is required. The load level and error frequency in ATM networks have a direct influence on the QoS parameters.

Table 7.5 Service Classes and Specified QoS Classes

B-ISDN Service Classes	
Service class A	Leased line service, constant bit rate video
Service class B	Service class B
Service class C	Service class C
Service class D	Service class D
Service Class Quality	
QoS class 1	QoS for class A applications
QoS class 2	QoS for class B applications
QoS class 3	QoS for class C applications
QoS class 4	QoS for class D applications

- ATM interface card defective
- ATM interface card incorrectly configured (interrupt, driver, timers)
- Cell streams with different priorities are being transmitted at high load, and cells with low priority are discarded
- Classical IP: ATM ARP server address not configured on the client systems
- Classical IP: Misconfigured ATM ARP server: clients are not registered at all or registered under a wrong address
- Faulty cable infrastructure: see Chapter 6
- Electromagnetic interference (ATM over UTP)
- Hardware or software problems on the switch
- High signal transit delay due to long transmission path
- ILMI not active on the client or on the ATM switch
- Incompatible ILMI software versions on client and server
- Incorrect port configuration: bit rate, scrambling, interface type, frame type (PLCP, G.804, SDH, SONET)
- Incorrect router configuration (port inactive, wrong operating mode, protocol not active)
- Incorrect router filters
- Insufficient buffering in the switch

Figure 7.10
Symptoms and causes of problems in ATM networks.

Figure 7.10 illustrates the variety of factors that may cause a deterioration of QoS parameters in operation.

7.2.4 Cell Rate Adaptation to the Transmission Bandwidth

When ATM cells from several connections are multiplexed into a single cell stream, the cell rate is decoupled from the data rate of the given physical medium by inserting idle cells in the cell stream. In this way a discontinuous user cell stream is converted into a continuous stream of user cells interspersed with idle cells. The receiving station simply discards the idle cells. (See Figure 7.11.) This cell rate adaptation is only required with physical communication that provides synchronous time slots for cell transmission, such as SDH/SONET and PDH. For systems with asynchronous time slots, such as some cell-based physical layers (e.g., ATM25, TAXI), no cell rate adaptation is necessary.

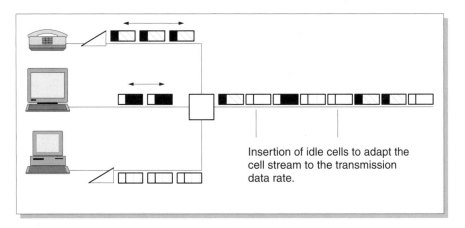

Insertion of idle cells to adapt the cell stream to the transmission data rate.

Figure 7.11
Adapting the cell rate to the transmission data rate.

7.2.5   Predefined Cell Types

All ATM implementations must be able to recognize certain cell types by reserved header values in the ATM layer. This allows signaling or OAM information cells to be immediately evaluated and forwarded to the appropriate functional module in the receiving system. Systems that do not support certain cell

Table 7.6   Payload Type Field

Payload Type Field	Meaning	
000	User data cell, no overload detected	SDU type = 0
001	User data cell, no overload detected	SDU type = 1
010	User data cell, overload detected	SDU type = 0
011	User data cell, overload detected	SDU type = 1
100	Segment OAM F5 cell	
101	End-to-end OAM F5 cell	
110	Reserved for future load management	
111	Reserved for future use	

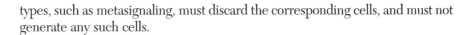

types, such as metasignaling, must discard the corresponding cells, and must not generate any such cells.

7.2.6 ATM Payload Types

Ordinary user data cells can be distinguished from special-purpose, nonuser cells by means of the Payload Type (PT) field. The PT values 0, 1, 2, and 3 (the most significant bit of the PT field = 0) identify user data cells; 4, 5, and 6 indicate virtual channel segment OAM, end-to-end OAM, and resource management (RM) cells, respectively; PT value 7 is undefined, so far. Table 7.6 lists the possible values of the payload type field.

7.2.7 Cell Loss Priority and Selective Discarding of Cells

To protect the network from users who produce unauthorized traffic loads or otherwise violate their traffic contract, each station's data stream is monitored by the "Usage Parameter Control" (UPC) or "policing" function. This entity analyzes and regulates the cell stream on each virtual path and virtual channel connection. The UPC function can act in three ways at the cell level to regulate the data stream: each cell can be passed along untagged (CLP = 0) or tagged (CLP = 1) or it can be discarded. Cell passing refers to the normal transfer of all cells that conform to the traffic contract. Cell tagging is performed on traffic that does not conform to the sustainable cell rate for a particular traffic contract type (VBR.3/SBR3). When such cells are tagged, their CLP value is changed by the Usage Parameter Control (UPC) function from 0 (normal priority) to 1 (low priority) (Figure 7.12). In case of network congestion, these cells will then be among the first to be discarded. If cell tagging is not supported, then cells that do not conform to any aspect of the traffic contract are discarded immediately. This subject is covered in much more detail in Chapter 20.

7.2.8 Traffic Shaping

The traffic contract negotiated during the connection setup includes a Connection Traffic Descriptor, which defines the parameters for permissible traffic, including peak cell rate, duration of the peak cell rate (maximum burst size, or MBS), and so on. A transmitting station can then help its virtual chan-

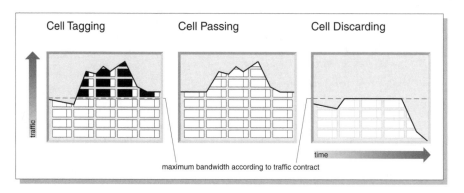

Figure 7.12
Usage Parameter Control (UPC).

nel stream(s) to conform to the negotiated traffic contract(s) by means of optional traffic shaping functions that smooth out the burstiness of these streams at the expense of some additional delay. Another user strategy would be to send all queued cells as they occur, and simply tolerate the inevitable loss of cells that will result when the traffic does not conform to the contract.

7.3 The ATM Layer: Management Plane Functions

Unlike the user plane functions, processes in the management plane serve to monitor and control cell transportation.

7.3.1 Monitoring in ATM Networks (OAM Flows)

Of the five ATM network operation and maintenance (OAM) information flows, F1–F5, F4 and F5 are situated in the ATM layer. All F4 and F5 OAM information is gathered and transmitted by means of special OAM cells. The F4 information flow is used for segment or end-to-end management at the virtual path (VP) level. A segment refers to one section of a connection, such as the link between two ATM switches (including any intermediate switches); end-to-end refers to the entire communication path between the two endpoints of the complete virtual path. Table 7.7 lists F4 and F5 functions.

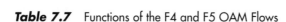

Table 7.7   Functions of the F4 and F5 OAM Flows

Layer	Function	Flow	Error Symptom
ATM path (VP)	Monitoring of path availability Network performance monitoring	F4	Path not available Low network performance
ATM channel (VC)	Network performance monitoring	F5	Low network performance

The information flow F5 is used for segment or end-to-end management at the virtual channel (VC) level. "End-to-end" refers here to communication between the two endpoints of the complete virtual channel, which is usually longer than the virtual path. As for F4, both segment and end-to-end F5 flows are defined. The purpose of F4 and F5 OAM cells is to provide the measurement data necessary to monitor the availability and performance of a given channel or path. See Figure 6.52 in Chapter 6 for an illustration of the information flows in the various protocol layers. See Figure 7.13 for F4 and F5 information flows.

Table 7.8 lists the individual OAM functions of the ATM layer.

Table 7.8   ATM Layer OAM Functions

OAM Function	Application
AIS	Transmit error reporting
RDI	Receive error reporting
Continuity check	Continous cell stream monitoring
Loopback	• For connection monitoring as neeeded • For error isolation • For link provisioning
Forward performance monitoring	Measurement of transmit performance
Backward performance monitoring	Measurement of receive performance
Activation/deactivation	Activation/deactivation of performance monitoring and continuity check
System management	System-dependent usage

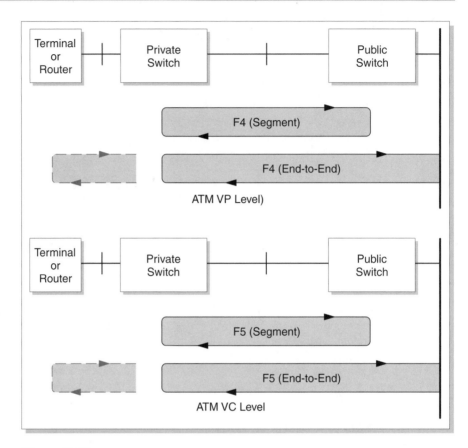

Figure 7.13
F4 and F5 information flow hierarchies.

7.3.2   The OAM Cell Format

The F4 OAM cells that transport management and monitoring information for VPCs have the same VPI value as the user cells on the virtual path being monitored. They are identified as F4 cells by the reserved VCI value 3 for F4 segment cells or 4 for F4 end-to-end cells. F5 OAM cells have the same VPI and VCI values as the user cells of the virtual channel connection being monitored. They are identified by the payload type field (PT). The PT value 100 (decimal 4) denotes F5 segment OAM cells; 101 (decimal 5) indicates an F5 end-to-end

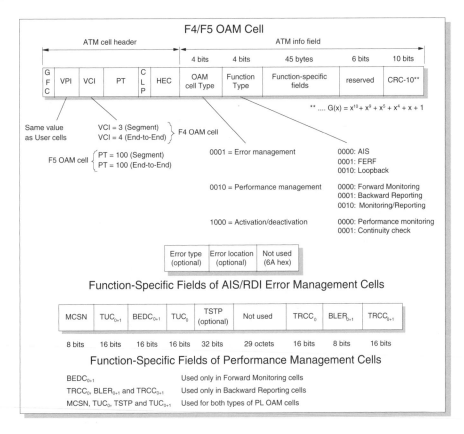

Figure 7.14
F4 and F5 OAM cell format.

OAM cell. End-to-end OAM cells must be forwarded transparently through all network nodes between the two connection endpoints. Only the endpoints may remove them from the cell stream. Segment OAM cells must be removed from the stream at the end of the given segment. There are five types of ATM-layer OAM cells: fault management OAM cells, APS coordination protocol OAM cells, performance management OAM cells, activation/deactivation cells, and system management OAM cells. The OAM cell type is indicated by a 4-bit field at the beginning of the OAM cell payload. Figure 7.14 shows F4 and F5 OAM cell format.

Fault management OAM cells are used to detect and localize communication errors and report them to the stations concerned. Performance management OAM cells detect parameters such as the cell block ratio, cell loss ratio, or the cell misinsertion rate, and thus provide information about the performance of a connection. APS coordination protocol OAM cells are used to manage ATM protection switching. Activation/deactivation cells are used to start and stop OAM functions such as fault or performance management. The fifth OAM cell type, system management cells, has no defined purpose in the specifications: its usage is left to individual manufacturers' implementations.

7.3.3   OAM Fault Management (AIS/RDI)

In analogy to SDH, fault management in the ATM layer involves two kinds of alarm signals: alarm indication signals (AISs) and remote defect indications (RDIs). The alarm indication signal (VP-AIS/VC-AIS) is sent by the channel or path node that detects the fault downstream to all network nodes directly affected. The AIS is transmitted at intervals of approximately 2 seconds as long as the fault persists. Immediately after the AIS, an RDI signal is sent upstream to the end nodes of the connections affected. These signals are also sent as long as the AIS condition persists. VP-AIS and VP-RDI messages are always sent in cells with VCI = 4, while VC-AIS and VC-RDI messages are sent in cells with PT = 101.

A fault at the virtual path level inevitably affects the virtual channels contained in that path. The faulty virtual path may terminate at a switch before the endpoint of the virtual channels, which go on from there in one or more other virtual paths as determined by the switching. For this reason, notification of the virtual path fault must be propagated further along the virtual channels. This is done not by propagating AIS or RDI in the F4 flows of the new virtual paths (which would incorrectly indicate that the channels' new paths are faulty), but by transferring the fault indication upward into the F5 flow, the virtual channel OAM flow, at the endpoints of the faulty virtual path. The RDI or AIS fault signals are then carried in VC-OAM cells over all the virtual channels that traveled through the faulty virtual path. This obviously results in a multiplication of fault indications, but this is inevitable if full fault management is to be achieved.

Fault conditions are detected by two mechanisms: continuity checks (CCs) and loopback tests. Continuity check cells can be inserted in the user data stream at regular intervals to provide continuous verification of the availability of a connection. ATM network nodes along the connection path can then monitor the presence of these cells. If the expected CC cells are not received, loss of continuity (LOC) is signaled by sending AIS OAM cells. The insertion of CC cells is useful where user traffic is intermittent, since the absence of user traffic does not necessarily mean that the virtual connection has been terminated. Without CC cells, there would be no mechanism to detect a fault occurring during a long period in which no data cells are transmitted in the virtual connection.

Loopback Cells

Loopback cells are used to verify connectivity to specific sections of the ATM network. There are five distinct kinds of loopback tests: end-to-end, access line, interdomain, network-to-endpoint, and intradomain.

End-to-end loopback cells sent to one endpoint of a VP or VC connection are sent back to the originating endpoint. The connection may lead across several subnetworks or "operator domains." In this way, the entire connection is tested from end system to end system. By contrast, access line loopback cells are returned by the first ATM network node that receives them. This tests exactly one connection section or segment. Interdomain loopback cells are reflected by the first network node of a neighboring operator domain. This makes it possible to test the connection of the neighboring network. Network-to-endpoint loopback cells can be used by a network operator to test the connection out of the network to an endpoint in an adjacent network. Finally, intradomain loopback cells can be sent from a segment node to any other node in another segment within the same operator domain. This tests the data flow across a certain sequence of segments within a domain.

Format of Loopback Cells

Loopback cells are F4 or F5 OAM cells that contain the value 1000 in the function type field (see Figure 7.14). The function-specific fields are the Loopback Indication, the Correlation Tag, the Loopback Location ID, and the Source ID.

The Loopback Indication (Figure 7.15) indicates whether or not the cell is to be sent back. If it contains the value 0000 0000, the cell is rejected. If the value is greater than 0000 0001, it is reduced by one and the cell is sent back to its source.

The Loopback Location ID field is 16 bytes in length and identifies the point or points along a connection at which the cell should be sent back. By default, all bits are set to 1. This indicates that the signal is to be reflected at the endpoint of the given connection.

Because several fault management cells may be in transit within a connection at the same time, a field is also required that allows the sender to identify which of its transmitted OAM cells was successfully returned. This field, the

Correlation Tag, is 4 bytes long. The sending station may set it to any value desired; the reflecting station must not modify it.

The 16-byte Source ID identifies the sender of the loopback cell. The sending station may set the Source ID field to any value desired. A station sending

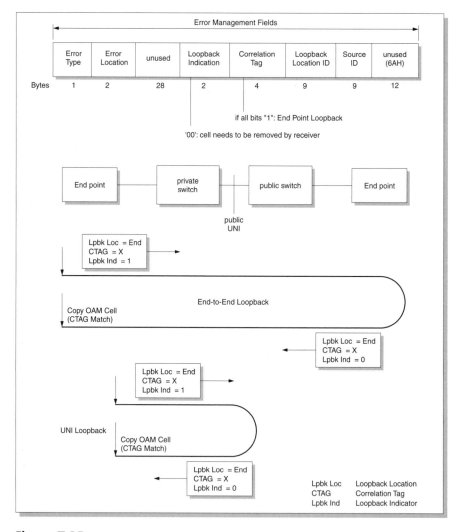

Figure 7.15
Format and function of loopback cells.

several loopback cells can identify its returning cells by their Source ID and distinguish between them on the basis of the Correlation Tag.

If a station receives a loopback OAM cell with a value other than 0 in the Loopback Indication field, it must return the cell within 1 second. Stations that transmit loopback cells must do so at such an interval that the management cell traffic is less than 1% of the capacity of each channel or path involved in the connection. User data cells are unaffected by loopback functions, so that loopback tests can be safely performed at any time.

7.3.4   OAM Performance Management

In addition to fault management, the performance of the individual VPs and VCs can also be monitored by the periodical insertion of special performance OAM cells in the user cell stream. Analysis of the special measurement data contained in these cells (cell sequence number, total user cell count, time stamp, cell loss count) yields direct information about the operating condition of the given ATM connection. OAM Performance Management involves two distinct functions known as Forward Monitoring and Backward Reporting. If both functions are activated, then information is transmitted in both directions when OAM performance information about a given cell block is determined. The individual fields of performance management cells are illustrated in Figure 7.14.

- Monitoring Cell Sequence Number (MCSN) (8 bits)
- Total user cell count for the CLP_{0+1} user cell flow (TUC_{0+1}, 16 bits). This is the number of cells transmitted with cell loss priority of 0 or 1 up to the time of OAM cell insertion.
- Total user cell count for the CLP_0 user cell flow (TUC_0, 16 bits). As TUC_{0+1}, but counting only cells with CLP = 0.
- Block error detection code for the CLP_{0+1} user cell flow ($BEDC_{0+1}$, 16 bits). This field is used only in forward-monitoring cells. It contains a BIP-16 checksum of the information fields of the cells transmitted since the last forward-monitoring cell.
- Time Stamp (TSTP, 32 bits). This is the time at which the OAM cell was inserted in the cell stream. At present the time stamp is optional, and its use has yet to be fully defined.
- Total received cell count for the CLP_{0+1} user cell flow ($TRCC_{0+1}$, 16 bits). This field is used only in backward-reporting OAM cells. It contains the number of cells received before the corresponding forward-monitoring cell.

- Total received cell count for the CLP_0 user cell flow ($TRCC_0$, 16 bits). This field is used only in backward-reporting OAM cells. It contains the number of cells with $CLP = 0$ received before the corresponding forward-monitoring cell.
- Block error result ($BLER_{0+1}$, 8 bits). This field is used only in backward-reporting OAM cells. It contains the number of incorrect parity bits determined on the basis of the BIP-16 code in the corresponding forward-monitoring cell.

Performance monitoring is done over blocks of cells of size N, where N is related to the peak cell rate of the virtual connection being monitored. A forward-performance monitoring OAM cell is inserted after every N user cell to transport information about the cell block. At the receiving end, the same analysis of the cell block is performed and the results compared with the information in the forward-performance-monitoring OAM cell. The results are then reported to network management and, optionally, to the originating end by means of a backward-reporting OAM cell.

The reason for using both forward-performance monitoring and backward-reporting cells is that the endpoints of the virtual path or virtual channel being monitored may lie in the domains of two different network operators. Normally, one operator does not have access to information in another operator's network management system, so the backward-reporting cell provides a means of transferring the results back across one or more domain boundaries between the network operators concerned. If no domain boundaries are crossed, backward-reporting cells are not necessary, since network management can access all nodes in the network.

7.3.5   Activation and Deactivation of OAM Functions

The performance monitoring and continuity check functions are started and stopped by means of special activation and deactivation cells. Figure 7.16 shows the format of these cells.

The Message-ID field contains the various commands of the OAM activation/deactivation cell:

Activate	000001
Activation confirmed	000010
Activation request denied	000011
Deactivate	000101

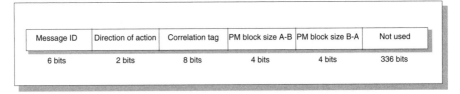

Message ID	Direction of action	Correlation tag	PM block size A-B	PM block size B-A	Not used
6 bits	2 bits	8 bits	4 bits	4 bits	336 bits

Figure 7.16
Function-specific fields of activation/deactivation cells.

Bit 8 7 6 5 4 3 2 1

Protocol Discriminator	Byte 1
Protocol Version	Byte 2
Message Type	Byte 3
Reference	Byte 4
Identifier	Byte 5
Signaling	Byte 6
Virtual Channel Identifier A	Byte 7
Signaling	Byte 8
Virtual Channel Identifier B	Byte 9
PSVC Cell Rate	Byte 10
Cause	Byte 11
Service Profile	Byte 12 to
Identifier	Byte 22
Null-fill	Byte 23 to
Null-fill	Byte 44
CRC	Byte 45 to
CRC	Byte 48

Protocol Discriminator (PF)	Identifies messaage as meta-signaling message
Protocol Version (PV)	Meta-signaling protocol version
Message Type (MT)	Identifies message type
Reference Identifier (RI)	Differentiates between meta-signaling processes such as ASSIGN REQUEST, ASSIGNED or DENIED
Signaling Virtual Channel Identifier A (SVCIA)	Contains either a PSVCI, a BSVCI or a GSVCI
Signaling Virtual Channel Identifier B (SVCIB)	Contains either a BSVCO or a GSVCI
Point-to-Point-SVC Cell Rate (PCR)	Contains the requested cell rate for the point-to-point connection of the virtual signaling channel
Cause (CAU)	Contains the cause for the sending of a particular message
Service Profile Identifier (SPID)	Contains the requested service type
Cyclic Redundancy Check (CRC)	Error checksum

Figure 7.17
Format of metasignaling cells.

Deactivation confirmed	000110
Deactivation request denied	000111

Commands are associated with the corresponding responses by means of the Correlation Tag. The Direction-of-Action field specifies the direction of transmission of the activated OAM cells. A–B indicates the direction away from the activator or deactivator; B–A indicates transmission toward the activator. The fields PM Block Size A–B and PM Block Size B–A specify the cell block length to be used for the given performance measurement.

7.4   Metasignaling

Because ATM networks require a great number of signaling procedures in order to support high bandwidths and a wide variety of services, a more flexible signaling mechanism was developed for ATM than the D-channel concept of N-ISDN. In ATM, new signaling channels can be set up as needed. The signaling process to control these signaling channels is called metasignaling. In actual practice, however, the standard signaling channel, VCI 5, has been found sufficient, so that metasignaling is only rarely used.

Metasignaling itself (ITU-T Q.2120) is a relatively simple procedure. Each message fits in one ATM cell and is sent over a reserved ATM channel (VCI = 1, VPI = 0; see Figure 7.17). (Metasignaling thus requires no ATM

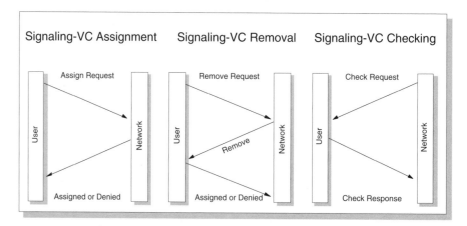

Figure 7.18
Metasignaling message flow.

Adaptation Layer.) Metasignaling fulfills three purposes: setting up, clearing down, and verifying signaling channels. These functions are performed by means of the messages ASSIGN REQUEST, REMOVE REQUEST, ASSIGNED, DENIED, CHECK REQUEST, and CHECK RESPONSE. If the remote station responds to an ASSIGN REQUEST message with an ASSIGNED message, the requested signaling channel is considered established. The connection is cleared down by a REMOVE REQUEST message. The remote station responds with REMOVED, whereupon the connection is cleared down. Figure 7.18 illustrates the flow of metasignaling messages.

Chapter 8

THE ATM PROTOCOL:
THE ATM ADAPTATION LAYER

The purpose of the ATM Adaptation Layer (AAL), shown in Figure 8.1, is to map the data structures of higher application layers to the cell structure of the ATM layer, and to provide the corresponding control and management functions. In order to meet the different requirements of various services, four AAL types were originally defined: AAL Type 1 for real-time sensitive services with constant bit rates; AAL Type 2 for real-time sensitive services with variable bit rates; and AAL Types 3 and 4 for connection-oriented and connectionless transmission of non-real-time-sensitive data. Later, AAL Type 5 was defined as a simplified version of AAL Type 3 (see Figure 8.2).

Early on it became apparent that there was no need for a distinction between connection-oriented and connectionless data communication at the AAL level. Consequently, AAL Types 3 and 4 were merged to form AAL Type 3/4. AAL types cannot be mixed within a virtual channel connection.

The reader may come across the term "AAL-0"; this term denotes the absence of any AAL capability. The application data is inserted directly in the payload fields of the ATM cells and transmitted. AAL-0 is thus not an AAL type at all, since the communication mechanisms are already cell-based and no adaptation layer functions are performed.

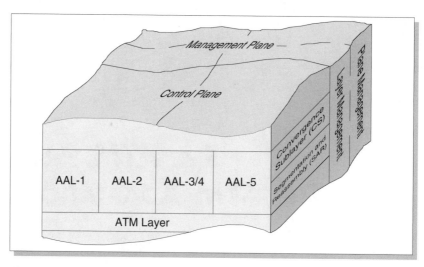

Figure 8.1
B-ISDN protocol reference model: The ATM Adaptation Layer (AAL).

Service Parameter	Class A	Class B	Class C	Class D
Time Compensation	required		not required	
Bit rate	constant	variable		
Communication mode	connection-oriented			connectionless
Example	circuit emulation	motion video	connection-oriented data communication	connectionless data communication
AAL type	AAL1	AAL2	AAL3, AAL5	AAL4

Figure 8.2
Service classes and AAL types.

8.1   ATM Adaptation Layer Type 1 (AAL-1)

The ATM Adaptation Layer Type 1 (ITU-T Recommendation I.363.1), or AAL-1, serves to transport data streams with constant bit rates (these include all the interfaces in the PDH hierarchy: T1, E1, T3, etc.), and provide them to the destination node in synchronization with the original service clock (that is, the clock associated with the constant bit rate service). This requires that the ATM network transport not only the data, but also the clock information. For this reason the AAL-1 protocol is capable of transporting both continuous bit streams and byte-structured data, such as data based on an 8-kHz sampling interval. Lost or erroneous data is not repeated or corrected. Events such as cell loss or the transmission of incorrect service data units (SDUs), loss of synchronization or clock signal, buffer overflow, or the occurrence of invalid AAL header information (AAL Protocol Control Information, or AAL-PCI) are passed from the user layer to the management layer. Figure 8.3 illustrates the various functions of AAL-1.

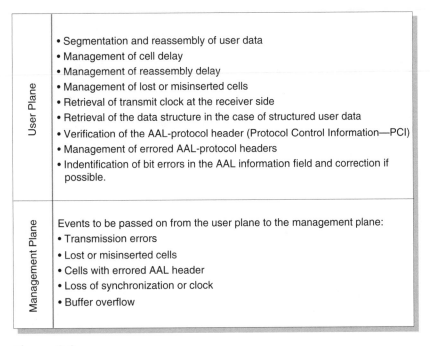

Figure 8.3
AAL-1 functions in the user and management planes.

8.1.1 Processes in AAL-1

AAL-1 is composed of two sublayers: the Segmentation and Reassembly Sublayer (SAR) and the Convergence Sublayer (CS). The data to be transported is first filled into 47-byte data blocks called CS-PDUs (Protocol Data Units). Each such data block is then given a 1-byte header, which contains a 3-bit sequence counter, a CRC-3 checksum with a parity bit, and a CSI bit, which is used to carry a multicell synchronous residual timestamp (SRTS; see "Transmission Frequency Regeneration" in section 8.2.4, below). The resulting 48-byte SAR PDU is then transported in the data field of an ATM cell.

8.1.2 The AAL-1 Segmentation and Reassembly Sublayer (SAR)

During AAL-1 generation, the SAR sublayer receives 47-byte data blocks from the convergence sublayer, supplies them with a SAR header, and passes the resulting SAR PDU to the ATM layer. Conversely, the receiving station's SAR removes the SAR header from the 48-byte SAR PDUs received from the ATM layer, and passes the 47-byte data blocks to the convergence sublayer. Figure 8.4 shows the structure of the SAR PDU.

The Sequence Number Field

With each 47-byte data block that the convergence sublayer passes to the SAR sublayer during the generation process, it also gives the SAR a corresponding sequence number, which is entered in the appropriate field in the SAR PDU's

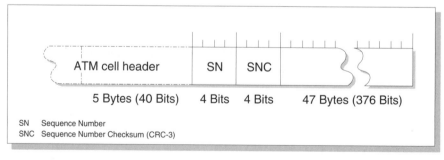

Figure 8.4
AAL-1 SAR PDU format.

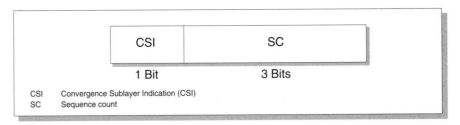

Figure 8.5
Format of the Sequence Number field.

header. In the reception process, the convergence sublayer analyzes the sequence numbers received in SAR headers to determine whether cells have been lost or incorrectly delivered. The Sequence Number field consists of two parts: the Sequence Count (SC) field and the Convergence Sublayer Indication (CSI) (Figure 8.5).

The sequence number of the given cell is entered in the Sequence Number field beginning with the most significant bit (MSB) at the left. The Convergence Sublayer Indication field is used to communicate information from sender to receiver for various sublayer functions, such as clock or data structure information. In order to minimize communication errors in the Sequence Number field, a checksum is calculated from this field and transported in the Sequence Number Protection (SNP) field. This CRC-3 checksum is calculated using the generator polynomial $G(x) = x^3 + x + 1$. Finally, the 7 bits comprising the Sequence Number field and the CRC-3 checksum are secured by a parity bit (Figure 8.6).

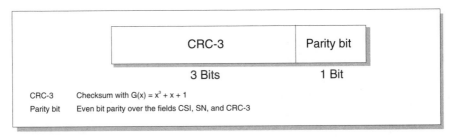

Figure 8.6
Sequence Number Protection (SNP).

8.1.3   The AAL-1 Convergence Sublayer (CS)

All of the AAL-1 functions represented in Figure 8.3, with the exception of segmentation and reassembly, are performed by the CS. Depending on the services that use the AAL-1 protocol, however, not all of the convergence sublayer functions are required. The convergence sublayer receives AAL SDUs (Service Data Units) from the application layer above it. Depending on the application, the length of these data units may be either 1 bit (as in the transportation of line interfaces such as E1, DS1, E3 etc.) or 1 byte (as in video or audio communication). The convergence sublayer then forwards these AAL SDUs to the SAR sublayer in the form of 47-byte data blocks, together with a sequence number.

Convergence Sublayer Functions for Private Data Lines

In leased-line applications, AAL-1 may be used to transport both asynchronous interfaces (such as all the signals in the PDH hierarchy—E1, DS1, J2, E3, DS3, etc.) and synchronous interfaces, such as SDH; in reality, transporting SDH over AAL-1 is probably never done. In these cases, the length of the AAL SDU (service data unit) is 1 bit; that is to say, the transmitter accepts service information (i.e., the constant bit rate service) one bit at a time at the service clock rate and at the receiver, it delivers service bits 1 bit at a time at the service clock rate. In asynchronousm data transport, the original bit rate (service clock) of the transmitter is regenerated at the destination node using the SRTS mechanism or by an adaptive clock method such as phase locked loop. If the data being transferred is structured, the structural information is entered in the CSI field. Cell delay variation is compensated for by buffering; this is the cause of some reassembly delay. In case of buffer underflow—when the buffer is exhausted in assembling user data from cells—dummy bits (set to "1") are generated to maintain the output bit rate. In the opposite direction, user data received for segmentation is discarded in case of a buffer overflow, as are cells with incorrect sequence numbers. When data is discarded or lost, bit rate integrity is maintained by generating dummy cells in which the Info fields are filled with bits set to 1.

Convergence Sublayer Functions for Video Signals

When the AAL-1 protocol is used to transport video signals, the length of the AAL SDU is 1 byte; that is to say, the transmitter accepts service information (i.e., the constant bit rate video service) one byte at a time at the service byte clock rate and at the receiver, it delivers service bits one byte at a time at the service byte clock rate. If the video data being transmitted is structured, the structural information is entered in the CSI field. As in leased-line emulation, described above, cell delay variation is compensated for by buffering. In case the transmission bit rate needs to be regenerated at the receiver, AAL-1 provides this function for video signals as well. Furthermore, an optional correction mode for cell loss and bit errors is also defined for video signal transport. This is required for services that cannot tolerate the ATM layer's values for cell loss and bit error rates. This option is called Forward Error Correction (FEC).

Convergence Sublayer Functions for Voice Signals

As for video signals, voice communication uses an AAL SDU of 1 byte. The voice data may be either A-Law or μ-Law-encoded 64 kbit/s voice band signals (ITU-T G.711) or 64 kbit/s ITU-T G.722 signals. Once again, cell delay variation is compensated for by buffering. No correction is provided for cell loss or bit errors. In addition to voice communication, AAL-1 can also be used to transport high-quality audio signals.

8.1.4　The Convergence Sublayer Protocol

The four basic functions of the AAL-1 convergence sublayer are described in detail below. These include sequence numbering, transmission frequency regeneration methods for the receiver, provisions for structured data transfer, and correction techniques for bit errors and cell loss.

Sequence Numbering

Every AAL-1 cell contains a sequence number in the 3-bit sequence number field (Figure 8.5). In accordance with the length of the sequence number field, the numbers are allocated in a modulo 8 cycle, beginning with zero. By analyzing sequence numbers, the receiver can detect the following conditions:

- Correct SAR PDU sequence
- One or more lost SAR PDUs
- The number of consecutive SAR PDUs lost (2–7 or more than 7)
- Misinserted SAR PDU (out of sequence)
- Location of lost information in the user data stream

Transmission Frequency Regeneration Methods for the Receiver

The receiver can regenerate the original transmission frequency after data transportation over the B-ISDN network by one of two methods: the SRTS method and the Adaptive Clock method.

Transmission Frequency Regeneration by SRTS

The Synchronous Residual Timestamp method of transmission frequency regeneration is based on the measurement of the frequency difference between the application data rate (the "service clock") and the ATM network data rate (the "network clock"). This method assumes that the network clock rate at the transmitting and receiving interfaces are locked (even if they are at different rates). If this is the case, then the measured difference between the application data rate and the ATM network data rate at the transmitting interface is all the information required for the receiving interface to recreate the original application data rate. If the network data rate is not the same everywhere in the ATM network, then transmission frequency regeneration must be performed by asynchronous methods, which are not specified in detail in this context.

The difference between the application and network data rates is measured by counting the number of phase cycles M_q of the network frequency f_n over a given period T. The period T is defined as N phase cycles of the service clock f_s. Since f_n and N are known at the receiving interface, only M_q needs to be determined in order to reproduce the application's original transmission data rate f_s (Figure 8.7).

$$f_s = \frac{N}{M_q} \times f_n$$

f_s	Service clock
f_n	B-ISDN network frequency
N	Number of f_s phase cycles during time period T
M_q	Number of f_n phase cycles during time period T

Figure 8.7
Relation between Application Data Rate and Network Data Rate.

M_q can be considered to be composed of a nominal part M_{nom} and a differential part M_{res}. The latter is also called the residual part: hence the name "residual time stamp." The nominal part M_{nom} is constant for a given application data rate, so that only the residual part of M_q needs to be communicated. Furthermore, the reference frequency used is not the actual ATM network frequency f_n, but rather a derived value f_{nx} such that

$$f_s \leq f_{nx} < 2f_s$$

In actual practice, a p-bit counter, which is continuously synchronized to the ATM network frequency f_n, is used to detect M_q. This counter is read at intervals of T (where T is the duration of N cycles of the service clock f_s). The result is equal to the value M_q. After subtraction of the nominal part, the residual part is sent to the receiver for transmission frequency regeneration (Figure 8.8).

In order to represent the frequency differential M_{res} with sufficient precision, this method requires an RTS parameter of a certain size, which is dependent on the ratio of f_s to f_{nx} as well as on the value of N and the tolerance of the application bit rate f_s.

The difference between M_{nom} and the maximum or minimum value of M is then calculated by the formula

$$y = N \times f_{nx} / f_s \times \varepsilon$$

To obtain M_{res} without ambiguity, the following condition must be met: $2(p - 1) > [y]$, where $[y]$ is the smallest integer greater than or equal to y. The following parameters are defined for the use of SRTS in transporting data streams from asynchronous line interfaces in accordance with ITU-T G.702:

- $N = 3008$
- $1 \leq f_{nx} / f_s < 2$
- Service clock tolerance: 200×10^{-6}
- Size of RTS: 4 bits

If the length of the SAR PDU's information field is reduced by the convergence sublayer header, this also reduces the RTS period T, since T is defined as a fixed number of SAR PDU information bits. The value of N can be adjusted accordingly in such cases. For example, if four information field bytes are occupied by convergence sublayer headers within eight SAR PDUs, this reduces the value of N to 2976 rather than 3008 bits.

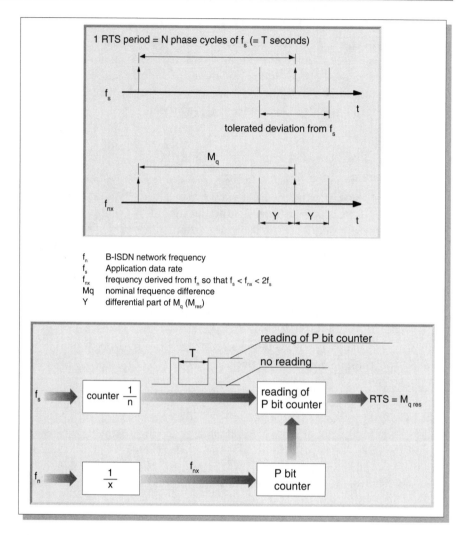

Figure 8.8
The Synchronous Residual Time Stamp concept.

As mentioned above, the reference frequency used for SRTS, f_{nx}, is not necessarily identical with the actual operational network frequency, f_n, but is rather derived from it in such a way that $1 \le f_{nx}/f_s < 2$, or $f_s \le f_{nx} < 2f_s$. For an SDH network with a data rate $f_n = 155.520$ MHz, for example, the following reference clock can be derived:

$$155.520 \text{ MHz} \times 2^{-k}, k = 0, 1, 2, ..., 11$$

For an application bit rate of 64 kbit/s, a network bit rate f_{nx} of 75.9375 kHz is obtained (k = 11); for 2.048 Mbit/s, f_{nx} is 2.430 Mbit/s (k = 6).

The four-bit RTS value M_{res} is transported in the CSI bits of consecutive odd-numbered SAR PDUs, that is, those with sequence numbers 1, 3, 5, and 7. The CSI bits of PDUs 0, 2, 4, and 6 remain available for other functions, and are set to 0 if not used.

Structured Data Transfer (SDT)

In addition to continuous data streams, AAL-1 also provides the capability for transporting byte-structured data. The boundaries of the structures are identified by means of pointers. For this reason, SAR PDU information fields are said to be in P format (if pointers are used), or in non-P (pointerless) format. In the format used to transport unstructured bit streams, every bit of the SAR PDU information field is filled with user data. To transport structured data, however, the pointer format is used. In this case, the first byte of the information field of even-numbered SAR PDUs functions as a pointer field.

The value of the pointer field is the number of bytes between the end of the pointer field and the beginning of the next structured data block within the next 93 Info field bytes. These 93 bytes are the remaining 46 bytes of the

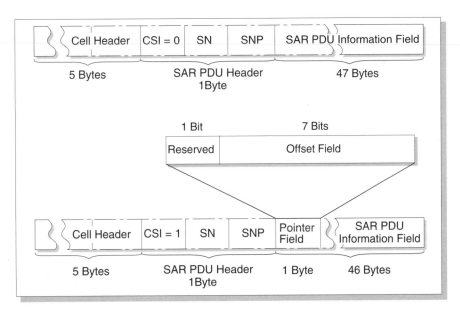

Figure 8.9
SAR PDU format for the transportation of structured data.

$$G(x) = (x - \alpha^{120}) \bullet (x - \alpha^{121}) \bullet (x - \alpha^{122}) \bullet (x - \alpha^{123})$$
$$\text{with } \alpha = x^8 + x^7 + x^2 + x + 1$$

Figure 8.10
Generator polynomial for the Reed-Solomon code.

present information field—that of the pointer PDU—and the 47 information field bytes of the following pointerless PDU. Permissible values for the pointer offset are 0 to 92. Bit one of the pointer field is reserved for future applications, and set to 0. If the SAR PDUs are only partially filled with user data to save reassembly time, then the rest of the information field is filled with padding bits. In calculating the pointer offset, however, both data bits and padding bits are counted. Furthermore, the number of user data bits in each cell must be constant. SRTS can also be used in the transportation of structured data. In this case, however, the RTS parameter N must be adjusted to the reduced number of SAR information field bits (Figure 8.9).

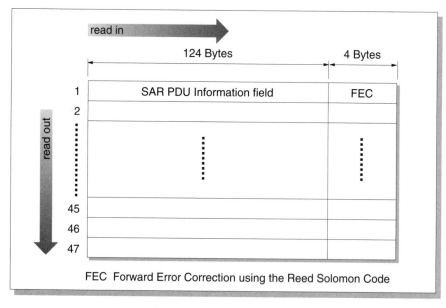

Figure 8.11
Byte interleaving in AAL-1 error correction.

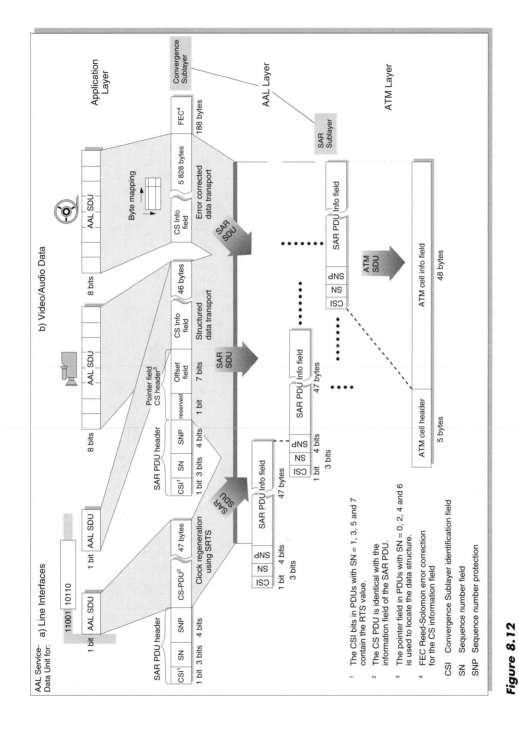

Figure 8.12
Structure of ATM Adaptation Layer Type 1.

Correction Techniques for Bit Errors and Cell Loss

The ATM layer's cell loss and bit error ratios can be too high for video communication. The error correction method provided for this case is a combination of Reed-Solomon coding and byte interleaving. This method can correct up to 2 errored or 4 lost bytes in a 128-byte block. First, the 4-byte Reed-Solomon code is calculated over 124 data bytes and appended to the data. The resulting 128-byte block is then interleaved over a matrix of 128 columns and 47 rows. This is done by reading in 47 data blocks line by line (where each line is one 128-byte block), and then reading them out again column by column. The number of bytes in the matrix, $128 \times 47 = 6016$, corresponds to the information fields of 128 47-byte SAR PDUs, which form one convergence sublayer PDU (CS-PDU) (Figures 8.10 and 8.11).

In order to identify the beginning of a CS-PDU, the CSI bit of the SAR PDU, which contains the first Info field of the CS-PDU, is set to 1. This use of the CSI bit is incompatible with the structured data transportation method described above, however. The following error combinations within a given CS-PDU can be corrected by this method:

- Four localized cell losses
- Two cell losses and one errored byte per row
- Two errored bytes per row if no cell loss occurs

The additional overhead generated by the 4-byte Reed-Salomon code for each 124 data bytes amounts to 3.1%. The cost of the technique also includes a cell transfer delay of 128 cells, since a whole CS-PDU must be received before data can be forwarded. Figure 8.12 summarizes the overall structure of AAL-1.

8.2 ATM Adaptation Layer Type 2 (AAL-2)

The ATM Adaptation Layer Type 2 (ITU-T Recommendation I.363.2), or AAL-2, is used for efficient transportation of delay-sensitive, narrowband applications with variable or fixed bandwidth (such as telephony). This means that the network must guarantee certain QoS parameters such as maximum cell delay or cell loss ratio for each connection while providing varying bandwidth. AAL-2 guarantees the traffic parameters for each connection using the QoS mechanisms of the underlying ATM layer.

The history of AAL-2 is complex. It was originally proposed by the ITU-T in the late 1980s as the adaptation layer to handle Class B services (variable bit-rate, connection-oriented services, specifically video), but later withdrawn. It returned in the latter half of the 1990s through the ATM Forum's and the ITU-T's initially separate, but later joint, efforts. First, to overcome AAL-1's problems with low bandwidth (and sometimes variable bandwidth), delay-sensitive services such as voice and compressed voice; and second, AAL-5's inefficiency in handling very short data packets. At one point the protocol was nearly named AAL-6 by the ATM Forum, before it was found to fulfill the original requirements defined for AAL-2 a decade earlier. Thus at the time of writing, two service types have been defined for AAL-2, namely narrowband services and SAR. ITU-T Recommendation I.366.2 describes the "AAL Type 2 Service-Specific Convergence Sublayer for Narrowband Services," the circuit emulation service used for transportation of narrowband, delay-sensitive traffic. AAL-2 also provides the means to handle very short data packets more efficiently, reducing the "cell tax"—the inefficient use of ATM cell payloads—inherent in AAL-3/4 and AAL-5. ITU-T I.366.1 thus describes the "Segmentation and Reassembly Service-Specific Convergence Sublayer for AAL Type 2." This allows the encapsulation of higher-layer, variable-length data packets over AAL-2 CPS-Packets in a similar way that the SAR function of AAL-5 allows encapsulation of data packets over ATM cells (see AAL Type 5, p. 228).

8.2.1   Processes in AAL-2

Like other ATM adaptation layers, AAL-2 consists of two sublayers. These are the common part sublayer (CPS) and the service-specific convergence sublayer (SSCS). AAL-2 is specified currently in three ITU-T recommendations: I.363.2 provides details of the CPS sublayer, and the generic features of the SSCS sublayer and layer management; I.366.1 provides details of the segmentation and reassembly service-specific convergence sublayer for handling packet-based services; I.366.2 provides details of the service-specific convergence sublayer for narrowband services (formerly known as "trunking"). Other types of SSCSs may be specified in the future.

The data to be transported is first filled into the payload of Common Part Sublayer Packets (CPS-Packets), which consist of 3 header bytes and up to 45 or up to 64 bytes of user data; these CPS-Packets may be thought of as "mini-cells" because such a term may help the reader understand the process (the ITU-T standards, however, never use this term). Multiple CPS-Packets (mini-cells), or parts thereof, are then inserted in CPS-PDUs, which consist of

1 header byte and 47 payload bytes. The CPS-PDU header contains an offset value (0 . . . 47), which points to the start of the next CPS-Packet within the CPS-PDU payload (i.e., within the cell). The CPS-PDUs are, in turn, transported in the payload fields of standard ATM cells. The process of mapping CPS-Packets into ATM cell payloads is analogous to the manner in which standard ATM cells are mapped into SDH/SONET frame payloads, where cells can be interrupted by the occurrence of SDH/SONET frame overhead bytes (SOH/TOH and POH). CPS-Packets can sometimes be split between one or two cells, so that at the ATM layer the 6 bytes comprising cell header plus cell payload header interrupt the PCS-Packet; of course, at the AAL, these effects are not visible.

Because each CPS-Packet (mini-cell) belongs to an AAL Type 2 channel, it is identified by an 8-bit channel IDentifier (CID); up to 248 values (8 . . . 255) of CID are available for user traffic, so there can be up to 248 "mini" virtual channels (officially called "AAL-2 channels") associated with each standard ATM virtual channel or VPI-VCI. A full label description of such a virtual channel would therefore be VPI-VCI-CID. There is a 5-bit user-to-user indicator (UUI) field, which plays a major part in AAL-2, as will become apparent. Now let us take a closer look at the CPS-Packet.

8.2.2   The AAL-2 CPS-Packet Format

The CPS-Packet (mini-cell) consists of a 3-byte header and a user data field with a default maximum length of 45 bytes. The maximum length can be increased to as much as 64 bytes through signaling or layer management actions, however. The default limit is set because a value greater than 45 would give rise to a CPS-Packet greater than 48 bytes (because of the 3-byte header); as we have said above, such a CPS-Packet could be split across three CPS-PDUs and therefore three ATM cell payloads (remember there is a 1-byte header in each ATM cell supporting AAL-2). To manage this, hardware implementations of the AAL-2 processes have to be more sophisticated. The 3-byte CPS header contains the following fields: Channel Identifier (CID), Length Indicator (LI), User-to-User Indication (UUI), and Header Error Control (HEC). Figure 8.13 shows the structure.

Channel Identifier (CID)

The CID is an 8-bit field that identifies the user channel ("AAL-2 channel") within an AAL-2 connection. Value 0 is not used; the CID value 1 is reserved for AAL-2 layer management peer-to-peer procedures; the CID value 2 is

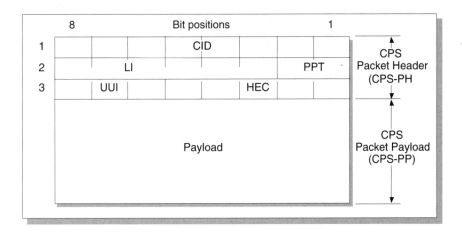

Figure 8.13
The AAL-2 CPS-Packet.

reserved for AAL-2 level signaling; the values 3 through 7 are reserved for future purposes. Values 8–255 can be used to identify user channels. *Note*: The ATM Forum prefers to ignore the CID values up to 7 and reserves the values 8 to 15 for its special purposes, in a similar way as to how the VCI values 0 to 15 are reserved for ITU-T use and values 16 to 31 are reserved for special proprietary use; that is, VCI = 16 is used by the ATM Forum for ILMI. Details of the ATM Forum's use of CIDs are given in af-vmoa-0145-000 (Loop Emulation Service Using AAL-2), which is discussed in section 12.4 in Chapter 12.

Length Indicator (LI)

The Length Indicator is a 6-bit field and contains the number of bytes in the CPS-Packet payload minus one. When the maximum CPS-Packet payload length is restricted to the default value of 45 bytes (LI = 44), LI values 45 . . . 63 are not allowed.

User-to-User Indication (UUI)

The UUI is a 5-bit field that is used either to transfer specific information between the CPS users (i.e., between the SSCS sublayers or between layer management). There are 32 codepoints (0 . . . 31); codepoints 0 . . . 27 are available for the SSCS sublayers; codepoints 28 . . . 29 are reserved for future use; codepoints 30 . . . 31 are used for layer management.

Header Error Control (HEC)

To guard against transmission errors in the first 19 bits of the CPS-Packet, a 5-bit header error control field is added. First, a polynomial of degree 31 is formed from the 19 header bits, which is then multiplied by x^5 and divided by the generator polynomial $x^5 + x^1 + 1$ modulo 2. The remainder of this division is the HEC checksum.

8.2.3 The AAL-2 CPS-PDU

The AAL-2 CPS-PDU consists of a 1-byte header (called the Start Field, or STF) and a 47-byte payload field; it occupies the 48 bytes of a standard ATM cell payload. The CPS header contains the 6-bit Offset (OSF) field, a 1-bit Sequence Number (SN), and a parity bit (P). The Offset field (with values 0 . . . 47) indicates the number of bytes between the header and the beginning of the next CPS-Packet within the CPS-PDU (i.e., within the same cell); the OSF exists to provide CPS-Packet delineation, particularly after the loss of an ATM cell transferring the CPS-Packets. If the Offset field contains the value 47, this indicates that the given CPS-PDU payload field does not contain the beginning of a CPS-Packet. This will only occur when a 48-byte CPS-Packet (i.e., one with the 45-byte default maximum payload size) starts in the last byte of an ATM cell or when a bigger CPS-Packet has been allowed, through signaling or layer management actions, to have a payload greater than the default maximum length of 45; such a CPS-Packet could be split across three ATM cells, so the middle of these cells would have no CPS-Packet boundary. Offset values greater than 47 are not allowed. The sequence number of the CPS-PDUs is modulo 2 (can have the value 0 or 1). The parity bit is used for error detection, and is set so that the parity of the complete CPS-PDU header byte is odd. Figure 8.14 shows the AAL-2 CPS-PDU.

The payload field of the CPS-PDU may contain zero, one, or more whole or partial CPS-Packets. As discussed above, a CPS-Packet can normally extend over two ATM cells or, exceptionally, over three ATM cells. Unused bytes of the CPS-PDU payload are filled with padding bytes of value zero. The use of padding is triggered by the expiration of a timer (Timer_CU), in order to avoid excessive delay in sending a CPS-Packet because of the unavailability of another CPS-Packet to fill the CPS-PDU (i.e., the cell payload). Figure 8.15 shows a diagram of the structure of AAL-2.

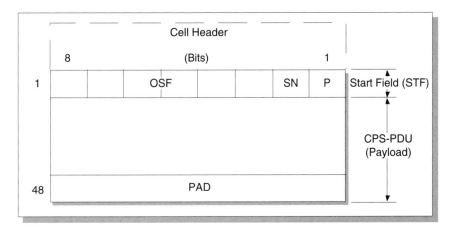

Figure 8.14
The AAL-2 CPS-PDU.

8.2.4 The Segmentation and Reassembly SSCS

ITU-T Recommendation I.366.1 defines the segmentation and reassembly service-specific convergence sublayer (SEG-SSCS) for AAL-2. This SSCS is designed to allow the transfer of short data packets (although packets similar in length to those handled by AAL-5 can also be accommodated) and has consequently been adopted for use in third-generation (3G) mobile wireless networks.

The SEG-SSCS has a basic functionality, covered by the service-specific segmentation and reassembly (SSSAR) sublayer, and two further optional sublayers, covered by the service-specific transmission error detection (SSTED) sublayer and the service-specific assured data transfer (SSADT) sublayer—the latter requires the SSTED to have been implemented too. Figure 8.16 shows the overall layered model for AAL-2 using the segmentation and reassembly service-specific convergence sublayer.

Service-Specific Segmentation and Reassembly (SSSAR)

The SSSAR operates as follows. A higher layer data packet (the SSSAR-SDU) to be transferred is first chopped into segments of the size that will fit in the CPS-Packet maximum payload set for the particular AAL-2 channel; the last segment will almost certainly be less than the full size permitted, so a CPS-Packet of appropriate size (probably less than the maximum permitted) is created to accommodate this. Remember, CPS-Packets have adjustable lengths,

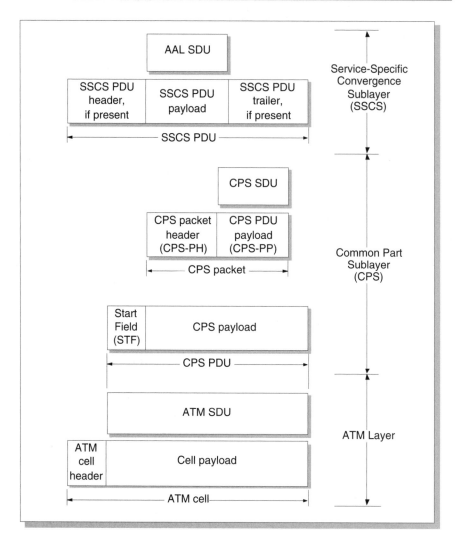

Figure 8.15
The structure of AAL-2.

the length indication being contained in the header. In all but the last CPS-Packet the UUI codepoint value is set to 27; in the last CPS-Packet the UUI is set to a codepoint value in the range 0 . . . 26 passed via the SSSAR-UUI parameter available for use by higher layer services. The default value of SSSAR-UUI is 26 if multiple codepoints are not required (Note: Because the SEG-SSCS [defined in I.366.1] often coexists with the narrowband services SSCS

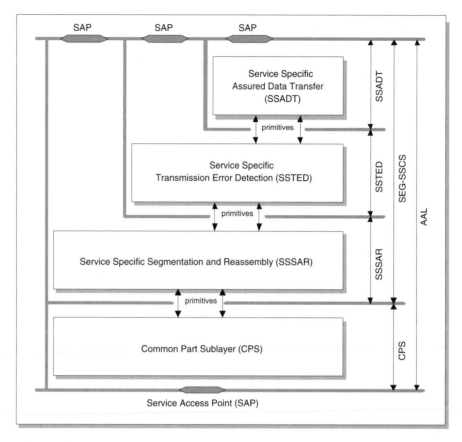

Figure 8.16
The structure of AAL-2 using the SEG-SSCS.

[defined in I.366.2], this default value is mandatory in such situations). The SSSAR-SDU can be up to 65,568 bytes long, though is usually substantially shorter. Because there is no header or trailer added to the SSSAR-SDU, this basic process forms the most efficient way to handle data packets over AAL-2, and is what is used in 3rd-generation (3G) wireless networks. Figure 8.17 shows an example of how the SSSAR-SDU is segmented into CPS-Packets.

Service-Specific Transmission Error Detection (SSTED)

If error detection is desired, the optional SSTED trailer is added before segmentation is performed (the UUI codepoint value *must* be 26 for the last CPS-Packet in this case). The SSTED-PDU trailer is 8 bytes long and has a similar

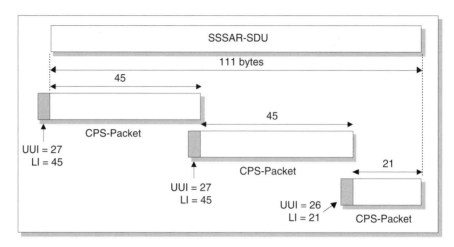

Figure 8.17
SSSAR-SDU segmented to CPS-Packets.

structure to that used for AAL-5. Like the AAL-5 trailer, the last 4 bytes form a 32-bit cyclic redundancy check (CRC-32). The CRC-32 is calculated from the entire SSTED-PDU, excluding the 4-byte CRC-32 itself. The generator polynomial used is

$$G(x) = x^{32} + x^{26} + x^{23} + x^{22} + x^{16} + x^{12} + x^{11} + x^{10} + x^{8}$$
$$+ x^{7} + x^{5} + x^{4} + x^{2} + x + 1$$

which is the same as that used in AAL-5. Figure 8.18 shows the arrangement.

Service-Specific Assured Data Transfer

A further sublayer can optionally be added above the SSTED sublayer to deliver an assured service. This is the service-specific assured data transfer (SSADT) sublayer and is specified to be the same service-specific connection-oriented protocol (SSCOP) specified for use with AAL-5 for the signaling adaptation layer (SAAL). At the receiver, CPS-Packets containing the segmented packet are extracted from the underlying ATM layer using AAL-2 CPS

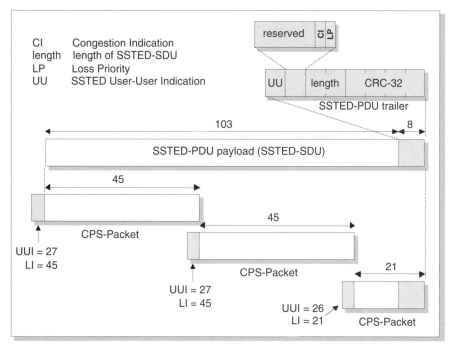

Figure 8.18
SSTED-SDU segmented to CPS-Packets.

procedures then processed to reassemble the SSSAR-PDU, SSTED-PDU, or SSADT-PDU, depending on which optional sublayers are being used.

8.2.5   The SSCS for Narrowband Services

ITU-T Recommendation I.366.2 defines the service-specific convergence sublayer for narrowband services for conveying voice, voice-band data, or circuit mode data. For voice services, it covers the use of low-rate voice using standard compression/encoding techniques (e.g., ITU-T G.728, G.729, etc.) with silence suppression, in-band channel associated signaling (CAS), dialed digits (DTMF, Signaling Systems R1 and R2), and facsimile. The ATM Forum's Loop Emulation Service specification (af-vmoa-0145.000) relies heavily on the features of this extensive recommendation. Recommendation I.366.2 covers far more than we will cover here, but we provide an overview of its main features.

CPS-Packet Types

There are currently two types of CPS-Packets ("mini-cell") defined for this SSCS, namely Type 1 and Type 3; in the original version of ITU-T Recommendation I.366.2, a Type 2 CPS-Packet was also defined, but this has been dropped from the revision published in November 2000. Type 1 CPS-Packets, the default type, are basic and have no protection of the payload data. These are used to carry user data and (encoded) voice samples. Type 3 CPS-Packets are, on the other hand, protected in that they contain a trailer containing a Message Type and a CRC-10 checksum to detect payload errors; the CRC-10 polynomial is identical to that used in standard ITU-T I.610 OAM cells. Type 3 CPS-Packets are used to carry critical control plane information such as channel associated signaling (CAS), facsimile demodulation control data, alarms, and so on. The 6-bit Message Type field is encoded in Table 8.1.

Because the Type 3 CPS-Packets for some message types are considered crucial, they are sent three times so that they survive the loss of up to two copies should ATM cells transferring them be lost or errors be detected. For these message types, the CPS-Packet payload also contains a 1-byte header, known as the Common Facilities header, comprising a 2-bit Redundancy field and a 6-bit timestamp. The Redundancy field is the only part of the CPS-Packet that is different for each of the three copies, apart from the CRC-10 (which, of course, changes *because* the Redundancy field is different). The

Table 8.1 Type 3 CPS-Packet Message Types

Information Stream	Message Type Code	Packet Format
OAM	000000	Alarm, loopback
User state control	000001	User state control
Dialed digits	000010	Dialed digits
Channel associated signaling (CAS)	000011	CAS bits
Rate control	000100	Rate control
Synchronization of change in SSCS operation	000101	Synchronization of change in SSCS operation
Facsimile demodulation control	100000 100001 100010 100011 100100	T.30_Preamble EPT Training Fax_Idle T.30_Data

coding of the Redundancy field uses the first three values 00, 01, 10; the value 11 indicates that redundancy is not being used and that only one copy of a message is being sent. When redundancy is being used, the Type 3 messages are timed to be dispatched at specific intervals, for example, 5 ms for CAS messages and 20 ms for facsimile demodulation control data; despite the different timing of their dispatch, all three CPS-Packets still retain the same timestamp value in the Type 3 CPS-Packet header to ensure that they are identified as being copies of the same message. Figure 8.19 shows the Type 3 CPS-Packet format, which includes the Common Facilities header.

Note that, for Type 3 CPS-Packets used for OAM, the Common Facilities header is omitted. All Type 3 CPS-Packets use UUI codepoint 24, except those used for OAM, for which the codepoint is 31.

Audio and Circuit Mode Data Services

Because of the use of short CPS-Packets, AAL-2 is much more suited than AAL-1 to handling low bandwidth, delay-sensitive streaming services such as 8 kb/s compressed voice; this is because it takes much less time to assemble the payload of a short CPS-Packet than it does to assemble the 47 bytes required to dispatch cells of an AAL-1 service. Many AAL-2 channels can be carried on the same ATM virtual channel (VPI-VCI), each being identified by a separate CID; the CPS-Packets associated with each CID are multiplexed such that efficient use is made of the bandwidth, despite the extra overhead implied by the CPS-Packet headers. Different types of traffic can be intermixed on the same ATM virtual channel; for example, 8 kb/s voice using encoding defined by G.729

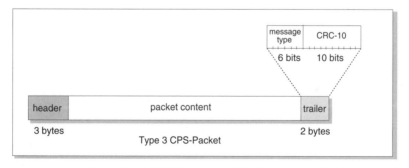

Figure 8.19
Type 3 CPS-Packet format.

211

might occupy one AAL-2 channel (identified by one CID), while a 64 kb/s circuit mode data service may occupy another (identified by another CID). This multiplexing is analogous to the ATM cell multiplexing that occurs at the ATM layer, except that the lengths of the CPS-Packets are adjusted to suit the service; in most cases so far defined, they are actually of fixed length within a given AAL-2 channel.

Much use is made of the UUI field for managing the timing associated with these streaming services. When the most significant bit (msb) is "0," it is used in combination with the length indicator (LI) to convey sequence numbers that imply timestamps, as we shall see, and silence suppression for the CPS-Packet; when the msb is "1" it is used to indicate that the CPS-Packet is conveying control and traffic management information, including the Type 3 CPS-Packets discussed earlier. Packet-mode AAL-2, discussed in section 8.2.4, also uses UUI values (26 and 27) in this range.

Audio and circuit mode data services use Type 1 CPS-Packets. For each service, a subfield of the UUI is used as a modulo n sequence counter (n = 1, 2, 4, 8, or 16) for successive CPS-Packets of a given AAL-2 channel. CPS-Packets are dispatched at regular intervals specific to the requirements of the particular service. For this reason, the sequence numbers double as timestamps, which help the play-out mechanisms at the receiver and helps cope with lost CPS-Packets due to lost ATM cells.

A couple of examples will help here. The 64 kb/s circuit mode data service standardized in ITU-T G.711 can be carried in CPS-Packets having a fixed payload length of 40 bytes (i.e., LI = 39). The CPS-Packets are dispatched regularly every 5 ms, which means that 200×40 bytes (= 8 kbytes = 64 kbits) are sent every second. Similarly, a 56 kb/s service would be sent using CPS-Packets having a payload length of 35 bytes (LI = 34), also dispatched every 5 ms. For both of these, a modulo-16 sequence number is used, encoded as the UUI values 0SSSS, where SSSS represents the sequence 0000, 0001, ... 1110, 1111, 0000, ... and so on. For the 8 kb/s G.729 compressed audio service, CPS-Packets having a payload length of 10 bytes (LI = 9) would be dispatched every 10 ms, which means that 100×10 bytes (= 1 kbyte = 8 kbits) are sent every second; there is also a provision with this service for sending longer CPS-Packets (LI = 19) at less frequent intervals (20 ms). To summarize, it is the CPS-Packet payload length plus the dispatch interval that determines the user data rate for a given AAL-2 channel. The embedded sequence number in the UUI, acting as a timestamp, provides an indication of lost CPS-Packets, should an ATM cell transferring the CPS-Packet be lost. The bigger the sequence number, the better the chances of maintaining the correct timing of the service in the event of loss. Dummy data has to be substituted for data missing with lost CPS-Packets.

Generic Silence Suppression

A great deal of bandwidth (possibly more than 50%) can be saved through the use of silence suppression in an audio service used for telephony, since one party is generally not speaking when the other is. Some encoding standards (e.g., G.729) specify how silence suppression should be used and Recommendation I.366.2 specifies how this can be implemented in AAL-2 narrowband services. Apart from silence suppression explicitly specified by some encoding standards, CPS-Packets with a payload length of 1 byte (LI = 0) are used for generic silence suppression and the fact that LI = 0 indicates that a period of silence is beginning or continuing. It is not necessary to send these "silence insertion descriptors" (SIDs) continuously, but in the background, the sequence number/timestamp encoded in the UUI is incremented at the same rate as CPS-Packets would be dispatched, but for the silence suppression so that the correct timing of voice play-out can be maintained after the silence period. SID CPS-Packets share the same UUI encoding so a SID packet following a voice packet would be dispatched after the standard interval and with the next sequential value of sequence number/timestamp. The content of the only byte of the generic SID CPS-Packet payload is encoded with a level indication for "comfort noise."

Channel Associated Signaling (CAS) and Dialed Digits

Because AAL-2 channels used for audio are generally dynamic, a method for conveying call setup and tear-down (signaling) has to be accommodated. In traditional communication systems based on T1 and E1 primary rate multiplexing, one type of signaling used is channel associated signaling (CAS). In T1 systems, CAS information is transferred through the use of a technique known as "bit stealing," in which the least significant bit of a 64 kb/s channel is reallocated to carry signaling information, which gives rise to the 56 kb/s clear channel (7 bits × 8 kHz rate). In the case of E1, timeslot 16 is used to contain signaling information. In both cases the information is coded such that 4 bits (A, B, C, D) are assigned to each user channel. When these traditional multiplexed services have to interwork with AAL-2, the audio part of the service can be processed to compress it and is carried in user CPS-Packets, as described earlier, but the CAS bits also need to be conveyed. This is done in Type 3 CPS packets in the same AAL-2 channel as the associated audio; the UUI codepoint is 24 and the message type is 3 (000011). Triple redundancy is used. The CAS CPS-Packet has the format shown in Figure 8.20.

8	Bit Positions				1
1	Redundancy	Time Stamp (upper 6 bits)			
2	Time Stamp (lower 8 bits)				
3	Reserved	A	B	C	D
4	0 0 0 0 1 1			CRC-10	
5	CRC-10 (continued)				

Figure 8.20
CAS CPS-Packet format.

For telephone links that need to carry tone dialing codes such as "dual tone multifrequency" (DTMF), another Type 3 CPS-Packet format is used (see Figure 8.21). This time the message type is 2 (000010). Three different tone dialing systems are supported (DTMF, MF-R1 dialed digit codes, and MF-R2 dialed digit codes). For all three systems, each dual tone combination is converted to deliver a 5-bit value, which is inserted into the Digit Code field. The system being used is indicated in the Digit Type field. Additionally, the received dual tone level is encoded in the Signal Level field so that regenerated tones at the receiver can be sent at the right level.

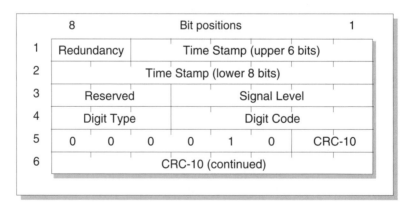

8	Bit positions	1
1	Redundancy	Time Stamp (upper 6 bits)
2	Time Stamp (lower 8 bits)	
3	Reserved	Signal Level
4	Digit Type	Digit Code
5	0 0 0 0 1 0	CRC-10
6	CRC-10 (continued)	

Figure 8.21
Dialed Digit CPS-Packet format.

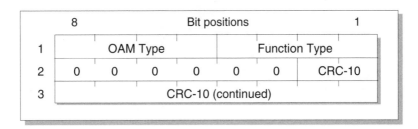

Figure 8.22
Alarm CPS-Packet format.

AAL-2 Channel OAM (Alarms and Loopback)

AAL-2 channel OAM messages are carried in Type 3 CPS-Packets but without the Common Facilities header; the UUI codepoint has the value 31 and the CID is the same value as the CID of user CPS-Packets in the AAL-2 channel for which these OAM functions are relevant. Two different CPS-Packet formats are used, one for alarms (see Figure 8.22) and one for loopback (see Figure 8.23).

AAL-2 channel level alarms supported are the alarm indication signal (AIS) and remote alarm indication (RAI). While the alarm condition exists, alarm CPS-Packets must be sent at least once a second.

AAL-2 loopback uses the same concept as ITU-T Recommendation I.68. Loopback CPS-Packets contain a 1-bit loopback indicator (LBI), which is initially set when the packet is first sent but is decremented at the loopback point. When a loopback packet is received with LBI set to 1, it is looped back; when set to 0, the arrival event is noted and the packet is discarded to prevent endless looping. Only the Loopback CPS-Packets are affected; user traffic with the same CID is not looped back.

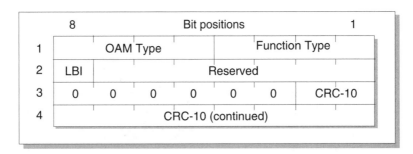

Figure 8.23
Loopback CPS-Packet format.

Table 8.2 Summary of AAL-2 SSCS Usage

	UUI		LI	Packet Type	Message Type Code	Time Stamp, Redundancy	M	Packet Time (ms)	Seq. No. Interval (ms)	Use	ITU-T Recommendation Details
User Stream Traffic	0SSSS	0-15	40	1	N/A	No	1	5	5	G.711-64 generic	I.366.2 Annex P
	00SSS	0-7	40	1	N/A	No	1	5	5	G.711-64 generic	I.366.2 Annex P
	0SSSS	0-15	1	1	N/A	No	1	5	5	Generic SID	I.366.2 Annex P
	0SSSS	0-15	24	1	N/A	No	1	30	5	G.723.1 - 6.4	I.366.2 Annex P
	0SSSS	0-15	20	1	N/A	No	1	30	5	G.723.1 - 5.3	I.366.2 Annex P
	0SSSS	0-15	4	1	N/A	No	1	30	5	G.723.1 SID	I.366.2 Annex P
	0SSSS	0-15	25	1	N/A	No	1	5	5	ADPCM G.726-40	I.366.2 Annex P
	0SSSS	0-15	20	1	N/A	No	1	5	5	ADPCM G.726-32	I.366.2 Annex P
	01SSS	8-15	40	1	N/A	No	1	10	5	ADPCM G.726-32	I.366.2 Annex P
	01SSS	8-15	20	1	N/A	No	1	5	5	ADPCM G.726-32	I.366.2 Annex P
	0SSSS	0-15	15	1	N/A	No	1	5	5	ADPCM G.726-24	I.366.2 Annex P
	0SSSS	0-15	10	1	N/A	No	1	5	5	ADPCM G.726-16	I.366.2 Annex P
	0SSSS	0-15	20	1	N/A	No	2	10	5	LD-CELP, G.728-16	I.366.2 Annex P
	0SSSS	0-15	16	1	N/A	No	2	10	5	LD-CELP, G.728-12.8	I.366.2 Annex P
	0SSSS	0-15	12	1	N/A	No	2	10	5	LD-CELP, G.728-9.6	I.366.2 Annex P
	0SSSS	0-15	10	1	N/A	No	1	5	5	LD-CELP, G.728-16	I.366.2 Annex P
	0SSSS	0-15	8	1	N/A	No	1	5	5	LD-CELP, G.728-12.8	I.366.2 Annex P
	0SSSS	0-15	6	1	N/A	No	1	5	5	LD-CELP, G.728-9.6	I.366.2 Annex P
	0SSSS	0-15	30	1	N/A	No	2	20	5	CS-ACELP, G.729-12	I.366.2 Annex P
	0SSSS	0-15	20	1	N/A	No	2	20	5	CS-ACELP, G.729-8	I.366.2 Annex P
	0SSSS	0-15	16	1	N/A	No	2	20	5	CS-ACELP, G.729-6.4	I.366.2 Annex P
	0SSSS	0-15	15	1	N/A	No	1	10	5	CS-ACELP, G.729-12	I.366.2 Annex P
	0SSSS	0-15	10	1	N/A	No	1	10	5	CS-ACELP, G.729-8	I.366.2 Annex P
	0SSSS	0-15	8	1	N/A	No	1	10	5	CS-ACELP, G.729-6.4	I.366.2 Annex P
	0SSSS	0-15	2	1	N/A	No	1	5	5	G.729 SID	I.366.2 Annex P
	00SSS	0-7	31	1	N/A	No	1	20	20	AMR 12.2	I.366.2 Annex P
	01SSS	8-15	31	1	N/A	No	1	20	20	AMR 12.2 (errored)	I.366.2 Annex P
	00SSS	0-7	26	1	N/A	No	1	20	20	AMR 10.2	I.366.2 Annex P
	01SSS	8-15	26	1	N/A	No	1	20	20	AMR 10.2 (errored)	I.366.2 Annex P
	00SSS	0-7	21	1	N/A	No	1	20	20	AMR 7.59	I.366.2 Annex P
	01SSS	8-15	21	1	N/A	No	1	20	20	AMR 7.59 (errored)	I.366.2 Annex P
	00SSS	0-7	19	1	N/A	No	1	20	20	AMR 7.4	I.366.2 Annex P
	01SSS	8-15	19	1	N/A	No	1	20	20	AMR 7.4 (errored)	I.366.2 Annex P
	00SSS	0-7	18	1	N/A	No	1	20	20	AMR 6.7	I.366.2 Annex P
	01SSS	8-15	18	1	N/A	No	1	20	20	AMR 6.7 (errored)	I.366.2 Annex P
	00SSS	0-7	16	1	N/A	No	1	20	20	AMR 5.9	I.366.2 Annex P
	01SSS	8-15	16	1	N/A	No	1	20	20	AMR 5.9 (errored)	I.366.2 Annex P
	00SSS	0-7	14	1	N/A	No	1	20	20	AMR 5.15	I.366.2 Annex P
	01SSS	8-15	14	1	N/A	No	1	20	20	AMR 5.15 (errored)	I.366.2 Annex P
	00SSS	0-7	13	1	N/A	No	1	20	20	AMR 4.75	I.366.2 Annex P
	01SSS	8-15	13	1	N/A	No	1	20	20	AMR 4.75 (errored)	I.366.2 Annex P
	0SSSS	0-15	2	1	N/A	No	1	—	20	AMR SID_First	I.366.2 Annex P
	00SSS	0-7	6	1	N/A	No	1	160	160	AMR SID Update	I.366.2 Annex P
	01SSS	8-15	6	1	N/A	No	1	160	160	AMR SID_Update (errored)	I.366.2 Annex P
Control & Management Traffic	10000	16-23	Undef	Undef	Undef	Undef	Undef	Undef	Undef	Reserved for future use	
	11000	24	6	3	000001	Yes	N/A	N/A	N/A	User state control	I.366.2 Annex O
	11000	24	6	3	000010	Yes	N/A	N/A	N/A	Dialed digits	I.366.2 Annex K
	11000	24	5	3	000011	Yes	N/A	N/A	N/A	CAS bits	I.366.2 Annex L
	11000	24	5	3	000100	Yes	N/A	N/A	N/A	Rate Control	I.366.2 Annex R
	11000	24	5	3	000101	Yes	N/A	N/A	N/A	Synchronization of change in SSCS operation	I.366.2 Annex S
	11000	24	4	3	100000	Yes	N/A	N/A	N/A	Fax demod control T.30_Preamble	I.366.2 Annex M-1
	11000	24	5	3	100001	Yes	N/A	N/A	N/A	Fax demod control EPT	I.366.2 Annex M-2
	11000	24	5	3	100010	Yes	N/A	N/A	N/A	Fax demod control Training	I.366.2 Annex M-3
	11000	24	4	3	100011	Yes	N/A	N/A	N/A	Fax demod control Fax_Idle	I.366.2 Annex M-4
	11000	24	>5	3	100100	Yes	N/A	N/A	N/A	Fax demod control T.30_Data	I.366.2 Annex M-5
	11001	25	Undef	Undef	Undef	Undef	Undef	Undef	Undef	Proprietary Use	I.366.2
	11010	26	Any	N/A	N/A	No	N/A	N/A	N/A	Framed data, final packet	I.366.1
	11011	27	Any	N/A	N/A	No	N/A	N/A	N/A	Framed data, more to come	I.366.1
	11100	28	Undef	Undef	Undef	Undef	Undef	Undef	Undef	Reserved (see I.363.2)	I.366.2 / I.366.2
	11101	29	Undef	Undef	Undef	Undef	Undef	Undef	Undef	Reserved (see I.363.2)	I.366.2 / I.366.2
	11110	30	Undef	Undef	Undef	Undef	Undef	Undef	Undef	Reserved (see I.363.2)	I.366.2 / I.366.2
	11111	31	5	3	000000	No	N/A	N/A	N/A	OAM packets (alarms & loopback)	I.366.2 Annex N

M: number of service units in a packet N/A: not applicable
SSS: 3 bit sequence number Undef: undefined
SSSS: 4 bit sequence number

Summary

Table 8.2 shows a summary of AAL-2 SSCS usage, including the SEG-SSCS discussed in section 8.2.4.

8.3 ATM Adaptation Layer Type 3/4 (AAL-3/4)

The ATM Adaptation Layer Type 3/4 (ITU-T Recommendation I.363.3) specifies connection-oriented and connectionless transportation of data packets in ATM networks. Both point-to-point and point-to-multipoint connections can be set up. The AAL-3/4 protocol is thus suitable for transportation of non-connection-oriented communications services such as SMDS/CBDS metropolitan area networks or Frame Relay. In practice, however, AAL-3/4 is now used only for legacy SMDS services, which are themselves obsolete. The much more efficient AAL-5 has supplanted AAL-3/4 for Frame Relay interworking and for most other services.

Like other ATM adaptation layers, the AAL-3/4 protocol consists of two sublayers. These are the Segmentation and Reassembly Sublayer (SAR) and the Convergence Sublayer (CS), although the Convergence Sublayer includes both a Common Part Convergence Sublayer (CPCS) and a Service-Specific Convergence Sublayer (SSCS), as shown in Figure 8.24.

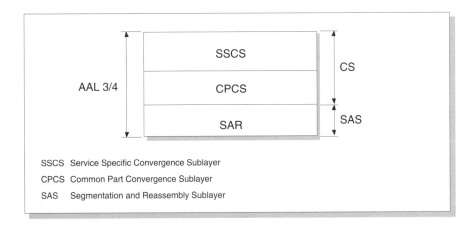

Figure 8.24
AAL-3/4 protocol layer model.

8.3.1 Processes in AAL-3/4

In the transmission process, the variable-length data packets (1 to 65,535 bytes) of the application building on AAL-3/4 are first padded to an integer multiple of 32 bits to permit an efficient, hardware-based implementation of the AAL processes; a 32-bit header and 32-bit trailer are then added. The resulting CS-PDU is then divided into 44-byte segments, each of which receives another header (16 bits) and trailer (16 bits), and is then passed to the ATM layer as a 48-byte SAR PDU.

This highly simplified description of AAL-3/4 may offer some orientation before the functional processes are examined in detail below. Two basic operating modes are defined for AAL-3/4: message mode and streaming mode (see Table 8.3).

8.3.2 Message Mode

In message mode, AAL SDUs can be of fixed or variable size. In either case, exactly one AAL SDU is transported in an AAL IDU (Interface Data Unit). Depending on the type of cells being transported, this can take place in one of two ways:

- In the case of short, fixed-length AAL SDUs, a blocking/deblocking buffer is activated so that several AAL SDUs can be transported within an SSCS-PDU.
- For variable-length AAL SDUs, a segmentation/reassembly function is activated that allows a single AAL SDU to be transported by one or several SSCS-PDUs.
- If the SSCS sublayer is not implemented, the AAL SDU is identical with the CPCS SDU (Figure 8.25).

8.3.3 Streaming Mode

In streaming mode communication, each AAL SDU is transported in one or more AAL IDUs. Moreover, the AAL IDUs that contain parts of a given AAL SDU can be transmitted at completely independent times. AAL SDUs that are not completely received through the AAL interface can be discarded. In streaming mode, as in message mode, a segmentation/reassembly function can be activated in order to transport an AAL SDU in one or sev-

Table 8.3 AAL-3/4 Operating Modes

	AAL-SDU Segmentation/ Reassembly	AAL-SDU Buffering (Blocking, Deblocking)	Pipelining
Message Mode: long SDUs, variable size	optional	—	—
short SDUs, fixed size	—	optional	—
Streaming Mode	optional	—	optional

eral SSCS-PDUs. Finally, streaming mode also provides a pipeline function. This function can be used to make the AAL convergence sublayer forward PDUs before the complete AAL SDU has been received. This reduces the size of the buffer required to store the individual IDUs that make up an AAL SDU. Once again, if the SSCS sublayer is not implemented, the AAL SDU is the same as the CPCS SDU (see Figure 8.26).

Both message mode and streaming mode permit a choice between guaranteed and nonguaranteed transmission, referred to in this context as assured and nonassured transmission. Assured transmission, which is intended primarily for point-to-point connections, provides retransmission of lost SDUs, as well as flow control functions. Nonassured transmission, on the other hand, provides no error correction. CPCS layer data transmissions are always nonassured. As-

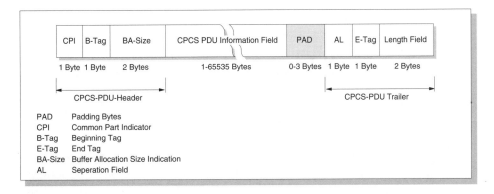

Figure 8.25
AAL-3/4 CPCS PDU.

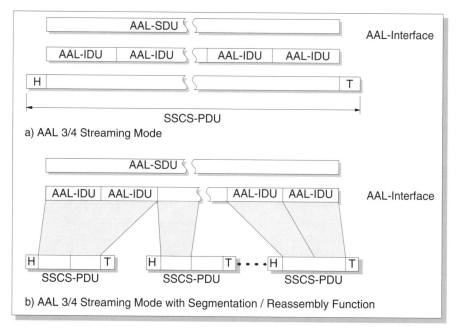

Figure 8.26
AAL Type 3/4 streaming mode.

sured transmission is reserved for the Service-Specific Convergence Sublayers (such as the Service-Specific Connection-Oriented Protocol, or SSCOP).

8.3.4 The AAL-3/4 Segmentation and Reassembly Sublayer

The AAL-3/4 segmentation/reassembly sublayer (SAR) is responsible for inserting and forwarding the SAR SDUs received from the CS in SAR PDUs *of variable length.* The SAR PDUs contain at most 44 bytes of SAR SDU data. The AAL-3/4 SAR sublayer comprises four functional areas:

- *Identification of the SAR SDU to be transported:* Each SAR SDU is identified using the Segment Type (ST) and Length Indication (LI) fields. The Segment Type field indicates whether the current SAR PDU contains the beginning of a SAR SDU (Beginning of Message, or BOM), an intermediate segment (Continuation of Message, or COM),

Table 8.4 Field Coding in the AAL-3/4 SAR PDU

Segment Type	Coding	Meaning
BOM	10	Begin of Message
COM	00	Continuation of Message
EOM	01	End of Message
SSM	11	Single Segment Message

or the end of the SDU (End of Message, or EOM). For SAR SDUs transported within one SAR PDU, the Segment Type value is Single Segment Message, or SSM (see Table 8.4).

- *Error detection, bit error handling, discarding SDUs:* The occurrence of bit errors at the receiver is monitored by means of a CRC-10 checksum. Corrupt SAR PDUs are discarded. Higher sublayer SAR SDUs that are incomplete due to lost SAR PDUs are also discarded. As an alternative option, however, the SAR may pass errored or incomplete SAR PDUs and SAR SDUs to the CPCS sublayer; this might be done where a real-time service would prefer to receive corrupt data rather than no data—it may have the capability to correct this at a higher layer.

- *SAR SDU sequence integrity:* This function preserves the order of SAR SDUs transported in the context of a CPCS connection.

- *Multiplexing/demultiblplexing:* The number of CPCS connections that are carried over an ATM connection (virtual channel) is defined during connection setup. In other words, several CPCS connections may be multiplexed over one ATM connection. The sequence integrity of SAR SDUs in each CPCS connection is preserved.

Structure of an AAL-3/4 SAR PDU

An AAL-3/4 SAR PDU consists of 2 header bytes, 2 trailer bytes, and 44 information bytes. Figure 8.27 illustrates the structure in detail.

The Segment Type Field

As mentioned above, the segment type (ST) identification field indicates which part of the SAR SDU is contained in each SAR PDU.

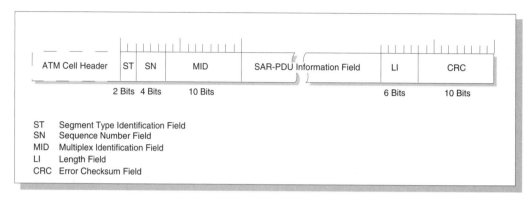

Figure 8.27
AAL Type 3/4 SAR PDU format.

The Sequence Number Field

In contrast to AAL-1, 4 bits are reserved for the sequence number field in AAL-3/4. Each SAR PDU in the transmission sequence of a SAR SDU is assigned a modulo 16 sequence number, beginning with zero. By analyzing the sequence numbers, the receiver can detect the loss of a SAR PDU or the receipt of a PDU that does not belong to the given sequence. If the receiving station does not evaluate the sequence number field, the sender may fill it with any value.

The Multiplexing Identification Field

The multiplexing identification (MID) field is used to bundle several CPCS connections over a single ATM connection. Such connection multiplexing is limited to an ATM connection between two users, however, and the multiplexed connections are still treated as a unit by the network. All SAR PDUs for the SDUs belonging to one connection are assigned the same MID value. This value can then be used to demultiplex the various SDUs into their respective connections.

Table 8.5   Permissible Values of the SAR PDU Length Field

Segment Type	Valid Values
BOM	44
COM	44
EOM	4,..., 44, 63 (abort)
SSM	8 ... 44

The Information Field

The 44-byte Info field is filled from left to right with SAR SDU bits. If the data does not fill the whole Info field, the remaining bits are set to zero, which are ignored at the receiver because the LI field is less than 44.

The Length Indication Field

The Length Indication (LI) field indicates the number of SAR SDU bytes contained in the Info field of the SAR PDU. Table 8.5 lists the permissible values of the length field. If an EOM (end of message) SAR PDU contains the length field value 63, it is treated as an Abort PDU.

The CRC Field

A CRC-10 checksum of the SAR PDU header, information, and length fields is calculated and inserted in the checksum field for use in detecting bit errors in the PDU. The checksum is calculated using the following generator polynomial:

$$G\,(x) = x^{10} + x^9 + x^5 + x^4 + x + 1$$

The Abort PDU

The communication of a SAR SDU can be cancelled by a special message in the form of an Abort PDU. The Abort PDU is a SAR frame whose MID field identifies it as an EOM (end of message), and whose length field contains the value 63. The Information field should contain zeroes, but it is ignored by the receiver in any case.

8.3.5   The AAL-3/4 Convergence Sublayer (CS)

The convergence sublayer consists of a part that is common to all higher applications—the Common Part Convergence Sublayer (CPCS)—and a part that is specific to a given application, the Service-Specific Convergence Sublayer (SSCS). The convergence sublayer contains basic signaling capabilities both for connectionless (Class D) data communication, such as the Connectionless Network Access Protocol (CLNAP), and for connection-oriented (Class C) data communication services, such as Frame Relay. The SSCS (Service-Specific Convergence Sublayer) does not need to be implemented for Class D protocols, but is necessary for Class C applications such as Frame Relay. As already mentioned, Frame Relay in reality never uses AAL-3/4, but instead uses the much more efficient (but less error tolerant) AAL-5.

The AAL-3/4 Common Part Convergence Sublayer (CPCS)

The following service characteristics are provided by the CPCS (and the SSCS that builds on it, if implemented):

- Nonassured transmission of variable-length frames (1 to 65,535 bytes)
- Simple or multiple connections between two CPCS endpoints
- Error detection and notification (bit errors and cell loss)
- Frame sequencing within a CPCS connection

The two AAL-3/4 modes described above, message mode and streaming mode, are also differentiated in the CPCS sublayer. In message mode, one CPCS SDU is transported by means of a CPCS IDU in exactly one CPCS PDU, whereas in streaming mode a CPCS SDU can be transported using one or several CPCS IDUs. The individual CPCS IDUs may arrive in a different sequence. Once they have been received, all of the IDUs that belong to a given SDU are sent in one CPCS PDU. The functions of the CPCS include:

- Identification of the CPCS SDU to be transported.
- Error detection and handling. The following errors are reported: B and E tag mismatch; PDU length different from that indicated in the length field; buffer overflow; CPCS PDU format errors; and bit errors reported by the SAR sublayer.

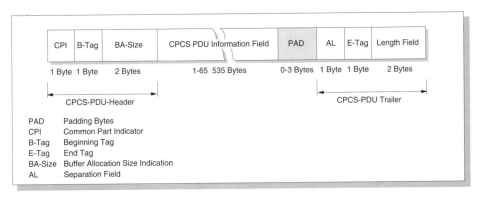

Figure 8.28
The AAL-3/4 CPCS PDU.

- Buffer allocation. The receiving station is told how much memory it should allocate to receive the given CPCS PDU.
- Discarding of incomplete CPCS SDUs.

Structure of an AAL-3/4 CPCS PDU. A CPCS PDU consists of a 4-byte CPCS PDU header, a CPCS PDU payload field of variable length (1 to 65,535 bytes), a padding field, and a 4-byte trailer. (See Figure 8.28.) The header contains the following fields: Common Part Indicator (CPI), Beginning tag (B tag), and Buffer Allocation Size (BASize). The CPCS PDU payload field contains the CPCS SDU. The trailer consists of the Alignment (AL), End tag (E tag), and Length (L) fields.

The CPI (Common Part Indicator) Field. The one-byte CPI field indicates the units (bytes, kilobytes, megabytes etc.) used in the BASize and length fields. At present, only one value is defined for this field: 00000000, indicating that the other parameters are given in bytes.

The B and E Tag Fields. The B tag and E tag fields allow the receiver to identify the end of the CPCS PDU header and the beginning of the trailer. Each tag is 2 bytes long. The contents of the B and E tags must be the same in each PDU, and consecutive PDUs must have different B/E tag values. One possible implementation is a modulo-256 cycle of B and E tag values.

BASize (Buffer Allocation Size) Field. The BASize field advises the receiving station of the appropriate buffer size to allocate for the incoming CPCS SDU. In message mode, the value of the BASize field is always the same as the CPCS PDU length. In streaming mode, however, the BASize value may be greater than the CPCS PDU length, since an SDU can be transported in one or more PDUs in streaming mode. The BASize field is 2 bytes long, and its value can thus range from 1 to 65,535 ($2^{16} - 1$). The units represented by the BASize value are determined by the CPI field.

CPCS PDU Payload.   This field can be of size 1 to 65,535 bytes and contains the CPCS SDU. Its actual length is indicated by the length field in the trailer.

The Padding Field.   Up to three padding bytes can be inserted between the CPCS PDU payload field and the 4-byte trailer to round the byte count of the information field to an integer multiple of 4 bytes. Consequently, the combined CPCS PDU payload and padding fields can have a length from 4 to 65,536 bytes in steps of 4 bytes.

The Alignment Field (AL).   The 1-byte Alignment field pads the CPCS trailer to 32 bits and contains no information.

The Length Field.   The 2-byte length field indicates the length of the PDU's information field. Like the BASize field, it can contain a value from 1 to 65,535. The units of length represented are also determined by the CPI field. Figure 8.29 illustrates the overall structure of the AAL-3/4 frame.

The Service-Specific Part of the AAL-3/4 Convergence Sublayer (SSCS)

For Class D communication protocols (connectionless communication), the nonassured transmission provided by the common part of the AAL-3/4 convergence sublayer (CPCS) is sufficient. Such applications do not require an implementation of the SSCS sublayer. For example, CBDS/SMDS metropolitan area network communication services that are transported over ATM networks build directly on the CPCS sublayer. Every Class C (connection-oriented) protocol, however, requires a service-specific AAL-3/4 convergence sublayer (SSCS). One example is the SSCS layer for B-ISDN signaling channels—the SSCOP protocol, which is described in section 8.6. Originally, it was intended that AAL-3/4 would be the ATM adaptation layer used for transporting signaling messages. Today, only AAL-5 is specified for this, so Class C operation of AAL-3/4 is probably not used at all. One could say, therefore, that "AAL-3" (for Class C services) is obsolete and that AAL-3/4 should become "AAL-4" (for Class D services).

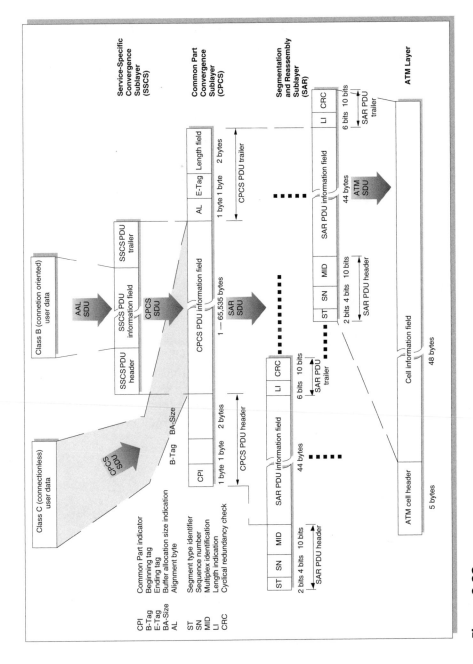

Figure 8.29
Structure of AAL-3/4.

8.4 ATM Adaptation Layer Type 5 (AAL-5)

AAL Type 5 was devised by the ATM Forum in the early 1990s to simplify the transportation of data protocols over ATM. The ITU-T later adopted it, and it is now defined in ITU-T Recommendation I.363.5. AAL-5 corresponds to a highly simplified implementation of AAL-3/4. Like AAL-3/4 it is suitable for both connection-oriented and connectionless transmission of data that does not require any synchronization between sender and receiver. And like AAL-3/4, the AAL-5 protocol also consists of the Segmentation and Reassembly Sublayer (SAR) and the Convergence Sublayer (CS), with the CS once again subdivided into a Common Part Convergence Sublayer (CPCS) and a Service-Specific Convergence Sublayer (SSCS), as shown in Figure 8.30.

8.4.1 Processes in AAL-5

The processes within the AAL-5 sublayers are significantly simpler than in AAL-3/4. There is no mechanism for cell multiplexing, for example. All cells that belong to a given AAL-5 CS-PDU are transmitted in one sequential cell stream. The variable-length data packets (1 to 65,535 bytes) of the application building on AAL-5 are first padded such that the total length of the resulting CPCS PDUs, including the 8-byte CPCS-PDU trailer (there is no CPCS PDU

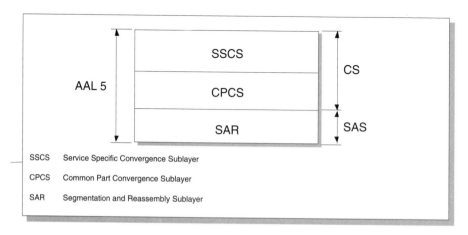

Figure 8.30
AAL-5 protocol layer model.

header), are multiples of 48 bytes. The resulting CPCS-PDU is then divided into 48-byte segments, which fit directly into the information field of ATM cells. The payload type (PT) field of the ATM header is "misused" to indicate whether further segments follow or whether the data field contains the end of the CPCS-PDU (see Figure 8.31).

Trailer-based PDUs such as those used in AAL-5 and in SAAL, described below, are efficient to process since the large amounts of higher-layer data often involved can be stored and further processed in memory-based implementations without being moved again. Furthermore, AAL-5 facilitates alignment on 32-bit boundaries: hence the 8-byte trailer length (2×32 bits), although there is no real need for more than 7 bytes—the CPCS UU and CPI fields are rarely used, and could have shared a single byte.

Like AAL-3/4, AAL-5 has two operating modes: message mode and streaming mode. Both modes provide two different communication methods: assured and nonassured transmission. The definitions of streaming mode, message mode, and assured and nonassured operation correspond exactly to those for AAL-3/4, and thus need not be repeated here. Here too, the CPCS sublayer provides only nonassured information transfer. The implementation of assured transmission is left to the appropriate SSCS sublayer.

8.4.2   The AAL-5 Segmentation and Reassembly (SAR) Sublayer

The SAR sublayer in AAL-5 comprises the following functions:

- *Identification of the SAR SDU to be transported:* The beginning and end of a SAR SDU are identified by the values of the ATM Payload Type (PT) header field. A Payload Type value of "1" means that the given SAR PDU contains the end of a SAR SDU. The value "0" indicates that the PDU Info is either the beginning or the continuation of a SAR SDU.

- *Congestion handling:* Upon receiving information about network congestion from the subordinate ATM layer, the AAL-5 SAR sublayer simply passes the information upward to the convergence sublayer.

- *Cell Loss Priority handling:* Likewise, the AAL-5 SAR sublayer does not evaluate Cell Loss Priority parameters, but simply forwards them upward from the ATM layer to the convergence sublayer.

- *SAR SDU sequence integrity:* This function preserves the order of SAR SDUs transported within a CPCS connection.

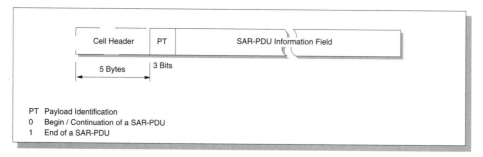

Figure 8.31
AAL Type 5 SAR PDU format.

Structure of the AAL-5 SAR PDU

The structure of the AAL-5 SAR PDU is identical with that of an ATM cell (Figure 8.31). No additional SAR header fields are defined within the ATM cell's Info field. The SAR protocol functions use only the Payload Type (PT) field of the ATM cell header. The value of this field indicates whether or not the SAR PDU contains the end of a SAR SDU. This is sufficient for a simplified version of the AAL-3/4 Segment Type field function.

Figure 8.32 illustrates the transmission of a SAR SDU in four SAR PDUs. In the first three SAR PDUs, the Payload Type field least significant bit (lsb) contains the value "0," indicating the beginning or continuation of a SAR SDU. The PT lsb value of "1" in the last SAR PDU identifies the end of the SAR SDU.

8.4.3   The AAL-5 Convergence Sublayer

As in AAL-3/4, the AAL Type 5 convergence sublayer is divided into a part that is common to all higher-order application layers (the Common Part Convergence Sublayer, or CPCS) and a part that is specific to a given application (the Service-Specific Convergence Sublayer, or SSCS).

The AAL-5 Common Part Convergence Sublayer (CPCS)

The following service characteristics are provided by the AAL-5 CPCS sublayer (and the SSCS sublayer that builds on it, if implemented):

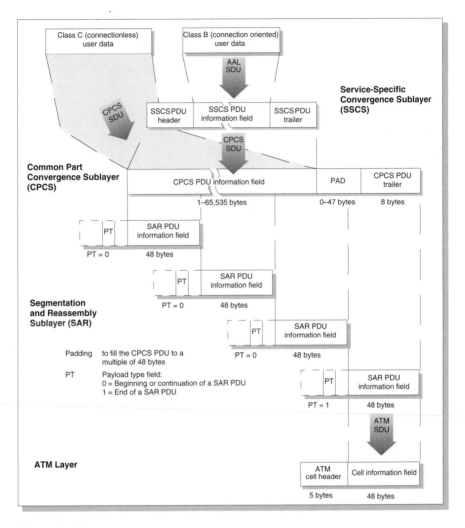

Figure 8.32
The structure of AAL-5.

- Nonassured transmission of variable-length frames (1 to 65,535 bytes), and of an additional byte of user-to-user information, the CPCS UU byte. (Note that there is no UU byte in AAL-3/4 CPCS.)
- Simple or multiple connections between two CPCS endpoints.
- Error detection and notification (bit errors and cell loss).
- Frame sequencing within CPCS connections.

The two operating modes described above in the section on AAL-3/4, message mode and streaming mode, are also distinguished by the ITU-T in the AAL-5 CPCS sublayer. In message mode, one CPCS SDU is transported by means of a CPCS interface data unit (IDU) in exactly one CPCS PDU, whereas in streaming mode a CPCS SDU can be transported using one or several CPCS IDUs. The individual CPCS IDUs may arrive in a different sequence. Once they have been received, all of the IDUs that belong to a given SDU are forwarded in one CPCS PDU.

The functions of the CPCS include:

- Identification of the CPCS SDU to be transported.
- Transmission of user–user information (in the CPCS UU byte).
- Error detection and handling. The following errors are reported: PDU length different from that indicated in the length field; buffer overflow; CPCS PDU format errors; CPCS CRC errors. (AAL-5 includes a CRC field in the CPCS, unlike AAL-3/4, which provides a checksum field in the SAR sublayer.)
- Discarding of incomplete CPCS SDUs.
- Padding bytes. The AAL-5 CPCS is rounded out to an integer multiple of 48 bytes by the addition of 0 to 47 padding bytes.
- Cell Loss Priority handling. The AAL-5 CPCS does not evaluate Cell Loss Priority parameters, but simply forwards them upward from the SAR sublayer to the SSCS.
- Congestion handling. Information about network congestion is not analyzed by the CPCS, but simply passed along.

Structure of the AAL-5 CPCS PDU

An AAL-5 CPCS PDU consists of an Info field of 1 to 65,535 bytes, a padding field of 0 to 47 bytes, and an 8-byte trailer. See Figure 8.33.

The Padding Field.   The CPCS PDU is rounded up to an integer multiple of 48 bytes by the addition of 0 to 47 padding bytes.

The CPCS UU field (CPCS User-to-User Indication).   The 1-byte CPCS UU field can be used to transmit user information.

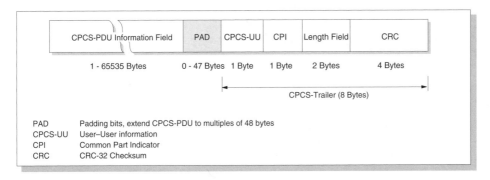

Figure 8.33
AAL Type 5 CPCS PDU Format.

The Length Field. The Length field indicates the length of the CPCS PDU's information field. The field is 2 bytes long, and can thus indicate a length of from 1 to 65,535 bytes. A CPCS PDU with the value 0 in the length field is called an "abort PDU," and is used to signal that the current CPCS SDU transmission has been aborted.

The CRC Field. The last 4 bytes of each CPCS PDU contain a cyclic redundancy check. The CRC-32, calculated from the entire CPCS PDU (the Information field, the padding field, and the first 4 bytes of the CPCS trailer), is transported in the CRC field of the CPCS PDU to monitor bit errors. The generator polynomial used is:

$$G(x) = x^{32} + x^{26} + x^{23} + x^{22} + x^{16} + x^{12} + x^{11} + x^{10} + \\ x^8 + x^7 + x^5 + x^4 + x^2 + x + 1$$

The Service-Specific Part of the AAL-5 Convergence Sublayer (SSCS). As in AAL-3/4, the nonassured transmission functions provided by the common part of the AAL-5 convergence sublayer (CPCS) are sufficient for Class D (connectionless) communication protocols. Such applications do not require an implementation of the SSCS sublayer (the SSCS sublayer is said to be "null"). Every Class C (connection-oriented) protocol, however, requires an AAL-5 service-specific convergence sublayer (SSCS). Examples of SSCS specifications building on the AAL-5 CPCS include FR-SSCS (Frame Relay service over ATM) and SSCOP (the service-specific connection-oriented protocol used for signaling channels and other services requiring assured delivery).

8.5 The Signaling ATM Adaptation Layer

As in narrowband ISDN, B-ISDN signaling is also handled in signaling virtual channels that are separate from the user connections. The SAAL (Signaling AAL; ITU-T Recommendations Q.2100–Q.2144) is the ATM Adaptation Layer used for all ITU-T signaling protocols (UNI and NNI) and for ATM Forum UNI signaling protocols 3.1 and 4.0. (UNI 3.0, which is now obsolete, used a prenormative version of SAAL because it was published about a year before the ITU-T had completed Recommendation Q.2931.) Figure 8.34 depicts the protocol layer model for signaling at the user–network interface (UNI) and the network–node interface (NNI) in ATM networks, with the position of the SAAL in the model.

The SAALs for UNI and NNI signaling have several features in common, but the NNI-SAAL has a more complex structure due to the greater number of mechanisms that need to be provided for MTP-3 and B-ISUP. The purpose of the SAAL is to provide the actual signaling layers situated above it in the protocol hierarchy (Q.2931 or MTP-3 and B-ISUP) with a reliable transportation service, since these signaling protocols have no other error compensation mechanisms. Fault tolerance is provided by SAAL's SSCS sublayer using SSCOP (the Service-Specific Connection-Oriented Protocol), which builds on the CPCS and SAR sublayers of AAL-5. Because the CPCS sublayer of AAL-5 only provides nonassured information transfer, a substantial part of the

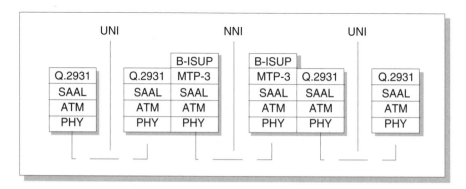

Figure 8.34
Protocol layer model for UNI and NNI signaling.

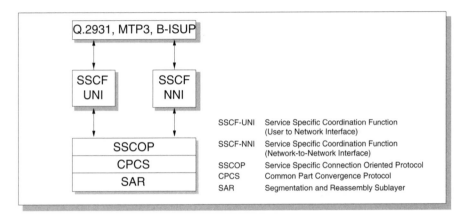

Figure 8.35
SAAL protocol layer model.

SSCOP protocol concerns procedures to guarantee transmission of the SSCOP information field contents. (This is analogous to the function of the TCP layer in providing reliable data transport over best-effort IP networks.) The given signaling layer's requests are translated to SSCOP by an appropriate Service-Specific Coordination Function (SSCF). See Figure 8.35.

8.5.1   Functions of SSCOP

SSCOP provides the following service characteristics as a platform for the Service-Specific Coordination Function:

- *Sequence integrity:* This function preserves the order of the SSCOP SDUs transmitted.
- *Error detection and correction:* PDUs are numbered sequentially so that lost packets are detected immediately. Such errors can be corrected by selective requests for retransmission.
- *Flow control:* The receiving station can control the sender's transmission rate by means of flow control information.
- *Error reporting:* Errors are reported to plane management.
- *Connection maintenance:* If no data is transported between two SSCOP nodes over a long period, they must transmit POLL PDUs periodically in order to maintain the connection. The maximum

interval between two POLL PDUs is determined by the KEEP-ALIVE timer.

- *Local data retrieval:* Individual SSCOP users may request retransmission of selected lost or unacknowledged PDU sequences.

- *Connection control:* Connection control is responsible for setting up and clearing down SSCOP connections, and for resynchronizing the sender's and receiver's buffers in case of problems.

- *Transmission of SSCOP user data:* The SSCOP protocol can also transport SSCOP user data, using either assured or nonassured transmission.

- *Detection of bit errors in the SSCOP header*

- *Exchange of status information between sender and receiver:* If the ATM protocol layer model is compared with that of SS7, SSCOP can be seen to fulfill similar functions to those of the older MTP-2 protocol specified for SS7. MTP-2 functions that are unnecessary in ATM networks have been omitted, however, while ATM-specific mechanisms have been added.

8.5.2   Basic Processes in SSCOP

The SSCOP protocol defines 15 distinct PDUs that are used to implement different functions. The PDUs Begin (BGN) and Begin Acknowledge (BGAK) are used to set up the SSCOP connection between two stations and reset the send and receive buffers of the receiving station. Assured data communication can then take place in two ways: The data packets can be sequentially numbered (SD PDUs), and each data packet may contain an individual request for confirmation of receipt (SDP PDUs). Such confirmation is sent by the receiver in a STAT PDU. After the receiver has analyzed the sequential numbers of the PDUs received, it can send USTAT PDUs if necessary to report lost PDUs, indicating the number range missing. Data can also be sent in a nonassured mode using UD (Unnumbered Data) PDUs. Table 8.6 lists the 15 types of SSCOP PDUs and their functions.

8.5.3   The SSCOP PDUs

The PDU type is identified by the PDU Type field, contained in the first byte of each SSCOP PDU. (The first 4 bits of this byte are reserved for future functions.) The values of the following bytes are dependent on the PDU type. The

Table 8.6   SSCOP PDUs and Their Functions

Function	Description	PDU Name	Coding
Establishment	Request Initialization	PDU BGN	0001
	Request Acknowledgement	PDU BGAK	0010
Release	Disconnect Command	PDU END	0011
	Disconnect Acknowledgement	PDU ENDAK	0100
Resynchronization	Command for resynchronization	PDU RS	0101
	Acknowledgement of resynchronization	PDU RSAK	0110
Reject	Rejection of connection establishment attempt	PDU BGREJ	0111
Recovery	Command for connection recovery	ER	1001
	Acknowledgement for recovery	ERAK	1111
Guaranteed transmission	Sequential numbered data	PDU SD	1000
	Request for receive status	PDU POLL	1010
	Receive status (requested)	PDU STAT	1011
	Receive status (not requested)	PDU USTAT	1100
Not guaranteed transmission	Unnumbered data	PDU UD	1101
Transmission of management data	Not guaranteed transmission of management data	PDU MD	1110

length of every SSCOP PDU must be an integer multiple of 32 bits (4 bytes). Header fields that consist of only 3 bytes are therefore extended by one padding byte. Each byte of the SSCOP PDUs is transmitted bitwise starting with the most significant bit (bit 8).

The Sequenced Data (SD) PDU

SD PDUs are used to transport SSCOP data in sequentially numbered frames. The sequential numbering makes it possible to detect lost PDUs. Retransmission of lost PDUs can then be requested by means of a USTAT PDU. An SD PDU consists of the 1-byte PDU Type field, a 3-byte sequence number field N(S), and an info field of up to 65,527 bytes. See Figure 8.36.

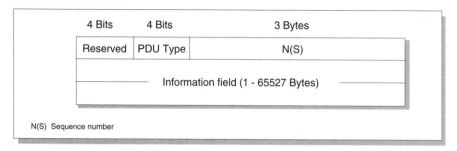

Figure 8.36
SD PDU format.

The Sequence Data with Poll (SDP) PDU

SDP PDUs transport sequentially numbered packets of SSCOP data and simultaneously request confirmation of receipt. Upon receiving an SDP PDU, a station must answer it with a STAT PDU. The STAT PDU contains the sequence number of the next PDU expected, N(R), the sequence number of the SDP PDU being acknowledged and, if necessary, a list of number ranges of lost PDUs. The SDP PDU consists of the 1-byte PDU Type field, a 3-byte long sequence number field N(S), and the 3-byte poll sequence number N(PS) (Figure 8.37). POLL PDUs thus have a separate sequence number in addition to the general sequence numbering of SD PDUs. This is the number used to identify the corresponding poll response.

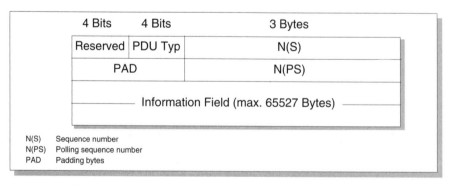

Figure 8.37
SDP PDU format.

4 Bits	4 Bits	3 Bytes
Reserved	PDU-Type	N(S)
PAD		N(PS)
PAD		N(MR)
PAD		List element 1
PAD		List element 2
PAD		List element L

N(R)   Next expected Sequence number
N(PS)   Polling sequence number
N(MR) Maximum value of M(R)

Figure 8.38
STAT PDU format.

The Solicited Status (STAT) PDU

STAT PDUs are sent in response to a status request, such as a SDP PDU or POLL PDU. The STAT PDU contains the sequence number of the next PDU expected, N(R), the sequence number of the status request PDU being answered, the maximum permissible value of N(R), N(MR), and, if necessary, a list of number ranges of lost PDUs (Figure 8.38). This list can contain up to 67 elements. In the AAL-5 CPCS sublayer, a STAT PDU with a list of 67 sequence numbers fills exactly 6 ATM cells: 70 PDU fields of 4 bytes each plus the 8-byte AAL-5 CPCS Trailer make 288 bytes, which is equivalent to the information fields of exactly 6 ATM cells: $48 \times 6 = 288$. Each pair of consecutive list elements represents a range of PDU sequence numbers that were not received. Thus each odd-numbered element in the list (the first, third, fifth, etc.) identifies the beginning of a lost sequence number range.

The Unsolicited Receiver State (USTAT) PDU

A USTAT PDU is a STAT PDU that is sent spontaneously rather than in response to a status poll. This is necessary, for example, if the receiving station has detected missing sequence numbers and needs to request retransmission of the lost PDUs. The structure of the USTAT PDU is identical to that of the

4 Bits	4 Bits	3 Bytes
Reserved	PDU-Type	N(R)
PAD		
PAD		N(MR)
PAD		List element 1
PAD		List element 2
PAD		List element L

N(R)   Next expected sequence number
N(MR) Maximum M(R) value
PAD   Padding bytes

Figure 8.39
USTAT PDU format.

STAT PDU, except that the field that contains poll sequence number N(PS) in the STAT PDU is filled with padding bytes in the USTAT PDU (Figure 8.39).

The Network Management Data (MD) PDU

MD PDUs are used to transport management information. The transmission of MD PDUs is nonassured: they contain no sequence number and thus may be lost without detection (see Figure 8.40).

4 Bits	4 Bits	3 Bytes
Reserved	PDU-Type	PAD
Information field (max. 65527 Bytes)		

PAD Padding bytes

Figure 8.40
MD PDU format.

The Unnumbered Data (UD) PDU

In addition to sequentially numbered data PDUs, data can also be sent in a nonassured mode by means of Unnumbered Data (UD) PDUs. The UD PDU is a more general form of the MD PDU.

The Begin (BGN) PDU

The BGN PDU initiates a connection setup between two SSCOP stations. The station that receives a Begin PDU initializes a receive buffer and the necessary protocol state variables (MR, S, P, etc.). The BGN PDU consists of the type field, the 3-byte N(MR) field indicating the maximum value of N(R), the maximum Send_Max_PDU and Receive_Max_PDU size fields, and the SSCOP User–User Info field (Figure 8.41). The Send_Max_PDU and Receive_Max_PDU size fields indicate the maximum length of the information field for PDUs transferred in both directions of communication. The default value for both is 4096 bytes.

The Begin Acknowledged (BGAK) PDU

The receiving station acknowledges a connection setup request (BGN) by sending a BGAK PDU. The BGAK PDU contains confirmation of the Send_Max_PDU size, Receive_Max_PDU size, and N(MR) parameters proposed by the initiating station in its BGN-PDU. With the exception of the PDU Type value, the structure of a BGAK PDU is identical with that of the BGN PDU.

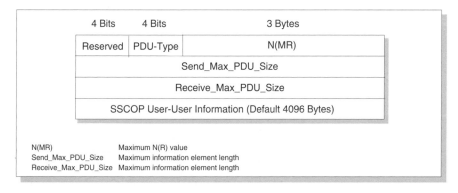

Figure 8.41
BGN PDU format.

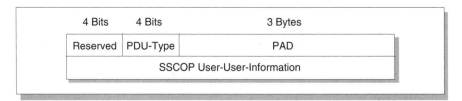

4 Bits	4 Bits	3 Bytes
Reserved	PDU-Type	PAD
SSCOP User-User-Information		

Figure 8.42
BGREJ PDU format.

The Begin Reject (BGREJ) PDU

The Begin-Reject PDU is used to refuse a connection setup attempt. The BGREJ PDU consists of the 1-byte type field and the SSCOP User–User Info field (see Figure 8.42).

The END PDU

The END PDU is used to clear down an existing connection between two SSCOP users. The structure of the END PDU is identical with that of the BGREJ PDU, with the exception of the PDU type field value.

The End Acknowledgment (ENDAK) PDU

A station that receives an END PDU confirms the requested connection clear-down by sending an ENDAK PDU. With the exception of the PDU type field value, the structure of the ENDAK PDU is identical with that of the END PDU.

The Resynchronization (RS) PDU

The RS PDU is sent to restore synchronization of the receive buffer and protocol state variables (MR, S, P, etc.) between the receiving and sending stations. With the exception of the PDU Type value, the structure of a RS PDU is identical with that of the BGN PDU.

The Resynchronization Acknowledge (RSAK) PDU

A station that receives an RS PDU confirms the requested resynchronization by sending an RSAK PDU. The structure of the RSAK PDU is the same as that of a BGAK PDU without the SSCOP User–User Info field.

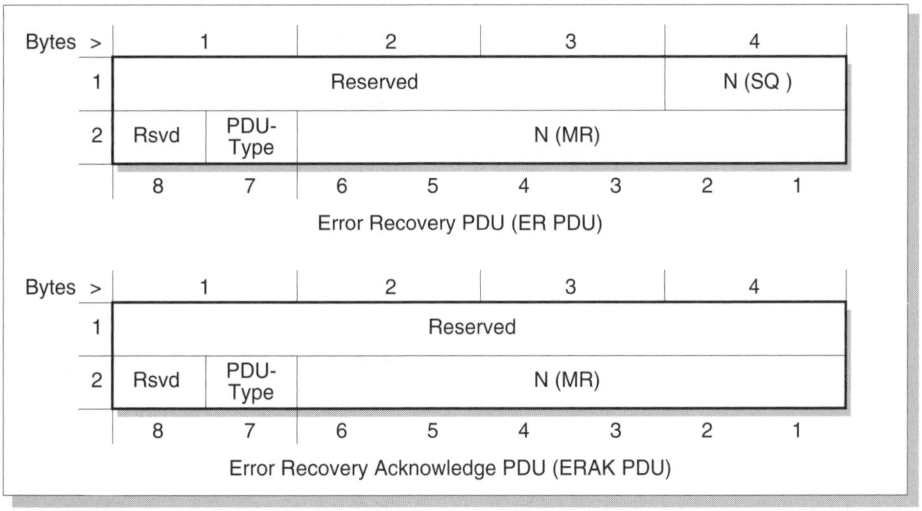

Figure 8.43
ER and ERAK PDU formats.

The Error Recovery (ER) and Error Recovery Acknowledge (ERAK) PDUs

The ER and ERAK PDUs are used to restore the connection after the occurrence of a protocol error (see Figure 8.43).

8.5.4 Error Correction Mechanisms in the SSCOP Protocol

The flow diagram in Figure 8.44 illustrates the error-handling mechanism for lost PDUs in the SSCOP protocol. The receiving station first fails to receive the PDUs with sequence numbers 2 through 5. The receiver does not detect this situation on its own, since the last PDU received, with $N(S) = 2$, follows the preceding sequence number, and no PDU was received out of order. The sending station then sends a POLL PDU to request receipt acknowledgment of the PDU with the sequence number 5 (POLL (5, 1)). Now the receiving station recognizes that packets are missing, and responds with STAT(3, 1, N(MR), {3, 5}). The list elements {3, 5} inform the sending station that the PDU sequence 3 through 5 has been lost. After sending the STAT PDU, the receiving station receives the

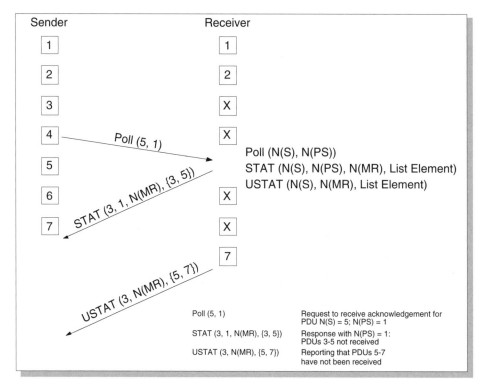

Figure 8.44
Error correction in the SSCOP protocol.

first SD PDU since the interruption, which has the sequence number 7. It then sends a USTAT PDU (3, N(MR), {5, 7}) to inform the sending station that the PDU sequence 5 through 7 was also not received.

8.5.5 The SSCOP Timers

The SSCOP protocol defines four timers that control the protocol process. These are the POLL, KEEP-ALIVE, NO-RESPONSE, and CONNECTION CONTROL (CC) timers.

The POLL Timer

The POLL timer monitors the maximum time interval between the transmission of successive POLL PDUs while SD or SDP PDUs are being transmitted.

The KEEP-ALIVE Timer

When no SD or SDP PDUs are being transmitted, the interval between successive POLL PDUs is controlled by the KEEP-ALIVE timer.

The NO-RESPONSE Timer

The NO-RESPONSE timer specifies the maximum delay between two POLL or STAT PDUs. The value of the NO-RESPONSE timer must be greater than both that of the KEEP-ALIVE timer and that of the POLL timer.

Table 8.7 SSCOP Error Codes

Error Type	Error Code	PDU or Event which Initiates the Error
Receipt of unsolicited or inappropriate PDU	A	SD PDU
	B	BGN PDU
	C	BGAK PDU
	D	BGREJ PDU
	E	END PDU
	F	ENDAK PDU
	G	POLL PDU
	H	STAT PDU
	I	USTAT PDU
	J	RS
	K	RSAK PDU
	L	ER
	M	ERAK
Unsuccessful retransmission	O	VT(CC) ≥ MaxCC
	P	Timer_NO_RESPONSE expires
Other list elements error type	Q	SD or POLL, N(S) error
	R	STAT N(PS) error
	S	STAT N(R) or list elements error
	T	USTAT N(R) or list elements error
	U	PDU length violation
SD loss	V	SD PDUs must be retransmitted
Credit condition	W	Lack of credit
	X	Credit obtained

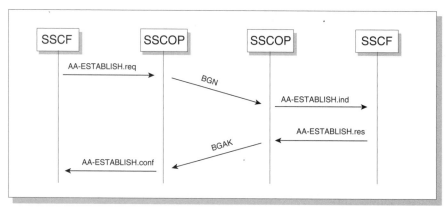

Figure 8.45
SAAL connection setup.

Furthermore, the value of the NO-RESPONSE timer must be more than twice the signal delay over the connection concerned.

The CC Timer

The CONNECTION CONTROL timer determines the maximum delay between the transmission of two BGN, END, or RS PDUs if no answering PDU is received. The CC timer must also have a value greater than twice the signal delay over the connection concerned.

8.5.6 SSCOP Error Messages to the Management Layer

Error codes are used to forward SSCOP error events to the management layer. Table 8.7 lists the various SSCOP error types.

8.5.7 SAAL Connection Setup

The connection setup between two SAAL system components is initiated by an AA-ESTABLISH message from the SSCF sublayer. This message contains the SSCOP UU (User to User) and BR (Buffer Release) parameters

Table 8.8 SSCOP Signals and Parameters

Signal Name	Signal Type			
	Request	Value	Response	Acknowledge
AA-ESTABLISH	SSCOP-UUBR	SSCOP-UU	SSCOP-UUBR	SSCOP-UU
AA-RELEASE	SSCOP-UU	SSCOP-UU Source	undefined	
AA-DATA	MU	MUSN	undefined	undefined
AA-RESYNC	SSCOP-UU	SSCOP-UU		
AA-RECOVER	undefined			undefined
AA-UNITDATA	MU	MU	undefined	undefined
AA-RETRIEVE	RN	MU	undefined	undefined
AA-RETRIEVE COMPLETE	undefined		undefined	undefined
M	Signal Type			
AA-ERROR	undefined	Code Count	undefined	undefined
MAA-UNITDATA	MU	MU	undefined	undefined
—	signal does not use parameter			

Message Unit (MU) Parameter	Reports message with variable length
SSCOP user-to-user information (SSCOP-UU) Parameter	Reports User-to-User message with variable length
Sequence Number (SN) Parameter	Reports N(S) value of received SD-PDU
Retrieval number (RN) Parameter	Initiates SD-PDU
Buffer release (BR) Parameter	Request for buffer availability at the sender side
Code Parameter	Reports protocol error type
Source Parameter	Reports call release initiated by SSCOP layer or SSCOP peer
Count Parameter	Number of retransmitted SD-PDUs

that are used by the SSCOP sublayer to create the BGN message. The receiver decodes the BGN message and passes the corresponding indication message, AA-ESTABLISH.ind, to the receiving SSCF. This sublayer responds with an AA-ESTABLISH.res command, which likewise contains the parameters SSCOP-UU and BR. The resulting BGAK message is sent back to the originating SSCOP, which passes an AA-ESTABLISH.conf to the initiating SSCF (see Figure 8.45).

Table 8.8 lists the various SSCOP signals and parameters exchanged in SSCOP-SSCF communication.

Frame-Based ATM

Although ATM is thought of as a cell-based technology, being cell-based is not an essential attribute. In the very early days of the ATM Forum, ATM over DXI was specified; later came FUNI (Frame-Based User-Network Interface), then more recently two new frame-based interface types were specified: FAST (Frame-Based ATM over SONET/SDH Transport) and FATE (Frame-Based ATM Transport over Ethernet). This section describes each of these interface technologies. Common to all these frame-based interfaces is the avoidance of the use of ATM cells; data is instead transferred in variable length frames based on the CPCS layer of AAL-5 and sometimes also on the CPCS layer of AAL-3/4. Any interworking with the cell-oriented interfaces described in Chapter 6 is done through SAR processes in interworking functions. Some of these frame-based interfaces also support frame fragmentation to enable delay-sensitive services, such as voice over frame, to be handled better.

9.1   ATM over DXI Interfaces

The Data Exchange Interface (DXI) is a simple communication protocol developed for interfaces such as V.35, EIA/TIA 449/530, or EIA/TIA 612/613 (HSSI). DXI was originally conceived as a data tributary protocol for

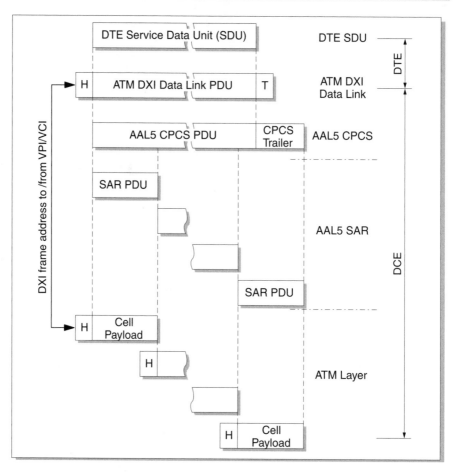

Figure 9.1
Encapsulation of ATM cells in DXI PDUs (Modes 1a and 1b).

Flag	DXI Header	DTE-SDU	DXI FCS	Flag
1	2	$0 < N \leq 9232$	2	1
		(Bytes)		

Figure 9.2
DXI frame for Modes 1a and 1b (DTE, AAL5).

metropolitan area networks (SMDS-DXI, SMDS Interest Group Technical Specification SIG-TS-005/1993). For lack of an ATM-specific DXI specification to connect their systems to ATM networks, many manufacturers began by implementing the simpler SMDS-DXI as an interface protocol. The ATM Forum subsequently developed a DXI variant tailored to the requirements of ATM (af-dxi-0014).

The functions of ATM DXI are divided into user-end processes (Data Terminal Equipment or DTE, Modes 1a and 1b) and network-end processes (Data Communications Equipment or DCE, Mode 2). In Mode 1a, user interfaces support up to 1023 virtual connections with data packets (Service Data Units, or SDUs) of up to 9232 bytes. The DTE SDUs, which correspond to AAL-5 PDUs, are encapsulated in DXI frames for transmission (see Figure 9.1). Mode 1b also supports AAL-3/4 with a maximum SDU length of 9224 bytes. The AAL-3/4 PDUs are encapsulated by the DTE, but all segmentation and reassembly (AAL-3/4 SAR) must be performed by the DCE.

In Mode 2, network interfaces support up to 16,777,215 virtual connections for AAL-5 and AAL-3/4. SDUs can be up to 65,535 bytes long.

The DXI frame address (DFA) is carried in the DXI header. It is used to convey the VPI and VCI information between DTEs and DCEs. The DFA is 10 bits long in Modes 1a and 1b (see Figure 9.2), and 24 bits long in Mode 2. Note that this interface deals only with AAL frames, not with ATM cells.

9.2   Frame-Based User-to-Network Interface (FUNI)

Frame-based User-to-Network Interface (FUNI) was developed by the ATM Forum for the efficient transfer of data over low bandwidth interfaces, specifically T1 and E1, though other interface rates, above and below these interface rates, are not precluded; fractional T1 and E1 are also supported. Those readers familiar with Frame Relay will recognize some similarities between FUNI and Frame Relay. Both rely upon an HDLC-like framing structure with frames separated by flags; both rely upon the same escape sequence procedures to handle the occurrence of reserved characters in the data to be transferred; extensions to FUNI also allow fragmentation to be used based on the Frame Relay FRF.12 specification for voice over Frame Relay. The current version of FUNI (v2.0) is specified by the ATM Forum in af-saa-0088.000, with multiservice extensions for handling fragmentation specified in af-saa-0109.000. The reference model for FUNI is shown in Figure 9.3.

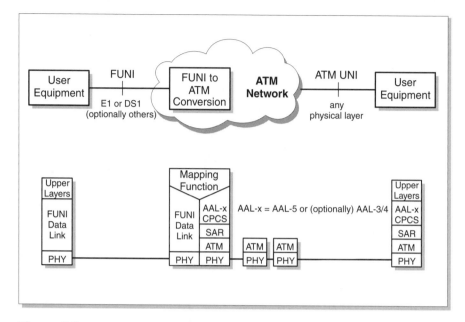

Figure 9.3
FUNI reference model.

9.2.1   FUNI Frame Structure

The FUNI frame comprises a header, a payload, and a trailer; frames are separated by at least one flag having the hexadecimal value 0x7E (binary 01111110), but any number of additional flags are used as frame separators when no data is available to send. Clearly, data making up the frame between these flags cannot have a sequence similar to the flag, so a bit-oriented solution is imposed to ensure data transparency. The bit sequence of the frame is examined and, following any occurence of five "1"s, a "0" is automatically inserted, preventing a 0x7E sequence from occuring; the only sequence of six "1"s found after this process must, therefore, be a flag. The bit-stuffing process is, of course, reversed when the frame is extracted from the bit stream.

There are several variants of the FUNI frame structure. The basic, mandatory variant for interface rates up to E1 (2 Mb/s) has a 2-byte FUNI header, a payload of up to 4096 bytes, a 2-byte trailer containing a 2-byte frame check sequence (FCS), and handles AAL-5 CPCS payload PDUs (the AAL-5 CPCS trailer is omitted as being redundant). Optionally, AAL-3/4 can also be handled, in which case the FUNI frame payload comprises the 4-byte AAL-3/4 CPCS_PDU header, the user payload, and the 4-byte AAL-3/4 CPCS_PDU

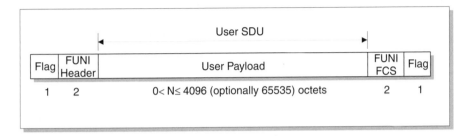

Figure 9.4
AAL-5-based FUNI frame (rate ≤ T1/E1).

trailer; the same 2-byte FUNI header and trailer is used. Because of the small size of the FUNI header, the number of virtual channel connections that can be handled is limited to a maximum of 512. Figure 9.4 shows the AAL-5-based FUNI frame and Figure 9.5 shows the optional AAL-3/4-based FUNI frame for interface rates ≤ T1/E1.

For interface rates from T1/E1 and upward, the mandatory frame structure has a 2-byte FUNI header, a payload of up to 9232 bytes, a 4-byte trailer containing a 4-byte FCS, and only handles AAL-5 CPCS payload PDUs (again, the AAL-5 CPCS trailer is omitted as being redundant); there is no AAL-3/4 option specified. Optionally, a 4-byte header is also permitted. Because of the larger size of a 4-byte FUNI header, the full 65,536 virtual channel connections can be handled. Figure 9.6 shows the AAL-5 frame for interface rates ≥ T1/E1.

The 2-byte FCS is a CRC-16 based on polynomial $x^{16} + x^{12} + x^5 + 1$ (the same as that used in ITU-T Q.921) and the 4-byte FCS is the same CRC-32 used in AAL-5, based on polynomial $x^{32} + x^{26} + x^{23} + x^{22} + x^{16} + x^{12} + x^{11} + x^{10} + x^8 + x^7 + x^5 + x^4 + x^2 + x + 1$.

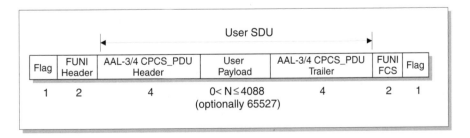

Figure 9.5
AAL-3/4-based FUNI frame (rate ≤ T1/E1 only).

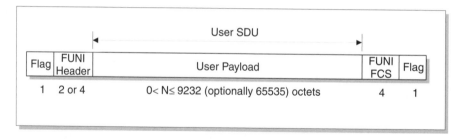

Figure 9.6
AAL-5-based FUNI frame (rate ≥ T1/E1).

The transfer of OAM cells is supported in FUNI. The complete OAM cell (all 53 bytes) is encapsulated as the payload of FUNI frames of any of the permitted FUNI header and trailer formats (2- and 4-byte headers and trailers), consistent with the format being used for user data.

9.2.2 FUNI Frame Addressing

As indicated above, the FUNI header can be 2 or 4 bytes long. ATM cell headers at the UNI can accommodate a VPI-VCI label field of 8 + 16 (= 24) bits, so clearly the shorter header cannot cope with a complete range of values equivalent to those in an ATM header. Indeed, only 10 bits are available for the "frame address" (FA) in 2-byte FUNI headers. These 10 bits are assigned as 4 bits for VPI and 6 bits for VCI, so only a subset of VPI and VCI values is supported. Figure 9.7 shows the mapping between the 2-byte FUNI header and the cell header.

The 4-byte FUNI header can accommodate the full range of VPI-VCI values; Figure 9.8 shows the mapping between the 4-byte FUNI header and the cell header.

Apart from the fixed value bits in the least significant bit position of each byte in both FUNI headers, other bits in both headers are as follows:

CN (congestion notification): This is zero in the FUNI header unless the PTI field in the header of last ATM cell arriving from the network and generating the FUNI frame has the value "01x"; it is always sent from the user equipment with the value zero.

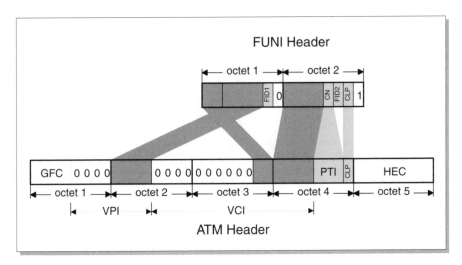

Figure 9.7
Mapping between 2-byte FUNI header and ATM cell header.

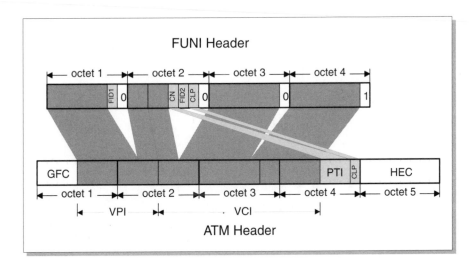

Figure 9.8
Mapping between 4-byte FUNI header and ATM cell header.

CPL (cell loss priority): The value of CLP in the FUNI header is mapped directly to the CPL bit in all constituent cells generated from the FUNI frame; FUNI frames generated from cells always have their CLP bit set to zero.

FID (frame identification): These bits are set to zero unless the FUNI frame is encapsulating an OAM cell, in which case FID1 is set to "1" and FID2 is set to "0"; the other two combinations of FID1 and FID2 are reserved for future use.

9.2.3 Signaling and Traffic Management

Normal ATM signaling can be used with FUNI. As FUNI frames can encapsulate AAL-5 CPCS_PDUs (less the trailer), the usual higher layers required for signaling (Q.2931/SSCF/SSCOP) are easily supported. Additionally, SNMP/ILMI can be supported for address registration purposes.

Because of the frame-based nature of FUNI, only certain traffic classes can be supported unless fragmentation is implemented: nrt-VBR (QoS class 3) and UBR (QoS class 0). Any attempt to set up FUNI-based switched virtual circuits (SVCs) with other QoS classes is rejected with Cause Code #49 ("quality of service unavailable").

In the direction FUNI frames to ATM cells, traffic shaping may be desirable to prevent bursts of cells, which may cause traffic contract nonconformance.

9.2.4 FUNI Frame Fragmentation

Recognizing the need to cope with the multiplexing of delay-sensitive data, the ATM Forum later developed an extension to the FUNI v2.0 specification to allow FUNI frame fragmentation; this is specified in af-saa-0109.000 (MultiService Extensions to FUNI v2.0 Specification). The ATM Forum based this specification on work already done for Frame Relay in FRF.12 ("Frame Relay Fragmentation Implementation Agreement") for better supporting Voice over Frame Relay (VoFR), specified earlier in FRF.11. The advantage of fragmentation is that, by breaking up long frames into shorter fragments, fragments from other FUNI virtual channels can be multiplexed so that delay-sensitive data is not held up excessively.

The method specified for fragmentation is to discard the original FUNI frame trailer, chop the FUNI frame payload into fragments, prepend a 2-byte fragmentation header to the 2- or 4-byte FUNI frame header, as appropriate, and prepend this combination to each fragment of the original FUNI frame. To each fragment is appended a 2- or 4-byte trailer, as appropriate, containing an FCS for that fragment. The encapsulated fragments are then sent in the same way as nonfragmented FUNI frames would be. The fragmentation header contains 2 bits ("B" and "E") and a 12-bit sequence number for tracking the progress of the fragmented frame sequence (a separate sequence counter is kept for each virtual channel). The "B" (beginning) bit is set for the first fragment, the "E" (end) bit is set for the last fragment, and, for fragments between the first and last fragments, both bits are reset. The sequence number starts at an arbitrary value for the very first fragment to be sent on the virtual channel, and it is incremented modulo-12 for every fragment thereafter, continuing in this way also between fragments belonging to sequential FUNI frames. See the format of a fragment from a FUNI frame having a 2-byte header and trailer in Figure 9.9.

Reassembling the fragmented FUNI frame is straightforward. The above process is reversed while the sequence number is checked. Assuming no fragments are lost, the original FUNI frame can easily be reconstituted. If one or more fragments is lost, the entire frame is discarded.

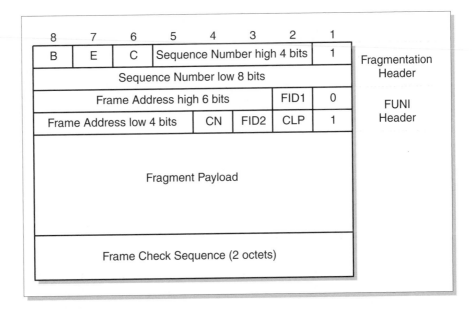

Figure 9.9
FUNI frame fragment format.

9.3   Frame-Based ATM over SONET/SDH Transport (FAST)

This interface technology is the ATM Forum's answer to Packet over SONET/SDH (PoS). One of the accusations leveled at ATM is that it is inefficient with the use of bandwidth, particularly at expensive high-rate network node interfaces (NNIs). The so-called "cell tax" results from the bandwidth occupied by the header of each cell plus the wasted bandwidth associated with the padding and trailer in AAL-5 CPCS PDUs. The worst-case example of this involves the handling of a 41-byte user data frame (CPCS-PDU payload) by AAL-5: two cells are required to carry this, as the user data frame is 1 byte longer than can be handled in a single cell AAL-5 CPCS PDU (remember that an 8-byte trailer also has to be accommodated). In this example, the first cell payload would contain the 41-byte user data frame plus 7 bytes of padding, and the second cell payload would contain 40 bytes of padding plus the 8-byte AAL-5 trailer, resulting in an overall efficiency of just $41 \div (53 \times 2) = 39\%$. Of course, as the user data frame gets bigger, the efficiency improves.

Frame-based ATM over SONET/SDH (FAST) is fully defined in the ATM Forum's specification af-phy-0151.000 (July 2000). As with other frame-based ATM interfaces, FAST usually involves sending data in frames based on AAL-5, although a cell encapsulation mode is also available and necessary for handling OAM cells or cells from AALs other than AAL-5. The value proposition of FAST is that, unlike PoS, it can deliver the guaranteed quality of service features of ATM, for which ATM is renowned, while providing a more data-efficient transfer mode than the ATM cell mode. FAST is specified for both UNI and NNI and for rates of 155.52 Mb/s and above in the SDH and SONET hierarchies.

9.3.1   FAST Reference Model

Figure 9.10 is probably the most useful in bringing understanding to how FAST relates to cell-based ATM, even though such a network with so many interworking options is unlikely in practice.

The process for sending data from the left-hand user equipment to the right-hand user equipment is as follows. User data is first turned into AAL-5 CPCS-PDUs and is then segmented into ATM cells by the SAR process. ATM cells cross the UNI and enter the FAST IWF (interworking function) where they are reassembled again. The user data, information from the cell header, and CPCS-PDU trailer are extracted for use in creating the HDLC-like FAST

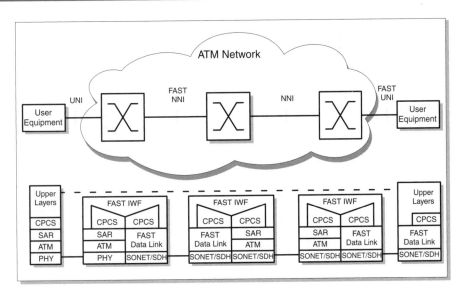

Figure 9.10
FAST interworking function options.

frame (described in detail later). The frame stream is then scrambled and mapped into the payload of SDH/SONET physical layer frames (this is the FAST Data Link process). It is then sent via a FAST NNI to a FAST IWF for conversion back into cell-based ATM, reversing the process just described. The rest of the process is hopefully obvious. Switching would be done in frame-based ATM switches, avoiding the need to return to ATM cell mode; FAST switches would be architecturally similar to Packet over SONET/SDH switches.

Figure 9.11 shows the FAST reference model for a purely frame-based ATM network. AAL-5 CPCS processes are assumed to occur in the user equipment.

9.3.2 FAST Frame Formats

The FAST frame and cell encapsulations use a simplified version of the IETF standard RFC 1662 ("PPP in HDLC-like Framing")—the address, control, protocol, and padding fields are omitted and the 32-bit frame check sequence (FCS) is mandated. Figure 9.12 shows the FAST frame format; note that FAST frames are separated by any number of flags, and that the frame-terminating flag of one frame can also be the opening flag of the next, just as in FUNI and other HDLC-like framing.

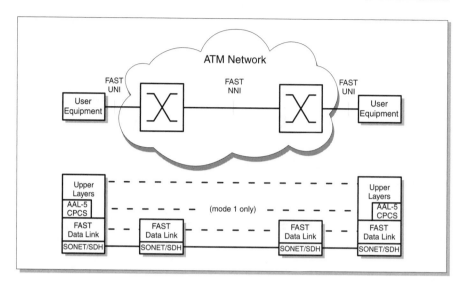

Figure 9.11
FAST reference model.

Because the value chosen for the flag (0x7e) cannot be allowed to occur in the frame information data, a process known as "escape sequencing" (or "octet stuffing") is used to replace any occurrence of 0x7e (hexadecimal 7e) in the information data as it is being formed from user data. Every occurrence of 0x7e is therefore replaced with the 2-byte sequence 0x7d5e. As 0x7d has now been used as the "escape" value, it also needs an escape sequence when it occurs, and this is 0x7d5d. The length of the information field is expanded by one every time one of these special characters occurs, but in the normal course of things, this does not have a big impact. At worst, the field can double in length if the user data is comprised of solely one or the other of these two characters. The reverse process is performed to recover the original data when the frame is delivered. This process is different from that used to ensure transparency for

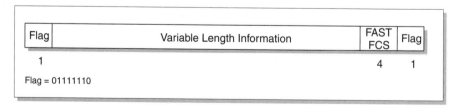

Figure 9.12
FAST frame format.

FUNI but is necessarily byte-oriented because SDH/SONET is byte (or "octet") oriented.

Two modes exist for coding the information field: Mode 0 and Mode 1. Mode 0 is the simplest and most efficient but also the less flexible. The first 4 bytes of the information field are a copy of the first 4 bytes of the cell header associated with the cells in the virtual channel that generated the AAL-5 frame from which the user data has been extracted, or a copy of the first 4 bytes of the OAM cell header; the HEC is not used. A user-to-user byte is appended to the user data frame or OAM cell, resulting in the structure in Figure 9.13.

The user-to-user byte is used only in frame encapsulation mode and it is mapped to the AAL-5 CPCS_UU byte. The user data field in frame encapsulation mode includes the CPCS-PDU payload data only; the CPCS-PDU trailer and any padding are not included. In cell encapsulation mode (used for sending OAM cells), the user-to-user byte is not used and is reset to zero. Note that in cell encapsulation mode, the cell header information actually occurs twice, once in the information field header and once in the encapsulated OAM cell. Though inefficient for a single cell, this scheme makes the overall FAST process simpler and is not seen as a serious efficiency issue, as OAM cells are sent relatively infrequently.

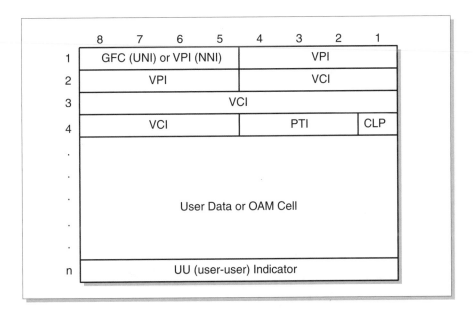

Figure 9.13
FAST Mode 0 information field.

Mode 1 is a more sophisticated mode and uses a longer information field header; it also includes the AAL-5 CPCS-PDU trailer (but does not include any padding from the CPCS-PDU frame); the structure is shown in Figure 9.14.

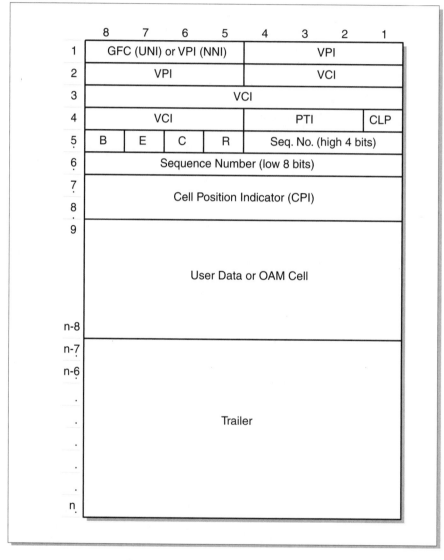

Figure 9.14
FAST Mode 1 information field.

Again, the first 4 bytes of the FAST Mode 1 information field contains a copy of the header from cells that generated the AAL-5 CPCS-PDU or a copy of the encapsulated ATM cell but there are 4 additional bytes, and in the frame encapsulation mode, a copy of the complete CPCS-PDU trailer; the trailer is omitted in the cell encapsulation mode.

The first 2 additional bytes (bytes 5 and 6) are associated with handling a fragmentation process, which is available with this mode and bears a strong similarity to the method used for FUNI described earlier. Fragmentation, if used, allows long packets to be cut down to shorter packets so that delay-sensitive information in multiple virtual channels can be interleaved, rather than having to wait until the complete CPCS-PDU (which could be as long as 65,535 bytes) is transmitted. Obviously, in the limit, we could end up with a situation equivalent to using ATM cells, but in reality, the fragments would be large compared with a standard cell, so the advantages of FAST would still be realized. The "B" (begin) bit in byte 5 is set for the first fragment and the "E" (end) bit is set for the last fragment; intermediate fragments have these bits reset. Bits "C" and "R" are reserved for future use. The 12-bit modulo-12 sequence number spread over bytes 5 and 6 is incremented for every successive fragment belonging to the same virtual channel and is allowed to fold over to zero when it reaches the all-"1"s state. A separate fragmentation sequence number counter is kept for each virtual channel. The actual starting value is arbitrary but the sequence number for fragments from successive frames are contiguous. The maximum fragment size is local to the link and is configured to meet the quality-of-service requirements for delay and delay variation.

Bytes 7 and 8 form a 16-bit cell position indicator (CPI), which is used to record the relative position of any OAM cell that occurred during the reassembly process, which generated the AAL-5 CPCS-PDU; this is used by the segmentation process at the termination of the FAST section to reinsert the OAM cells in the correct position with respect to the cells resulting from the segmentation.

9.3.3   FAST Physical Layer

FAST is specified for SDH/SONET rates of 155.52 Mb/s and above (Figure 9.15). FAST uses the same IETF standard as Packet over SONET/SDH for mapping FAST frames to SDH/SONET physical layer frame payloads, RFC 2615 ("PPP over SONET/SDH"). This RFC requires that the entire FAST frame stream (including flags) be scrambled before it is inserted into the SDH/SONET payload using the self-synchronizing scrambler $x^{43} + 1$, the same scrambler used for scrambling cell payloads in cell stream. This is done to minimize the possibility that a bit sequence could accidentally occur (or be

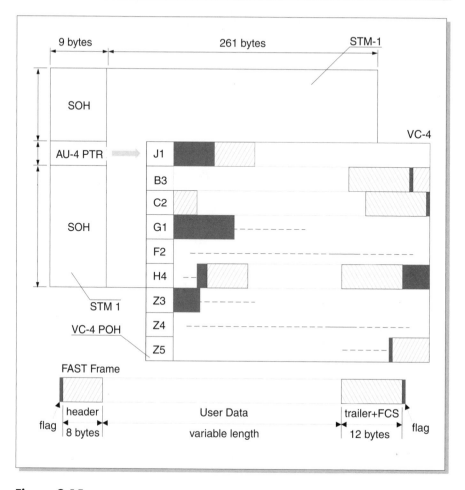

Figure 9.15
FAST frame mapping to SDH.

maliciously created) that would "anti-scramble" the SDH/SONET frame synchronous scrambler based on the polynomial $x^7 + x^6 + 1$ (details in ITU-T Recommendation G.707). The frame synchronous scrambler is used to ensure that long sequences of "1"s or "0"s do not occur, for such an occurrence would prevent the successful extraction of the bit clock at the remote end of a transmission line, which relies upon the detection of bit transitions. The Path Signal Label (C2 byte) in the SDH/SONET path overhead (POH) is set to 0x16 to indicate that the SDH/SONET payload is a variable length HDLC frame with scrambling.

9.3.4   Signaling and Traffic Management

Signaling, including ILMI address registration, is straightforward for FAST, as FAST relies upon AAL-5-related processes. The higher sublayers of the SAAL (SSCOP and SSCF) map directly to the HDLC frame payload, as does SNMP/ILMI. Unlike FUNI, no restrictions are placed on traffic types, so signaling messages can support all traffic types, in principle, including traffic types for delay-sensitive services (FUNI, using fragmentation, could also do this, of course).

9.4   Frame-Based ATM Transport over Ethernet (FATE)

FATE is defined in the ATM Forum's specification af-phy-0139.000 (February 2000); this specification is not one of the ATM Forum's finest (the FAST specification, on the other hand, is well written and complete). This interface is, today, UNI focused on the SOHO (small office, home office) market and is closely associated with ATM over ADSL (asymmetrical digital subscriber link), today the most common mode of ADSL for such environments (PPP/ADSL is largely confined for use in domestic PC environments). FATE allows ATM services to be provided over Ethernet; it makes use of FATE UNI Converters to interface a stream of ATM cells arriving over a cell-based UNI (usually ATM/ADSL) to an Ethernet LAN. One or more PCs can then be connected to the LAN via Ethernet. FATE frames are encapsulated as the data field in Ethernet frames with a FATE specific Ethertype value.

9.4.1   FATE Reference Model

The diagram in Figure 9.16 shows the FATE reference model.

9.4.2   FATE Frame Formats

Like the FAST interface, two modes of operation are available: frame mode and cell mode, the latter for handling OAM and RM (resource management) cells. FATE supports two versions of Ethernet (DIX Ethernet and IEEE 802.3). The DIX Ethernet or IEEE 802.3 frame payload encapsulates the FATE frame, which is comprised of a header and payload. The FATE frame

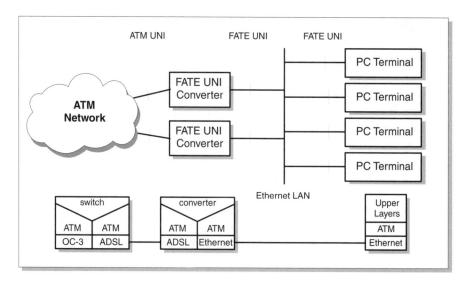

Figure 9.16
FATE reference model.

header is identical to the first 4 bytes of the ATM cell header common to cells whose payloads are either AAL-5 reassembled (frame mode) or used explicitly (cell mode), in the case of OAM or RM cells. Fragmentation of frame mode FATE frames is always enabled and is based on the fragmentation scheme described earlier for FUNI frames. When frame mode is used, the payload is comprised of the AAL-5 SSCS-PDU less the CRC-32 field, which is not required, as the Ethernet frame provides a frame check sequence (FCS). Figures 9.17 and 9.18 show the frame arrangements.

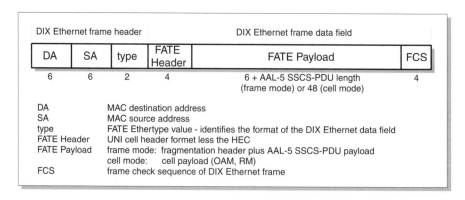

Figure 9.17
FATE frame format in DIX Ethernet frames.

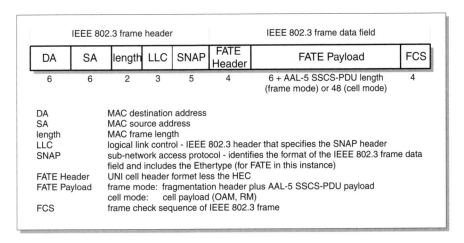

Figure 9.18
FATE frame format in IEEE 802.3 frames.

In frame mode the frame format is as shown in Figure 9.19. The first 2 bytes form the fragmentation header (see the description earlier in the FUNI section). Fields from the AAL-5 CPCS trailer are copied to fields following the fragmentation header and the CPCS payload (that is, the SSCS-PDU) is copied to the data field (any AAL-5 CPCS padding is discarded).

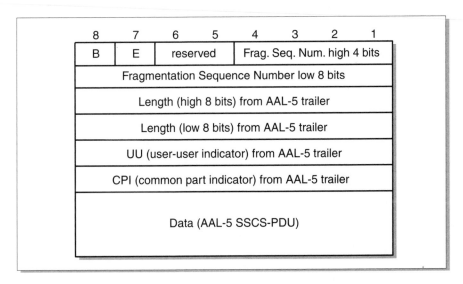

Figure 9.19
FATE frame mode frame format.

9.4.3   FATE Discovery Messages

Two types of discovery messages exist: DISCOVER-REQ and DISCOVER-ACK. The 8-byte DISCOVERY-REQ is sent to the FATE UNI Converter from the end station (PC) to request a DISCOVER-ACK from the converter. The PC suggests what size the fragmentation length should be. The DISCOVER-ACK is sent to the PC to advertise the MAC address and service capabilities of the FATE UNI Converter. The converter will set the fragmentation size so that it is no greater (though it may be smaller) than the size suggested by the PC. It also conveys other details, such as upstream and downstream data rates and ATM cell link type (e.g., 155 Mb/s ATM, 25.6 Mb/s ATM, ADSL, etc.).

9.4.4   Traffic Management

Guaranteeing quality of service (QoS) of ATM over Ethernet is difficult because of the nature of Ethernet but certain parameters have an influence that tends to enhance the QoS. Shorter fragmentation frame sizes help, as does the ratio of the traffic-to-Ethernet rate (the smaller the traffic bandwidth, the better).

Chapter 10

THE **ATM** PROTOCOL: UNI SIGNALING

Signaling in ATM refers to all processes necessary to set up a connection between two or more stations. Compared with conventional signaling mechanisms, signaling in ATM networks is an extremely complex procedure. All kinds of traffic parameters—such as the AAL type, streaming or message mode, assured or nonassured transfer, average and peak bit rates, cell loss ratio, and cell delay—must be negotiated and guaranteed over all segments of the connection path. Moreover, connection-oriented topologies, such as point-to-multipoint or broadcast connections, must also be handled. For this reason the existing UNI and NNI signaling protocols (Q.931 and Q.933 or ISUP) on which ATM signaling is based, and which were originally developed for narrowband ISDN, have undergone major extension for ATM networks to produce Q.2931 (and Q.2971) or B-ISUP.

Signaling at the user–network interface (UNI) is based either on ITU-T Recommendations Q.2931 (B-ISDN DSS2 point-to-point signaling) and Q.2971 (B-ISDN DSS2 point-to-multipoint signaling) or on one of the ATM Forum specifications, UNI 3.0, 3.1, 4.0, or 4.1. At the network node interface (NNI), public networks use B-ISUP (ITU-T Q.2761–Q.2764) or the corresponding ATM Forum protocols, B-ICI, AINI, or even PNNI (although this was originally developed for the private NNI, hence its name, Private

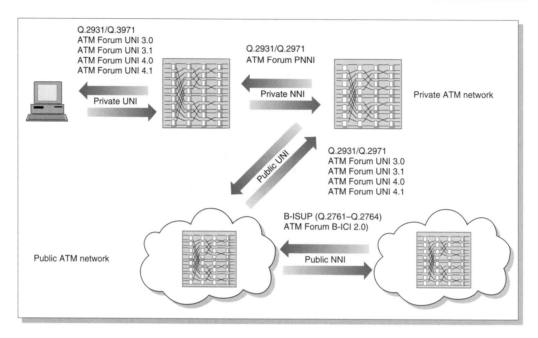

Figure 10.1
Signaling in public and private ATM networks.

Network–Network Interface). Figure 10.1 shows the relationship between the different types of signaling.

Connection setup can take place either on the reserved signaling channel, VPI = 0/VCI = 5, or, theoretically, over VCs selected by means of metasignaling. In this case, any signaling VCs could be set up without an existing AAL connection, since the simple metasignaling messages can be transferred in one cell. Once the signaling channel has been determined, the AAL for the signaling channel (SAAL) is established. At this point the signaling protocol becomes active. In practice, the signaling channel VPI = 0/VCI = 5 is generally used, and metasignaling is not necessary and has probably never been implemented by any vendor.

Basically two types of signaling have been defined by the ITU-T: associated signaling, in which the signaling VC controls only the VP in which it is allocated, and nonassociated signaling, in which the signaling VC controls its VP as well as other VPs. While Q.2931 and Q.2971 support both signaling types, the ATM Forum specifications only allow for nonassociated signaling.

10.1   The UNI Signaling Message Format

ITU-T Recommendations Q.2931 and Q.2971, and the ATM Forum UNI 3.0 and 3.1 specifications define signaling messages for point-to-point and route (caller)-initiated join point-to-multipoint signaling, which can be classified in groups for connection setup, connection clear-down, and other messages. Additionally, the ATM Forum UNI 4.0 specifies leaf (additional caller) initiated join point-to-point signaling, though support for this has now been removed in UNI 4.1. For all point-to-point signaling processes, the following 11 message types are available (messages marked ° have modifications in Q.2971 from the definitions in Q.2931):

Connection Setup

ALERTING°

CALL PROCEEDING°

CONNECT°

CONNECT ACKNOWLEDGE

CONNECTION AVAILABLE (added in Q.2931 amendment 4 12/99)

SETUP°

Connection Clear-down

RELEASE

RELEASE COMPLETE

Other

NOTIFY°

STATUS°

STATUS ENQUIRY°

For point-to-multipoint signaling processes, the following XX message types are available (messages marked ° are for leaf-initiated join signaling, which is only supported in the ATM Forum's UNI 4.0 specification; the ITU-T has so far not specified leaf-initiated join signaling):

Connection Setup

ADD PARTY

ADD PARTY ACKNOWLEDGE

LEAF SETUP REQUEST*
LEAF SETUP FAILURE*
PARTY ALERTING
ADD PARTY REJECT

Connection Clear-down

DROP PARTY
DROP PARTY ACKNOWLEDGE

For interoperability with narrowband ISDN, three more messages have been defined by the ITU-T in addition to those listed above (none of these is supported by the ATM Forum UNI signaling specifications):

Connection Setup (Additional Messages for N-ISDN Interworking)

SETUP ACKNOWLEDGE
PROGRESSING

Other (Additional Messages for N-ISDN Interworking)

INFORMATION

Furthermore, the messages RESTART and RESTART ACKNOWLEDGE are defined for the purpose of requesting a new connection setup attempt (in the event that a connection enters an undefined state, for example). These messages may be used only with the global call reference 0.

Every signaling message consists of the following five sections, called information elements:

- Protocol discriminator
- Call reference
- Message type
- Message length
- Message-specific information elements

The first four information elements (protocol discriminator, call reference, message type, and message length) are mandatory, and must be contained in every signaling message. The usage of other information elements is dependent on the message type. The diagram in Figure 10.2 illustrates the structure of a UNI signaling message.

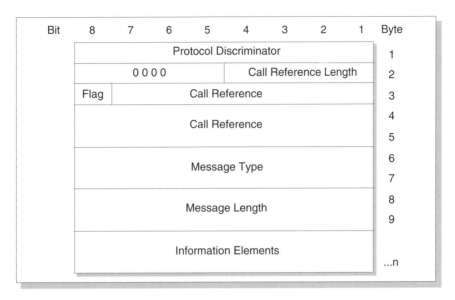

Figure 10.2
UNI signaling message format.

10.1.1   Protocol Discriminator

The protocol discriminator is the first element in every signaling message. It identifies the signaling protocol used, and is coded as 00001001 (decimal 9) for ITU-T Q.2931 and Q.2971. The ATM Forum signaling variants (UNI 3.x, 4.x) share the same protocol discriminator value. Figure 10.3 shows the protocol discriminator values for different signaling systems and highlights the one used for ATM.

10.1.2   Call Reference

The call reference identifies the connection affected by a UNI signaling message. From the time a new connection is established, all messages concerning that connection have the same call reference value. When the connection has been cleared down, the call reference is released and can be used again. The same call reference can be used by two connections within an ATM channel (VC) only if the respective connection setups took place in opposite directions. The length of the call reference field is measured in bytes, with a default length of 3 bytes. The call reference flag identifies the sending and receiving

Bit	8	7	6	5	4	3	2	1
	0	0	0	0	1	0	0	1

Protocol discriminator value for Q.2931/Q.2971 messages

Bit 8765 4321	
0000 0000 to 0000 0111	Reserved
0000 1000	Q.931/ I.415 user network call control
0000 1001	**Q.2931/Q.2971 user network call/connection control**
0001 0000 to 0011 1111	Reserved for other Layer 3 protocols (X.25 etc.)
0100 0000 to 0100 1111	For national use
0101 0000 to 1111 1110	Reserved for other Layer 3 protocols (X.25 etc.)

Figure 10.3
The protocol discriminator field.

stations. The station that initiated the connection always sets this flag to 0 in its messages, while messages originating from the receiving station have the flag set to 1. The call reference value 0 is known as the global call reference, and refers to all connections within a signaling channel (see Figure 10.4).

10.1.3   Message Type

This field indicates the message type. All message types except SETUP ACKNOWLEDGE and INFORMATION are also supported by the corresponding ATM Forum specification UNI 4.0 and 4.1 (see Figure 10.5).

10.1.4   The Message Length Field

The message length field indicates the length of the signaling message in bytes, not counting the protocol discriminator, call reference, message type, and message length fields. The length field itself can be one or two bytes long. In the first byte, only the first 7 bits can be used. Bit 8 indicates whether the

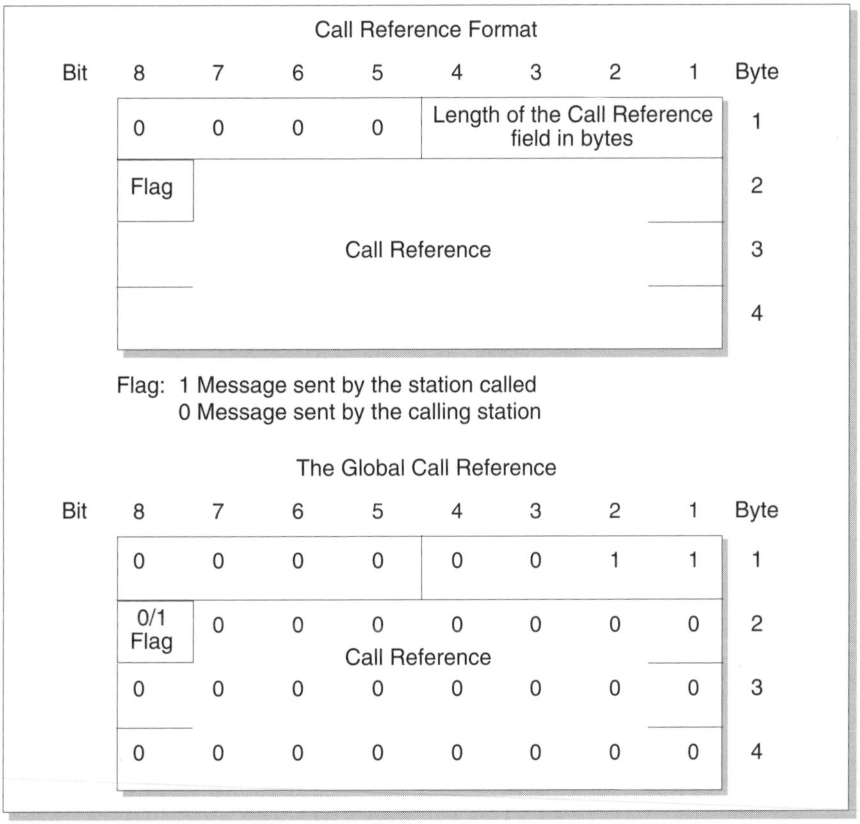

Figure 10.4
Call reference and global call reference.

length field includes a second byte. If bit 8 is set to 0, the length field is continued in the following byte; otherwise the length field is a single byte. If the message contains no other information elements after the length field, the length field has the value 1000 0000.

10.1.5 UNI Information Elements

After the four mandatory information elements, the various message types use specific information elements of varying lengths to fulfill their respective functions. Each of these information elements consists of an information element identifier, a length field, a compatibility indicator, and the actual information

Bit	8	7	6	5	4	3	2	1	Byte
	Message Type								1
	1 Ext.	0	0	Flag	0		1	Msg. Action Indicator	2

Bits 8765 4321	UNI Signaling Message
0000 0000	Escape sequence for national message types
Connection set-up	
0000 0001	ALERTING[1]
0000 0111	CONNECT
0000 1111	CONNECT ACKNOWLEDGE
0000 0010	CALL PROCEEDING
0000 0011	PROGRESS[1]
0000 0101	SETUP
0000 1101	SETUP ACKNOWLEDGE[1]
1000 0000	ADD PARTY[2]
1000 0001	ADD PARTY ACKNOWLEDGE[2]
1000 0101	PARTY ALERTING[2]
1000 0010	ADD PART REJECT[2]
1001 0001	LEAF SETUP REQUEST[3]
1001 0000	LEAF SETUP FAILURE[3]
Connection clear-down	
0100 1110	RESTART ACKNOWLEDGE
0100 0110	RESTART
0101 1010	RELEASE COMPLETE
0100 1101	RELEASE
1000 0011	DROP PARTY[2]
1000 0100	DROP PARTY ACKNOWLEDGE[2]
Other Messages	
0110 1110	NOTIFY[1]
0111 1011	INFORMATION[1]
0111 0101	STATUS ENQUIRY
0111 1101	STATUS

[1] Not supported in UNI 3.0 or UNI 3.1
[2] Point-to-multipoint (route-initiated join)—Q.2971, UNI 3.0, 3.1, 4.0, 4.1
[3] Point-to-multipoint (leaf-initiated join)—UNI 4.0, 4.1

Figure 10.5
UNI signaling messages.

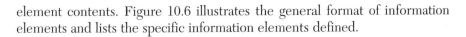

element contents. Figure 10.6 illustrates the general format of information elements and lists the specific information elements defined.

The Information Element Identifier

The first field of the information element contains the 8-bit information element identifier. The information elements shown in Table 10.1 are defined for the various signaling versions plus addenda.

The Compatibility Indicator Field

The 1-byte compatibility indicator field contains information about the coding standard used in the information element (also called the codeset), as well as the action indicator field, which indicates how errors are to be handled, and an extension flag. Table 10.2 shows details of this field.

The action indicator can have the following values:

000   Clear call
001   Discard information element and proceed
010   Discard information element, proceed, and report status
101   Discard information element and ignore
110   Discard information element and report status

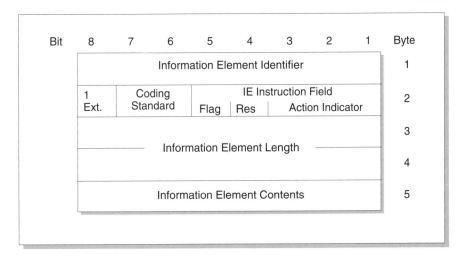

Figure 10.6
Format and coding of information elements.

Table 10.1 Information Element Indicator

	Information Element Identifiers						
Bits 8 7 6 5 4 3 2 1	Information Element Identifier	Q.2931	Q.2971	UNI 3.0	UNI 3.1	UNI 4.0	UNI 4.1
0 0 0 0 0 1 0 0	Narrowband Bearer Capability	X				X	X
0 0 0 0 1 0 0 0	Cause	X		X	X	X	X
0 0 0 1 0 1 0 0	Call State	X		X	X	X	X
0 0 0 1 1 1 1 0	Progress Indicator	X				X	X
0 0 1 0 0 1 1 1	Notification Indicator	X				X	X
0 1 0 0 0 0 1 0	End-to-End Transit Delay	X				X	X
0 1 0 0 1 1 0 0	Connected Number					X	X
0 1 0 0 1 1 0 1	Connected Subaddress					X	X
0 1 0 1 0 1 0 0	Endpoint Reference		X	X	X	X	X
0 1 0 1 0 1 0 1	Endpoint State		X	X	X	X	X
0 1 0 1 1 0 0 0	ATM Adaptation Layer Parameters	X		X	X	X	X
0 1 0 1 1 0 0 1	ATM Traffic Descriptor	X		X	X	X	X
0 1 0 1 1 0 1 0	Connection Identifier	X		X	X	X	
0 1 0 1 1 0 1 1	OAM Traffic Descriptor	X					X
0 1 0 1 1 1 0 0	Quality of Service Parameter	X		X	X	X	X
0 1 0 1 1 1 0 1	Broadband Bearer Capability	X		X	X	X	X
0 1 0 1 1 1 1 0	Broadband Low Layer Information (B-LLI)	X		X	X	X	X
0 1 0 1 1 1 1 1	Broadband High Layer Information (B-HLI)	X		X	X	X	X
0 1 1 0 0 0 0 0	Broadband Locking Shift	X		X	X	X	X
0 1 1 0 0 0 0 1	Broadband Non-Locking Shift	X		X	X	X	X
0 1 1 0 0 0 1 0	Broadband Sending Complete	X		X	X	X	X
0 1 1 0 0 0 1 1	Broadband Repeat Indicator	X		X	X	X	X
0 1 1 0 1 1 0 0	Calling Party Number	X		X	X	X	X
0 1 1 0 1 1 0 1	Calling Party Sub-address	X		X	X	X	X
0 1 1 1 0 0 0 0	Called Party Number	X		X	X	X	X
0 1 1 1 0 0 0 1	Called Party Sub-address	X		X	X	X	X
0 1 1 1 1 0 0 0	Transit Network Selection	X		X	X	X	X
0 1 1 1 1 0 0 1	Restart Indicator	X		X	X	X	X
0 1 1 1 1 1 0 0	Narrowband Low Layer Compatibility	X				X	X
0 1 1 1 1 1 0 1	Narrowband High Layer Compatibility	X				X	X
0 1 1 1 1 1 1 0	User-User						X
0 1 1 1 1 1 1 1	Generic Identifier Transport					X	X
1 0 0 0 1 0 0 1	Broadband Report Type	X					X
1 0 0 0 0 0 0 1	Minimum Acceptable Traffic Descriptor					X	X
1 0 0 0 0 0 1 0	Alternative ATM Traffic Descriptor					X	X
1 0 0 0 0 1 0 0	ABR (now ATC) Setup Parameters					X	X
1 1 1 0 0 0 0 0	ABR (now ATC) Additional Parameters					X	X
1 1 1 0 0 0 1 1	Called Party Soft PVPC or PVCC						X
1 1 1 0 0 1 0 0	Calling Party Soft PVPC or PVCC						X
1 1 1 0 0 1 1 1	Security Services					X	X
1 1 1 0 1 0 0 0	Leaf-Initiated Join Call Identifier					X	
1 1 1 0 1 0 0 1	Leaf-Initiated Join Parameters					X	
1 1 1 0 1 0 1 0	Leaf sequence Number					X	
1 1 1 0 1 0 1 1	Connection Scope Selection					X	X
1 1 1 0 1 1 0 0	Extended QoS Parameters					X	X
1 1 1 0 1 1 0 1	PHY/MAC-Layer Identifier					X	X
1 1 1 0 1 1 1 1	Network Call Correlation Identifier					X	X
1 1 1 1 0 0 0 0	Minimum Desired Cell Rate					X	X
1 1 1 1 0 0 0 1	Optional Traffic Attributes					X	X
1 1 1 1 0 0 1 0	Rerouting Services					X	X
1 1 1 1 0 1 0 0	Rerouting Cause					X	X
1 1 1 1 0 1 0 1	Reference List						X

Table 10.2 Compatibility Indicator (Byte 2 of Information Element)

Information Field Coding: Byte 2 Compatibility Indicator	
Extension Indicator, bit 8	Set to 1; reserved for future use
Coding standard, bits 7 6	
0 0	ITU-T coding
0 1	ISO/IEC standard
1 0	National standard
1 1	Network-specific standard (private, public)
Flag bit 5	
0	Ignore instruction indicator
1	Obey instruction indicator
Reserved field, bit 4	Set to 0; reserved for future use
Action indicator, bits 3 2 1	
0 0 0	Clear Call
0 0 1	Discard info element and proceed
0 1 0	Discard info element, proceed and report status
1 0 1	Discard info element and ignore
1 1 0	Discard info element and report status

The Information Element Length Field

Information elements contain a 1- or 2-byte length field, which indicates the length of the information element in bytes, not counting the first three fields (the Information Element Identifier field, the Compatibility Instruction Identifier field, and the length field itself). As in the message length field described above, bit 8 serves as an extension flag, indicating whether the length field includes a second byte.

Extended Codesets

The set of all permissible information elements in a given operating mode is called a codeset. The 29 information elements specified in Q.2931 and Q.2971 or the 41 information elements currently specified in UNI 4.0 and 4.1 (plus addenda) form the default codeset, Codeset 0. A total of seven other codesets of up to 125 information elements each can be defined as alternatives or extensions to Codeset 0. A permanent codeset shift can take place only from a lower- to a higher-numbered codeset. The currently active codeset is indicated in the codeset section of the compatibility indicator field:

Codesets 1–3	Reserved for future use by ITU-T
Codeset 4	Reserved for future use by ISO/IEC
Codeset 5	Reserved for national use
Codeset 6	Reserved for use in private networks
Codeset 7	Reserved for user-specific information elements

Two methods of changing codesets are defined: the locking shift and the nonlocking shift.

The Locking Shift Procedure. The locking codeset shift changes the active codeset permanently to a higher-numbered codeset. For example, if Codeset 0 (the default codeset) is active, the "broadband locking shift" information element can be used to specify a permanent change to Codeset 5. All subsequent information elements are then interpreted in accordance with the new codeset. At present, only the default Codeset 0 and Codesets 5, 6, and 7 are defined. Codeset 5 is reserved for national use, Codeset 6 for use in local area networks, and Codeset 7 for user-specific purposes. Figure 10.7 illustrates the format of the locking shift information element.

The Nonlocking Shift Procedure. The nonlocking codeset shift changes the active codeset temporarily to a different codeset. The specified codeset is then applied only for the single information element that immediately follows the nonlocking shift information element. After that element has been interpreted, the previously active codeset is active once again. If the info element received immediately after the nonlocking shift is a locking shift, however, then the receiver must ignore the nonlocking shift and proceed as if it had received only the locking shift information element. Figure 10.8 illustrates the format of the nonlocking shift information element.

10.2 The Basic Signaling Processes

The signaling procedures defined in point-to-point signaling can be classified in two groups: those that take place between the calling station and the network, and those between the network and the station called. As mentioned

Bit	8	7	6	5	4	3	2	1	Byte
	Broadband Locking Shift								

Bit	8	7	6	5	4	3	2	1	Byte
				Broadband Locking Shift					
	0	1	1	0	0	0	0	0	1
				Information Element Identifier					
	1 Ext.	Coding Standard		Flag	Res.	IE Action Ind.			2
									3
			Length of Broadband Locking Shift Content						4
	1 Ext.	0	Spare 0 0		0	New Codeset Identification			5

Structure of the Broadband-Locking-Shift information element

New Codeset Identification (Byte 5)	
Bits 3 2 1	
0 0 0	Not used
0 0 1 to 0 1 1	Reserved
1 0 0	Codeset 1: ISO/IEC information elements
1 0 1	Codeset 5: Information elements for national use
1 1 0	Codeset 6: Information elements for local use
1 1 1	Codeset 7: Vendor-specific information element

Figure 10.7
Format and coding of the locking shift information element.

above, the signaling protocol at the calling station assumes that an AAL signaling connection has already been established between the user and the network. There are minor differences between the ITU-T procedures and those of the ATM Forum's UNI 3.x specifications (which omit some of the steps); UNI 4.0 comes back into line with the ITU-T, and is in fact derived from ITU-T rather than UNI 3.1, and UNI 4.1 is based on UNI 4.0 (more on all this later). The following describes the ITU-T procedures.

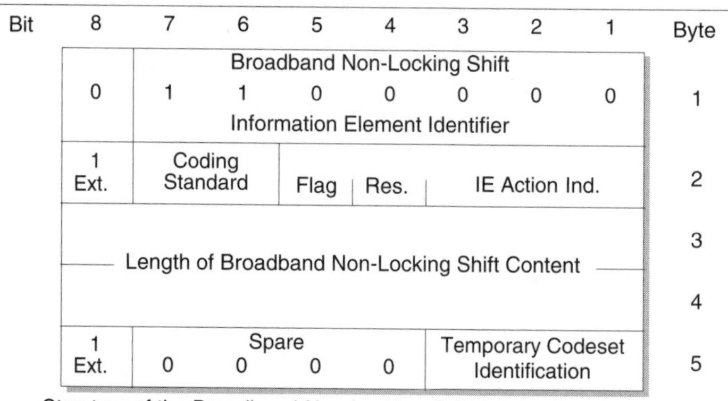

Bit	8	7	6	5	4	3	2	1	Byte
		Broadband Non-Locking Shift							
	0	1	1	0	0	0	0	0	1
		Information Element Identifier							
	1 Ext.	Coding Standard	Flag	Res.		IE Action Ind.			2
									3
	— Length of Broadband Non-Locking Shift Content —								
									4
	1 Ext.	0	Spare 0	0	0	Temporary Codeset Identification			5

Structure of the Broadband-Non-Locking-Shift information element

Temporary Codeset Identification	
Bits 3 2 1	
0 0 0	Codeset 0: Q.2931 information elements
0 0 1 to 0 1 1	Reserved
1 0 0	Codeset 1: ISO/IEC information elements
1 0 1	Codeset 5: Information elements for national use
1 1 0	Codeset 6: Information elements for local use
1 1 1	Codeset 7: Vendor-specific information element

Figure 10.8
Format of the nonlocking shift information element.

10.2.1   Connection Setup at the Calling Station

The caller initiates the connection setup by transmitting a SETUP message containing the desired ATM virtual path, virtual channel, quality-of-service, and traffic parameters. If the network is able to provide the service requested, and if the specified ATM virtual path and virtual channel are available, the network answers with a CALL PROCEEDING message and forwards the setup request to the receiving station.

If the station called is able to receive the request, the network sends the caller an ALERTING message. If the station called accepts the call, the network sends the caller a CONNECT message. The caller may optionally respond with a

CONNECT ACKNOWLEDGE. This completes the connection setup, and the call is then in the Active state. If the calling station receives a Broadband Report Type information element in the CONNECT message, with "End-to-end connection completion indication requested" following the sending of the CONNECT ACKNOWLEDGE message, the calling user must send a CONNECTION AVAILABLE message to successfully finish the connection establishment.

10.2.2 Connection Setup at the Station Called

After the receiving station has been notified of an incoming call by a SETUP message from the network, it performs a compatibility check. This test compares the address information, the QoS parameters, and the traffic parameters of the SETUP request with the local services available. If the SETUP parameters requested are not locally available, the receiving station responds with a RELEASE COMPLETE message and Cause #88, "Incompatible Destination." If the SETUP parameters are compatible, the receiving station can respond with a CALL PROCEEDING, ALERTING, or CONNECT message, depending on the type of end system. The network confirms a CONNECT message with a CONNECT ACKNOWLEDGE, and the connection enters the Active state. The diagram in Figure 10.9 illustrates the basic Q.2931

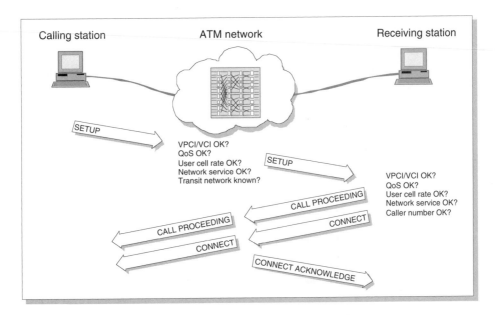

Figure 10.9
UNI connection setup.

signaling procedures. This is merely a general outline of the UNI signaling mechanism. We can now examine the connection setup process in more detail from the points of view of both the caller and the station called.

10.3 UNI Connection Setup: The Calling Station

As described in the previous section, the calling station initiates the connection setup by sending a SETUP message. At the same time, it starts its timer T303.

Table 10.3 Information Elements in the SETUP Message

Information Element	Direction	Type	Length (Byte)
Protocol Discriminator	U ↔ N	M	1
Call Reference	U → N	M	1
Message Type	U → N	M	2
Message Length	U ↔ N	M	2
QOS Parameter	U ↔ N	M	6
BB Sending Complete	U ↔ N	O	1–5
B-Bearer Capability	U ↔ N	M	6–7
End-to-End Transit Delay	U ↔ N	O	1–10
ATM Traffic Descriptor	U → N	M	12–20
AAL Parameter	U ↔ N	O	1–21
Calling Party Number	U ↔ N	O	1–
Calling Party Sub-Address	U ↔ N	O	1–25
Called Party Number	U ↔ N	O	1–
Called Party Sub-Address	U ↔ N	O	1–25
Transit Network Selection	U → N	O	1–n
BB Low Layer Information	U → N	O	1–17
BB High Layer Information	U ↔ N	O	1–13
Connection Identifier	U ↔ N	O	1–9
BB Repeat Indicator	U ↔ N	O	1–5
Notification Indicator	U ↔ N	O	1–n
OAM Traffic Descriptor	U ↔ N	O	1–6
Broadband Report Type	U → N	O	–5

M   Mandatory
N   Network
O   Optional
U   User

10.3.1 The SETUP Message

The SETUP message must contain the following mandatory information elements:

- Protocol discriminator
- Call reference
- Message type
- Message length
- ATM cell rate (indicating the user's peak cell rate)
- Broadband bearer capability (specifying the service class for the requested connection, e.g., Class A–connection-oriented with constant bit rate)
- AAL protocol parameter (specifying the requested ATM Adaptation Layer type)

The remaining information elements required to set up the connection can be transferred in one of two ways. If the connection setup is performed using overlap sending and receiving, then the remaining information elements can be transported in several successive SETUP messages. Under the en-bloc setup method, however, all of the required information elements must be contained in the initial, single SETUP message. Table 10.3 lists the information elements specified for the SETUP message.

Communication Paths and Channels (Caller–Network)

The Connection Identifier information element in the SETUP message specifies the local communication path in the ATM layer, that is, the virtual path and virtual channel (VP and VC). The calling station can determine the virtual path connection identifier (VPCI) and virtual channel identifier (VCI) in one of the following four ways.

1. The caller may specify a VPCI, and accept no alternatives, but not specify any VCI.
2. The caller may specify a VPCI, but still accept alternative values, and not specify a VCI.
3. The caller may specify a VPCI and accept no alternatives, and also indicate a value for the VCI.

285

4. The caller may specify a VPCI, but still accept alternatives, and also indicate a value for the VCI.

If the sending station does not accept alternative values for the virtual path (VPCI), but the value it requests is not available, or if no alternative VPCI or VCI is available, then the network answers the SETUP message with a RE-LEASE COMPLETE message. If the VPCI and VCI are successfully allocated, then the network continues the connection setup dialog by sending a CALL PROCEEDING message. At the user–network interface, channels are identified by Virtual Path Connection Identifiers (VPCI) rather than Virtual Path Identifiers (VPIs), since virtual path cross-connects with several interfaces require that both the path (VPI) and the interface to be used be designated. For a cross-connect with two user interfaces, for example, the VPCI value is composed of an interface ID as well as the path ID (Figure 10.10). If signaling between users and network takes place over only one interface, then no interface identification is necessary and the value of the VPCI is identical with the VPI.

The virtual channel ID number (VCIs) may have a value from 16 to 65,535. VCIs 0 through 15 are reserved. These reserved VCIs include VCI = 0 for unassigned cells, VCI = 1 for metasignaling, VCI = 3 and VCI = 4 for OAM-F4 cells, and so on.

Quality-of-Service Class

A Quality-of-Service class is selected by means of the Quality-of-Service information element in the SETUP message (Figure 10.11). If the QoS class requested by the caller is available, the call is forwarded to the receiving station and the connection setup continues. If the specified QoS class cannot be provided, then the network responds by sending the caller a RELEASE COMPLETE message with Cause #49, "Quality of Service unavailable."

Transit Network

If a connection needs to be set up across several networks, one or more transit networks can be specified in the SETUP message by means of transit network selection information elements (Figure 10.12). Up to four transit networks can be specified. Each transit network is identified in a separate information element. The call is then routed through the individual transit networks in the order in which the corresponding transit network selection information elements occur in the SETUP message. If a network is unable to switch the transit connection due to traffic loads, the connection setup is

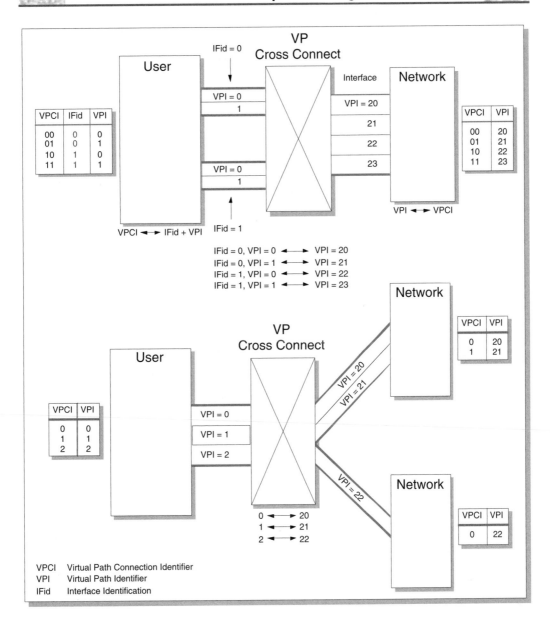

Figure 10.10
Signaling over cross-connects with one and two interfaces.

287

Bit	8	7	6	5	4	3	2	1	Byte
	Quality of Service Parameter								
	0	1	1	0	0	0	0	0	1
	Information Element Identifier								
	1 Ext.	Coding Standard		Flag	Res.		IE Action Ind.		2
	Length of QoS Parameter Contents								3
									4
	QoS Class Forward								5
	QoS Class Backward								6

Format of the QoS information element

QoS Class Forward
Bits 8 7 6 5 4 3 2 1
    0 0 0 0 0 0 0 0 Unspecified QoS-class
    1 1 1 1 1 1 1 1 Reserved

QoS Class Backward
Bits 8 7 6 5 4 3 2 1
    0 0 0 0 0 0 0 0 Unspecified QoS-class
    1 1 1 1 1 1 1 1 Reserved

Figure 10.11
Format of the QoS information element.

aborted with the message "Bandwidth not available." If the specified transit network is unknown, the connection setup is aborted with Cause #2, "No route to specified transit network." If the transit network selection information element contains errors, the connection setup is rejected with Cause #91, "Invalid transit network selection."

Maximum Cell Rate

The maximum cell rate of the requested connection is indicated in the ATM user cell rate information element. If the specified throughput is not available, the connection setup is rejected with a RELEASE COMPLETE message containing the cause "User cell rate not available."

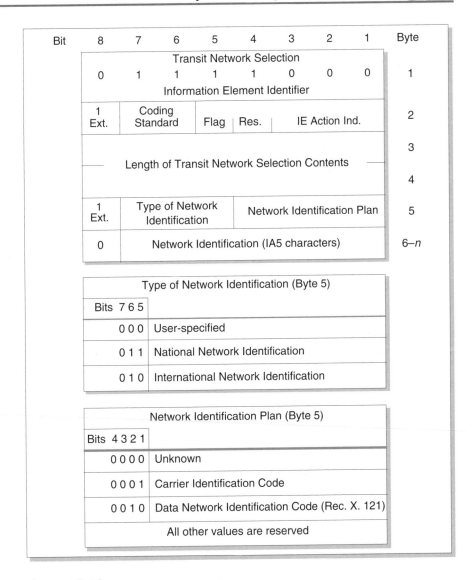

Figure 10.12
Format of the transit network selection information element.

Caller and Called Party Numbers

The SETUP message identifies the station called by its number in the "Called Party Subaddress" and "Called Party Number" information elements. The network verifies that this is a valid number. If not, the network sends a RELEASE COMPLETE message with one of the following causes:

Cause #1   Unassigned (unallocated) number

Cause #2   No route to destination

Cause #3   Number changed

Cause #28   Invalid number format (incomplete number)

ATM Addressing

Six types of ATM addresses are specified in Q.2931:

* Unknown
* International number
* National number
* Network-specific number
* Subscriber number
* Abbreviated number

The format of the address types "abbreviated number" and "network-specific number" is different from case to case, depending on the given network. "Network-specific numbers" can be used for administrative services (such as operator numbers). An "abbreviated number" address contains a shortened form of a complete ATM address, and may be defined by the network operator as appropriate for the internal structure of the network. All other address types use one of the following address formats:

* Unknown
* ISDN Telephony Numbering Plan (E.164)
* ATM end system address (AESA) (a subclass of an NSAP address, which is always 20 bytes long [ISO8348])
* Data numbering plan (ITU-T Recommendation X.121)
* Private Numbering Plan

The address format "unknown" is used when an ATM end system address is indicated in the addressing/numbering plan identification or when the user or the network indicates the type of number using the number digits field. Fig-ure 10.13 illustrates the ISO NSAP DCC and ICD address formats and the E.164 format.

The DCC (Data Country Code) Address Format. The data country code indicates the country in which the address is registered. The values for this field are defined in accordance with ISO 3166.

The ICD (International-Code Designator) Address Format. International organizations can obtain unique addresses by means of International Code Designators. ICD codes are assigned centrally by the British Standards Institute.

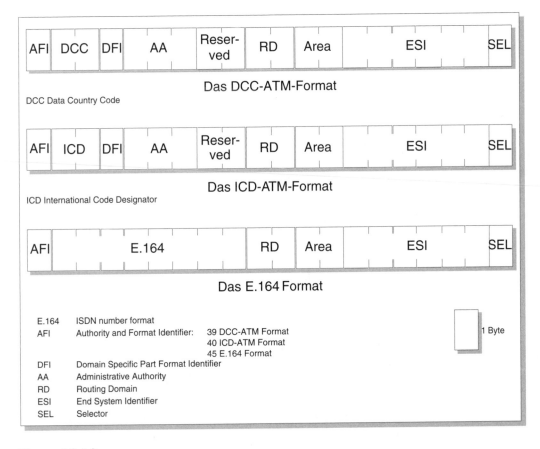

Das DCC-ATM-Format

DCC Data Country Code

Das ICD-ATM-Format

ICD International Code Designator

Das E.164 Format

E.164	ISDN number format	
AFI	Authority and Format Identifier:	39 DCC-ATM Format
		40 ICD-ATM Format
		45 E.164 Format
DFI	Domain Specific Part Format Identifier	
AA	Administrative Authority	
RD	Routing Domain	
ESI	End System Identifier	
SEL	Selector	

1 Byte

Figure 10.13
The ATM number formats.

The E.164 Address Format.   E.164 describes the subscriber number system in ISDN. ATM uses the international number format. These numbers can contain up to 15 digits. The E.164 address field is 8 bytes in length.

Domain-Specific Part Format Identifier (DFI): The DFI indicates the structure of the remaining address fields (the AA, RD, AREA, ESI, and SEL fields).

Administrative Authority (AA): The AA field identifies a national organization such as an ATM network operator, an ATM user, or an ATM equipment vendor.

Routing Domain (RD): The two-byte Routing Domain field specifies an address range that must be unique within E.164, DCC/DFI/AA or ICD/DFI/AA.

AREA: An area refers to a unique address range within a routing domain.

End System Identifier (ESI): The End System Identifier designates a single end system within an area. Each ESI must be unique in its area. The ESI field is 6 bytes long.

Selector (SEL): The selector is an addressing element provided for use by the terminal equipment.

Network Services

Finally, the calling station's SETUP message also specifies the requested network service in the Broadband Bearer Capability and Bearer Capability information elements. If the specified service is unavailable in the network or if the sending station is not authorized to use it, the network responds with a RELEASE COMPLETE message containing one of the following causes:

#57	Bearer capability not authorized
#58	Bearer capability not presently available
#63	Service or option not available or unspecified
#65	Bearer service not implemented

Alerting Ring and Completion of the Connection Setup

If the number is valid and the network is able to provide the services and traffic parameters requested in the SETUP message, then the call is forwarded to the station called, and the network sends the calling station a CALL PROCEEDING message. The sending station then starts its timer T310 and waits for the completion of the call set-up process. If the network is able to deliver the setup request to the station called, it sends the caller an ALERTING message.

When the station called has accepted the connection, the network sends the caller the CONNECT message. The caller may respond with an optional CONNECT ACKNOWLEDGE message. The connection setup is then completed. The connection is established and the caller stops the T310 timer. If the receiver is unable to accept the call, the network sends the caller a RE-LEASE COMPLETE message with the cause indicated by the station called. Table 10.4 lists the information elements of the CALL PROCEEDING, CONNECT, and CONNECT ACKNOWLEDGE messages.

Table 10.4 Information Elements of CALL PROCEEDING, CONNECT, and CONNECT ACKNOWLEDGE

Information Element	Direction	Type	Length (Byte)
CALL PROCEEDING			
Protocol Discriminator	U ◄► N	M	1
Call Reference	U ◄— N	M	4
Message Type	U ◄► N	M	2
Message Length	U ◄► N	M	2
Connection Identifier	U ◄► N	O	4–9
Notification Indicator	U ◄► N	O	4–*
CONNECT			
Protocol Discriminator	U ◄► N	M	1
Call Reference	U ◄► N	M	4
Message Type	U ◄► N	M	2
Message Length	U ◄► N	M	2
AAL Parameters	U ◄► N	O	4–21
Broadband Low Layer Information	U ◄► N	O	4–17
Connection Identifier	U ◄► N	O	4–9
End-to-end Transit Delay	U ◄► N	O	4–10
Notification Indicator	U ◄► N	O	4–*
OAM Traffic Descriptor	U ◄► N	O	4–6
Broadband Report Type	U —► N	O	–5
CONNECT ACKNOWLEDGE	U ◄► N		
Protocol Discriminator	U ◄► N	M	1
Call Reference	U ◄► N	M	4
Message Type	U ◄► N	M	2
Message Length	U —► N	M	2
Notification Indicator		O	4–*

M Mandatory
N Network
O Optional
U User

10.4 Connection Setup at the Station Called

Upon receiving a connection request, the network selects a VPCI/VCI combination and transmits the SETUP message over this channel to the receiving station. If no response is received from the station called before the T303 timer expires once, T303 is restarted.

10.4.1 Number Verification

If the station called has been assigned a subaddress, it compares this to the corresponding contents of the "Called Party Subaddress" and "Called Party Number" information elements with its number and subaddress (Figure 10.14). If the information element contents are not compatible with its number and subaddress, the station does not accept the call. If the receiving station has no subaddress, then the called party number is not verified. The connection setup process continues with compatibility verification.

10.4.2 Compatibility Verification

Two kinds of compatibility verification are performed, called Broadband Category 1 and Broadband Category 2 compatibility verification. Broadband Category 1 information affects both users and the network, and must therefore be tested by both. The information elements examined are:

- Broadband Bearer Capability
- End-to-End Transit Delay
- ATM User Cell Rate
- Quality-of-Service Parameter

Broadband Category 2 information only concerns the user, and need not be verified by the network. The information elements examined are:

- AAL Parameter
- Broadband Low Layer Information (optional)

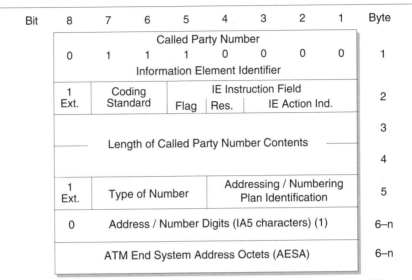

Bit	8	7	6	5	4	3	2	1	Byte
			Called Party Number						
	0	1	1	1	0	0	0	0	1
			Information Element Identifier						
	1 Ext.	Coding Standard		Flag	Res.	IE Instruction Field / IE Action Ind.			2
									3
			Length of Called Party Number Contents						4
	1 Ext.	Type of Number		Addressing / Numbering Plan Identification					5
	0	Address / Number Digits (IA5 characters) (1)							6–n
		ATM End System Address Octets (AESA)							6–n

(1)   The numbers are transmitted in the sequence in which they would be entered.
In case of AESA addresses, coding as described in ITU-T E.191 is to be used.

Type of Number (Byte 5) (1)	
Bits 7 6 5	
0 0 0	Unknown (2)
0 1 1	International number
0 1 0	National number
0 1 1	Network specific number
1 0 0	Subscriber number
1 1 0	Abbreviated number
1 1 1	Reserved

Addressing/Numbering Plan Identification (Byte 5)	
Bits 4 3 2 1	
0 0 0 0	Unknown (2)
0 0 0 1	ISDN Numbering Plan (E.164)
0 0 1 0	ATM End System Address
1 0 0 1	Private Numbering Plan
0 0 1 1	Data Numbering Plan
All other values are reserved	

(1)   International, national and user numbers are defined in ITU-T I.330.

(2)   Number type »unknown« indicates the default numbering plan of the network.

Figure 10.14
Format of the Called Party Number information element.

If the station called determines that it is incompatible with the parameters specified in the information elements listed above, it transmits a RELEASE COMPLETE message with Cause #88, "Incompatible destination," to the network.

10.4.3 Communication Paths and Channels (Caller–Network)

In the network's SETUP message to the station called, the communication path and channel (VPCI and VCI) can be indicated in two ways:

1. The network may specify a VPCI and accept no alternatives, and also indicate a value for the VCI.
2. The network may specify a VPCI, but accept any alternative, and also indicate a value for the VCI.

In case 1, if the specified VPCI or the specified VCI within the VPCI is unavailable, the receiving station must respond with a RELEASE COMPLETE message. In case 2, however, if the specified values are not available, the receiver can respond to the network's SETUP message by indicating any available VPCI/VCI combination. It is then up to the network to send a RELEASE COMPLETE to the station called if these values are not acceptable. If the user specifies a given VPCI/VCI value in a SETUP message to the network at the same time that the network is sending a SETUP message to the user over the same VCI in the same VPCI, then the network's SETUP message to the user takes priority. In its answer to the user's SETUP message, the network assigns the user's outgoing call a new VCPI/VCI combination. Collisions of this type can be avoided, however, by having users select low VPCI/VCI values in SETUP messages while network stations select high values.

10.4.4 Confirmation of Quality-of-Service (QoS) and User Cell Rate

If the station called is unable to provide the QoS parameters specified in the SETUP message received from the network, it responds with a RELEASE COMPLETE message indicating Cause #49, "Quality of Service not available." Similarly, if the requested maximum cell rate is not available, the station responds with a RELEASE COMPLETE message with the cause "Bandwidth not available."

10.4.5   Connection Available Confirmation

If the called user wants a success confirmation of the call setup procedure during the establishment of the call, the Broadband report type information element needs to be included in the CONNECT message, as mentioned in the signaling overview section. In addition to the connect timer T313, this event starts timer T333, which stops when the CONNECTION AVAILABLE message indicating "End-to-end connection completed" has been received.

10.4.6   Call Acceptance and Completion of the Connection Setup

Once the station called has received all the information necessary to set up the connection and verified that the connection parameters are compatible with its local capabilities, it can answer the network with a CALL PROCEEDING, ALERTING, or CONNECT message. The CALL PROCEEDING message is used only by users that are unable to answer with ALERTING, CONNECT, or RELEASE before the T303 timer expires. ALERTING only needs to be sent if the user requires other VCPI/VCI values than those proposed in the SETUP message. In other cases, the station can reply immediately with the CONNECT message. If the parameters of the incoming connection request are compatible with the receiving station, but the station is not ready to establish a connection, it sends the network a RELEASE COMPLETE message with Cause #17, "User busy." If the party called chooses not to accept the call, it can reply with a RELEASE COMPLETE message indicating the cause "Call rejected."

As soon as the network receives the called station's CALL PROCEEDING message, it stops T303 and starts the T310 timer. If the station called sends the network an ALERTING message, then T303 or T310—whichever is running—is stopped and timer T301 is started. If the network receives a RELEASE COMPLETE or a RELEASE before the connection is shifted into the active state by means of a CONNECT message, then the active timer (T303, T310, or T301) is stopped and the connection to both the calling station and the station called is cleared down. If the network receives no response

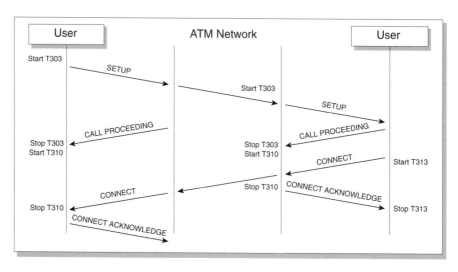

Figure 10.15
Connection setup processes at the UNI interface.

from the call destination before T303 expires, the connection to the calling station is cleared down with Cause #18, "No user responding," and the connection to the destination is also terminated. Likewise if the network receives a CALL PROCEEDING but no ALERTING, CONNECT, or RELEASE message before T301 expires, the calling station's connection is cleared down with Cause #18, "No user responding." If timer T301 expires after the network has received an ALERTING message, then the connection setup is aborted with Cause #19, "No answer from user."

Upon sending the network a CONNECT message, the station called starts its T313 timer. When the network receives the CONNECT message, it stops its T301, T303, or T310 timer. At this point the connection is established. Optionally, the network may confirm the called station's CONNECT message by sending it a CONNECT ACKNOWLEDGE. In any case, however, the network sends a CONNECT message to the station that initiated the connection setup. When the receiving station receives the CONNECT ACKNOWLEDGE, it stops the last timer, T313, and changes to the "connection active" state. If T313 expires before a CONNECT ACKNOWLEDGE is received, however, the connection is cleared down. Figure 10.15 shows the entire call setup procedure.

10.5   Connection Clear-Down

Before describing the processes involved in clearing down a connection, we must define the three states "Connected," "Disconnected," and "Released." An ATM virtual channel is in the "Connected" state when it forms part of an active ATM connection. The channel is in the "Disconnected" state when it is not part of such a connection, but is not available for any other connection. If an ATM channel is in the "Released" state, then it is not part of an existing ATM connection and is available for use.

Connection clear-down is normally initiated by a "RELEASE" command, except in the following three cases:

1. If a SETUP message is received without a mandatory information element, the receiver may refuse the connection setup by sending a RELEASE COMPLETE message with Cause #96, "Mandatory information element is missing."

2. If a SETUP message is received with an incorrect mandatory information element, the receiver may refuse the connection setup by sending a RELEASE COMPLETE message with Cause #100, "Invalid information element contents."

3. After VPCI/VCI negotiation has failed, the system that initiated the call may terminate the connection setup with a RELEASE COMPLETE.

10.5.1   Connection Clear-Down by the User

In all cases except the three mentioned above, the connection clear-down is begun by sending a RELEASE message. If the connection clear-down is initiated by the user, the user's timer T308 is started when the RELEASE message is sent. The first time T308 expires, the user repeats the RELEASE command and starts T308 again. If no RELEASE COMPLETE is received from the network in answer to the second connection clear-down attempt, the user treats the channel as out of order and enters the Null state. If the user receives a RELEASE COMPLETE from the network before T308 expires, it clears down the virtual channel, releases the Call Reference, and enters the Null state.

10.5.2 Connection Clear-Down by the Network

The network can initiate a connection clear-down by sending a RELEASE message and starting its timer T308. The user responds with a RELEASE COMPLETE, whereupon the network stops T308, clears down the virtual channels, and releases the Call Reference. The connection clear-down is then complete. If T308 expires before the network receives a RELEASE COMPLETE, the RELEASE message is repeated and T308 restarted. If T308 expires a second time before a RELEASE COMPLETE is received, the network marks the ATM channel as out of order and clears the Call Reference.

10.6   Connection Restart

The restart process is used to reset a virtual channel to its original Idle state after bit errors have occurred. A restart can be initiated by the user or by the network. The Restart process is triggered by sending a RESTART message and simultaneously starting a T316 timer. A RESTART ACKNOWLEDGE message received in response to the RESTART indicates that the Restart procedure was successful, and that the given virtual channel and call reference are ready to use again. If no RESTART ACKNOWLEDGE is received before T316 expires, the RESTART message may be repeated up to two more times. If the repeat attempts are also unsuccessful, the given channel must be treated as out of order.

On receiving a RESTART message, the user or network starts timer T317, performs the necessary internal operations to clear the virtual channel, and then sends a RESTART ACKNOWLEDGE message. Table 10.5 illustrates the format of the RESTART and RESTART ACKNOWLEDGE messages.

10.7   Error Handling

The most important error states that can occur during the connection setup and clear-down processes are described below, with the appropriate actions taken by the communication partners involved.

Table 10.5 RESTART and RESTART ACKNOWLEDGE Messages

Information Element	Direction	Type	Length (Byte)
RESTART			
Protocol Discriminator	U ◄─ N	M	1
Call Reference	U ◄─ N	M	1
Message Type	U ◄─► N	M	2
Message Length	U ◄─► N	M	2
Connection Identifier	U ◄─► N	O	1–9
Restart Indicator	U ◄─► N	M	5
RESTART ACKNOWLEDGE			
Protocol Discriminator	U ◄─► N	M	1
Call Reference	U ◄─ N	M	1
Message Type	U ◄─► N	M	2
Message Length	U ◄─► N	M	2
Connection Identifier	U ◄─► N	O	1–9
Restart Indicator	U ◄─► N	M	5

M Mandatory
N Network
O Optional
U User

10.7.1   Invalid Protocol Discriminator

Messages with an invalid protocol discriminator are simply ignored.

10.7.2   Short Messages

Messages that are too short to contain a complete information element are also ignored.

10.7.3   Invalid Call Reference Format

If bytes 1 and 5 through 8 of the call reference information element are not set to the value 0, or if the call reference length field contains a value other than 3, the entire message is ignored.

Invalid Call Reference

1. Whenever any message except SETUP, RELEASE, RELEASE COMPLETE, STATUS ENQUIRY, or STATUS is received with a call reference that does not refer to an active call or to a call in progress, the receiver clears down the connection by sending a RELEASE COMPLETE message with Cause #81, "Invalid call reference value."

2. If a RELEASE COMPLETE message is received with a call reference that does not refer to an active call or to a call in progress, the message is simply ignored.

3. A SETUP message with a call reference that does not refer to an active call or to a call in progress, and with a call reference flag incorrectly set to 1, is likewise ignored.

4. If a SETUP message is received with a call reference that does refer to an active call or to a call in progress, the message is ignored.

5. If any message except RESTART, RESTART ACKNOWLEDGE, or STATUS is received with the global call reference, no action should be taken on this message, but a STATUS message is returned using the global call reference, indicating the current state associated with the global call reference and Cause #81, "Invalid call reference."

6. A STATUS or STATUS ENQUIRY message with a call reference that does not refer to an active call or to a call in progress is simply ignored.

7. If a RESTART message is received specifying the global call reference with the call reference flag incorrectly set to 1, or if a RESTART ACKNOWLEDGE message is received specifying the global call reference with the call reference flag incorrectly set to 0, no action should be taken on the message, but a STATUS message should be returned indicating Cause #81, "Invalid call reference."

10.7.4   Message Type Errors

Whenever an unrecognized or unexpected message is received, except RELEASE or RELEASE COMPLETE, the receiver returns a STATUS message with Cause #97, "Message type non-existent or not implemented," or Cause #101, "Message not compatible with call state."

If the unexpected message is a RELEASE, however, the network connection and the call to the remote user must be cleared down with the cause contained in the RELEASE message received, or if no cause was included, with Cause #31, "Normal, unspecified." The network then releases the call reference, stops all timers, and enters the Null state. If a user receives an unexpected RELEASE message, the user must release the virtual channel, return a RELEASE COMPLETE message to the network, release the call reference, stop all timers, and enter the Null state.

If the network receives an unexpected RELEASE COMPLETE message, it must disconnect and release the virtual channel, and clear down the network connection and the call to the remote user indicating the cause given in the message received or, if no cause was included, Cause #111, "Protocol error, unspecified." The network also releases the call reference, stops all timers, and enters the Null state. Whenever a user receives an unexpected RELEASE COMPLETE message, the user must disconnect and release the virtual channel, release the call reference, stop all timers, and enter the Null state.

10.7.5   General Information Element Errors

Information Element Sequence

Information elements must be sent in the following order:

- Protocol Discriminator
- Call Reference
- Message Type
- Message Length
- Other information elements

Information elements of variable length can be sent in any order.

Duplicate Information Elements

If an information element is repeated in a message in which repetition of the information element is not permitted, only the contents of the information element appearing first shall be handled. All subsequent repetitions of the information element are ignored.

Mandatory Information Element Missing

When a message other than SETUP, RELEASE, or RELEASE COMPLETE is received that lacks one or more mandatory information elements, no action is taken on the message. A STATUS message is then returned with Cause #96, "Mandatory information element missing." If a SETUP message is received that lacks one or more mandatory information elements, a RELEASE COMPLETE message is returned with Cause #96, "Mandatory information element missing."

Mandatory Information Element Content Errors

If a message other than SETUP, RELEASE, or RELEASE COMPLETE is received in which one or more mandatory information elements have invalid contents, no state change occurs. A STATUS message is returned with Cause #100, "Invalid information element contents."

If a SETUP message is received in which one or more mandatory information elements has invalid contents, a RELEASE COMPLETE message is returned with Cause #100, "Invalid information element contents."

Unrecognized Information Elements, Optional Information Element Content Errors

If a message is received that contains one or more unknown information elements, action is taken on the message and those information elements that are recognized and have valid contents. If the message received is not a RELEASE or RELEASE COMPLETE, a STATUS message is returned that contains Cause #99, "Information element non-existent or not implemented," along with the information element identifier of each unrecognized information element. RELEASE and RELEASE COMPLETE messages with unknown information elements are treated as follows:

1. If a RELEASE message is received that has one or more unrecognized information elements, a RELEASE COMPLETE message with Cause #99, "Information element non-existent or not implemented," is returned.

2. A RELEASE COMPLETE message with unknown information elements is ignored completely.

If a message contains one or more information elements with invalid contents, then action is taken only on those information elements that are valid. A STATUS message is also sent containing Cause #100, "Invalid information element contents," with the information element identifier of each invalid information element in the diagnostic field. If the corrupt information includes the address information fields, then Cause #43, "Access information discarded," is sent rather than Cause #100. If an information element is recognized but should not be present in the given message, it is treated as an unrecognized information element.

AAL Signaling Errors

If an AAL signaling error occurs, all connections not yet started are initialized and a T309 timer is started for each active connection. Then a restart of the AAL signaling layer is initiated. If any connection's T309 timer expires before the AAL signaling layer can be restarted, that connection is deactivated with Cause #27, "Destination out of order." The ATM channel is placed in the "released" state and the call reference is deleted.

STATUS ENQUIRY

Users may send a STATUS ENQUIRY message to determine the state of a call at a peer station. When the STATUS ENQUIRY message is sent, timer T322 is started in anticipation of an incoming STATUS message. Only one unanswered STATUS ENQUIRY message may be outstanding at any given time. A station that receives a STATUS ENQUIRY message must respond with a STATUS message containing Cause #30, "Response to STATUS ENQUIRY," and indicating the current call state. When the STATUS ENQUIRY sender receives the STATUS message, it stops its T322 timer and evaluates the call state information received. If no STATUS response is received before T322 expires, the STATUS ENQUIRY can be repeated one or more times, depending on the implementation. If the timer expires after the last attempt, the connection is cleared down with Cause #41, "Temporary failure."

Procedure on Receipt of a STATUS Message

If a STATUS message is received that indicates that the peer station is in an incompatible state for call handling, the connection can be cleared down with Cause #101, "Message not compatible with call state," or the implementation may attempt to correct the fault. The decision as to whether the two stations' call states are incompatible with one another is left to the given implementation, except in the following three cases:

1. If a STATUS message is received indicating that the peer station is in a state other than Null, and the station receiving the STATUS message is in the Null state itself, then the receiver responds with a RELEASE message and Cause #101, "Message not compatible with call state."

2. If a STATUS message is received signaling that the peer station is in a state other than Null, and the station receiving the STATUS message is in the "Release Request" state, the receiver shall not respond.

3. If a STATUS message is received signaling that the peer station is in the Null state, and the station receiving the STATUS message is not in the Null state, then the receiver of the STATUS message shall change to the Null state.

If a STATUS message is received that signals a compatible call state but contains Cause #96, #97, #99, #100, or #101, the response is left to the given implementation. If no particular action is specified, the connection in question should be cleared down using the Cause indicated in the STATUS message received.

10.8 Comparing ITU-T and ATM Forum UNI Signaling

10.8.1 History

To enable manufacturers to develop ATM components before the definitive adoption of international standards by the ITU-T, the ATM Forum also developed specifications for ATM signaling in its UNI 3.0, 3.1, 4.0, and 4.1 documents. The signaling specification in UNI 3.0 was published before ITU-T Recommendation Q.2931 in the second half of 1993, and is incompatible with Q.2931 because the service-specific connection-oriented protocol (SSCOP) sublayer of the SAAL used with UNI 3.0 is different from that used with Q.2931. The reason for this situation was that, after the ATM Forum had adopted a prenormative version of the ITU-T's SSCOP sublayer, believing it to be finished, the ITU-T made a last-minute change in its definition to turn the SSCOP sublayer into a trailer-based protocol from one that had used both a header and a trailer. This change was done to make processing more efficient, as AAL-5 is also a trailer-based protocol and higher layer contents of the AAL-5 PDU did not, consequently, have to be moved in memory because the PDUs at both layers started with the payload. The adopted ITU-T recommendation for the SSCOP was standardized in Recommendation Q.2110 in July 1994. The ATM Forum quickly updated its UNI 3.0 specification to use this version of SSCOP and the resulting specification became UNI 3.1, which was published late in 1994, still before Q.2931 (February 1995) and a sister recommendation Q.2971 (November 1995), the latter of which standardizes route-initiated join point-to-multipoint signaling. Note that UNI 3.0 and UNI 3.1 already supported point-to-point and point-to-multipoint signaling. Work continued in the ATM Forum to add leaf-initiated join point-to-multipoint signaling; this resulted in the publication of UNI 4.0 in July 1996. The reader might be forgiven for wondering why this apparent competition existed between the ATM Forum and the ITU-T. In reality, the work on the ATM Forum signaling specifications and the ITU-T signaling recommendations was largely done by the same core people, who attended both bodies; the ITU-T tends to move more slowly than the ATM Forum because its procedures are more cumbersome; it is a subcommittee of the United Nations and, as such, requires the agreement of member countries for a recommendation to be approved. This can take lots of time, although in recent years, new procedures have speeded this up. In case the reader has any doubts, the work of both organizations has been focused on compatible standards and specifications—there are not two completely separate signaling systems! ATM Forum UNI 4.0 is actually based on the ITU-T Recommendations Q.2931 and Q.2971 rather than UNI 3.1, as is clear from the text of that specification, so in many ways UNI 4.1 (plus UNI 4.0 addenda) is the superset and most useful specification from either body, as UNI 4.1 is a further development of UNI 4.0, incorporating two of the UNI 4.0 addenda plus other changes from the ATM Forum and the ITU-T. Figure 10.16 shows graphically the history for signaling standards development.

10.8.2 Signaling: ATM Forum UNI 3.1 versus ITU-T Q.2931/Q.2971

The ATM Adaptation Layer for signaling (SAAL) as specified in UNI 3.1 is based only on AAL5. Nonetheless, the sublayer definitions for this SAAL, CP-AAL, and SSCS with the Service-Specific Coordination Function (SSCF) and the Service-Specific Connection-Oriented Peer-to-Peer Protocol (SSCOP) are identical with those in the corresponding ITU-T Recommendation.

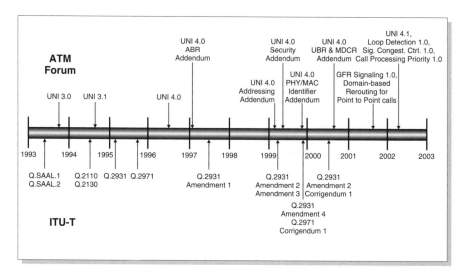

Figure 10.16
UNI signaling developments over time.

UNI 3.1: Signaling Channels and Metasignaling

The default channel for all signaling is a point-to-point-channel with the fixed values VCI = 5 and VPI = 0. In addition, however, metasignaling and broadcast (point-to-multipoint) signaling are also supported.

UNI 3.1: VPI, VPCI, and VCI

While VPCIs may be used to identify the ATM virtual path used for data transmission, these VPCIs are limited to a length of 8 bits (as opposed to 16 bits in Q.2931) in order to be identical with the VPI. Furthermore, no negotiation is possible between user and network regarding the VPCI/VCI values to be used.

UNI 3.1: Addressing

UNI 3.1 addressing also differs from the Q.2931 specification in that it uses only two number types ("Unknown" and "International number") and the numbering plans E.164 (the ISDN numbering system) and ISO NSAP. When E.164 numbers are used, the number type is "International Number." ISO NSAP numbers are designated as "Unknown."

UNI 3.1: Protocol States in Connection Setup and Active Connections

The UNI 3.1 specification supports all of the user and network protocol states defined in Q.2931, with the following exceptions:

- Call Delivered (user state U4; network state N4): Used on outgoing calls when a ring tone has been generated at the receiving station, but the call has not yet been answered
- Call Received (user state U7; network state N7): Used on incoming calls when a ring tone has been generated, but the call has not yet been answered

Furthermore, UNI 3.1 does not support "overlap" signaling, which Q.2931 provides for internetworking applications that require additional connection information:

- Overlap Sending (state U2/N2)
- Overlap Receiving (state U25/N25)

Q.2931 and UNI 3.1 Message Types and Information Elements

The following Q.2931 signaling messages are not supported by UNI 3.1:

- ALERTING
- PROGRESS
- SETUP ACKNOWLEDGE
- INFORMATION
- NOTIFY

Because UNI 3.1 has no NOTIFY message, the information element "Notification Indicator" is also not supported. This information element is used in the Q.2931 NOTIFY message to obtain information about the connection state. This affects the messages CALL PROCEEDING, CONNECT ACKNOWLEDGE, RELEASE, and SETUP.

UNI 3.1 supports only the default codeset 0, while Q.2931 also supports codesets 5, 6, and 7. Furthermore, the definitions of certain UNI 3.1 information elements are slightly modified with respect to Q.2931. The maximum length of the "Traffic Descriptor" information element in the SETUP message, for example, is increased to 30 bytes (as opposed to 20 in Q.2931), while the length of the "Transit Network Selection" element is limited to 8 bytes. A complete list of the differences between UNI 3.1 and Q.2931 signaling is found in Appendix E of the ATM Forum UNI specification.

UNI 3.1: Permissible Virtual Channel Identifier (VCI) Values

The ATM Forum signaling protocol divides up the range of VCI values as follows: VCIs 0 through 15 are reserved for ITU-T, 16 through 31 are reserved for the ATM Forum, and values from 32 through 65,535 are available to users.

UNI 3.1: Point-to-Point Connection Setup at the Calling Station and at the Station Called

Due to the reduced set of message types, point-to-point connection setup is simpler in ATM Forum signaling, as described below.

Connection Setup at the Calling Station. The caller initiates connection set-up by sending a SETUP message with the QoS and traffic parameters, but *without* specifying an ATM path or channel to use. (If the SETUP message does contain VPCI/VCI values, they are ignored.) The network selects the VPCI/VCI value for the connection. As mentioned above, the VPCI is restricted to 8 bits, so that the value is the same as that of the corresponding VPI. Permissible VPCI values are thus in the range from 0 to 255. If the network is able to provide the service requested, it answers with a CALL PROCEEDING message and forwards the setup request to the receiving station. If the network is unable to provide the specified QoS parameters, the connection setup is aborted with a RELEASE COMPLETE message indicating Cause #49, "Quality-of-service unavailable." If the network cannot provide the requested user cell rate, a RELEASE COMPLETE message is returned with Cause #51, "User cell rate unavailable." If the network is able to complete the call successfully, it returns a CONNECT message to the sending station. This completes the connection setup, and the connection is active. Acknowledgment of the CONNECT message by the calling station is not supported.

Connection Setup at the Station Called. The network signals an incoming call by sending a SETUP message to the station called. This SETUP message contains the VPCI/VCI values to be used by the receiving station. These values are not negotiable. If the station called cannot accept these values, it must abort the connection setup with a RELEASE COMPLETE message and Cause #35, "Requested VPCI/VCI unavailable." The station called does not perform any address or compatibility checking. Only the requested QoS parameters and user cell rate are verified. If these setup parameters are available locally, the station responds with a CALL PROCEEDING or a CONNECT message. As in Q.2931, the CONNECT message completes the connection setup and activates the connection. The network does not acknowledge the CONNECT message by sending a CONNECT ACKNOWLEDGE, however.

UNI 3.1 and Q.2971 Point-to-Multipoint Connections

A point-to-multipoint connection begins with the establishment of a root connection from one station, the "root node," to another, the "first leaf node." Once this connection is active, the ADD PARTY message can be used to connect other leaf nodes to the existing root link. The ADD PARTY message must contain the same QoS and traffic parameters as the SETUP message that was sent to initiate the root connection. Stations that receive an ADD PARTY message can respond with ADD PARTY REJECT or ADD PARTY ACKNOWLEDGE. When the root node has received the ADD PARTY ACKNOWLEDGE message, the new connection enters the active state. The root node does not need to wait for an ADD PARTY message to be answered before sending another. Thus several ADD PARTY messages may be outstanding at the same time. Unlike point-to-point-connections, point-to-multipoint connections permit only symmetrical bandwidth allocation—that is, the same communication bandwidth is available on the outgoing and incoming channels.

ATM Forum UNI Timers

The ATM signaling timers defined in UNI 3.1 are the same as those in Q.2931 and Q.2971, with the exception of T301, T302, T304, and T397, which are not supported by UNI 3.1, and timers T333 and T334, which were added to Q.2931 in amendment 4 of the standard. The ATM Forum defines an additional timer for point-to-multipoint processes: T331 (UNI 4.0 and 4.1). Tables 10.6 and 10.7 list the UNI protocol timers.

Table 10.6 Timers for UNI Signaling Processes: Q.2931, Q.2971, and ATM Forum (User Side)

Timer Number	Default Value	Start	Stop	On First Expiration	On Second Expiration	Implemetation
T301 (Q.2931 only)	≥ 3 min	ALERT received	CONNECT received	Clear call		M (if symmetrical connections supported)
T302 (Q.2931 only)	10–15 s	SETUP ACK sent	Sending Complete indication	If information incomplete, clear call Otherwise, CALL PROCEEDING		M (if overlap sending and receiving supported)
T303	4 s	SETUP sent	CONNECT, CALL PROCEEDING, ALERT RELEASE COMPLETE received	Repeat SETUP restart T303	Abort call set-up	M
T304 (Q.2931 only)	30 s	SETUP ACK received; restart when INFO received	CALL PROCEEDING; ALERT; CONNECT received	Clear call		M
T308	30 s	RELEASE sent	RELEASE COMPLETE or RELEASE received	Repeat RELEASE, restart T308		
T309	10 s	SAAL aborted	SAAL active again	Clear call; delete VCIs and call references		M
T310	30–120 s	CALL PROCEEDING received	ALERT, CONNECT or RELEASE received	Send RELEASE		M
T313	4 s	CONNECT sent	CONNECT ACK received	Send RELEASE		M
T316	2 min	RESTART sent	RESTART ACK received	Repeat RESTART several times	Repeat RESTART several times	M
T317	Implementation specific, but < T316	RESTART received	All call references deleted	Report error		M
T322	4 s	STATUS ENQUIRY sent	STATUS, RELEASE or RELEASE COMPLETE received	Repeat STATUS ENQUIRY	Repeat STATUS ENQUIRY	M
T397	≥ 3 min	ALERTING or ADD PARTY ALERTING received	ADD PARTY ACKNOWLEDGE received	Drop the Party (DROP PARTY or RELEASE)	Timer is not restarted	Only mandatory if Annex A of Q.2971 supported
T398	4 s	DROP PARTY sent	DROP PARTY ACK or RELEASE received	Send DROP PARTY ACK or RELEASE COMPLETE	Timer is not restarted	M
T399	14 s UNI 3.0/3.1 34–124 s (UNI 4.0)	ADD PARTY sent	ADD PARTY ACK, ADD PARTY REJECT, or RELEASE received	Delete party	Timer is not restarted	M
T331 (ATM Forum 4.0 only)	60 s	LEAF SETUP REQUEST sent	SETUP, ADD PARTY, or LEAF SETUP FAILURE received	Repeat LEAF SETUP REQUEST and restart T331	Delete connection	M
T333 (Q.2931 Amendment 4)	10 s	Sending of "End to End conn. compl. indication requ."	Receipt of "End to End connection completion indication requested"	Implementation specific		M

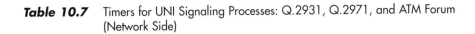

Table 10.7 Timers for UNI Signaling Processes: Q.2931, Q.2971, and ATM Forum (Network Side)

Timer Number	Default Value	Start	Stop	On First Expiration	On Second Expiration	Implemetation
T301 (Q.2931 only)	≥ 3 min	ALERT received	CONNECT received	Clear call		M (if symmetrical connections supported)
T302 (Q.2931 only)	10–15 s	SETUP ACK sent; restart when INFO sent	Sending Complete indication	If information incomplete, clear call Otherwise, CALL PROCEEDING		M (if overlap sending and receiving supported)
T303	4 s	SETUP sent	CONNECT, CALL PROCEEDING, ALERT SETUP ACK, RELEASE COMPLETE received	Repeat SETUP restart T303	Abort call set-up	M
T304 (Q.2931 only)	20 s	SETUP ACK received	INFO sent or CALL PROCEEDING, ALERT, CONNECT received	Clear call		
T306 (Q.2931 only)	20 s	RELEASE with Progress Indicator 8 sent	RELEASE COMPLETE received	Stop ringing		M (if inband alarms supported)
T308	30 s	RELEASE sent	RELEASE COMPLETE or RELEASE received	Repeat RELEASE, restart T308	Set VC to maintenance state	M
T309	10 s	SAAL aborted	SAAL active again	Clear call; delete VCIs and call references		O
T310	10 s	CALL PROCEEDING received	ALERT, CONNECT or RELEASE received	Clear call		M
T316	2 min	RESTART sent	RESTART ACK received	Repeat RESTART several times	Repeat RESTART several times	M
T317	Implementation specific, but < T316	RESTART received	All call references deleted	Report error		M
T322	4 s	STATUS ENQUIRY sent	STATUS, RELEASE or RELEASE COMPLETE received	Repeat STATUS ENQUIRY	Repeat STATUS ENQUIRY	M
T397	≥ 3 min	ALERTING or ADD PARTY ALERTING received	ADD PARTY ACKNOWLEDGE received	Drop the Party (DROP PARTY or RELEASE)	Timer is not restarted	M
T398	4 s	DROP PARTY sent	DROP PARTY ACK or RELEASE received	Send DROP PARTY ACK or RELEASE COMPLETE	Timer is not restarted	M
T399	14 s	ADD PARTY sent	ADD PARTY ACK, ADD PARTY REJECT, or RELEASE received	Delete party	Timer is not restarted	M
T334 (Q.2931 Amendment 4)	1 s	Connect sent with "End-to-End conn. compl. indictation requ."	CONNECTION AVAILABLE received	No action		M

10.8.3 ATM Forum Signaling: UNI 3.0

The most important difference between the UNI 3.0 and UNI 3.1 signaling specifications is that the adaptation layer for signaling (SAAL) in UNI 3.1 is compatible with the corresponding definition in Q.2931. This is not true of UNI 3.0, which uses the older SAAL specifications Q.SAAL1 and Q.SAAL2. Furthermore, UNI 3.0 signaling supports neither metasignaling nor broadcast signaling.

10.8.4 ATM Forum Signaling: UNI 4.0

The ATM Forum signaling specification, UNI 4.0, closely approximates ITU-T Recommendations Q.2931 and Q.2971. UNI 4.0 supports all of the Q.2931 signaling messages with the exception of SETUP ACKNOWLEDGE and INFORMATION, which in any case are only required at transitions between narrowband and broadband ISDN networks. In addition to the UNI 3.1 messages specific to the ATM Forum, UNI 4.0 also defines the messages LEAF SETUP REQUEST and LEAF SETUP FAILURE, as well as the corresponding protocol states. Other important differences from Q.2931 and Q.2971 include the following:

- Restarting all VCs in a VP is not supported.
- The protocol states U2, N2, U15, N15, U17, N17, U25, and N25, are not supported.
- The locking and nonlocking shift mechanisms for changing between different codesets are not supported.
- Compatibility verification is not supported.
- VCI values 16 through 31 are reserved for use by the ATM Forum.
- The address registration mechanism defined in UNI 4.0 is not present in Q.2931 or Q.2971.
- UNI 4.0 defines new information elements to support the following services: Direct Dial-in (DDI), Multiple Subscriber Numbers (MSN), Calling Line Identification Presentation (CLIP), Calling Line Identification Restriction (CLIR), Connected Line Identification Presentation (COLP), Connected Line Identification Restriction (COLR), Subaddressing (SUB), and User-to-User Signaling (UUS).
- UNI 4.0 defines new procedures for proxy signaling. This mechanism allows a proxy signaling agent (PSA) to perform signaling processes for

one or more other users that lack signaling capabilities. In this case the users share the same ATM address. A server connected to the ATM network over four 155 Mbit/s interfaces, for example, could use the same ATM address for all of them.

- UNI 4.0 defines processes to support several virtual UNIs over a single physical user–network interface. With this feature wireless ATM can be implemented.

- Processes, timers, and protocol states were also added for connection requests initiated by a leaf node in a point-to-multipoint connection (LEAF SETUP REQUEST).

10.8.5   ATM Forum Signaling: UNI 4.0 Addenda

Since the publication of the UNI 4.0 specification, a number of changes and additions have been made and were published in several ATM Forum addenda. Two of these addenda are integrated into the new UNI 4.1 signaling specification, as discussed in the next section. The most significant of these modifications are described below.

Modification of Active Connections

To allow traffic parameter modification for existing calls, the following new message types were defined by the ATM forum, complementing the old ATM UNI 4.0 signaling specification. (With the exception of CONNECTION AVAILABLE, which as been added to Q.2931 in amendment 4, 12/99), these messages are not supported in the Q.2931 specification):

MODIFY REQUEST
MODIFY ACKNOWLEDGE
MODIFY REJECT
CONNECTION AVAILABLE

A connection modification can now be initiated sending a MODIFY RE-QUEST message. If the called station is capable of fulfilling the request, it replies with a MODIFY ACKNOWLEDGE. If requested by the calling party, the called party concludes the process by sending CONNECTION AVAIL-ABLE to confirm the successful completion of the connection modification. Parameters that can be modified include SCR, MBS, MFS, BCT, MDCR,

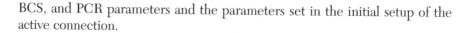

BCS, and PCR parameters and the parameters set in the initial setup of the active connection.

Specification of a PHY MAC Identifier

ATM physical layers with multiple physical layer connections such as ADSL or shared media topologies require the capability to assign a (local) ATM virtual connection to a physical or MAC layer entity. For this purpose a new information element, the PHY/MAC layer identifier, was defined. Currently there are two PHY/MAC layer information element types specified: IEEE 802.14 and ADSL. These information elements are used in the network's SETUP message, to send the selected PHY MAC identifier to the end user. If supported by the implementation, the PHY MAC indentifier value can be negotiated between network and end user, otherwise the default value of the network is being used.

Support for UBR Connections with Minimum Desired Cell Rate (MDCR)

For the purpose of allowing the specification of a minimum desired cell rate between two parties, the ATM Forum defined the Minimum Desired Cell Rate (MDCR) information element, which can be used within a SETUP or ADD PARTY message to request an MDCR. Nodes that do not support the MDCR capability can ignore the information element and proceed with their operation.

Behavior Class Selector Support

By adding the information element Optional Traffic Attributes, the ATM Forum adds the capability to transmit a Behavior Class Selector (BCS) with a UBR connection setup. For this, an Optional Traffic Attributes information element needs to be sent within the SETUP or ADD PARTY message along with the desired BCS value.

Guaranteed Frame Rate (GFR) Signaling Support

Another new feature added is the capability to request a guaranteed frame length by including a Broadband Bearer Capability information element indicating GFR.1 (no tagging allowed) or GFR.2 (tagging allowed) in the ATM transfer capability field.

Hard and Soft Rerouting

Finally, a new rerouting services information element was designed to handle the negotiations for rerouting procedures. The rerouting information element is included in the SETUP and the CONNECT message during the initial call setup process. Two types of rerouting services are defined: interdomain (scope: end-to-end) and intra-domain (scope: local to the rerouting domain). Hard rerouting is intended to be used for failure recovery and soft rerouting for administrative purposes.

10.8.6 ATM Forum Signaling: UNI 4.1

UNI 4.1, which was published as this book was going to press, is based on UNI 4.0 and incorporates corrected versions of the Addendum to UNI Signaling V4.0 for ABR parameter negotiation (af-sig-0076.000) and the Addressing Addendum to ATM User-Network Interface (UNI) Signaling Specification Version 4.0 (af-cs-0107.000). It also includes some technical and editorial changes made by the ATM Forum, as well as changes resulting from developments in the ITU-T since the publication of UNI 4.0. Other addenda to UNI 4.0 are also relevant to UNI 4.1; UNI 4.1 contains some changes to these addenda. One major change in UNI 4.1 is the removal of support for leaf-initiated join for point-to-multipoint connections, which was introduced in UNI 4.0 but never standardized by the ITU-T.

Chapter 11

THE ATM PROTOCOL: NNI SIGNALING (B-ISUP, PNNI, AINI)

For connection setup between two NNI interfaces, the ITU-T developed the broadband protocol B-ISUP (ITU-T Q.2761–Q.2764), modeled after the narrowband ISDN protocol ISUP (ISDN User Part). B-ISUP contains many of the proven mechanisms and functions of ISUP. Only the characteristic parameters and processes of broadband networks with their virtual connections were added. By the same token, ISUP functions that are only practical in conventional connection-oriented networks were omitted. While B-ISUP is used primarily for NNI signaling in wide area networks, the ATM Forum Private Network–Network Interface (PNNI), though designed for the private user network, and based on UNI signaling, has been used in both private and public ATM networks. Unlike B-ISUP, PNNI is able to select routes for the desired connections, a function that has to be implemented completely independently by manufacturers of B-ISUP switching systems. In ATM networks based on PNNI, ATM components can run immediately, whereas networks with B-ISUP signaling first require the definition and implementation of route selection and bandwidth monitoring functions. A recent development of signaling is the introduction of the ATM Inter-Network Interface (AINI), used for interfacing two networks based on different NNI protocols (B-ISUP and PNNI); this is discussed briefly at the end of the chapter.

11.1   B-ISUP Signaling

The B-ISUP protocol is the NNI counterpart to the UNI protocols Q.2931/Q.2971 (or ATM Forum UNI 4.0/4.1) and extends virtual UNI connections across the ATM network to the end system called. There the NNI connection is translated back into a UNI connection. However, B-ISUP is unable to provide other functions, such as:

- Bandwidth management
- Route selection
- Routing table maintenance or
- OAM process control for existing virtual connections.

The implementation of these functions is left to the component manufacturers or the operators of B-ISDN networks. The B-ISUP protocol builds on Message Transfer Part, Level 3 (MTP-3), specified especially for ATM, which in turn uses the NNI SAAL layer to transport its data packets (Figure 11.1).

Communication between B-ISUP and MTP-3 uses only the following four messages:

MTP-3 B-ISUP Messages	Parameters
MTP TRANSFER	(OPC, DPC, SLS, SIO, Signaling information)
MTP PAUSE	(DPC)
MTP RESUME	(DPC)
MTP STATUS	(DPC, Cause)

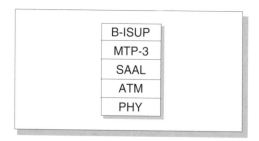

Figure 11.1
The B-ISUP protocol layer model.

B-ISUP uses the MTP-TRANSFER message to request MTP-3 message transport services. The MTP-3 layer uses this message to announce signaling message transfers to the B-ISUP layer. Each MTP-TRANSFER contains the following parameters: Originating Point Code (OPC), Destination Point Code (DPC), Signaling Link Selection Code (SLS), Service Information Octet (SIO), and the actual signaling information. MTP-PAUSE is used by the MTP layer to notify B-ISUP that no signaling information can be transferred to the specified DPC. MTP-RESUME is used to announce that the DPC is addressable again. Finally, MTP-STATUS is used to convey the reason why a DPC is not reachable.

11.1.1 Basic Signaling Processes in B-ISUP

In B-ISDN networks, ATM switches are connected to one another over one or more virtual paths. The bandwidth available for these interswitch paths must be specified by the network operator, and depends in practice on the traffic volume between the switches concerned. (In narrowband ISDN networks such interswitch paths are called trunk groups.) The purpose of the B-ISUP protocol is to accept incoming connection requests from the UNI interfaces and to set up appropriate virtual connections with the requested bandwidth over the VPs available at that moment. The first step in this process is to assign a VPCI (Virtual Path Connection Identifier) to the connection being set up. One of the two switches involved is then responsible for setting up the virtual connection and reserving the required bandwidth. Which switch performs these functions depends on the VPCI chosen: by default, the switch with the higher signaling point code (SPC) is responsible for all even VPCIs. The switch with the lower SPC manages the odd-numbered connections. The appropriate switch then designates a virtual channel in the VP and reserves the required bandwidth. If this process is successful, the connection is activated.

11.1.2 B-ISUP Messages

Each B-ISUP message consists of the following fields: Routing Label, Message Type, Message Length, Message Compatibility Information, and Payload (Figure 11.2).

The Answer Message (ANM): This message is sent to the calling station and indicates that the station called has answered the connection setup request (see Table 11.2). It corresponds to the CONNECT message in the UNI protocol.

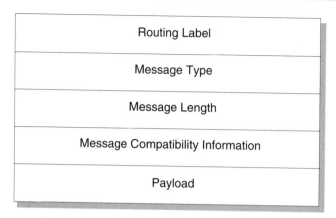

| Routing Label |
| Message Type |
| Message Length |
| Message Compatibility Information |
| Payload |

Figure 11.2
B-ISUP message format.

Blocking Message (BLO): A switch that receives a BLO message stops all further connection setup attempts. Incoming connections can still be received, however.

Blocking Acknowledgement Message (BLA): A BLA message acknowledges that a BLO was received and all connection setup attempts have been blocked.

Call Progress Message (CPG): The CPG message is sent on entering certain protocol states to indicate the correct progress of the connection setup procedure.

Confusion Message (CFN): The CFN message is sent by a system that has received an unknown or unidentifiable message.

Consistency Check End Message (CCE): This message announces the completion of the link verification that must be performed before the virtual connection is activated for data communication.

Consistency Check End Acknowledge Message (CCEA): The CCEA message is sent to acknowledge the receipt of a CCE message.

Consistency Check Request Acknowledgement Message (CCRA): The CCRA message acknowledges the receipt of a CCR message.

Consistency Check Request Message (CCR): The CCR message instructs the remote switch to perform the verification test for a virtual path. After receiving the CCR, the switch verifies the VPCI value of the specified VP and begins monitoring the ATM cells received over the path.

Table 11.1 B-ISUP Message Types

Message Type	Coding
Address Complete	0000 0110
Answer	0000 1001
Application Transport	0100 0001
Blocking	0001 0011
Blocking Acknowledgement	0001 0101
Call Progress	0010 1100
Call Transfer	0011 1001
Confusion	0010 1111
Connection Available	1000 1011
Consistency Check End	0001 0111
Consistency Check End Acknowledgement	0001 1000
Consistency Check Request	0000 0101
Consistency Check Request Acknowledgement	0001 0001
Facility	0011 0011
Forward Transfer	0000 1000
IAM Acknowledgement	0000 1010
IAM Reject	0000 1011
Identification Request	0011 0110
Identification Response	0011 0111
Initial Address	0000 0001
Loop Prevention	0100 0000
Modify Acknowledge	0011 1010
Modify Reject	0011 1011
Modify Request	0011 1100
Network Resource Management	0011 0010
Pre-release Information	0100 0010
Release	0000 1100
Release Complete	0001 0000
Reset	0001 0010
Reset Acknowledgement	0000 1111
Resume	0000 1110
Segmentation (national use)	0011 1000
Subsequent Address	0000 0010
Suspend	0000 1101
Unblocking	0001 0100
Unblocking Acknowledgement	0001 0110
User Part Available	0011 0101
User Part Test	0011 0100
User-to-User Information	0010 1101

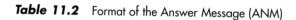

Table 11.2 Format of the Answer Message (ANM)

ANM-Parameter	Length (Bytes)
AAL Parameters	?–22
Access Delivery Information	5–6
Additional Connected Number	6–15
Backward Narrow-Band Interworking Indicator	5–6
Broadband Low Layer Information	10–?
Call History Information	6–7
Charge Indicator	5–6
Connected Number	6–15
Connected Sub-Address	7–27
Destination Signaling Identifier	8–9
Echo Control Information	5–6
In-Band Information Indicator	5–6
Narrow-Band Bearer Capability	11–?
Narrow-Band High Layer Compatibility	11–?
Narrow-Band Low Layer Compatibility	11–?
Notification (Note)	5–6
OAM Traffic Descriptor	6–7
Progress Indicator	11–?
Redirection Number Restriction	5–6
Segmentation Indicator (National Use)	5–6
User-to-User Indicators	5–6
User-to-User Information	7–136

Connection Available: CONNECTION AVAILABLE is used to confirm the successful completion of the traffic parameter modification of an active connection (see also MODIFY messages).

Exit Message (EXM): The EXM message is returned by a switch that functions as an edge gateway—a component on the boundary between the ATM network and a neighboring network—and indicates that the outbound call was successfully set up (defined only in ANSI T1.648).

Forward Transfer Message (FOT): This message is used by the calling station in semiautomatic systems when operator support is required to set up the connection.

IAM Acknowledgement Message (IAA): The IAA message is sent in response to an IAM (Initial Address Message) to indicate that the required switching capacities are available, that the IAM was accepted,

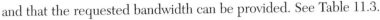

and that the requested bandwidth can be provided. See Table 11.3.

IAM Reject Message (IAR): An IAM Reject message indicates that a connection request initiated by a prior IAM must be denied due to insufficient capacities.

Initial Address Message (IAM): The IAM message is the first message sent to initiate a B-ISUP connection setup. It instructs the remote station to assign a VPCI/VCI and to reserve the required bandwidth. The IAM message corresponds to the SETUP message at the UNI interface. See Table 11.4.

Modify Request, Modify Acknowledge, Modify Reject: The MODIFY messages are used to alter traffic parameters of an existing connection.

Network Resource Management Message (NRM): This message can be used to obtain information about network availability.

Release Message (REL): The RELEASE message initiates a connection clear-down. See Table 11.5.

Release Complete Message (RLC): Release Complete acknowledges the receipt of a Release message and completes the connection clear-down. See Table 11.6.

Reset Message (RSM): A Reset message is used to initialize a connection when one of the communicating parties no longer knows the status of the connection. This may be due to overloads, memory problems, or other extraordinary operating conditions.

Reset Acknowledgement Message (RAM): RAM is sent to acknowledge the reception of an RSM and confirms that the connection concerned has been reset.

Resume Message (RES): The Resume message indicates that the calling station or the station called is operational again after temporary inactivity.

Table 11.3   Format of the IAM Acknowledgement Message (IAA)

IAA-Parameter	Length (Bytes)
Connection Element Identifier	8–9
Destination Signaling Identifier	8–9
Origination Signaling Identifier	8–9

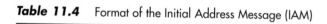

Table 11.4 Format of the Initial Address Message (IAM)

IAM-Parameter	Length (Bytes)
AAL Parameters	?–22
Additional Calling Party Number	6–15
ATM Cell Rate	8–21
Broadband Bearer Capability	7–11
Broadband High Layer Information	?–17
Broadband Low Layer Information	10–?
Called Party Number	7–15
Called Party Sub-Address	7–27
Calling Party Number	6–15
Calling Party Sub-Address	7–27
Calling Partys Category	5–6
Closed User Group Information	9–10
Connected Line ID Request	5–6
Connection Element Identifier	8–9
Echo Control Information	5–6
Forward Narrow-Band Interworking Indicator	5–6
Location Number	7–15
Maximum End-to-End Transit Delay	6–7
MLPP Precedence	10–11
Narrow-Band Bearer Capability	11–?
Narrow-Band High Layer Compatibility	11–?
Narrow-Band Low Layer Compatibility	11–?
National/International Call Indicator	5–6
Notification (Note)	5–6
OAM Traffic Descriptor	6–7
Original Called Number	6–15
Origination ISC Point Code	6–7
Origination Signaling Identifier	8–9
Progress Indicator	11–?
Propagation Delay Counter	6–7
Redirecting Number	6–15
Redirection Information	5–7
Segmentation Indicator (national use)	5–6
Transit Network Selection (national use)	6–?
User-to-User Indicators	5–6
User-to-User Information	7–136

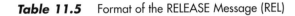

Table 11.5 Format of the RELEASE Message (REL)

REL-Parameter	Length (Bytes)
Access Delivery	5–6
Automatic Congestion Level	5–6
Cause Indicators	6–?
Destination Signaling Identifier	8–9
Notification (Note)	5–6
Progress Indicator	11–?
Redirection Information (national use)	5–7
Redirection Number (national use)	7–15
Redirection Number Restriction (national use)	5–6
Segmentation Indicator (national use)	5–6
User-to-User Indicators	5–6
User-to-User Information	7–136

Segmentation Message (SGM): If a message has to be segmented into several parts, then SGM is used to indicate that the given message is part of a larger message.

Subsequent Address Message (SAM): An SAM message is used to send the number of a station called after the IAM has been sent.

Suspend Message (SUS): SUS indicates that the given station is temporarily inactive.

Unblocking Message (UBL): The UBL message reactivates a component that was blocked by a prior BLO message.

Unblocking Acknowledgement Message (UBA): The UBA message is sent to acknowledge a UBL.

User Part Available Message (UPA): UPA is the response to a User Part Test (UPT) message.

User Part Test Message (UPT): A UPT message is used to verify that a given ISUP component is active.

Table 11.6 Format of the Release Complete Message (RLC)

RLC-Parameter	Length (Bytes)
Cause Indicators	7–?
Destination Signaling Identifier	8–9

User-to-User Information Message (USR): USR messages are used to transport data addressed to the users, not to the network.

11.1.3   Connection Setup in B-ISUP

B-ISUP connection setup begins with the transmission of an Initial Address message (IAM) by a switch A (Figure 11.3). The IAM message corresponds to the setup message at the UNI interface. On sending the IAM, station A starts timer T40b and allocates an Originating Signaling ID (OSID) for the connection. When switch B receives the IAM message, it tests whether the called party number is valid and the corresponding station is active. If so, the VPCI/VCI parameters selected by switch A are now assigned to the receiving end of the connection. Switch A or B, whichever is responsible for managing the connection, now sets up a virtual connection along an appropriate route. (As mentioned above, the switch with the higher SPC is responsible for all even VPCIs, and the switch with the lower SPC manages the odd VPCIs.) The route selection algorithm is not specified in B-ISUP. If the exchange determines that the connection is to be routed to another exchange, it has to select appropriate routing information, which is either stored at the exchange itself, or at a remote database, which then has to be accessed. The selection of the route depends on the Called Party Number, Broadband Bearer Capability, ATM Cell Rate; and, when present, Additional ATM Cell Rate, Minimum ATM Cell Rate, or Alternative ATM Cell Rate, and other optional requested traffic capabilities (QoS). Additionally, if the Maximum End-to-end Transit Delay parameter is present, this is used together with the Propagation Delay Counter as well to select the route.

The information used to determine the routing of the call/connection by the originating exchange will be included in the Set_Up request primitive to enable the correct routing at intermediate exchanges. The Set_Up request primitive implicitly confirms that performance parameter objectives have been met. It indicates the reservation of ATM connection elements. The other connection parameters, such as the AAL parameter, Broadband Low and High Layer Information, Narrowband High Layer Compatibility, and OAM Traffic Descriptor, are transported to the receiver as part of the IAM message, and are analyzed during the receiver's compatibility check. After these procedures have been successfully completed, switch B responds with an IAM Acknowledge message (IAA), which contains its Connection Element ID, the Destination Signaling ID, and the Origination Signaling ID. The Connection Element ID in turn contains the VPCI and VCI of the connection as set up by switch B. These values must be identical with those assigned by switch A.

When A receives them, it stops timer T40b. The Destination Signaling ID (DSID) in the IAA conforms to A's OSID, and the OSID in the IAA is the one assigned to this connection by switch B. After the IAA message, B also sends an Address Complete message (ACM) notifying A that the IAM message was received and completely processed. The most important information elements contained in the ACM message are the Backward Narrowband Interworking Indicator, the Called Party Indicator, the Charge Indicator, and the Destination Signaling Indicator. On receiving the ACM message, switch A starts timer T9b. When the called party answers, switch B stops sending the ring tone (if implemented) and sends the Answer message (ANM) to A. While transporting this message from B to A, all the intermediate links and switches that have been on standby along the connection route are activated. When the ANM message reaches A, timer T9b is stopped and the connection is available for data communication.

Either of the two communicating parties can terminate the connection by sending a Release (REL) message. The station that sends a Release message to initiate the connection clear-down also starts timer T1b. The connection is cleared as soon as the Release message is answered by a Release Complete (RLC). The bandwidth allocation and the assigned VPCI/VCI values are then deleted, and timer T1b is stopped.

Table 11.7 lists all the timers involved in B-ISUP signaling.

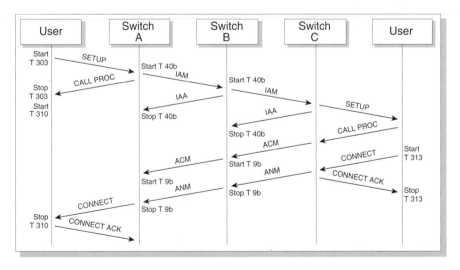

Figure 11.3
Connection setup and clear-down in the UNI/NNI network.

Table 11.7 Timers in B-ISUP

Timer	Time-out	Trigger	Stop	After Expiration
Await Release Complete (T 1b)	15–60 sec	Sending of RELEASE	Receipt of RELEASE COMPLETE	Release of resources, start of maintenance proc. and sending of RESET
User Part Availability (T4b)	5–15 min	Receipt of MTP-STATUS with cause »remote user unavailable«	Expiration or receipt of User-Part-Available message	Sending of a User-Part-Test message and start of T4b
Await Network Resume (T6b)	See Rec. Q.118	The active switch receives SUSPEND-(SUS)	Receipt of RESUME (RES) or RELEASE (REL)	Start of Connection setup
Await Address Complete (T7b)	20–30 s	After sending of the last IAM	Receipt of address complete acknowledgement	Release of all connections (sending of RELEASE)
Await answer (T9b)	See Rec. Q.118	National or international switch receives Address-Complete	Receipt of ANSWER (ANM)	Release of all connections (sending of RELEASE)
Await Blocking Acknowledge (T12b)	15–60 s	Sending of BLOCKING (BLO)	Receipt of BLA-Nachricht	Activation of alarm and maintenance procedures
Await Unblocking Acknowledge (T14b)	15–60 s	Sending of UNBLOCKING (UBL)	Receipt of UBA	Activation of maintancenance procedures
Await Reset Acknowledge (T16b)	15–60 s	Sending of RESET	Receipt of RESET-ACKNOWLEDGE-(RAM)	Resending of RESET
Repeat Reset (T17b)	5–15 M	RAM is not received within »Await Reset Acknowledgement« timer	—	Resending of RESET and activation of maintenance procedures
Short SC (T29b)	300–600 ms	Receipt of congestion indication (T29b not active)	—	Logging of overload message
Long SCC (T30b)	5–10 s	Receipt of congestion indication (T29b not active)	—	Increase of traffic capacity by one level and start of T30b
Segmentation (T34b)	2–4 s	Indication of segmented message received	Receipt of segmented message	Continuation of call setup
Address incomplete (T35b)	15–20 s	If the last number of the calling number (ST) was received and the minimum calling number length was not reached	If the minimum length of a calling number was reached	Sending of RELEASE
Await Network Resume-Inter-national (T38b)	See Rec. Q.118	If then incoming international switch sends SUSPEND	Receipt of RESUME	Sending of RELEASE
Await IAM Acknowledge (T40b)	4–6 s	Sending of a IAM-message	Receipt of a IAM-ACKNOWLEDGEMENT-or IAM-REJECT-message	Release of all resources, activation of maintenance procedures and sending of RESET
Await Consistency Check Request Acknowledgement (T41b)	15–60 s	Sending of a CONSISTENCY-CHECK-REQUEST message (CSR)	Receipt of a CCEA message	Activate maintenance procedure
Await Consistency Check End Acknowledgement (T42b)	15–60 s	Sending of a CONSISTENCY-CHECK-REQUEST-END message (CCE)	Receipt of a CCEA message	Activate maintenance procedures
Await Modify Acknowledge (T43b)	20–30 s	When Modify message is sent	At receipt of Modify message or Modify Reject messsage	Initiate release connection procedure

11.2   The PNNI Protocol

Because the B-ISUP protocol, developed for intranetwork communication in public ATM networks, leaves important functions such as route selection, topology analysis, and the propagation of route information up to the network operator or the switching implementation, a separate NNI protocol had to be created for private networks. For this reason the ATM Forum developed PNNI, an NNI protocol especially tailored to private networks in which the components missing from B-ISUP are specified, as well as several functions that are important in operating large networks. Today, PNNI is used not only in private local area and wide area networks, but also in public ATM networks, especially in North America. At the time of writing, PNNI v1.1 (af-pnni-0055.002) had just been approved and is mainly a consolidation of PNNI v1.0 and four addenda published subsequently. It can be used with UNI 4.0 or UNI 4.1, also just approved.

11.2.1   PNNI Signaling

PNNI (Private Network-to-Network Interface) signaling consists of two protocols: a topology protocol, which distributes information about the network topology to the individual network stations, and a signaling protocol, required for connection setup between PNNI nodes. The signaling protocol is mainly based on the UNI 4.0/4.1 signaling specification. The network topology distribution process consists of the Hello protocol (through which a PNNI node reports its existence to the rest of the network) and the exchange of a sequence of database summary packets, containing the information of all PNNI Topology State Elements of the node's topology database. These topology state parameters provide information about the availability of connections to adjacent nodes, and are continuously updated by the "hello" procedures carried out between all PNNI nodes.

In addition to the signaling and topology distribution mechanisms, PNNI also contains a number of important functions for efficient network operation. These include searching for alternative routes, crankback procedures (in which a switch that is unable to route a call refers it back to the upstream switch, which will then try another route), maintenance of connection matrices for ascertaining routes, and the operation of a dedicated routing control channel, used only to distribute routing information.

11.2.2   The PNNI Concept

PNNI topologies are hierarchically structured in order to minimize the overhead traffic necessary to propagate topology information. At the lowest level,

ATM switching systems are aggregated in peer groups (PG), which are represented on the next higher topological level by their peer group leader. Each PNNI network node (generally an ATM switch) exchanges "hello" packets with its immediate neighbors, thus communicating its own identity and the status of its links to its other neighbors. Such an information block is known as a PNNI Topology State Element (PTSE). Network nodes that have links leading outside their peer group are called border nodes. On the next higher hierarchical level, peer group leaders send out abridged topology information on all the network nodes they represent, and receive similar information from other peer group leaders. The peer group leader then distributes the information thus received to the nodes in its peer group, so that each network node possesses a map of the whole network. The topology information about a given destination node is less precise as the distance increases, however. If a station now wants to set up a connection to a network node in another peer group, it composes a SETUP message that indicates the intermediate nodes to be used in the connection in a "Designated Transit List" (DTL), created using the available topology information. Thus PNNI uses a source-routing mechanism. If necessary, the DTL is modified during the switching procedure by switches in the transit networks (Figure 11.4).

11.2.3   PNNI Messages

The PNNI signaling messages are taken directly from UNI 4.0/4.1 (which are based on Q.2931 and Q.2971):

Connection Setup

SETUP

CALL PROCEEDING

CONNECT

ALERTING

CONNECTION AVAILABLE

Connection Clear-down

RELEASE

RELEASE COMPLETE

Other

NOTIFY

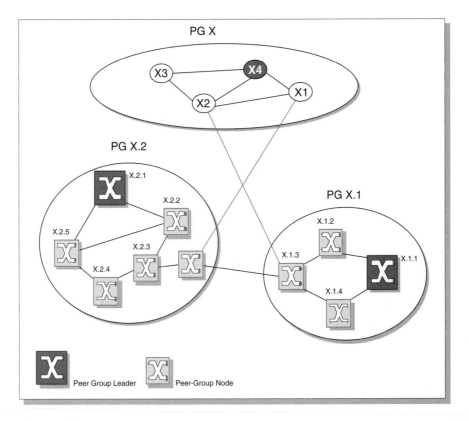

Figure 11.4
Hierarchical structure of PNNI networks.

STATUS

STATUS ENQUIRY

The differences from UNI signaling are reflected in a number of information elements used in the implementation of PNNI functions such as route selection and crankback signaling. Table 11.8 lists the information elements used in PNNI.

11.2.4   PNNI Addressing

The format for PNNI node addresses is the ATM End System Address (AESA). For transport and routing of public networks address information, embedded E.164 NSAP addresses are being used. Of the 20 AESA bytes,

333

Table 11.8 Information Elements in PNNI

Bits 8 7 6 5 4 3 2 1	Information Element	Maximum Length	Maximum occurence within message
0000 0100	Narrowband bearer capability	14	3
0000 1000	Cause	34	2
0001 0100	Call state	5	1
0001 1100	Facility	34	see specification
0001 1110	Progress indicator	6	2
0010 0111	Notification indicator	see specification	see specification
0100 0010	End-to-end transit delay	13	1
0100 1100	Connected number	26	1
0100 1101	Connected subaddress	25	1
0101 0100	Endpoint reference	7	1
0101 0101	Endpoint state	5	1
0101 1000	ATM adaptation layer parameters	21	1
0101 1001	ATM traffic descriptor	30	1
0101 1010	Connection identifier	9	1
0101 1011	OAM traffic descriptor	6	1
0101 1100	Quality of service parameter	6	1
0101 1101	Broadband high layer information	13	1
0101 1110	Broadband bearer capability	7	1
0101 1111	Broadband low-layer information	17	3
0110 0000	Broadband locking shift	5	see specification
0110 0001	Broadband non-locking shift	5	see specification
0110 0011	Broadband repeat indicator	5	3
0110 1100	Calling party number	26	1
0110 1101	Calling party subaddress	25	2
0111 0000	Called party number	25	1
0111 0001	Called party subaddress	25	2
0111 1000	Transit network selection	9	1
0111 1001	Restart indicator	5	1
0111 1100	Narrowband low layer compatibility	20	2
0111 1101	Narrowband high layer compatibility	7	2
0111 1110	User-user	133	1
0111 1111	Generic identifier transport	33	3
1000 0001	Minimum acceptable ATM traffic descriptor	20	1
1000 0010	Alternative ATM traffic descriptor	30	1
1000 0100	ATC (was ABR) setup parameters	36	1
1000 1001	Broadband report type	5	2
1110 0000	Called party soft PVPC or PVCC	11	1
1110 0001	Crankback	72	1
1110 0010	Designated transit list	546	10
1110 0011	Calling party soft PVPC or PVCC	10	1
1110 0100	ABR additional parameters	14	1
1110 0101	Generic Application Transport	512	5
1110 0110	Transported Address	53	5
1110 0111	Security Services	512	1
1110 1011	Connection scope selection	6	1
1110 1100	Extended QoS parameters	25	1
1110 1110	Trace Transit List	1466	1
1110 1111	Network Call Correlation Identifier	38	1
1111 0000	Minimum Desired Cell Rate	13	1
1111 0001	Optional Traffic Attributes	14	5
1111 0010	Rerouting Services	8	1
1111 0011	Rerouting	80	1
1111 0100	Rerouting Cause	5	1
1111 0101	Reference List	3007	1

PNNI processes only the first 19 bytes. The last byte only distinguishes destinations, which can be reached at the same ATM end system interface, which therefore is not relevant to the routing process.

Rather than advertising every single end system a PNNI node can reach to the rest of the network, so-called groups of end systems are being used. These groups are formed through prefixes. This approach allows to advertise the connectivity to a large number of destinations with a single prefix.

11.2.5 Routing Control Channels in PNNI

To exchange PNNI routing protocol messages (Hello Packets, Topology State Elements, etc.), a special AAL-5 virtual channel connection called Routing Control Channel (RCC) is being used. These RCCs are exclusively dedicated to carry PNN routing control data. Any service categories (nrt-VBR, rt-VBR, CBR, ABR, UBR) can be selected.

11.2.6 PNNI Connection Setup

The PNNI connection setup (Figure 11.5), like the corresponding UNI procedure, begins when a switch A transmits a SETUP message and starts its T303 timer. If no answer is received from switch B before T303 expires, the SETUP message may be sent one more time. If the timer expires again, switch A transmits a RELEASE COMPLETE with Cause #102, "Recovery on timer expiry." Otherwise, if the network and the remote station are able to provide the QoS and traffic parameters specified in the SETUP message, and the specified VPCI/VCI combination is available, then switch B responds with a CALL PROCEEDING message. On receiving CALL PROCEEDING, switch A stops timer T303 and starts T310. If B does not support one or more of the QoS parameters (ATM traffic descriptor, end-to-end transit delay, etc.), it responds with a RELEASE COMPLETE containing Cause #73: "Unsupported combination of traffic parameters," and the crankback information element, which contains crankback message #73. If the network or the remote station is unable to provide the requested traffic parameters, then switch B again sends a RELEASE COMPLETE, but in this case with Cause #37, "User cell rate unavailable."

After successfully transmitting the CALL PROCEEDING message, B sends an ALERTING message to A and enters the Alerting Delivered state. As soon as switch A receives the ALERTING message, it stops T310 and starts T301. Switch B now sends a CONNECT message. On receiving this, switch A stops timer T301.

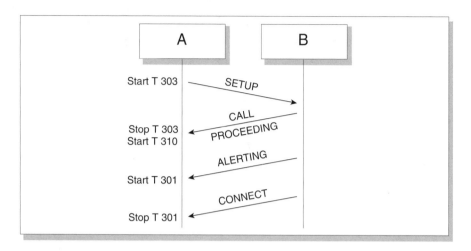

Figure 11.5
Connection setup processes at the PNNI interface.

11.2.7   ATM InterNetwork Interface (AINI)

The AINI protocol, specified in af-cs-0125.000, is heavily based on the PNNI v1.0 specification (af-pnni-0055.000) and various addendums; it defines the signaling that can be used between ATM networks. Only the briefest discussion is included here of this specification, as it is used only in rare situations; it is mentioned to explain how the ATM Forum has solved the problem that arises when PNNI is used as a public network NNI. Thus the main purpose of the AINI specification is to allow the interfacing of two ATM networks which are running different NNI signaling systems (B-ISUP and PNNI). Table 11.9 shows the capabilities of AINI.

Protocol interworking supported by AINI is as follows:

PNNI to AINI to B-ISUP

B-ISUP to AINI to PNNI

PNNI to AINI to PNNI

The latter case would occur when routing information is not transferred between two PNNI networks. A potential fourth case (B-ISUP to AINI to B-ISUP) can already be done through direct connection between B-ISUP networks or through B-ICI procedures.

Table 11.9 Capabilities of AINI

Capabilities	Mandatory/Optional
Point-to-Point Calls	M
Point-to Multipoint Calls	O
Signaling of Individual QoS Parameters	O*
Crankback	O*
Alternate Routing as a Result of Crankback	O
Associated Signalling	O
Negotiation of ATM Traffic Descriptors	O
Switched Virtual Path (VP) Service	O
Soft PVPC and PVCC	O
ABR Signaling for Point-to-Point Calls	O
Generic Identifier Transport	O
Transport of Frame Discard Indication	O*
AINI/PNNI Interworking	O
AINI/B-ISUP Interworking	O
Security Signaling	O
Transported Address Stack	O
Generic Application Transport	O

*Support is mandatory when AINI/PNNI interworking is supported and optional otherwise.

The AINI to B-ISUP interworking procedures mainly involve the interpretation of UNI signaling to B-ISUP signaling messages and NNI to UNI messages. PNNI to PNNI interworking involves no signaling interpretation but does have to handle routing.

Chapter 12

ATM INTERWORKING

ATM networks are capable of transporting practically all data and telecommunication services. Specifically, these include both WAN and LAN data services (Frame Relay, DQDB MANs, PDH leased lines; Ethernet, Token Ring, FDDI) as well as the various telecommunications services for audio and video applications (telephony, video-conferencing, cable television, etc.). In order to connect ATM with these legacy communication systems, which are based on completely different transport mechanisms, ATM networks must be able to emulate the corresponding interfaces. From the point of view of the services transported over it, the ATM network should appear as a native transport network. In order to achieve this, however, extraordinarily complex protocols and processes must be implemented in the ATM interworking components. The following sections discuss interworking of ATM with local area networks, with Frame Relay, and with DQDB MANs.

12.1   ATM–LAN Interworking

Traditional LAN infrastructures can be connected to ATM by three different methods:

- LLC Encapsulation (RFC 2684)
- Classical IP-over-ATM (RFC 2225)
- LAN Emulation (LANE)

In LLC encapsulation, LAN packets are transported over virtual channels in the ATM network. Data transport is transparent to the ATM network: in other words, ATM only provides the transport capacity, without regard to the contents of the data transferred. Classical IP-over-ATM (CIP), on the other hand, provides a complete implementation of the Internet protocol for ATM networks. Functions such as address resolution (ARP) are emulated by appropriate protocol components in the ATM network. The two main drawbacks of CIP, however, are that no broadcasts are supported and all nodes of a workgroup must be connected to the network by ATM. Both of these limitations are overcome by LAN Emulation. Finally, emulated LANs can be connected transparently by means of MPOA (Multiprotocol over ATM). LANE and MPOA can thus be used in a heterogeneous network, consisting of various conventional LAN and ATM segments, to form virtual LANs as desired, regardless of the individual network nodes' location and type of network connection.

12.1.1   LAN ATM: LLC Encapsulation (RFC 2684)

The first specifications for connecting LANs to ATM networks were two RFCs (Requests for Comments) published by the Internet Engineering Task Force in 1993, RFC 1483 and RFC 1577. These specifications were updated in 1998 with the publication of RFCs 2684 and 2225, mainly to account for the progress made in signaling procedures during the intervening 5 years. RFC 2684 specifies two methods for the encapsulation of LAN data packets in ATM:

- LLC encapsulation
- VC-based multiplexing

The first method transports all LAN protocols by encapsulating the LLC data packets in AAL-5 CPCS PDUs. The entire data stream is transmitted within one VC. All protocols based on Ethernet, Token Ring, FDDI, or DQDB (IEEE 802.6 MAN) can be transported over ATM networks in this way (see Figure 12.1).

This method is used mainly in networks that only support permanent virtual connections (PVCs), and that are unable to manage constantly changing VCs in use. In networks using SVCs, which typically have no trouble dynamically managing a large number of VCs, VC-based multiplexing can be used. This method avoids transporting the LLC header by setting up a separate virtual channel (VC) for each protocol. This makes transportation significantly more efficient overall, which is why this method is preferable to LLC encapsulation wherever possible (Figure 12.2).

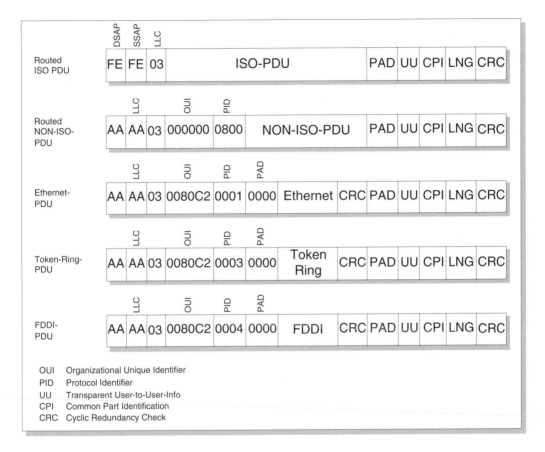

Figure 12.1
ATM LAN: LLC encapsulation (RFC 2684).

12.1.2 LAN ATM: Classical IP over ATM (RFC 2225)

Classical IP over ATM goes beyond the RFC 2684 encapsulation technique to provide a complete implementation of the Internet protocol for ATM. IP address resolution, which is realized in Ethernet by ARP and Reverse Address Resolution Protocol (RARP), is handled by ATMARP and InATMARP functions. The mapping tables for the ATMARP and InATMARP functions are stored in an ATMARP server, which must be present in each logical IP subnet (LIS). The ARP client itself is responsible for registering its own IP/ATM address information with the ATMARP server, and for obtaining the IP/ATM address of the desired destination system from the server. Entries in clients' and

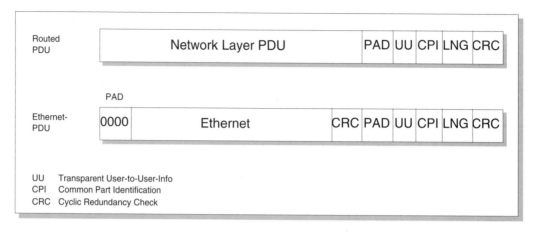

Figure 12.2
VC-based multiplexing (RFC 2684).

servers' ATMARP tables are subject to an aging process. Client ATMARP entries are valid for a maximum of 15 minutes; server ATMARP entries for at least 20 minutes. ATMARP PDUs, like the IP data packets themselves, are transported in AAL-5 CPCS PDUs according to the rules of LLC encapsulation (see Figure 12.3).

The following rules govern the design and operation of logical IP subnetworks (LISs):

- All IP nodes of an LIS must be directly connected to the ATM network.
- All IP nodes of an LIS must have the same IP network or subnetwork address.
- Network nodes outside the LIS must be accessible only through routers.

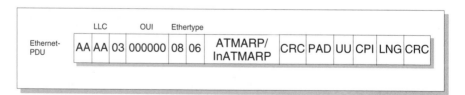

Figure 12.3
ATMARP and InATMARP (RFC 2225).

- All IP nodes in an LIS must be able to resolve addresses by ATMARP.
- Every IP node in an LIS must be able to communicate with every other IP node.
- Address resolution must function both for PVCs and for SVCs.

The default packet size in Classical IP networks is 9180 bytes. Adding the 8-byte LLC/SNAP header yields a default AAL-5 PDU size of 9188 bytes in CIP networks.

12.1.3   LAN Emulation

ATM–LAN Emulation Techniques

The most universal method for efficiently integrating ATM networks in existing, conventional LAN infrastructures involves a complete emulation of the LAN MAC layer, since this allows all existing LAN applications to be extended across ATM networks without modification. From the point of view of traditional local area networking, the LAN emulation service behaves the same as a conventional MAC LAN driver. The LAN Emulation (LANE) specification was developed by the ATM Forum to provide such a function for ATM networks.

Basic Challenges in ATM–LAN Emulation

Due to the completely different functional principles of ATM on the one hand and Ethernet, Token Ring, or FDDI on the other, ATM networks cannot be directly connected to conventional LAN topologies. The crucial problem is not one of different data speeds or incompatible frame formats; differences of these kinds can be overcome by means of bridges with appropriate capabilities, which already exist to interconnect Ethernet, Token Ring, and FDDI LANs. The key difference between ATM and traditional LAN technologies is that ATM networks are based on connection-oriented communications, whereas all the traditional LAN MAC protocols are connectionless.

In conventional LANs, MAC frames are simply placed on the shared communication medium in the hope that they will reach and be read by the destination node. There is no confirmation of receipt, much less a quality-of-service agreement for the communication channel. Retransmission of lost frames can only be requested by appropriate mechanisms in higher-layer protocols, such as TCP. Because all hosts communicate over one and the same medium, each frame not only reaches its actual destination node, but also every other node connected to the same network segment. The user's perception of an exclusive communication with a remote host is only due to the filtering by destination address performed by the network interface card. Furthermore, if the destination address of a given frame is a broadcast address, the frame is processed by all hosts. In this way, all hosts on a LAN segment can be addressed with just a single frame transmission. LAN protocols make use of this broadcast capability in implementing numerous functions. For example, X-Window terminals using the BOOTP protocol obtain their IP addresses by means of broadcast messages upon starting. The ARP protocol, which resolves IP addresses to Layer 2 MAC addresses, is also broadcast based. These broadcast mechanisms, which are "natural" in shared-media LANs, are completely at odds with the connection-oriented principle of ATM networks, and are accordingly quite complicated to emulate.

ATM provides each pair of communicating hosts with a logical connection (VP/VC) whose characteristics, such as bandwidth and transfer delay, are negotiated during the connection setup phase. Each frame sent over this virtual connection is delivered only to its exact destination node, and cannot be observed by the other hosts. A broadcast transmission to n hosts would therefore require setting up n connection paths, one to each receiver host. For this reason, the emulation of conventional LAN topologies in ATM is a complex and extraordinarily resource-intensive process, which can lead to a network overload if broadcast rates are high.

LAN Emulation: Structure and Functional Principles

The ATM Forum's LAN Emulation (Version 2) is defined in the two documents *LAN Emulation over ATM Version 2—LUNI Specification* (af-lane-0084_000), and *LAN Emulation over ATM Version 2—LNNI* (af-lane-0112_000), which specify emulated Ethernet and Token Ring LANs. FDDI is also supported indirectly through interworking with Ethernet or Token Ring.

LANE is based on five ATM service modules that build on AAL-5:

- LAN Emulation Client (LE Client or LEC)
- LAN Emulation Server (LE Server or LES)
- LAN Emulation Configuration Server (LE Configuration Server or LECS)
- Broadcast and Unknown Server (BUS)
- Selected Multicast Server (SMS)

LUNI (LANE User–Network Interface) describes the processes at the interface to the LEC, while LNNI (LANE Network–Network Interface) specifies the protocols for interconnected LEC, LES, BUS, and SMS components (Figure 12.4). LNNI components can be used to coordinate several LES, LECS, and BUS systems in order to build redundant LANE structures. LECs can also be grouped in subnetworks regardless of their location or the LES or BUS used, which makes it possible to build virtual emulated LANs (ELANs).

LANE emulates the most widely used end system protocol stacks, NDIS (Network Driver Interface Specification), ODI (Open Data Link Interface), and DLPI (Data Link Provider Interface). The LAN frames themselves (IEEE 802.3 Ethernet or IEEE 802.5 Token Ring frames) are transported over AAL-5 in LAN emulation frames. No special LANE frame type is defined for FDDI: either Ethernet or Token Ring frames can be used. Using the Token Ring frame format yields better results since the MAC address format is the same as in FDDI. LANE also provides Quality-of-Service functions for communication between LANE hosts connected by ATM.

LEC (LAN Emulation Client).   The LAN emulation client software, shown in Figure 12.5, performs all the necessary control functions as well as the actual

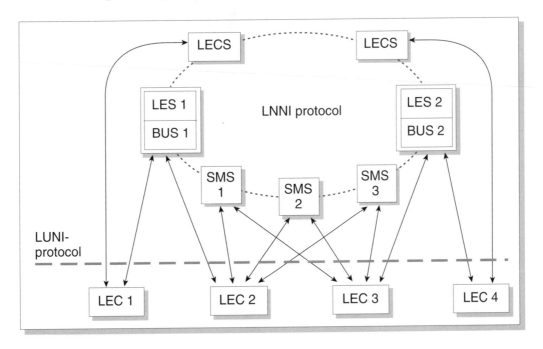

Figure 12.4
LAN emulation: LUNI and LNNI.

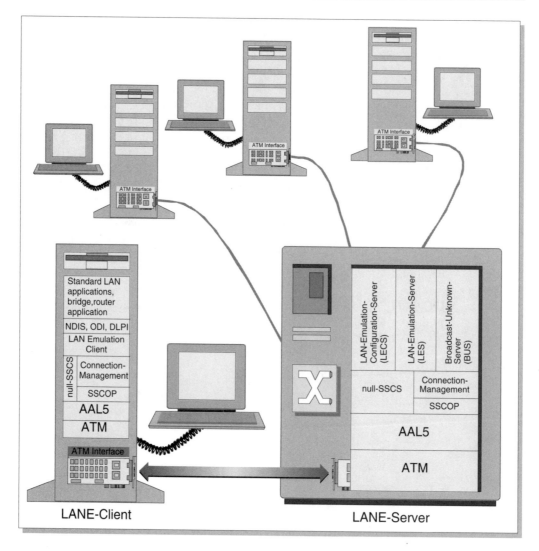

Figure 12.5
Components of the LAN emulation service.

data communication over the ATM interface, providing a standard LAN MAC interface (NDIS, ODI, or DLPI) to higher-layer applications. LE clients consist of the following components:

- System hardware (PC, workstation, router, etc.)
- Standard LAN software (MAC address, protocol stack, drivers, etc.)

- LE client software
- ATM interface with ATM address

LES (LAN Emulation Servers). The LAN emulation server (LES) module controls the emulated LAN. It includes such functions as registration of LE clients and MAC-to-ATM address resolution for all registered hosts. Every LE client participating in an emulated LAN reports its LAN MAC address, the corresponding ATM address, and any necessary route information to the LAN emulation server. When a LAN data packet needs to be sent, the ATM address of the destination is first sought in the address table of the LES. If it is not found there, address resolution must be performed by BUS server broadcasts.

LAN Emulation Configuration Server (LECS). The LAN emulation configuration server manages the LECs' membership in the various emulated LANs by maintaining configuration information on the emulated LANs in a configuration database. A LEC can belong to several emulated LANs simultaneously.

Broadcast and Unknown Server (BUS). The Broadcast and Unknown server module retransmits all the LE clients' broadcast and multicast data packets. These include:

- All data packets with broadcast or multicast addresses
- Data packets sent to a MAC address for which the LE client does not know the corresponding ATM address and that could not be resolved by the LES
- The source routing mechanism's explorer data packets, used to determine optimum routes.

Data packets received by the BUS are retransmitted in sequence to the appropriate group of destination LECs. This is necessary in order to avoid overlapping of AAL-5 data packets from different senders.

Functional Processes in LAN Emulation

Process control between the individual LAN emulation servers takes place by means of control VCCs and data VCCs. Control channels are used to connect LAN emulation clients with LAN emulation servers and with LAN emulation configuration servers. Communication between LAN emulation clients, as well as between broadcast/unknown servers and LAN emulation clients, takes place over data channels (data VCCs). Unlike LANE Specification 1.0, LANE v2 also supports LCC multiplexing. This means that the data streams of several emulated LANs, and of several different protocols, can be transported over a single VC.

When a new LAN emulation client is added to an emulated LAN, the LEC first sets up a Configuration Direct VCC to the LE configuration server in order to register as a member of a certain emulated LAN. Optionally it may also use the LE configuration protocol to negotiate various parameters (addresses, name of the emulated LAN, maximum frame size).

Next, the Control Direct VCC to the LAN emulation server is set up. After registering, the LAN emulation client should possess all the information necessary in order to participate in the LAN emulation service, including the LE client identifier (LECID), the LAN type (802.3 Ethernet, 802.5 Token Ring), and so on. If necessary, the LAN emulation server may also set up a one-way, point-to-multipoint Control Distribute VCC to several LE clients. (Point-to-multipoint connections are supported in LANE Version 2.0, but not in LANE 1.0). Finally, communication with the Broadcast/Unknown Server is opened over a data-direct VCC. The LAN emulation client is then ready for operation under the LAN emulation service (see Figure 12.6). The various connections are set up and cleared down using the ATM Forum UNI signaling protocols (UNI 3.0, UNI 3.1, UNI 4.0, UNI 4.1).

In LAN emulation, data can flow either between the LEC and the BUS, or between one LEC and another. If a LEC needs to send a packet to a host whose ATM address is unknown, it first sends an LE ARP message to the LES. The LES either forwards the LE ARP request directly to the desired host, or provides the sender with the desired ATM address in the form of an LE ARP response. Multiple data VCCs may be set up between two LECs, if both of them support this. The application layer may specify Quality-of-Service parameters for the connections, such as ATM Traffic Descriptor, Alternative ATM Traffic Descriptor (only in UNI 4.0/4.1), Minimum Acceptable Traffic Descriptor (only in UNI 4.0/4.1), Broadband Bearer Capability, QoS parameters, End-to-End Transmit Delay (only in UNI 4.0/4.1), and so on. If no specific QoS parameters are requested, the default QoS parameters for LANE data VCCs must be used (UBR or ABR, QoS class 0).

The Flush Message Protocol.   Because LAN emulation clients can send data packets to the same destination by different paths—via the BUS or over different data VCCs, for example—the Flush Message protocol is used to preserve the order of the LAN data packets during transmission over the emulated LAN. The Flush Message protocol in effect "deletes" the old transmission path when communication is moved to a new path. The LE client performs this operation by sending an LE flush request message over the

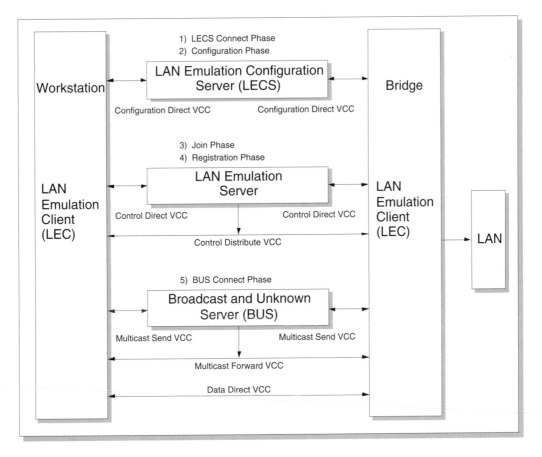

Figure 12.6
LANE functional processes.

given VCC to ensure that all data packets sent over that channel have arrived at the receiving host, and that no more will follow. On receiving the Flush response, the LEC knows that no more data will be sent to it over the initial VCC, and can begin using the new VCC.

All LANE components must support one of the following maximum sizes for AAL-5 SDUs: 1516, 1580, 4544, 9234, or 18190 bytes for nonmultiplexed data packets, and 1528, 1592, 4556, 9246, or 18202 bytes for multiplex LLC data.

The SDU length of 1516 is due to the fact that LANE data packets contain the 2-byte LAN emulation header (LEH), but not the 4-byte checksum. For Token Ring, the maximum frame sizes of 4450 bytes (for 4 Mbit/s) and 18200 bytes (for 16 Mbit/s) are calculated based on a Token Holding Timer value of 9.1 ms.

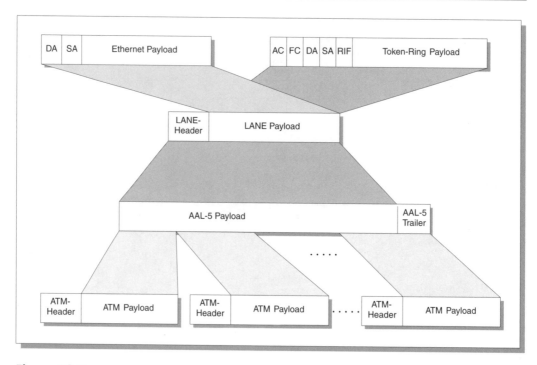

Figure 12.7
LANE frame format.

However, LANE frames contain no SD, FCS, ED, or FS fields and no inter-frame spacing gap, so that the resulting lengths are 4544 and 18190 bytes. Figure 12.7 shows the LANE frame format for Ethernet and Token Ring, and Figure 12.8 illustrates a heterogeneous LAN/ATM network based on LAN emulation.

12.1.4 MPOA: Multiprotocol over ATM

ATM networks can use LAN emulation to emulate Ethernet and Token Ring topologies. Such emulated LANs (ELANs) can then form the basis of subnetworks (virtual LANs) that include network nodes of all three LAN topologies: Ethernet, Token Ring, and ATM. Any ATM network can contain several ELANs, but LAN emulation does not make it possible to connect ELANs to one another, except through the use of conventional routers. The Multiprotocol Over ATM Version 1.1 Specification (af-mpoa-0114.000) does away with this restriction. MPOA integrates LANE v2 with NHRP (the Next Hop Resolution Protocol, RFC 2332) and the Multicast Address Resolution

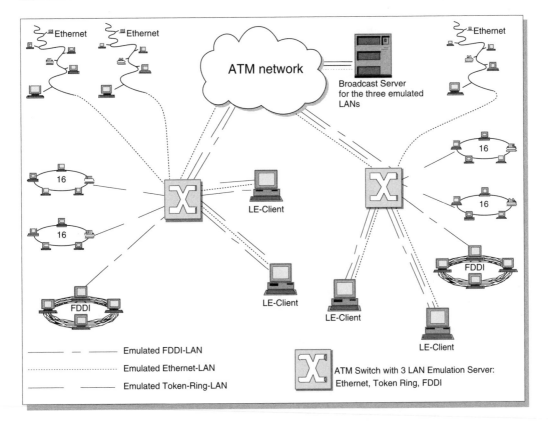

Figure 12.8
Heterogeneous LAN/ATM network with LAN emulation.

Server (MARS) protocol (RFC 2022), and permits inter-ELAN communication without the use of additional routers. By separating route selection from the data forwarding function, MPOA is able to provide efficient routing even in large, complex networks.

Every MPOA network consists of MPOA servers (MPS) and MPOA clients (MPC). MPOA servers are responsible for route selection, while MPOA clients perform the actual forwarding of data from their LAN emulation client interfaces (LECs), requesting the appropriate routes from the MPS as necessary.

Prerequisites for the use of MPOA in the LAN include support for

- ATM UNI signaling (UNI 3.0, UNI 3.1, UNI 4.0, UNI 4.1)
- LANE v.2
- the Next Hop Resolution Protocol (NHRP, RFC 2332)

351

MPOA Components

MPOA components serve to connect emulated LANs to one another. Because this implies that they are situated at the edges of the ELANs, they are also called "edge devices." Such an edge device may be an ATM switch, a router, or a host system that provides at least the MPC and LEC functions. Such a minimum system must obtain its route information from a separate MPOA server. The MPS may, however, be integrated in the same system with the MPC and LEC, so that the full MPOA capability is implemented in just one physical component. Every MPC or MPS can serve several LECs but a LEC can only be associated with one MPOA component.

Basic MPOA Processes

As in LANE, all MPOA processes are managed through virtual control channels, while the actual data transport takes place through separate virtual data channels. All control and data flows are transported over VCCs with LLC encapsulation (RFC 2684). Channels are set up and cleared down in accordance with one of the UNI signaling specifications, UNI 3.0, UNI 3.1, UNI 4.0, or UNI 4.1. Four kinds of virtual control channels are defined:

- MPS/MPC configuration VCs
- MPC–MPS control VCs
- MPS–MPS control VCs
- MPC–MPC control VCs

MPOA components obtain configuration information from the LAN Emulation Configuration Server (LECS). The MPOA clients obtain route information from the MPOA server over the MPC–MPS control VC. The MPS–MPS control VCs are used by standard routing protocols and NHRP to exchange route information. MPCs exchange control information directly only if one MPC receives misrouted data packets from another. In this case, the sender MPC is notified so that it can delete the incorrect routing information from its cache. MPOA networks are characterized by the following five basic operating processes:

- Configuration
- Discovery
- Target resolution

- Connection management
- Data communication

MPOA obtains all its configuration information from the ELAN's LAN Emulation Configuration Servers. Additionally, MPOA components can also be directly configured by means of the MPOA MIB. All MPCs and MPSs automatically detect each other's existence through an extended LE ARP protocol. This protocol transports not only the ATM addresses of the individual hosts, but also information about the MPOA type (MPC or MPS). The target resolution process serves to determine the route to the destination, and is carried out using modified NHRP Resolution Request messages. The connection management process is responsible for setting up and operating the virtual control and data connections, while the data transport process consists of transmitting the user data over the selected routes. The various MPOA processes are controlled by means of eight MPOA and two NHRP control messages:

- MPOA Resolution Request
- MPOA Resolution Reply
- MPOA Cache Imposition Request
- MPOA Cache Imposition Reply
- MPOA Egress Cache Purge Request
- MPOA Egress Cache Purge Reply
- MPOA Keep-Alive
- MPOA Trigger
- NHRP Purge Request
- NHRP Purge Reply

Route Selection and Shortcuts in MPOA Networks

In selecting routes for data packet transport, MPOA distinguishes between default routes and shortcuts. Data packets initially enter the MPOA network through an MPC. Because the MPC generally does not know the ATM address that corresponds to the Layer 3 destination address of the packet, it does not attempt to set up a direct VC to the destination. By default, the data is first encapsulated in a LANE frame and forwarded to the default MPS router by the MPC's LEC unit. This router forwards the data to the destination MPC according to the information available in its routing tables. Then the MPC attempts to resolve the network address of the packets by sending an MPOA

Resolution Request message to the MPS. The MPS obtains the corresponding ATM address, along with the information whether a direct connection (shortcut) is available for the given connection, from its assigned next-hop server (NHS). If a shortcut is available, the MPS sends an Imposition Request message to the destination MPC to ask whether it is able to accept the shortcut connection. The destination MPC responds with an Imposition Reply message, which the MPS forwards to the originating MPC in the form of an MPOA Resolution Reply. The originating MPC can then set up the shortcut connection. The shortcut route information is entered in the MPC's routing cache, and all data packets for the given destination address are then sent directly over the shortcut. Figure 12.9 shows a schematic illustration of the

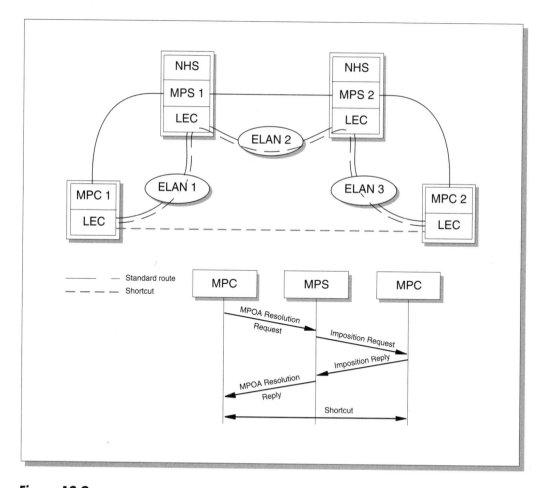

Figure 12.9
Route selection and shortcuts in MPOA networks.

MPOA route selection process. The default route between the MPOA clients MPC1 and MPC2 leads first to the LEC interfaces of the three MPOA components connected to one another over the three ELANs. Once the shortcut has been obtained from the next-hop server, a direct connection can be set up between the LEC interfaces of the two MPOA clients.

The Next Hop Resolution Protocol (NHRP)

Route optimization in MPOA networks is performed by means of the Non-Broadcast Multiple Access (NBMA) and Next Hop Resolution Protocols, since broadcast-based address resolution mechanisms are completely unsuitable for ATM networks. The purpose of NHRP is to find the ATM address that corresponds to a given network address (such as an IP address) so that a direct connection (shortcut) can be set up between two communicating hosts. NHRP is based on a client server model in which next-hop clients (NHC) send address resolution requests to a next-hop server (NHS). In MPOA, the MPOA servers play the part of NHCs and initiate Next-Hop Resolution requests to the NHS as required by MPCs. Every NHR request contains the following information:

- Network address (e.g., IP address) of the target
- Network address (e.g., IP address) of the sender
- ATM address of the sender

The NHS analyzes the incoming address resolution request and verifies whether it is itself competent to resolve the given destination. If not, it forwards the request to another NHS. Next-hop servers may forward address resolution requests only to other next-hop servers that are not more than one hop away—hence the name "next-hop" server. If the NHS is competent for the destination indicated in the request, it resolves the address and sends a reply packet containing the next-hop network address and the ATM address of the destination to the MPS, which forwards the information to the MPC. The MPC can then set up a direct VCC, or shortcut, to the destination.

12.2   ATM–Frame Relay Interworking

Frame Relay is a connection-oriented communication service that supports data packets of up to 8 kilobytes. Two main types of interworking between ATM and Frame Relay have been defined: network interworking and service interworking. Both are specified in Recommendation ITU-T I.555 (Frame Relaying Bearer Service Interworking). The Frame Relay Forum, working with the ATM Forum, has created two implementation agreements, FRF.5 (Frame Relay/ATM PVC Network Interworking Implementation Agreement) and FRF.8 (Frame Relay/ATM PVC Service Interworking Implementation Agreement), which conform to this and other ITU-T recommendations.

12.2.1   Network Interworking

Network interworking occurs when ATM is used as a transport mechanism for Frame Relay. Frame Relay frames (minus the CRC-16 check sequence) are encapsulated into CPCS frames of AAL-5 in the ATM network. The mapping process is performed in the Frame Relay Service-Specific Convergence Sublayer (FR-SSCS) that sits above the CPCS sublayer in AAL-5; the FR-SSCS is specified in ITU-T Recommendation I.365.1. The reason that the CRC-16 check sequence is omitted is one of efficiency; the CRC-32 check sequence of the AAL-5 CPCS sublayer provides an even more rigorous error detection method, so the Frame Relay CRC-16 check sequence is redundant. Figure 12.10 shows the layered model for the AAL-5 incorporating the FR-SSCS.

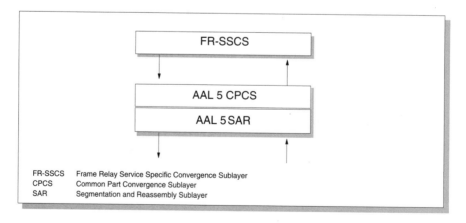

Figure 12.10
Protocol layer model for ATM–Frame Relay interworking.

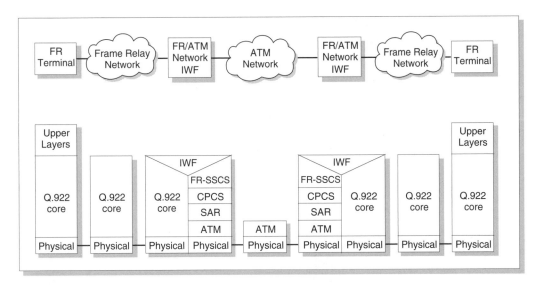

Figure 12.11
Frame Relay to ATM network interworking (user plane)—scenario 1.

Functions of the Frame Relay Service-Specific Convergence Sublayer

The FR-SSCS sublayer provides the following functions.

Multiplexing/Demultiplexing. Several FR-SSCS connections can be multiplexed over a single CPCS connection. Either one-to-one or many-to-one multiplexing may be used. In many-to-one multiplexing (ITU-T's Scenario 1), the individual channels are distinguished only by the encapsulated DLCIs. All many-to-one connections must end at the same ATM end system or be re-interworked to become native Frame Relay again. Figure 12.11 shows the reference model.

One-to-one multiplexing (ITU-T Scenario 2) takes place in the ATM layer using multiple ATM VCCs. The values of the Frame Relay DLCIs may range from 16 to 991, unless the default DLCI 1022 is used. (No default DLCI is specified for use with the optional 3 and 4-byte headers. In this case the DLCIs must be negotiated.) Figure 12.12 shows the reference model for this.

Note that in this case, because of the one-to-one relationship between ATM VPI-VCIs and the encapsulated Frame Relay DLCIs, ATM switching can be used to route the encapsulated Frame Relay to any terminal, or to join another Frame Relay network, although this would have to be done via a

357

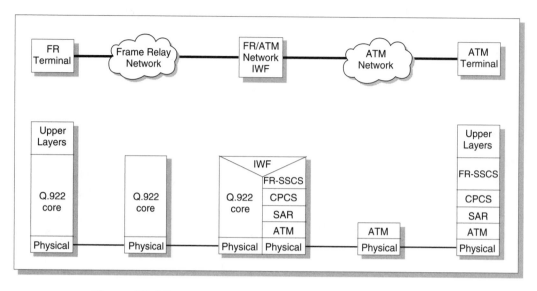

Figure 12.12
Frame Relay to ATM network interworking (user plane)—scenario 2.

switch so that the DLCI can be translated into an appropriate value for the local link.

Formatting of Variable-Length PDUs.   Overload monitoring adapts Frame Relay's Forward/Backward Congestion Control functions to ATM as follows.

Congestion Indication (Forward)

- Frame Relay to ATM
- ATM to Frame Relay

Congestion Indication (Backward)

- Frame Relay to ATM
- ATM to Frame Relay

The forward congestion indication is implemented using the Frame Relay Forward Explicit Congestion Indication FR-SSCS FECN) bit and the ATM Explicit Forward Congestion Indication bit (EFCI). For Frame Relay–ATM interworking, the FECN bit of the Frame Relay frame is copied into the FECN field of the FR-SSCS PDU. The ATM EFCI bit must always be set to 0, "Congestion not experienced." In ATM–Frame Relay interworking, a value of 1 in the SSCS FECN bit is copied to the FECN bit of the corresponding Frame Relay frame. Regardless of the value of the SSCS FECN bit, however, the Frame Relay FECN is also set to 1 if the EFCI bit of any cell in the given FR-SSCS PDU is set to 1:

FR→ATM		
Q.922 ECN	FR-SSCS FECN	ATM EFCI
0	0	0
1	1	0

ATM→FR		
ATM EFCI	FR-SSCS FECN	Q.922 ECN
0	0	0
X	1	1
1	X	1

X: Ignored by the interworking function

The backward congestion indication is supported only by means of the Frame Relay or FR-SSCS BECN bit. At the transition from ATM to Frame Relay, the value of the FR-SSCS BECN bit is copied directly to the BECN of the Frame Relay frame. In the opposite direction, the FR-SSCS BECN bit is set to 1 in the following two cases:

- If the BECN bit of the incoming Frame Relay frame is set to 1
- If the EFCI bit of the last ATM cell of the last segmented FR-SSCS PDU is set to 1

Mapping of Frame Relay Discard Eligible (DE) and ATM Cell Loss Priority (CLP). The Discard Eligible bit can be translated to ATM in two ways. In the case of Frame Relay–ATM interworking, the DE bit can be mapped either to the DE bit of the FR-SSCS PDU and then to the CLP field of the corresponding ATM cells, or it may be mapped only to the FR-SSCS PDU field while the value of the ATM CLP field is set to a constant 0 or 1 on connection setup, and only changed when the status of the ATM connection itself changes. For the first of these two cases, in ATM–Frame Relay interworking the Frame Relay DE bit is set to 1 whenever either a CLP bit or the DE bit of the FR-SSCS PDU is set to 1. In the second case, only the FR-SSCS PDU bit is mapped to the Frame Relay DE bit.

FR→ATM (1)			FR→ATM (2)		
Q.922 DE	FR-SSCS DE	CLP	Q.922 DE	FR-SSCS DE	CLP
0	0	0	0	0	Y
1	1	1	1	1	Y

Y: Constantly set to 0 or 1, depending on the ATM connection

ATM→FR (1)			ATM→FR (2)		
CLP	FR-SSCS DE	Q.922 DE	CLP	FR-SSCS DE	Q.922 DE
0	0	0	X	0	0
1	X	1	X	1	1
X	1	1			

X: Ignored by the interworking function

Error Detection.   Bit error detection for Frame Relay interworking is based on the AAL-5 checksum, which is calculated for the FR-SSCS PDU.

Structure of the FR-SSCS PDU

Figure 12.13 illustrates the structure of an FR-SSCS PDU. Its format corresponds exactly to the Frame Relay specification, with the exception of the missing CRC-16 check sequence and the start and end flags. Every implementation must support at least the 2-byte header. Support for the 3- and 4-byte headers is optional. The coding of the PDU's individual fields is also different from the Q.922 Frame Relay specification in that a zero does not need to be inserted after five successive ones, as is required by the HDLC protocol.

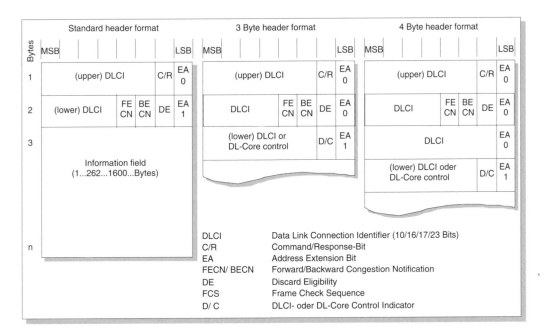

Figure 12.13
Format of an FR-SSCS PDU.

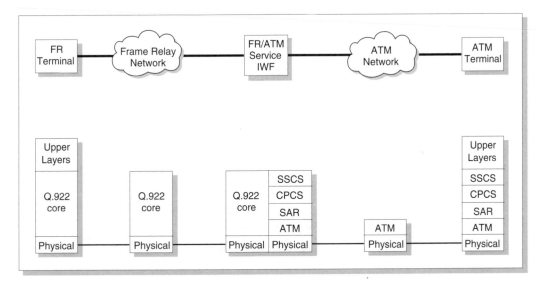

Figure 12.14
Frame Relay to ATM service interworking (user plane).

12.2.2 Service Interworking

In Frame Relay to ATM service interworking, the interworking occurs at a higher layer than in network interworking. The payload content of the Frame Relay frame is extracted and re-encapsulated directly in the appropriate service-specific convergence sublayer for the service being carried (e.g., data or voice), that is, the FR-SSCS is not used. Figure 12.14 shows the reference model.

Note that with service interworking, there is no encapsulation of any Frame Relay-specific features, so either end is unaware that the service was initially transported over a different technology.

12.3   ATM–MAN Interworking

Even before specifications for LAN emulation were developed, wide area network operators sought a method for transporting connectionless protocols over ATM. Most importantly, a way to transport the popular Dual Queue Dual Bus (DQDB) protocol for metropolitan area networks over ATM was needed. Two methods were developed: an indirect technique based on semi-permanent connections, and a direct method using the "connectionless server" principle.

12.3.1 Indirect, Connectionless Communication over Wide Area ATM Networks

In indirect connectionless communication, a semi-permanent connection is set up between two users with connectionless, non-ATM-compatible systems that are connected to the ATM network by interworking components (Figure 12.15). The users' "connectionless" communications are then transported over this link. The ATM network simply provides encapsulated transport of all data transmitted by the hosts, without regard to their connectionless communication behavior.

12.3.2 Direct, Connectionless Communication over ATM Networks: Connectionless Servers

The direct method of connectionless communication over ATM involves a connectionless service function (CLSF) by which the ATM network itself supports connectionless communication. This function requires a "connectionless

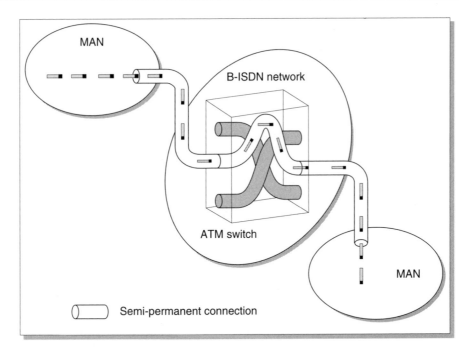

MAN

B-ISDN network

ATM switch

MAN

⬭ Semi-permanent connection

Figure 12.15
Indirect, connectionless communication over ATM networks.

server" (CLS), which can operate in message mode or streaming mode. In message mode, the CLS first stores the ATM cells pertaining to a frame of the connectionless service in a buffer. Only when all the cells of a frame have been received is a connection to the destination set up and the data sent. This method ensures that the network is not burdened with the transmission of useless incomplete frames. If the CLS detects that even just one cell of a frame is missing, it discards all the other ATM cells of that frame. In streaming mode, on the other hand, data transmission begins as soon as the first cell of a frame has been received and the destination is known (Figure 12.16).

12.3.3   CLNAP and CLNIP

The connectionless service function (CLSF) provides transportation for connectionless communication over wide area ATM networks. This is done by means of the two protocols CLNIP (Connectionless Network Interface

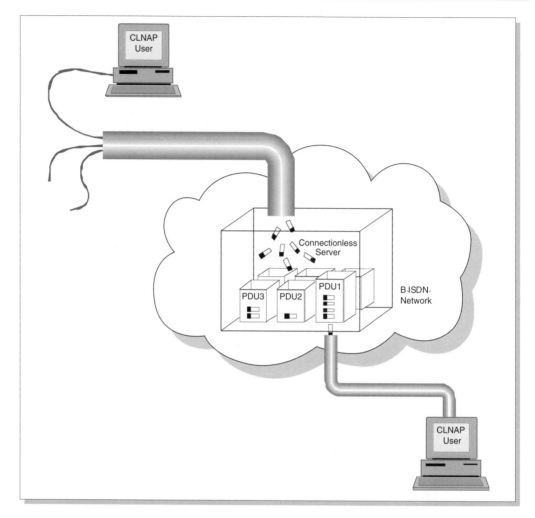

Figure 12.16
Connectionless server principle.

Protocol) and CLNAP (Connectionless Network Access Protocol), both of which build on AAL-3/4. CLNIP is used for communication between two connectionless server hosts, and as an interface to the MAN, while CLNAP provides the interface between ATM nodes and the connectionless servers (Figure 12.17).

Thus if two ATM nodes communicate using the Connectionless Network Access Protocol (CLNAP) over two or more connectionless servers, the

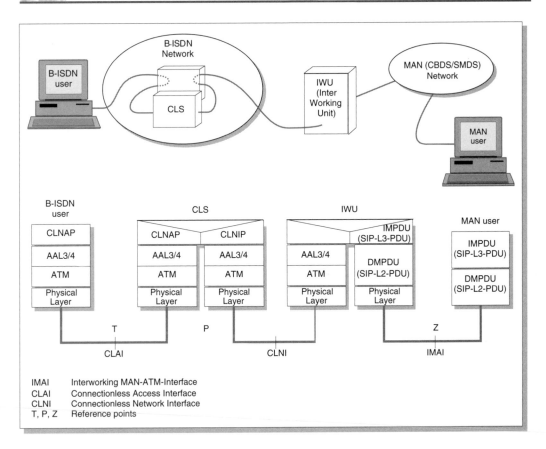

Figure 12.17
ATM–MAN interworking.

CLNAP PDUs are encapsulated in CLNIP PDUs, then segmented in the SAR sublayer for transportation in ATM cells. The destination host's connectionless server reassembles and unpacks the CLNAP frame, and forwards it without the CLNIP overhead to the receiving host. In the case of a connection between a MAN and an ATM network, an interworking unit packs the MAN's Layer 3 PDUs—that is, the IMPDUs (Initial MAC PDUs) in CBDS MANs or the SIP L3 PDUs (SMDS Interface Protocol, Level 3, PDU) in SMDS—in CLNIP PDUs, which are then segmented into ATM cells for insertion into the ATM network (Figure 12.18).

Because SMDS SIP L3 PDUs and IMPDUs have the same structure as CLNAP PDUs (with the exception of the first four header bytes and the last

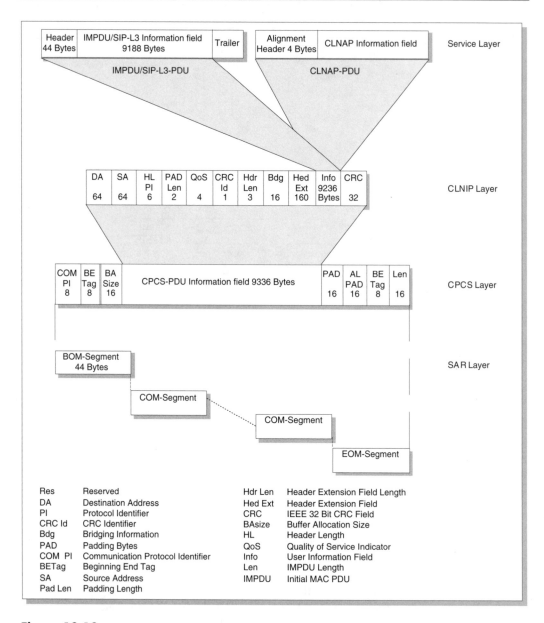

Figure 12.18
ATM encapsulation of CLNAP, CLNIP, and SMDS.

Res	BE Tag	BA Size	DA	SA	X	PAD Len	X	CRC Id	Hdr Len	X	Hed Ext	Info 9188 Bytes	PAD	X	Res	BE Tag	Len
8	8	16	64	64	6	2	4	1	3	16	96	Bytes	16	32	8	8	16

SIP-L3-PDU

DA	SA	X	PAD Len	X	CRC Id	Hdr Len	X	Hed Ext	Info 9188 Bytes	PAD	X
64	64	6	2	4	1	3	16	96	Bytes	16	32

CLNAP-PDU

Res	BE Tag	BA Size	DA	SA	HL PI	PAD Len	QoS	CRC Id	Hdr Len	Bdg	Hed Ext	Info 9188 Bytes	PAD	CRC	Res	BE Tag	Len
8	8	16	64	64	6	2	4	1	3	16	160	Bytes	16	32	8	8	16

IMPDU

Res	Reserved	Pad Len	Padding Length
DA	Destination Address	Hdr Len	Header Extension Field Length
PI	Protocol Identifier	Hed Ext	Header Extension Field
CRC Id	CRC Identifier	CRC	IEEE 32 Bit CRC Field
Bdg	Bridging Information	BAsize	Buffer Allocation Size
PAD	Padding Bytes	HL	Header Length
X	not used by network	QoS	Quality of Service Indicator
BETag	Beginning End Tag	Info	User Information Field
SA	Source Address	Len	IMPDU Length

Figure 12.19
SMDS, CBDS, and CLNAP frame formats.

four trailer bytes—see Figure 12.19), ATM–SMDS interworking is quite straightforward.

12.4 Loop Emulation Service

So far in this chapter we have discussed interworking between ATM and different types of data-carrying technologies, whether LAN, MAN, or WAN. In July 2000, the ATM Forum published its "Voice and Multimedia Over ATM— Loop Emulation Service Using AAL2" specification (af-vmoa-0145.000); this specifies interworking between ATM and legacy public-switched telephone network (PSTN) circuit-based technologies. An important use of this service is to allow multiple "local loops" to make use of digital subscriber line (DSL) technologies for efficient communication between the public telephone system and small offices where perhaps a few dozen phone lines are available. Figure 12.20 shows the general arrangement and positioning of customer premises (CP) and telephone exchange/central office (CP) interworking functions (IWFs).

AAL-2, using the service-specific convergence sublayer specified in ITU-T Recommendation I.366.2, is used to transfer the voiceband data on multiple AAL-2 channels, each identified by a separate CID in the associated CPS-Packets. Figure 12.21 shows the protocol stacks and ITU-T recommendations involved.

Familiarity with the details given in the earlier chapter on the ATM Adaptation Layer, specifically AAL-2, is an advantage when considering the ATM Forum's Loop Emulation Service.

The ATM Forum specification is quite extensive and specifies several different interworking scenarios, covering different types of legacy signaling, both analog and digital. One example is given here to provide the reader with the general concept of this kind of interworking.

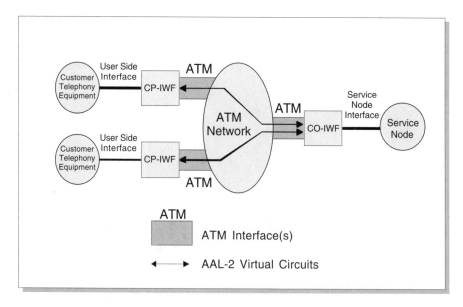

Figure 12.20
Loop emulation service using AAL-2 reference model.

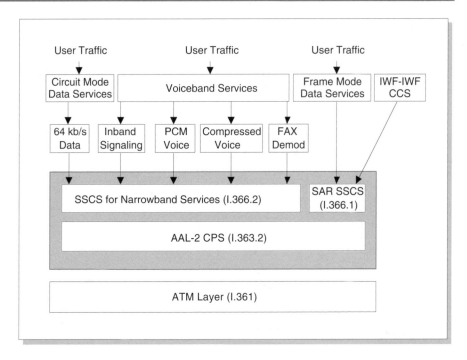

Figure 12.21
Loop emulation service protocols.

Figure 12.22 shows interworking between analog telephony using channel-associated signaling (CAS) and ATM AAL-2.

The analog voice signal is converted to a 64kb/s digital signal then mapped to an AAL-2 channel with a CID value in the range 16 to 127; mapping and coding is in accordance with one of the I.366.2 Annexes in the range A to I (e.g., Annex B for uncompressed G.711 A-law or m-law encoding).

The CAS information ("ABCD" codewords) is extracted from the analog telephone signal by the Analog Signaling Convertion block, which interprets on-hook, off-hook, and pulse dialing; in accordance with ITU-T Recommendation I.366.2, the CAS is carried in the same AAL-2 Channel (CPS-Packets with the same CID) as the bearer channel. The CAS CPS-Packets have UUI value 24 and the CPS-Packets are type 3 (i.e., they include CRC-10 error detection and involve triple redundancy) with message type 000011, in accordance with Annex L of I.366.2.

For tone dialing using dual tone multifrequency (DTMF), the DTMF Conversion block information is again sent over the same AAL-2 channel as the bearer channel with UUI value 24 and type 3 CPS-Packets but with message type 000010, in accordance with I.366.2 Annex K.

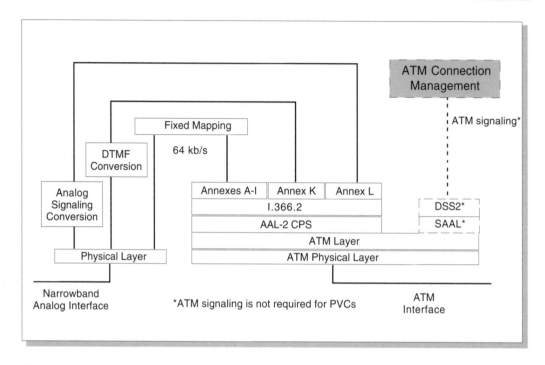

Figure 12.22
Protocol reference model for interworking analog telephony using channel-associated signaling with AAL-2.

Figure 12.22 shows an additional stack, only required where ATM UNI (DSS2) signaling is required; this signaling must not be confused with the telephone signaling carried over the AAL-2 bearer channel—it is there only in the event that the underlying ATM virtual channel needs to be set up. Normally, PVCs are more likely, so this extra stack is omitted.

At the time of this writing, this specification was in the process of being revised. The main new capability being added in the revised version will be support for Primary Rate Interfaces (E1 30B + D and DSI 23B + D).

Chapter 13

ATM Network Management

Management of ATM network components uses an ATM implementation of the Simple Network Management Protocol (SNMP) and the ATM systems' Management Information Base (MIB). ATM MIBs are databases that contain current status and configuration information about the ATM component. SNMP is the communication protocol used to read and edit the contents of MIBs. This concept was taken in large part from the standards for the management of IP networks (SNMP, RFC 1157; MIB II, RFC 1213), on which most network management solutions today are based, and codified by the ATM Forum in the Integrated Local Management Interface (ILMI) Specification Version 4.0 (af-ilmi-0065.000). (ILMI was formerly called "Interim Local Management Interface.") Every ATM interface used in the public network must contain a MIB and the accompanying ATM Interface Management Entity (IME). The IME represents the software agent that grants SNMP access to the interface's MIB. ILMI defines four ATM MIB modules; the Textual Conventions MIB, Link Management MIB, Address Registration MIB, and Service Registry MIB. The Textual Conventions MIB specifies the formats and names of the MIB objects in the ASN.1 language. The Link Management MIB provides general management of the ATM interface. The Address Registration MIB is used in registering ATM addresses with ATM switching components, and the Service Registry MIB is used to register ATM network services such as the LAN Emulation Configuration Server

(LECS). (Note that ATM *addresses* are not the VPI-VCIs of ATM cells (these are *routing labels*) but correspond more to phone numbers used in call setup.) The MIB modules contain 32-bit counters that can hold values from 0 to $2^{32} - 1$ (decimal 4294967295). The ATM Forum's Network Management Working Group has for years worked on MIBs for different network components and the number of these MIBs continues to increase as new extensions to ATM technology occur. A current list of MIBs is available on the ATM Forum public website at www.atmforum.com.

13.1   The ATM MIB Groups

The information in the ATM MIB (Figure 13.1) is grouped as follows:

- System
- Physical Layer
- ATM Layer
- Virtual Path (VP) Connections
- Virtual Channel (VC) Connections

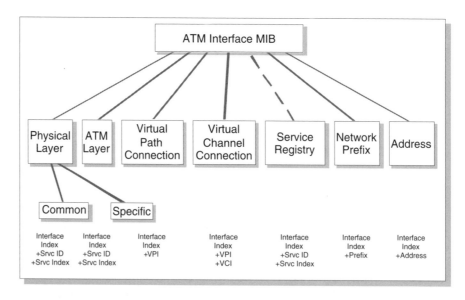

Figure 13.1

The tree structure of the ATM interface MIB.

- Address Registration Information
- Service Registry

The System MIB group is mandatory for all ATM components. It contains objects for identification (sysObjectID), location (sysLocation), services (sysServices), and operator (sysContact) of the system, as well as the elapsed time since the component was started (sysUpTime):

- sysDescr
- sysObjectID
- sysUpTime
- sysContact
- sysName
- sysLocation
- sysServices

The Physical Layer group contains the operating parameters and statistics of the physical or virtual ATM interfaces. The ATM Layer group contains ATM configuration information such as the number of permanent VPCs and VCCs, or the maximum number of VPCs and VCCs supported by the given ATM interface. Status information and QoS configuration information for the VPCs and VCCs are stored in the Virtual Path Connections and Virtual Channel Connections groups.

13.2   ILMI and SNMP

The SNMP protocol defines four commands for handling management information:

Get	Reads out the management information contained in a specific MIB object.
Get-Next	Reads successive objects from the MIB.
Set	Changes the value of MIB variables.
Trap	Reports events (a bit like an *interrupt*).

In ILMI, the functions of these four commands are implemented by means of the following five ILMI PDU types:

GetRequest PDU	Transports a Get command.
GetNextRequest PDU	Transports a Get-Next command.

GetResponse PDU   Contains the response to a Get, Get-Next, or Set command.

SetRequest PDU   Transports a Set command.

Trap PDU   Reports a Trap event.

The ILMI PDUs are transferred between IMEs (Interface Management Entities) over the default VCC VPI = 0, VCI = 16, encapsulated in AAL5 frames. All ILMI messages are sent with the Cell Loss Priority (CLP) set to 0, and must not take up more than 1% of the ATM interface's communication bandwidth. The message format conforms to that of SNMP Version 1 (RFC 1157). All ILMI SNMP messages use the community name "ILMI." In Trap PDUs, the agent-addr field contains the IP address 0.0.0.0, and the value of the MIB object sysUpTime as the timestamp. The maximum size of the SNMP messages is 484 bytes.

13.2.1   ILMI Traffic Profile

The VCC used for ILMI may have a Sustainable Cell Rate of no more than 1% and a peak cell rate of no more than 5% of the physical ATM interface's bandwidth. The response time must be under 1 second for 95% of all ILMI requests. The MIB values should be updated at least every 30 seconds, and a trap should be sent within 2 seconds after the occurrence of the event reported.

13.3   The Link Management MIB Module

The Link Management MIB implements three component management functions:

* Connectivity monitoring
* Attachment point monitoring
* Automatic interface configuration

The connectivity monitoring function serves to inform the network manager whether ILMI connectivity to a given component exists. For this purpose, every IME periodically sends a GetRequest or GetNextRequest to poll the remote station's ATM MIB objects atmPortMyIdentifier, atmMySystemIdentifier, and

sysUpTime. These polls take place at 1-second intervals during the auto configuration and address registration processes, and at 5-second intervals thereafter.
If the IME fails to respond to four polls in succession, then ILMI connectivity
is considered lost. The poll intervals and the number of unanswered MIB requests are variable, and can be set to other than the default values indicated.

The attachment point monitoring function can be used to detect when a
component (such as an ATM switch) changes its attachment point to another
port. Actually, a change of attachment point should terminate all connections.
However, because a very brief interruption of the physical layer may not clear
down the connection at the signaling level, it is possible that a quick physical
port change could result in a connection being routed to the wrong station.
For this reason, every IME stores a local copy of the remote interface's
atmfPortMyIdentifier, atmfMySystemIdentifier, and sysUpTime values.
Attachment point monitoring compares these locally stored values with the
values of these three MIB objects obtained at regular intervals by the connectivity monitoring poll. If the IME finds that the atmfPortMyIdentifier or
atmfMySystemIdentifier values have changed, or that the remote sysUpTime
is now less than the last recorded sysUpTime, then the IME reports a change
of attachment point to the local system, and all signaling channels routed
over the port in question are cleared down. The new values of atmfPortMy-
Identifier, atmfMySystemIdentifier, and sysUpTime are then saved locally; the
remote IME is asked to initialize the link, and the automatic port configuration and address registration processes are started. Then ILMI connectivity
can be declared reestablished. If the remote station does not support ILMI,
then the IME can only report the loss of ILMI connectivity, not a point of attachment change, since it has no access to the remote station's MIB values. In
environments with high security requirements, all virtual connections can be
optionally cleared down any time ILMI connectivity is lost. This policy is
known as Secure Link Procedures.

For network nodes operated in private networks, ILMI also defines
processes for automatic configuration of the ATM interfaces. Until the configuration process has been completed, such network components are only
allowed to send ILMI messages. If the MIB object atmfAtmLayerUniType
contains the value "private," then the values of the "per ATM-layer interface
attributes" can be read out by the remote interface's IME:

- Interface Index
- Maximum Number of Active VPI Bits
- Maximum Number of Active VCI Bits
- Maximum Number of VPCs
- Maximum Number of VCCs

- Number of Configured VPCs
- Number of Configured VCCs
- Maximum SVPC VPI
- Maximum SVCC VPI
- Minimum SVCC VCI
- ATM Interface Type (Public/Private)
- ATM Device Type (User/Node)
- ILMI Version
- UNI Signaling Version
- NNI Signaling Version

The same is true for automatic configuration of the traffic parameters of the signaling channel, unless the parameters specified in UNI 4.0/4.1 are used. The local IME first initializes its own signaling VCC parameters. Specifically, these are

- atmfVccServiceCategory
- atmfVccBestEffortIndicator
- atmfVccReceiveTrafficDescriptorType
- atmfVccReceiveTrafficDescriptorParam1
- atmfVccReceiveTrafficDescriptorParam2
- atmfVccReceiveTrafficDescriptorParam3
- atmfVccReceiveTrafficDescriptorParam4 and
- atmfVccReceiveTrafficDescriptorParam5 for VPI=0, VCI=5

Afterward, the corresponding MIB objects are requested from the remote interface and compared with the local values. The traffic contract for the signaling channel is then based on the minimum of the values for the two systems. The only exception is the CDVT, which is set directly to the value of the remote interface's MIB object atmfVccReceiveTrafficDescriptorParam.

13.4 The Address Registration MIB Module

ILMI allows end systems to register automatically with ATM switches by means of the Address Registration MIB module. The network and user end ATM address parts are exchanged and agreed upon in an initialization process.

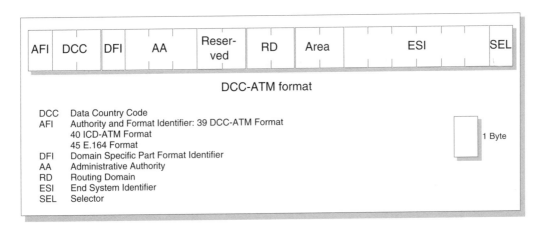

Figure 13.2
The NSAP DCC ATM address format.

ATM addresses consist of a network part (the network prefix) and a user part. If private ATM addresses are used, the user part of the ATM address is composed of the fields ESI and SEL. All other fields form the network part (Figure 13.2).

If addressing is based on the E.164 number plan, then the whole address is considered as a network part. The address part referring to the ATM network is configured on installation of the ATM switch. The user address part is stored in the given end system. When an end system is connected to an ATM switch, an exchange of user and network address parts takes place. Only when this has taken place can connections be set up using the complete ATM addresses. The user system receives the network address information from the switch and creates an MIB file of network prefixes. This is the NetPrefix group, which is mandatory in user systems and optional in network systems. Conversely, the switch maintains an ATM user address MIB, the Address group, which is mandatory in network systems and optional in user systems. Furthermore, every IME must also implement the Address Registration Admin MIB group, which documents whether the NetPrefix and Address groups are present. When the system is initialized, the ATM switch first communicates the network prefix to the end system by means of a SetRequest message. The end system then submits its system address for entry in the ATM switch's MIB. When the end system is deactivated, all registered addresses are deleted again (Figure 13.3).

The NetPrefix and Address Registration Admin groups contain the following MIB objects:

- NetPrefix Group (atmfNetPrefixGroup)
  - Interface Index (atmfNetPrefixPort)

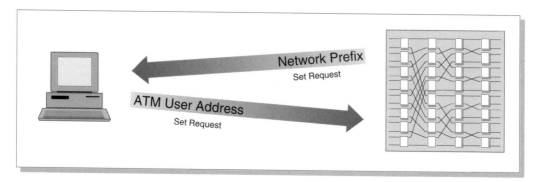

Figure 13.3
The ATM address registration process.

- Network Prefix (atmfNetPrefixPrefix)
- Network Prefix Status (atmfNetPrefixStatus)
- Address Group (atmfAddressGroup)
  - Interface Index (atmfAddressPort)
  - ATM Address (atmfAddressAtmAddress)
  - ATM Address Status (atmfAddressStatus)
  - ATM Address Organizational Scope Indication (atmfAddressOrgScope)
- Address Registration Admin Group (atmfAddressRegistrationAdmin Group)
  - Interface Index (atmfAddressRegistrationAdminIndex)
  - Address Registration Admin Status (atmfAddressRegistrationAdminStatus)

13.4.1   The Address Registration Procedure

Before communicating the NetPrefix to the user, the ATM switch first sends a

```
GetRequest {atmfAddressRegistrationAdminStatus}
```

to verify whether the user supports automatic address registration (1 = supported, 2 = unsupported). If automatic registration is supported, the network prefix is transported by means of a SetRequest message:

```
SetRequest {atmfNetPrefixStatus.port.prefix=valid(1)}
```

The user address part is entered in the ATM switch's Address group in a similar way:

```
GetRequest {atmfAddressRegistrationAdminStatus}
SetRequest { atmfAddressStatus.port.address=valid(1)}
```

Part III

ATM Networks:
Design and Planning

Chapter 14

DESIGNING AND PLANNING ATM NETWORKS

ATM network planning is a complex process, and should be carried out with great care. Data throughput on a scale corresponding to ATM bit rates can only be attained when high-performance equipment is connected over the right ATM infrastructures.

14.1   ATM End Systems

A number of conditions must be met when connecting end systems to a high-speed ATM network. Even today's computer systems can easily reach their performance limits when connected as ATM network nodes. Every component in the communication path between two data communication endpoints must therefore be examined to determine whether it is suitable for use in an ATM network. Thus it is not a good idea to connect computer systems with insufficient CPU capacity, slow memory access, or obsolete bus architectures to a network with data speeds of 155 Mbit/s and more per network node. In order to attain the high communication bandwidth possible in ATM, every system used must be examined and equipped for maximum data throughput. The following four areas in particular must be examined:

- CPU performance (instruction set, registers, cache, second-level cache)
- System bus

- Mass storage interfaces (hard disk controller, host adapter)
- Network interface

14.1.1 CPU Performance

Computer systems in high-speed networks must have a CPU architecture designed for maximum performance. Attention must be given not only to the CPU bus width and clock rate, but also to the size and efficiency of the on-chip cache memory and of the second-level (external) cache. Furthermore, the system's application software should be optimized for the given processor type wherever possible. Running 16-bit applications on 32-bit Pentium processors, for example, reduces performance to a significant degree.

14.1.2 System Bus

The system bus is another key component of a computer system. Its width and clock rate determine the attainable data throughput between the CPU on the one hand and adapter cards and peripheral devices on the other hand. The system bus standards most widely used today are PC-AT (ISA), MicroChannel, EISA, VESA, and PCI (33 or 66 MHz). Table 14.1 lists the various bus types with their maximum throughput rates. The throughput obtained in actual practice with various chipsets is indicated in another column. These figures provide the first important guideline to be observed in ATM network design. The PCI bus is the only technology capable of delivering the communication bandwidth necessary for ATM. In Fast Ethernet networks, in which the maximum communication throughput of a given station generally does not exceed 5 megabytes per second, ISA or VESA-based systems can also be used.

14.1.3 Mass Storage Interfaces

Not only the computer system itself, but also its access to mass storage is often a performance bottleneck in high-speed networks. According to Amdahl's Law, a computer requires one Mbit/s of input/output capacity for every MIPS of processing speed. The disk I/O architectures most widely used today are EIDE, SCSI, and Fiber Channel. EIDE (Enhanced Integrated Drive Electronics) components are found almost exclusively in systems based on Intel CPUs. The EIDE bus can transfer from 2 to 16.7 MB/s, but supports only two storage media per controller, and can only carry out one command at

Table 14.1 Bus Interfaces in Comparison

System bus	Maximum throughput in Mbyte/s		Typical throughput of commercial systems in MByte/s	
PC-AT (ISA)	8 (8 MHz Clock, 16 bit Transfer)		3	
Micro Channel	160 (2 MHz doubled Clock)		40	
EISA	33		8–33	
VESA	10533 MHz Clock, 486-Processor		33–40	
PCI	528 64 bit Bus, 66 MHz Clock)		33–133	
Network topology	Maximum theoretical throughput		Maximum throughput in operation	
ATM	19.4 MByte/s (=155 Mbit/s)		19 Mbyte/s	
Fast Ethernet	12.5 MByte/s (=100 Mbit/s)		5 Mbyte/s	
Bus technologies	Fiber Channel	SCSI	Ultra SCSI	IBM SAA
Transfer rate	25–100 MByte/s	5–20 MByte/s	5–40 MByte/s	20–40 MByte/s
Distance	≤ 10 km	≤ 25 m	6–25 m	≤ 2.5 km

a time. In order to manage the extremely high data throughput demanded between servers and clients in ATM networks, however, a great number of disk drives must be connected in parallel to form "disk arrays." The topology and management of such disk arrays have been standardized in seven different performance classes in the RAID (Redundant Array of Inexpensive Disks) standards. In order to support up to 15 simultaneously addressable disk drives per controller, at speeds from 5 to 40 MB/s, RAID arrays use the SCSI-II bus rather than EIDE. Like the original SCSI standard, SCSI II is a parallel interface with a defined maximum cable length and data speed. Because serial architectures are less subject to such limitations, SCSI commands have also been adapted to serial interface specifications such as SSA (Series Storage Architecture), IEEE P1394, and Fiber Channel.

Fiber Channel components (shown in Figure 14.1) which operate at data rates of over 100 MB/s (equivalent to 60,000 pages of text per second), outstrip the capabilities of SCSI by a factor of 2.5 to 40. Furthermore, Fiber Channel links can be up to 10 kilometers long, whereas SCSI can only bridge a maximum distance of 25 meters. Like SCSI, Fiber Channel is also suitable for building large disk arrays and redundant storage systems. Because Fiber Channel is actually a point-to-point technology, this is done using Fiber Channel switches. In addition to the SCSI protocol, Fiber Channel links can also be used to transport the IP, IEEE 802, ATM, HIPPI, IPI-3, and SBCCS protocols. Thus bandwidth-intensive network applications such as telemedicine and 3D CAD are also implemented over Fiber Channel infrastructures.

Fiber Channel is thus the optimum technology for connecting storage media in ATM networks with high data throughput requirements. In smaller

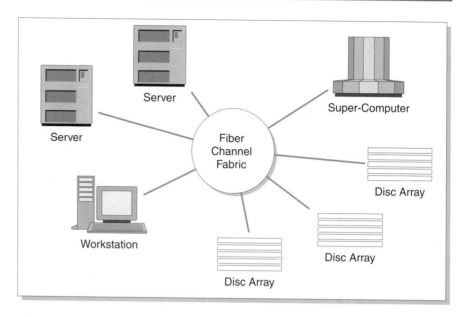

Figure 14.1
High-speed Fiber Channel–based network.

and medium-scale networks, however, SCSI-based disk arrays are also suitable.

14.1.4   Network Interface

The fourth key component in a high-performance ATM end system is the network interface, which includes both the interface hardware and the driver software. The hardware extracts the ATM cells from the incoming SDH/SONET frame, reassembles them, and makes the data available to the driver software. Outgoing data must be processed in the opposite order. The SDH/SONET frame processing is performed by appropriate SDH/SONET chipsets, which differ only slightly from one manufacturer to another. The segmentation and reassembly, however, can take place using one of three different techniques. First, this process can run on the host system's CPU and memory. This results in a significant system load on the ATM station, however, so that the data throughput only reaches a fraction of the speed that is theoretically possible. A second method is to perform cell assembly on the interface card using on-board processors. A number of manufacturers use the Intel i960 for this purpose—a very powerful but also relatively expensive microprocessor. Finally, since more and more ATM interface cards are being sold, special-purpose SAR (Segmentation and Reassembly) chips are in-

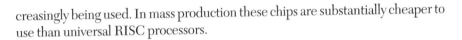

creasingly being used. In mass production these chips are substantially cheaper to use than universal RISC processors.

ATM Driver Software

The performance of the ATM interface depends not only on the hardware, but also on the driver software used. The driver software mediates between the ATM card and the host system's protocol stack. Today's ATM driver software must include all common ATM network operating modes, such as Classical IP-over-ATM (CIP) and LAN emulation. The lighter the load placed on the host CPU by these driver functions, the more resources the computer system can devote to other processes, optimizing its overall performance.

Choosing the Maximum Transfer Unit (MTU) Size

Data throughput can be further increased by making the MTU (maximum transmission unit) as large as possible. If the end system communicates with Ethernet clients using LAN emulation, then the MTU must not exceed the Ethernet limit of 1516 bytes. If connections are made only to other ATM end systems, on the other hand, a much higher MTU value can be configured. An MTU of 1516 bytes, for example, forces the system to process almost six times as many packets as it would with an MTU value of 9180 bytes. As a result of the lower overhead processing, the attainable throughput with an MTU of 9 kilobytes is up to 250% higher than with an MTU of 1.5 kilobytes.

Logical ATM Interfaces

Another factor to consider is the number of logical interfaces supported by the ATM interface card. Current ATM cards can support up to 32 logical interfaces with different addresses. This is very important for the ultimate design of the network, since this feature increases the ATM end system's ability to communicate directly with other subnetworks and end systems without having to use intermediate router components.

14.2 Planning ATM Workgroups

Due to the sharply increased bandwidth needs of today's client systems, ATM has become established at the workgroup level as an alternative to conventional 10/100 Mbit/s Ethernet and 4/16 Mbit/s Token Ring topologies. A large selection of ATM workgroup switches is available. The price per port for such ATM switches is 30 times that of 10 Mbit/s Ethernet hubs, and 10 times as high as for 100 Mbit/s Fast Ethernet hubs. If the prices per Mbit/s of throughput capacity are compared, however, ATM is by far the most economical technology (see Table 14.2).

14.2.1   ATM Workgroups with Classical IP over ATM

Communication within an ATM workgroup can take place either by means of Classical IP over ATM (CIP) or based on LAN emulation (LANE) (see Table 14.3). Classical IP over ATM is less complex to operate and administer than LANE, but has two significant drawbacks. CIP does not support broadcasts, and it requires that all nodes in the workgroup be connected by ATM interfaces. Nodes connected to the network over other topologies cannot be part of such a workgroup. LANE overcomes both of these limitations. On the other hand, Classical IP over ATM has the advantage of supporting large packet lengths. The MTU value of most routers and switches is 4470 bytes, although some interface cards only support a lower MTU. Yet if all stations in the workgroup can be so configured, an MTU of up to 65536 bytes is possible. Because Classical IP does not support broadcasts, a special ATMARP server is necessary to resolve the stations' IP addresses to ATM numbers. This server is usually located in the ATM switch or in the IP router. Because the ATMARP service generates a relatively low CPU load, which component it runs on is not of primary importance. Under maximum loads, however, it is preferable to use the ATM switch's ARP server.

Table 14.2   Comparison by Throughput: Ethernet, Fast Ethernet, Switched Ethernet, and ATM

Classical IP over ATM (CIP)	LAN-Emulation
+ Simple configuration and administration	− Complex administration and troubleshooting
+ Support of long packets	− High CPU load for ATM switch
− No broadcasts	+ Broadcasts
− No integration of Ethernet-, TR-, FDDI nodes	+ Integration of Ethernet-, TR-, FDDI nodes

Table 14.3 ATM Workgroup Design: Classical IP versus LAN Emulation

MTU (recommended maximum)	1518 Bytes
Broadcasts / Multicasts	< 10%
Installation of LES and BUS	On ATM-Switch
Configuration	Selection of meaningful names for eLAN and subnet nodes which belong together
LECS, LES, BUS topology	Redundant with fail-safe function

14.2.2 Heterogeneous LAN ATM Workgroups with LAN Emulation

LAN Emulation is a significantly more complex protocol than Classical IP. It does allow broadcasts and the integration of Ethernet, Token Ring, or FDDI nodes in the ATM subnetwork, however. (*Note*: Only Ethernet and Token Ring are fully supported by the ATM Forum LANE specifications but FDDI can be supported indirectly through the use of an internetworking function with either Ethernet or Token Ring; for details, see af-lane-0084.000.) In order to implement broadcast support, a LANE subnetwork requires a Broadcast and Unknown Server, or BUS. The LAN emulation processes, such as client registration, MAC–ATM address resolution, and so on, are performed by means of a LAN Emulation Server (LES). Finally, every LANE network must have a LAN Emulation Configuration Server (LECS), which manages the individual LANE stations' membership in the various emulated LANs. All three of these server components can be located either in the ATM switch or in a router or LAN switch connected to ATM. For LAN emulation, the recommended MTU size is the Ethernet frame length of 1518 bytes. This prevents problems that could arise when network nodes from traditional LAN topologies are integrated in the ATM workgroup. The administrator of an emulated LAN must take special care that the proportion of broadcast or multicast traffic is not too high. Otherwise the BUS may become a bottleneck, restricting the network's performance. The LANE stations can be grouped in virtual LAN segments regardless of the subnetworks to which they are physically connected. In this way the ATM workgroup can be completely integrated with traditional LAN topologies.

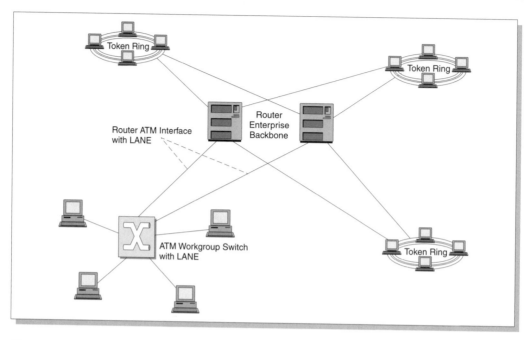

Figure 14.2
Recommendations for connecting ATM workgroups using LANE.

Note that, since a failure of one of the LANE components LECS, LES, or BUS brings all communication in the workgroup to a halt, the network design should include redundant backup components. All leading ATM component manufacturers offer LANE solutions with appropriate LEC fail-safe functions. Each ATM node (LEC) can then be assigned to several redundant LECS/BUS pairs. Cisco Systems has developed a special protocol, the Simple Server Redundancy Protocol for LAN Emulation (SSRP), to manage these functions. Other manufacturers integrate redundancy functions directly in their LANE implementations. Figure 14.2 shows the interconnection of workgroups using LANE.

14.2.3   Connecting ATM Workgroups

Connection to a Conventional Backbone Router or Switch

How an ATM workgroup can be connected to the corporate backbone depends on the type of backbone structure and the LAN mechanism used in the ATM workgroup. Today's routers and LAN switches generally support both LANE

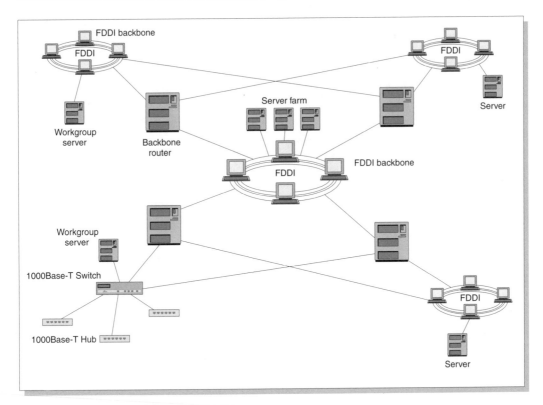

Figure 14.3
Connecting ATM workgroups to a router backbone.

and Classical IP over ATM. If LAN emulation is chosen for the workgroup, then it is recommended that the BUS and LES, which require substantial CPU performance, be implemented on the ATM switch rather than the router or LAN switch. Otherwise the backbone connection component's throughput could be impaired under high network loads. If the ATM workgroup is connected to the backbone by more than one router, then these routers should also be connected to one another for the sake of redundancy. Thus two Cisco routers, for example, can monitor one another using HSRP (the Hot Stand-by Router Protocol) for LANE. If one of the routers is no longer available, the other can then take over its functions immediately (see Figure 14.3).

Connection to an ATM Backbone

An ATM workgroup can be connected to an ATM backbone directly at one of the backbone ATM switches. Because PNNI, the classic ATM signaling and routing protocol for backbones, only supports routing on the ATM layer, not for

CIP or LANE, the MPOA protocol (Multiprotocol over ATM) must be used on the backbone ATM switch. An MPOA ATM backbone can interconnect several ATM workgroups with any desired degree of transparency. If MPOA is not available on the ATM backbone network, then a conventional router with appropriate ATM interfaces and LANE support on the workgroup side must be connected between the workgroup and the backbone switch. In a solution of this type, special attention must be given to the router's performance and throughput to avoid possible bottlenecks under heavy loads. Prior traffic measurements on the backbone and the connected ATM workgroups are useful in obtaining an exact idea of the expected load on the connecting router. In case of doubt, it is generally advisable to avoid the intermediate router by upgrading or replacing the ATM backbone switch to add support for MPOA.

14.3   Design and Planning of ATM Backbones

ATM as a backbone technology offers a number of advantages compared with routers and traditional network topologies (FDDI, LAN switching, 10/100Base-TX, Gigabit Ethernet). The most important of these are:

- Better traffic management
- Scalable bandwidth
- Greater range
- Efficient transportation of different types of traffic (voice, data, image, video)
- Highly flexible change management (virtual LANs)
- Direct integration with WAN and MAN ATM services
- Optimum network and resource utilization through the use of ATM PNNI routing rather than independent routing protocols
- Faster fall-back routing based on SVCs and SPVCs compared with the Spanning Tree algorithm

The migration of a backbone to ATM is generally a gradual process. At first only the backbone routers are connected to one another over an ATM network, which optimizes router-to-router communication. Inter-router bandwidth can now be guaranteed, and when individual links fail, fall-back routes can be activated more quickly. In the second phase, the backbone routers themselves are replaced by ATM switches with LAN emulation. This means that the departmental LAN switches and routers are directly connected to the ATM backbone. In large networks, several emulated LANs are interconnected by means of MPOA. After successful migration to ATM, department and campus servers can be concentrated in the data-processing center. This simplifies server maintenance, operation, and management. The workgroup servers remain decentralized. The establishment of the enterprise data center completes the migration to an ATM backbone.

14.3.1　The ATM Router Backbone

In the first step toward the deployment of ATM as a backbone technology, the ATM network is used only as a router backbone. The advantages here lie in the guaranteed bandwidth that ATM provides for inter-router communication, and in immediate switching to alternative paths in case of link failure—assuming, of course, that alternative paths exist within the ATM cloud, and that SPVCs (smart permanent virtual connections) are used. The fail-over speed of SPVCs is significantly faster than switching to backup routes by OSPF over an Ethernet connection. Yet the critical factor in the performance of the ATM router backbone is the throughput capability of the ATM modules in the switches used. The technical data on router ATM modules should therefore be carefully analyzed before a selection is made. Other qualities to look for in ATM router modules include:

- *Support for multiple ATM ports:* If the given router only supports one ATM port, then any physical redundancy must be implemented using a different interface (such as 100Base-TX). Support for at least two ATM interfaces per router is preferable.
- *OAM support:* A complete implementation of OAM cell functions is necessary for effective fault management and performance monitoring.
- *Automatic neighbor discovery:* The newest generation of routers are able to identify the next router reachable over their ATM interfaces automatically. This simplifies router configuration in the backbone network significantly.

Router Backbone Architecture

The routers can be connected to the ATM backbone in one of three ways:

- Using PVCs
- Using SPVCs
- Using SVCs

The use of LAN emulation, as in ATM-based LAN switching backbones, is not necessary in an ATM router backbone since the path of the outgoing frames is predetermined by the router. At the same time, the routers retain their function of structuring the network. When LAN switches are connected by PVCs or SPVCs, on the other hand, the network is comparable to one big LAN segment. This is why LAN emulation must be used to structure a network that uses a LAN switch backbone (see section 14.3.2).

In a router backbone, Permanent Virtual Circuits (PVCs) are recommended, especially if only a few (i.e., 5 to 10) routers are being connected to one another over a relatively small ATM network, with one or two ATM switches. The PVCs are statically configured connections between individual pairs of routers. In order for the router traffic to be transported over the various PVCs, static PVC-IP address lists must be maintained on each router.

"Smart PVCs" (SPVCs) are an improvement over ordinary PVCs, and can automatically divert traffic to alternative routes when link failures occur. The ATM switches used in the router backbone continuously monitor which PVCs are available, and provide alternative paths as needed. SPVCs should therefore be used if the router backbone consists of more than two ATM switches.

Switched Virtual Circuits (SVCs) are used in the backbone only if a greater number of routers (over 20, for example) need to be networked with one another, yet permanent inter-router connections are not desired. This can be the case if the communication bandwidth of the ATM backbone is not sufficient for a very great number of simultaneous PVCs, for example. Drawbacks of using SVCs include more frequent errors than with PVCs, and especially a noticeable delay on connection setup, which may take from 1 to 10 milliseconds depending on the performance of the ATM switch and the router interface. Figure 14.4 illustrates a sample router backbone's migration from FDDI to ATM. As shown in Figure 14.4, the ATM backbone should consist of at least two ATM switches with redundant links.

14.3.2   ATM LAN Switch Backbone with LANE

If the enterprise backbone consists of networked LAN switches (such as 100Base-TX switches), it may also be a good idea to convert the inter-switch network to ATM. Whether this is worthwhile must be determined case by case, however. In smaller switch backbones in particular, full duplex 100Base-TX or 100Base-FX connections may be a more economical solution. Another consideration is the additional delay of about 100 µs, which is caused by segmentation and reassembly when data packets are transported over an ATM backbone. Furthermore, each ATM switch in the communication path adds another 10 to 20 µs to the total transfer delay. In backbones with many

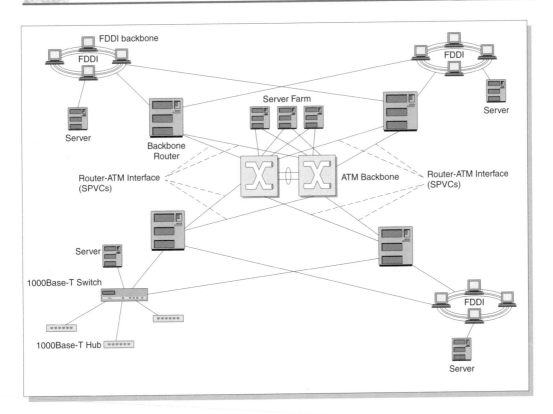

Figure 14.4
ATM router backbone with SPVCs.

switches and high bandwidth requirements, however, ATM rapidly becomes the more efficient solution. In LAN switch backbones, an ATM solution based on LAN emulation is generally chosen. The use of SPVCs would make sense only with a low number of switches (fewer than five), but for most of these small backbones it is not worth migrating to ATM in the first place.

All leading LAN switch manufacturers now offer ATM uplinks with support for LAN emulation. Note once again that the LANE components (LES, BUS, and LECS) should run on the ATM switch and not on the LAN switching hardware. And here too, the ATM backbone consists of at least two redundant ATM switches. ATM then provides significant advantages over a conventional switching solution. Virtual ELANs can be formed of any subset of the LAN switches, regardless of their location in the backbone. The data traffic can be controlled flexibly and dynamically. Bandwidth can be augmented where needed, and bandwidth reserves can be cleared down. If at some future time the network of 155 Mbit/s links in the ATM cloud is no longer sufficient, it can easily be upgraded to data speeds of 622 Mbit/s or 2.4 Gbit/s (depending on switch models). In operating ATM backbones between LAN switches, as in operating LANE workgroups, it is very important to monitor the proportion of broadcast and multicast traffic, especially in the post-transition phase, to avoid performance losses due to an overloaded BUS.

14.3.3   The ATM MPOA Enterprise Backbone

Where several department or building backbones based on LAN emulation are connected to an ATM enterprise backbone, MPOA (Multiprotocol over ATM) is used. MPOA extends PNNI (the ATM signaling and routing protocol for backbones) and the original LAN emulation standard to permit efficient routing of all the protocols emulated in LANE over the ATM backbone, across any number of LANE subnets. With MPOA in place, virtual LANs can be formed across the entire enterprise network. The users in these LANs can be grouped without regard to their physical location or their type of network connection, whether ATM or a traditional LAN technology. Furthermore, the extensive bandwidth and traffic management capabilities of ATM are now available in the enterprise backbone as well. At this point, the final step in optimizing the enterprise backbone architecture can be taken: concentrating all enterprise and departmental servers in an enterprise data center. Only the workgroup server remains at the location of the workgroup itself. This simplifies a number of processes in server operation, maintenance, and administration. Depending on the ATM adapter card, ATM servers support up to 32 logical interfaces with 32 different addresses. This means that ATM servers can communicate with a great number of clients or subnetworks without intermediate routers. Moreover, ATM links can bridge very long distances. Thus the data passes through fewer network nodes than with conventional enterprise backbones. Over single-mode fiber, for example, an ATM segment may extend up to 60 km, so that a subnetwork can be directly connected to an enterprise data center located at a great distance. The complexity and number of interfaces in the network is thus drastically reduced.

14.3.4   ATM Enterprise Backbone with Router Support

If MPOA is not available for the ATM switches used, then routing functions in the ATM backbone must be provided by conventional routers. This is achieved by connecting routers with appropriate ATM LANE interfaces between the emulated LANs and the ATM backbone, as described above in the section on connecting ATM workgroups. This solution is preferable only in backbone structures with limited traffic loads, however, and should be carefully analyzed on a case-by-case basis.

Chapter 15

TESTING AND CHOOSING NETWORK COMPONENTS

The testing and selection of network components and end systems to be used in high-speed networks is an extremely important process. While today's components have no trouble attaining the theoretical maximum data throughput in traditional networking technologies, such as 100 Mbit/s Ethernet, this is not always the case with ATM. The products available vary widely in performance, so that a detailed analysis of their technical characteristics is imperative before a decision can be made for or against a specific product. Furthermore, the accuracy of the manufacturer's specifications should be tested on site if appropriate test instruments are available. Vendors often provide technical data that are erroneous, imprecise, or incomplete, and also list technical parameters that make their particular product appear in a favorable light, but that are not found in any other comparable device. For these reasons, the ATM Forum Test Working Group and the IETF Benchmarking Methodology Working Group (IETF-BMWG *http://www.ietf.org/html.charters/bmwg-charter.html*) have developed documents designed to establish a uniform nomenclature for measuring the performance of network components, thus making comparable performance measurements possible. These documents include:

- RFC 1242 Benchmarking Terminology for Network Interconnection Devices
- RFC 2285 Benchmarking Terminology for LAN Switching Devices

- RFC 2761 Terminology for ATM Benchmarking
- RFC 2544 Benchmarking Methodology for Network Interconnect Devices
- RFC 2889 Benchmarking Methodology for LAN Switching Devices
- ATM Forum Performance Testing Specification (af-test-0131.000)
- ATM Forum UNI Signaling Performance Test Suite (af-test-0158.000)

The performance parameters defined and discussed in these documents describe all the major functions of ATM network components. They should be ascertained and if possible verified by on-site testing before any network component is deployed. All key performance parameters and the appropriate tests are explained below.

15.1 Application-Related Performance Parameters for ATM Components

Due to the tremendous complexity of processes in ATM networks, the definitive evaluation of the performance of ATM components is a very involved task. The results of individual tests must always be weighed and interpreted in the context of the other known performance parameters. Evaluating the performance of ATM systems with regard to actual applications is especially difficult. For example, even though one ATM switch shows a lower cell loss ratio than another, the second switch may still drop fewer higher-layer packets, which is the decisive criterion for the user. Similar difficulties may arise in evaluating LAN emulation or signaling performance. The decisive parameters from the user's point of view are therefore primarily those that refer to data packets, not ATM cells:

- Frame throughput
- Frame latency
- Fairness
- Frame loss ratio
- Frame burst size
- Signaling performance parameters

ATM network performance parameters on the physical and ATM cell layers, which are especially important to measure while the ATM network is in service, are explained in detail in Chapter 19.

15.1.1   Frame Throughput

In testing frame throughput, three distinct quantities are measured (Figure 15.1):

- Lossless throughput (the maximum data rate at which no frames are lost)
- Peak throughput (the maximum attainable throughput, regardless of packet loss)
- Full-load throughput (throughput at a load of 100% of the line rate on the input ports)

Throughput is measured by counting only those frames that are transported completely without errors. Partial frames or frames with checksum errors are not counted. Throughput is defined in bits per second, counting only the bits in successfully transported packets. The overhead generated by the ATM cell format or the switching system is not counted.

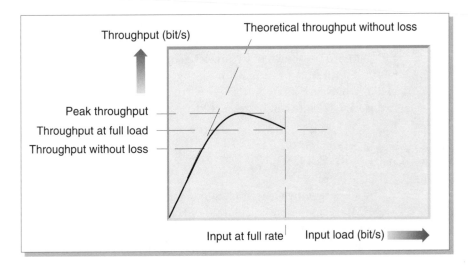

Figure 15.1
Lossless, peak, and full-load throughput.

Testing Frame Throughput

Frame throughput testing is performed in several steps. First, the data flow through the ATM switch must be defined. The following scenarios (shown in Figure 15.2) are possible:

- n-to-n straight connections
- n-to-$(n − 1)$ full-cross connections
- n-to-m partial cross connections $(1 \leq m \leq n − 1)$
- k-to-1 $(1 < k < n)$
- 1-to-$(n − 1)$ multicast connections
- n-to-$(n − 1)$ multicast connections

The connection configurations n-to-$(n − 1)$ full cross and n-to-$(n − 1)$ multicast place the highest demands on the switching fabric of ATM components. For each of the scenarios listed, the corresponding connections are created with AAL payload frames of various lengths (64 bytes, 1518 bytes, 9188 bytes, and 65,535 bytes). The traffic is low at first, and is gradually increased until the frame count at the switch input ports no longer matches the number received at the output ports. The load at which this occurs is the lossless throughput limit. Then the traffic is increased further until throughput no longer increases, regardless of packet loss. This determines the switch's peak throughput. Finally, a 100% line rate load is applied to the connections to measure the full-load throughput.

The test equipment necessary to generate and evaluate the test traffic can be reduced by looping the output ports of the switch under test back into its input ports, as shown in Figure 15.3. In this way an 8-port switch can be tested with 8-to-8 straight connections using just one test device. Due to the fixed cabling, however, only permanent virtual connections (PVCs) can be tested in this way. Results can be tabulated as shown in Table 15.1.

15.1.2 Frame Latency

The most significant frame latency measurement is message in–message out (MIMO) latency. If the cell rate of the input port is less than or equal to that of the output ports, then the MIMO latency is the time that elapses between the arrival of the first bit and the transmission of the last bit of the packet, and thus equal to the FILO (first in–last out) latency. If the interface cell rate at the switch's output ports is lower than that of the input ports, however, then the delay time due to the different input and output interface cell rates, which

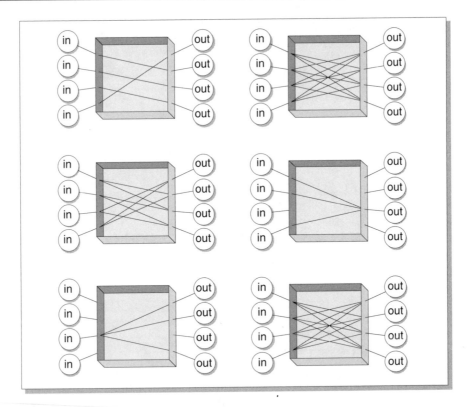

Figure 15.2
Different connection configurations for ATM switch testing.

Table 15.1 Frame Throughput Results

Foreground traffic PVPC, SVPC, PVC, SVC	VCCs within a switch module	VCCs between two switch modules	Connection topology	Service class (UBR, ABR, VBR)	Packet length	Fixed packet length, random distribution	Lossless free packet throughput	Peak packet throughput	Full load packet throughput
PVC		**X**	**n-to-m partial meshed**	**UBR**	**1518 Byte**	**fixed**	**... Mbit/s**	**... Mbit/s**	**... Mbit/s**
SVC		X	n-to-n direct	UBR	64 Byte		... Mbit/s	... Mbit/s	... Mbit/s

Bold: Recommended by ATM forum as minimum requirement

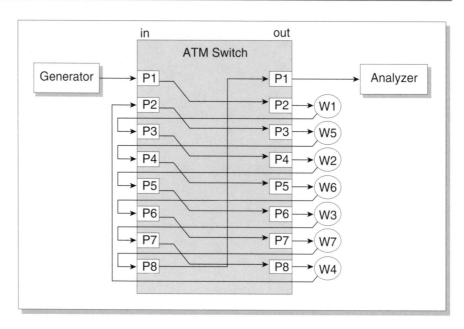

Figure 15.3
Load testing with loopback cabling.

would occur even in an ideal zero-delay switch, must be subtracted from the FILO latency. This adjusted delay is called the Nominal Frame Output Time (NFOT). The important issue to understand here is that cells passing across higher rate interfaces do so more quickly than cells passing across slower interfaces. Obviously the cell rate for the test channel must be low enough such that the lower rate interface can cope, and consequently the test channel occupies a smaller percentage of the available bandwidth of the high rate interface than of the lower rate interface. But it is just because of this almost uniquely ATM-related artifact that the MIMO measurement is preferred over the FILO measurement.

Input port rate $\leq$ output port rate:
  Frame latency (MIMO) $= t_1 - t_2$ (FIFO)
    t_1: the first bit of the frame enters the switch
    t_2: the last bit of the frame exits the switch

Input port rate $>$ output port rate:
  Frame latency (MIMO) $= t_1 - t_2 - \text{NFOT}$
    t_1: the first bit of the frame enters the switch
    t_2: the last bit of the frame exits the switch
    NFOT: Nominal Frame Output Time (latency in an ideal zero-delay switch)

If the MIMO latency M is measured for p packets, the mean MIMO latency M_M and the empirical $(n-1)$ standard deviation M_D can be calculated as follows:

$$M_D = \sum_{i=1}^{p} \frac{M_i}{p}$$

$$M_D = \sqrt{\frac{\sum_{i=1}^{p}(M_i - M_M)^2}{p - 1}}$$

The standard deviation is an approximate value for the error of individual measurements. An approximation for the error of the mean itself is obtained by

$$M_E = \frac{M_D}{\sqrt{n}}$$

If over 30 measurements are performed, then the measured mean latency has a 68% probability of lying within the error value M_E of the theoretical mean of an infinite number of measurements. This probability is also called the confidence interval:

$$\text{Confidence interval} = M_M \pm t\frac{M_D}{\sqrt{n}}$$

For a set of 30 measurements, the following values for the parameter t can be used:

Confidence interval 68%: $t = 1$

Confidence interval 80%: $t = 1.31$

Confidence interval 90%: $t = 1.70$

Confidence interval 80%: $t = 2.76$

Frame Latency Testing

Frame latency testing differs from throughput testing in that a distinction is made between foreground and background traffic. The actual delay measurements are performed on connections defined as foreground traffic at varying background loads. In this way the effect of the switch's overall traffic load on frame latency can be tested. Two switch ports are selected for foreground traffic, and PVC or SVC connections are set up between them with different bandwidths and packet lengths (64 bytes, 1518 bytes, 9188 bytes, 65,535 bytes). The foreground traffic load is gradually increased, beginning at half the maximum foreground load, until packet loss occurs. The full foreground traffic load (FFL) is equal to the link rate of the output port (P_O) or of the input port, P_I, whichever is less.

The switch ports not devoted to foreground traffic are subjected to varying background traffic loads during the packet delay tests. Like the foreground traffic, the background load can also consist of different connection types (PVC, SVC) and topologies as well as varying frame sizes. The background load is generated at all but two of the switch's ports. Once again, to minimize the traffic generating equipment necessary, the background load can be looped from output ports back to other input ports (Figure 15.4 and Table 15.2).

15.1.3 Fairness

The "fairness" of a switch in transporting user data refers to the degree to which it provides optimum distribution of the available bandwidth to the individual connections. For example, if n connections are active simultaneously and the available switch throughput is T, then a bandwidth allocation of T/n to each of these connections is defined as optimum (assuming, of course, that the connections have the same bandwidth requirements). If the measured throughput of n connections is $\{T_{f1}, T_{f2}, T_{f3}, T_{f4}, \ldots T_{fn}\}$ and the ideal throughput is $\{T_{i1}, T_{i2}, T_{i3}, T_{i4}, \ldots T_{in}\}$, then the fairness index is defined as follows:

$$\text{Fairness index} = \text{Fairness index} = \frac{\Sigma\, x_i}{n \Sigma x_i^2}$$

$$\text{where } x_i = \frac{T_i}{T_{fi}}$$

Note, however, that fairness does not necessarily refer to throughput. Fairness is a dimensionless quantity, and can be calculated with respect to other parameters, such as the latency in a switch. Fairness ranges from zero to one, so that maximum fairness is defined as 100% and minimum fairness as 0%. If a switch allocates its entire capacity to 75% of the existing connections, the resulting fairness index equals 0.75.

Measuring Fairness

From a user's point of view, fairness measurements are especially significant under peak throughput and under full-load conditions. To perform such measurements, the peak throughput must first be determined, as described in sec-

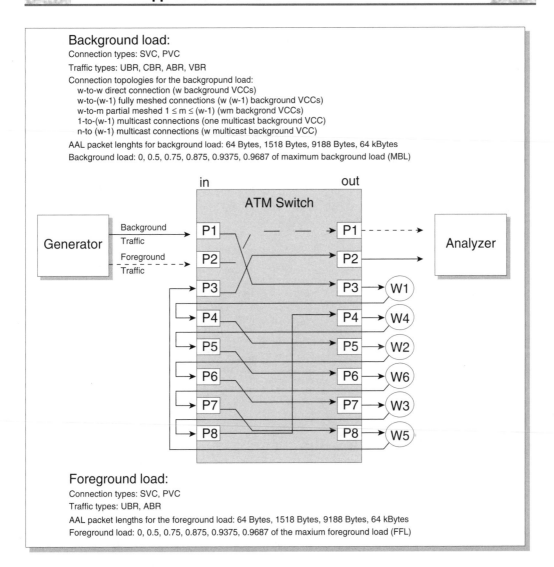

Background load:

Connection types: SVC, PVC

Traffic types: UBR, CBR, ABR, VBR

Connection topologies for the backgropund load:
  w-to-w direct connection (w background VCCs)
  w-to-(w-1) fully meshed connections (w (w-1) background VCCs)
  w-to-m partial meshed 1 ≤ m ≤ (w-1) (wm backgrond VCCs)
  1-to-(w-1) multicast connections (one multicast background VCC)
  n-to (w-1) multicast connections (w multicast background VCC)

AAL packet lenghts for background load: 64 Bytes, 1518 Bytes, 9188 Bytes, 64 kBytes

Background load: 0, 0.5, 0.75, 0.875, 0.9375, 0.9687 of maximum background load (MBL)

in   out

ATM Switch

Generator — Background Traffic → P1 ⋯ ⋯ → P1 ⤏ Analyzer
Foreground Traffic → P2 → P2 →

P3 → W1
P4 → W4
P5 → W2
P6 → W6
P7 → W3
P8 → W5

Foreground load:

Connection types: SVC, PVC

Traffic types: UBR, ABR

AAL packet lengths for the foreground load: 64 Bytes, 1518 Bytes, 9188 Bytes, 64 kBytes

Foreground load: 0, 0.5, 0.75, 0.875, 0.9375, 0.9687 of the maxium foreground load (FFL)

Figure 15.4
Frame latency test configuration.

tion 15.1.1. The relative throughput of selected virtual connections is measured at a traffic load corresponding to the peak throughput rate, and the fairness index is calculated from the results. Then the traffic is increased to full load, and similar measurements are made in order to calculate the full-load throughput fairness index.

Table 15.2 Frame Latency Test Results

Configuration for foreground traffic and latency							
Foreground traffic PVPC, SVPC, PVC, SVC	Foreground traffic VCCs within one switch module	Foreground traffic VCCs within two switch modules	Service class (UBR, ABR, VBR)	Packet length	Packet distance fixed, random distribution	Foreground traffic ratio to FFL	Packet delay
PVC		X	UBR	1518 Byte	fixed	0.75 FFL	... Mbit/s
Configuration for background traffic							
Foreground PVPC, SVPC, PVC, SVC	Foreground traffic VCCs within one switch	Foreground traffic VCCs between two modules	Service class (UBR, ABR, VBR)	Packet length	Packet distance fixed, random distribution	Load ratio to MBL	
PVC		X	UBR	9188 Byte	fixed	0 0.85 MBL	
PVC		X	CBR	9188 Byte	fixed	... Mbit/s	

Bold: Recommended for test by ATM forum

15.1.4   Frame Loss Ratio

The frame loss ratio provides a measure the of frames that could not be forwarded due to insufficient switch capacity:

Frame loss ratio = (frame input rate – frame throughput)/frame input rate

Clearly, if no frames are ever lost (an unlikely situation), the frame loss ratio is zero. Here again, the most significant frame loss ratio quantities for the user are those measured under peak throughput and full-load conditions. The test parameters for frame loss ratio tests—background traffic, AAL frame size, service classes, and so on—are varied as described above.

15.1.5   Maximum Frame Burst Size

The maximum frame burst size (MFBS) refers to the number of frames that can be sent at the peak rate before losses occur. The MFBS is especially significant for UBR traffic, since the UBR service category permits bursts at the peak rate.

Measuring the Maximum Frame Burst Size

The MFBS is measured using a k-to-1 connection configuration with k VCCs, as shown in Figure 15.5.

Once the VCCs are set up, fixed-length cell bursts—sequences of a given number of user cells with no interspersed idle/unassigned cells—are sent over all connections simultaneously. If no cell loss is detected, the burst length is increased until cell loss occurs. The longest burst with no loss represents the maximum cell burst size (MCBS). Since a given frame fills the payload of a known number of cells, the maximum frame burst size—the maximum number of frames that can be sent in succession before losses occur—is obtained by dividing the maximum cell burst size by the frame length. The minimum MFBS test parameters recommended by the ATM Forum are as follows:

- Connection setup between different network modules
- k-to-1 connection configuration
- Frame lengths: 64 bytes, 1518 bytes, 9188 bytes, 65,535 bytes

15.1.6   Signaling Performance Parameters

When the traffic over a switch includes a high number of SVCs of relatively short duration, the connection establishment time becomes a critical parameter affecting the maximum attainable throughput. The connection establishment time is defined as the time that elapses between the transmission of the SETUP message and the reception of the CONNECT message. The time required by the station called to decide whether to accept the connection

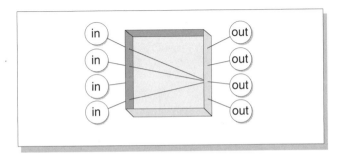

Figure 15.5
Maximum frame burst size test configuration.

request is subtracted, however. Since both the SETUP and CONNECT messages extend across several cells, the precise definition of connection establishment time (Figure 15.6) for an ATM system is as follows:

Connection establishment time = MIMO(SETUP) + MIMO(CONNECT)

Note, however, that the use of MIMO is problematic since the message received at the destination is not the same as that sent from the source, so a modified definition is required. At the time of writing, this is still under study.

Other measurements that characterize the performance of a system in relation to signaling include:

- *Connection tear-down time:* The time required to clear down a connection: MIMO(RELEASE) + MIMO(RELEASE COMPLETE)
- *Connection setup rate:* The maximum number of connections that can be established per second
- *Connection tear-down rate:* The maximum number of connections that can be successfully cleared down per second

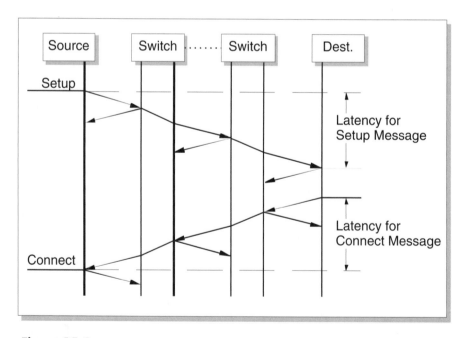

Figure 15.6
Definition of connection establishment time.

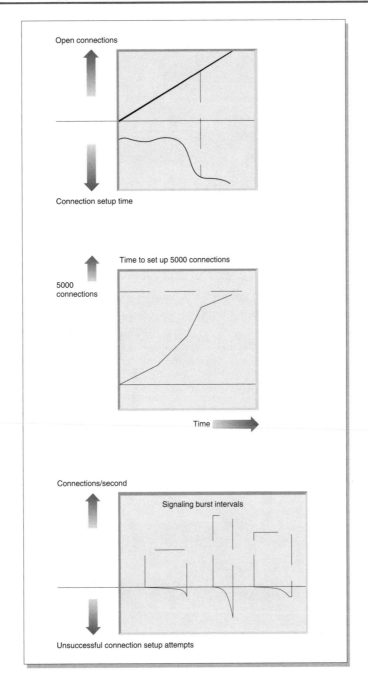

Figure 15.7
Test criteria for signaling performance.

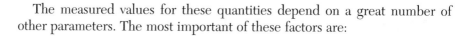

The measured values for these quantities depend on a great number of other parameters. The most important of these factors are:

- The number of intermediate switches
- The number of connection requests to be processed simultaneously in the switch
- The background traffic level
- The traffic contract and QoS parameters

Specialized signaling load generators can be used to measure the parameters listed under all kinds of conditions. Most relevant from the user's point of view, however, are the following switch characteristics:

- How many connection setups per second can be processed before the connection establishment time begins to increase?
- How many active connections can the switch have before it begins to reject connection requests?
- How long does a switch take to set up and clear down a large number of connections (100, 500, 1000, 2000, 4000, etc.)?
- How long is the maximum signaling burst that the switch can process without rejecting setup requests?

Figure 15.7 lists several examples of typical signaling load procedures.

Chapter 16

SECURITY IN ATM NETWORKS

In recent years, data network security has developed into one of the most important strategic aspects of commercial data processing. This is because the risk of lasting damage through sabotage or abuse of data networks increases along with businesses' growing dependency on increasingly complex networks. The danger to corporate networks is exacerbated by the trend toward greater use of the public Internet in business computing, as well as in-house use of Internet technologies in the form of intranets. At the same time, today's high throughput rates and the enormous volume of data transported make it more and more difficult to monitor data networks.

16.1 Risk Factor: Internet

With the explosive growth of the Internet as a global medium for information and communication, it has become a must almost overnight for nearly every company to participate in the world's largest network, and to implement an appropriate connection between the Internet and its own networking infrastructure. E-commerce and e-business are the catchwords for the Internet-based sales, marketing, service, and communication infrastructures currently being set up throughout whole industries. However, the increasing commercial use of the Internet is also leading to a significant increase in willful abuse and criminal activity in these newly created data infrastructures. Consequently, the need for network security mechanisms to meet these dangers has also grown rapidly.

16.2   Risk Factor: Intranet

"Intranet" is the name given to an internal corporate network using Internet technologies, an increasingly common phenomenon. The Internet's transport mechanisms (TCP/IP, HTTP, SMTP, FTP, etc.), presentation formats, and services are used as a universal platform for internal company data communications. In addition to a number of advantages, however, this strategy brings with it certain security problems. For example, the standardization of communication protocols and data formats can make it simpler for unauthorized persons to gain access to confidential data as the intranet is deployed. Cracking tools once used on the Internet can now be used in the LAN to obtain access to systems and databases. This fact implies a significant increase in the company's security risks, since studies show that more than two thirds of all computer system abuse is committed by the owning company's employees. For this reason, intranet migration must be accompanied by appropriate internal security measures, including internal firewalls, intrusion detection systems, and encryption. Another consequence of the introduction of intranets is the accelerated migration from paper and telephone communication toward electronic information transported over the intranet in the form of video and audio conferencing, newsgroups, messaging and voice mail systems, and so on. Because an increasing proportion of internal business communication and data is thus stored in electronic form, it can be used more efficiently on the one hand— thanks to search engines and other tools—but on the other hand, the potential consequences of abuse become more serious. Intranets therefore place special demands on a company's internal security architecture.

16.3   Risk Factor: High-Speed Networks

Due to rapidly increasing bandwidth demands on LANs, a marked trend toward high-speed data networks has been observable since the mid-1990s. At the workgroup level, the traditional Ethernet and Token Ring network topologies are increasingly being replaced by switched LAN structures, while ATM and Gigabit Ethernet have taken the place of FDDI in backbones. The rapid increases in data throughput and data speeds make it harder to implement security mechanisms with the necessary performance reserves. For example, at data rates of several hundred megabits per second, internal firewalls between a server farm with intranet web or file servers and neighboring segments with lower security requirements can be extremely difficult to implement. The same is true of other internal security measures, such as the use of antivirus software or intrusion detection systems, which can be overloaded by the enormous amount of data to be processed.

16.4 ATM Networks: Vulnerabilities and Risk Analysis

In ATM networks, as in any other network topology, the greatest risk is that of unintended security breaches caused by such procedures as:

- Administration and configuration errors
- Insufficient or faulty backups
- Operator error

These risks can be addressed primarily by intensive training programs and by well-planned and explicitly defined operating procedures. The following discussion, however, deals primarily with malicious acts and with the security mechanisms provided to prevent them in ATM networks. Threats to ATM networks can be classified according to the following scenarios:

- Unauthorized recording of data communications ("sniffing")
- Unauthorized access to network components
- Manipulation of data and communication (deletion, falsification)
- Sabotage to the communication infrastructure
- Sabotage to network components

Each of these scenarios describes a number of known methods of attack, each of which in turn can be met by various strategies. ATM networks are to some extent even more susceptible to attacks than networks based on conventional shared-media technologies such as Ethernet or FDDI.

16.4.1   ATM Network Attacks

The ATM networking principle of connection-oriented communication, which on the surface seems to offer a greater degree of security than shared-media network topologies, in fact makes it possible to implement traditional intrusion techniques, such as spoofing or TCP sequence number guessing, much more efficiently than in conventional networks. For example, a spoofing attack, in which the sender replaces the source IP address with another, can be an even more dangerous weapon in a Classical IP over ATM (CIP) network than in IP over Ethernet environments.

Spoofing in CIP ATM Networks

If the attacker knows the ATM address of the target system, he first sets up a connection to it directly. The attacker then responds to the target system's reverse ARP (InATMARP) request (which IP address is mapped to your ATM address?) with a modified InATMARP reply message that shows the IP address of a system with access authorization. Once this registration has been completed, the attacker can send other spoofed IP frames to the server. Furthermore, the attacker receives the server's reply packets, since they are sent over the existing connection. TCP sequence number guessing is therefore superfluous. IP spoofing is thus significantly simpler to perform and harder to detect in CIP ATM environments than in shared-media networks.

ATMARP Server Attack

An attacker who knows the ATM address of the ATMARP server can use it to access the complex IP address list of all systems registered as belonging to the given logical IP segment (LIS). The attacking system can then register itself with the ATMARP server using any unassigned IP address. Because each IP address can only be registered once, a system that was temporarily inactive cannot rejoin the IP over the ATM network if its address was registered by the attacker. This technique can be used on a large scale—the attacker assigns itself every address that becomes temporarily inactive—to sabotage whole networks.

The Man-in-the-Middle Attack in ATM Networks

The ARP server attack described above can also be used to mount a classic man-in-the-middle attack. Every IP address that is registered on the ARP server results in an ARP server list entry that maps the IP address to the ATM

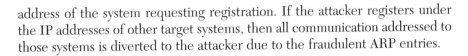

address of the system requesting registration. If the attacker registers under the IP addresses of other target systems, then all communication addressed to those systems is diverted to the attacker due to the fraudulent ARP entries.

ATM Network Load Attacks

Another denial-of-service technique is based on establishing connections with extremely high bandwidth requirements. Attacks of this kind are easy to carry out, since bandwidth is reserved for the established connection even if no actual traffic is generated. This is sufficient to undermine the availability of the network. If a connection crosses several ATM switches, it can sabotage several networks simultaneously. A variation on this attack involves setting up a large number of simultaneously active connections. Although the number of theoretically possible simultaneous ATM connections is very high, many ATM device drivers are limited to a maximum of 1024 or 2048 connections. When this limit is reached, no more connections can be set up, and traffic on the ATM network comes to a standstill.

Attacks on ATM Switches

Another category of attacks involves the manipulation of ATM switching mechanisms. First, SNMP commands are sent to the switch to make it initialize its MIB tables. In the automatic ILMI configuration process that ensues, the attacker pretends to be another ATM switch (atmfAtmLayerDeviceType = 2) using the PNNI (MPOA) protocol (atmfAtmLayerNniSigVersion = 3). In this way the attacker is able to manipulate the peer group database containing information about ATM subnetworks. Paths can then be routed through the attacker's system, and whole peer groups' communications can be disrupted.

16.5 Security Strategies for ATM Networks

All studies on security in data networks indicate that a large proportion of malicious security violations are committed by persons who are employed by the company attacked, or who at least have had physical access to the network at some time. An effective security strategy must therefore guard against attacks conducted from outside (over the Internet, leased lines, dial-up lines) as well as against attacks originating in the company network itself. Methods of protecting data networks can be classified in three groups:

- Firewalls
- Intrusion detection systems
- Encryption and authentication

16.5.1   Firewalls in High-Speed Networks

A firewall system is a network component that connects a security-sensitive data network to an unsecured or less secure network. The purpose of the firewall is to afford local users the best possible access to the public network, while at the same time protecting the private data network from intrusion. The firewall system comprises the physical and logical interface between sensitive and unprotected networks. Depending on the network topology, the connection may be between LAN segments, between two WAN segments, or between several LAN segments and a WAN link.

Behind these communication interfaces (LAN/WAN, WAN/WAN, LAN/LAN) are mechanisms that permit, control, or prohibit connection setup between the data networks joined by the firewall, depending on the service and user. The systems that perform these functions are called access control systems. Firewalls can be equipped with one or more access control systems of three basic kinds:

- Packet filters
- Protocol relays (also called circuit relays)
- Application relays

Access Control Systems: Packet Filters

Access control systems based on packet filtering are able to forward or reject packets according to such criteria as:

- Source and destination addresses
- Protocols
- Protocol ports
- User-defined bit masks

The filtering takes place in Layers 2 and 3 of the OSI communication protocol model. A well-designed and correctly configured packet filter can provide a first line of defense. In complex networks, however, filter tables can quickly become unclear and incorrect. Furthermore, the static nature of filter tables prohibits the secure operation of services such as FTP and X.11. For these reasons, packet filters are often used as preliminary filters in front of other firewall components based on the circuit or application relay principles. In ATM environments, packet-filtering functions are generally performed by the ATM switches themselves. After all, the ATM switch already has the task of examining and forwarding each incoming cell. Filtering based on ATM routing labels can thus be implemented simply by configuring the ATM switch appropriately. Other systems to control access based on the network address or service must be implemented by connecting specialized firewall systems, however, since the necessary information is not available at the ATM switching level.

Access Control Systems: Protocol Relays

Network security can be enhanced considerably through the use of firewall components based on protocol relaying. Such systems permit the use of applications based on communication protocols such as HTTP or FTP without creating an end-to-end network-layer (OSI layer 3) connection. The circuit relay functions as a proxy for the given protocol. All incoming connections end here, and are recreated at the opposite interface. Firewall systems for ATM networks operate on the same principle as protocol relays. The firewall sets up an outbound ATM connection as a continuation of each incoming connection, and thus acts as an ATM relay.

Access Control Systems: Application Relays

Application relays (Figure 16.1) go one step further than protocol relays. Like protocol relays, they allow applications to be used without allowing a connection through the firewall at the protocol level. However, the relaying takes place at the level of the application, not the underlying protocol. This technique achieves the highest degree of security of all three firewall architectures. However, an application relay must be provided for every service operated across the firewall. This places high demands on the firewall's hardware platform.

Most firewall systems today are designed for use at Internet access interfaces with a bandwidth of up to 2–45 Mbit/s, so that they are barely suitable for use between two Gigabit Ethernet segments. These systems cannot be

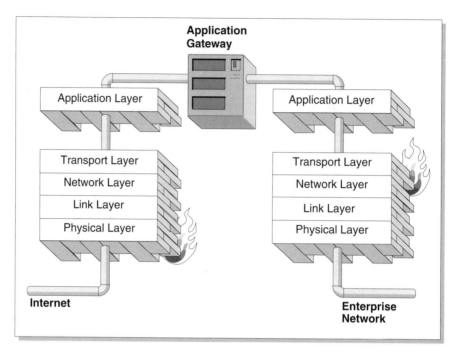

Figure 16.1
Application relays in the seven-layer OSI model.

used to connect high-speed networks. In the case of ATM firewalls, the connection-oriented principle increases the performance requirements still further. All incoming connections must be received individually, the data tested against the access control rules, then forwarded over the corresponding outgoing connections. To achieve the high data throughput found in ATM networks, ATM firewall designs combine an ATM switch and a dedicated firewall computer. The switch provides packet-filtering access control, while the firewall computer performs the ATM relaying.

16.5.2   ATM Firewalls

Firewalls in ATM networks are connected directly to the ATM switch. The ATM switch is then configured to allow only local communication among the connected segments. This is done either by defining appropriate PVCs or, if SVCs are used, by defining access control lists (ACLs) to restrict signaling (Figure 16.2).

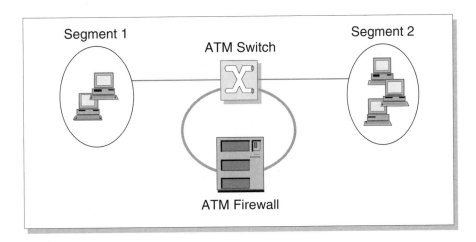

Figure 16.2
ATM firewall topology.

Each connection between two network segments must then pass through the firewall system, which is connected to two interfaces of the ATM switch. The ATM switch filters the data traffic by ATM addresses, and forwards it accordingly. Inter-segment traffic is forwarded to the firewall, which applies the access control rules based on host IP addresses or network services (TCP ports, etc.).

16.5.3   Intrusion Detection

Even sophisticated firewall systems and authentication procedures are of little use when the attack comes from within, as is often the case. In recent years this hazard has led to the strategy of concentrating not only on preventive measures, but also on minimizing the delay between a security violation and its discovery. The systems developed for this purpose are known as intrusion detection systems (IDSs). These systems monitor a number of network activities in real time, including traffic loads, connection matrices, activity at specific port addresses, and so on, and watch for the traffic profiles typical of a network attack, or "signatures." The problem in the case of ATM, however, is that the amounts of data to be analyzed are enormous. In order to analyze a 155-Mbit/s full-duplex ATM connection, 310 megabits, or 40 megabytes, of data have to be processed every second.

16.5.4   Encryption and Authentication

If every network node can be protected by means of strong cryptography and authentication methods, then all other security measures such as firewalls or IDS systems are superfluous. (Naturally this applies only if communication can be restricted to authenticated systems. Because this is rarely the case in actual practice, encryption systems are generally used in combination with firewalls and IDSs.) Every network node then communicates only with positively identifiable partners, and identifies itself to them in return. Data encryption also eliminates the danger of malicious activity during communication. An additional requirement, however, is that every network user have a nonspoofable digital identity that the network node can verify by analyzing biometric data, such as fingerprint or voice patterns. High-performance cryptography systems have recently become available, which are able to encrypt ATM cell streams even at a throughput of up to 622 Mbit/s. Together with the security techniques standardized for ATM by the ATM Forum, this permits secure operation of ATM networks to meet the most stringent requirements.

16.6   Security Functions in ATM Networks

The security functions for ATM include the following four services:

- Authentication (unilateral or bilateral)
- Confidentiality of data
- Integrity of data
- Access control for network services

16.6.1   Authentication

The authentication process tests the identity of the participants at the beginning of a connection. This protects network users against spoofing attacks and provides the foundation for all secure communication. Authentication can be either unidirectional or bidirectional. Unidirectional authentication may be sufficient if a user only retrieves data from a server, but does not send any data in the opposite direction. If the client is not interested in authenticating the operator of the data server, then server-side authentication is sufficient. In bidirectional authentication, both communicating parties must identify themselves. Each virtual channel (VC) can be configured individually to use an authentication mechanism or not. The authentication procedure to use is negotiated either over the data channel (in-band) or over the signaling channel (out-of-band). In either case, the required security information is transported by means of a specially defined Security Services information element (SSIE). The authentication itself takes place using either symmetrical or asymmetrical algorithms.

Symmetrical and Asymmetrical Encryption Methods

Two basic cryptographic methods are currently in use: symmetrical and asymmetrical encryption.

Symmetrical algorithms use one key for encryption and decryption. The sender and the receiver of the encrypted message must both know the same key. In asymmetrical methods, the encryption and decryption keys are different, and only one is published. Symmetrical encryption methods are significantly faster than asymmetrical algorithms (by a factor of 100 to 10,000), but have the obvious drawback that the key must first be conveyed to the receiver by a secure channel. For communication with many partners, a key has to be generated for each receiver, and transmitted to the receiver before encrypted messages are sent. Key management and distribution are thus the main problems involved with symmetrical encryption algorithms.

Asymmetrical or public-key cryptography techniques were developed in the mid-1970s. In 1976, Martin E. Hellman and Whitfield Diffie were the first to propose such an asymmetrical technique in their now-legendary paper, "New Directions in Cryptography." Their idea was not to use the same key for encrypting and decrypting messages, as in the known symmetrical techniques, but to use two complementary keys, one of which would be kept private while the other was made public. The two keys were constructed so that messages encrypted with the public key could only be decrypted with the corresponding private key. Thus anyone who wants to send an encrypted message must possess the addressee's public key. The public key need not be kept secret, since it is only used to encrypt, not to decrypt, messages.

In addition to encryption, public-key algorithms can also be used to certify the authenticity of a message by generating a digital signature. When a message is encrypted with the sender's private key, it can be decrypted with the matching public key. If the receiver of the message is able to decrypt it, then it must have originated with the holder of the private key. Finally, both methods can be combined: If a message is encrypted first with the receiver's public

419

key, then with the sender's private key, both confidentiality and authenticity are guaranteed. Furthermore, the integrity of a document or file can be secured by generating a "digital fingerprint" using a "message digest." The digital fingerprint is produced by calculating special hash functions of the document. Such functions have the property that the corresponding inverse operations are extremely difficult. Certain hash functions for use as message digests, named MD2, MD4, and MD5, are specified in RFCs 1319, 1320, and 1321. An average of 2^{64} trials are necessary in order to find two input values that yield the same MD hash result. This is a comparable effort to that required to crack a 512-bit RSA key. The standard message digest algorithm proposed by NIST is SHS (Secure Hash Standard). This function generates a string of 160 bits with security comparable to MD4.

Authentication Algorithms for ATM

The following algorithms have been specified for authentication in ATM:

- Asymmetrical algorithms
  - RSA
  - DSA (Digital Signature Algorithm)
  - ESIGN
- Symmetrical algorithms
  - DES (CBC)
  - DES40 (CBC)
  - FEAL (CBC)
- Hash functions
  - SHA
  - MD5

16.6.2 Confidentiality

The secrecy of data is ensured by encrypting it. As with authentication, data encryption in ATM can be configured for every VC individually. The encryption takes place at the ATM cell level using one of the following symmetrical algorithms:

- DES (56-bit keys)
- DES (40-bit keys)
- Triple DES (112 bits)
- FEAL (64 bits)

420

The supported encryption modes are ECB (Electronic Code Book), CBC (Cipher Block Chaining), and CM (Counter Mode). Negotiation of an encryption method and key exchange can take place either in-band or out-of-band during the ATM connection setup using the Security Services information elements. In order to retain their functions, special ATM cells such as OAM cells must be exempted from encryption. Hence all cells in a VCC (virtual channel connection) with a Payload Type value of 1xx and all cells in a VPC (virtual path connection) with a VCI of 3 or 4 are left unencrypted.

16.6.3   Data Integrity

The integrity of data is guaranteed by means of hash functions. ATM allows the options of activating hash functions either at the level of VCCs (whether SVCs or PVCs) or at the AAL level. Signaling for this purpose once again can be performed either in-band or out-of-band. Data integrity can be assured either with or without replay detection. If replay detection is not required, then a cryptographic signature, known as a message authentication code or MAC, is added to the AAL frame. The receiver calculates the same signature and accepts the frame only if its result matches the signature received; otherwise, the frame is discarded. Replay protection provides the same integrity assurance, with the additional capability of detecting and rejecting a second transmission of the same data, as would occur in a replay attack. Replay detection is achieved by adding a 6-byte sequence number to the AAL frame before calculating the digital signature hash. This sequence number is incremented with every second AAL PDU. The cryptographic signature is calculated over both the AAL PDU and its sequence number together, and is also attached. The following hash algorithms are specified:

- Keyed MD5 MAC
- DES/CBD MAC
- FEAL/CBC MAC

16.6.4   Access Control for Network Services

As a fourth security function, access to certain services can also be restricted in ATM. Once again, this access control function can be configured for every VC individually. This is done by transporting an identification label, which grants access to a certain service, in the Security Services information element during connection setup. ATM supports the "Standard Security Label for Information Transfer," as defined in the standard FIPS 188.

16.6.5 Negotiation and Exchange of Security Parameters

The parameters necessary for the four ATM security functions can be exchanged according to either a two-way or a three-way protocol. Both protocols support the following functions:

- Unidirectional and bidirectional authentication
- One-way and two-way key exchange
- Certificate exchange

The three-way exchange protocol also allows for the negotiation of various security options.

The Three-Way Security Message Protocol

In the first step, A sends B its own ID (A), that of the remote station (B), the desired security options ($SecNeg_a$), a random number (R_a), and its own certificate ($Cert_a$) in order to allow B to verify A's identity (parameters enclosed in braces {} are optional):
  Protocol sequence 1–3, A → B:

```
A, {B}, Ra, SecNega, {Certa}
```

B then verifies whether the indicated destination ID matches its own ID, determines its response to A's requested security options, and verifies the validity of the certificate $Cert_a$. In the second step, B sends A both parties' IDs (A, B), the security options $SecNeg_b$ determined in response to $SecNeg_a$, a random number of its own R_b alongside R_a, and if an exchange of symmetrical keys is necessary, it sends the key encrypted with A's public key (Enc_{ka} ($ConfPar_b$)). In addition, all parameters can be fingerprinted with a hash function and encrypted with B's private key (if asymmetrical encryption is used) or with a symmetrical key (Sig_{Ka} (Hash(...)).
  Protocol sequence 2–3, B → A:

```
A, B, SecNegb, {Certb}, {Ra, Rb, {EncKa(ConfParb)},
SigKb(Hash(A, B, Ra, RB, SecNega, SecNegB,
{ConfParB})))}
```

A then analyzes B's security parameters B ($SecNeg_b$), verifies the signatures and the returned random number R_a, and authenticates B's certificate. A then sends the IDs of A and B, B's random number R_b, and, if encrypted keys are being exchanged, its key, $(Enc_{Kb}(ConfPar_a))$.

Protocol sequence 3–3, A → B:

```
{A, B, Rb, {EncKb(ConfPara)}, SigKa(Hash(A, B, Rb,
{ConfPara})))}
```

After receiving the third protocol sequence, B checks its integrity, verifies the returned random number R_b, and processes $ConfPar_a$. This concludes the security handshake sequence.

The Two-Way Security Message Protocol

The two-way security handshake uses a random number and a timestamp for authentication. First A transmits both communicating parties' IDs, the security options, a timestamp T_a and a random number R_a, and, if necessary, a symmetrical key in encrypted form, $(Enc_{Kb}(ConfPar_a))$.

Protocol sequence 1–2, A → B:

```
A, B, SecOpt, {TaRa, {EncKb(ConfPara)},
SigKa(Hash(A, B, Ta, Ra, SecOpt, {ConfPara})))}
```

Upon receiving the first protocol sequence, B verifies its signature and makes sure that the timestamp is current. Then B transmits both IDs, the random number received from A (R_a), and, if necessary, an encrypted symmetrical key, $(Enc_{Ka}(ConfPar_b))$.

Protocol sequence 2–2, B → A:

```
A, B, Ra, {EncKa(ConfParb)}, SigKb(Hash(A, B, Ra,
{ConfParb})))}
```

A then verifies the signature $(Sig_{Kb}(Hash(A ...))$ and the random number R_a, and extracts the symmetrical key, if any.

16.6.6   The Security Services Information Element (SSIE)

The security message exchange protocol for ATM connections uses an information element that was especially defined for this purpose: the Security Services Information Element (Figure 16.3). This information element is used for both in-band and out-of-band signaling of security options.

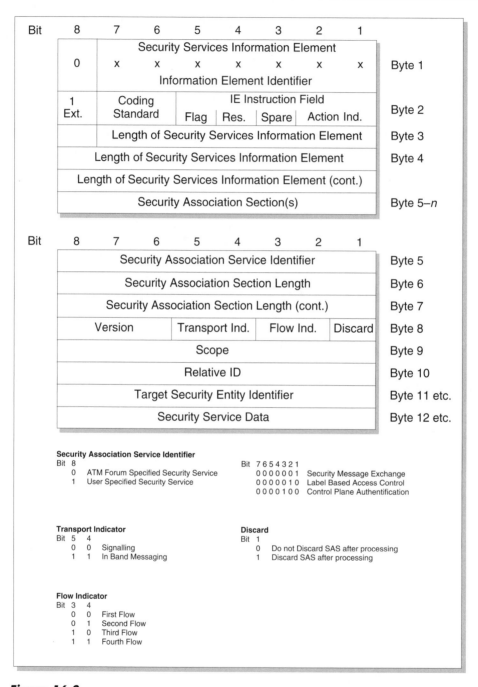

Figure 16.3
The Security Services Information Element (SSIE).

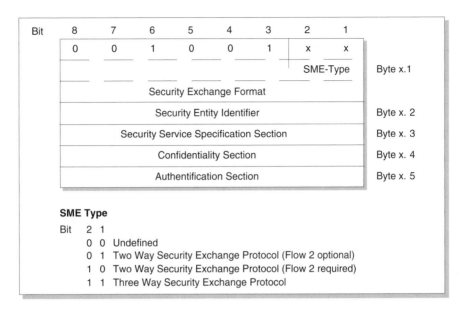

Figure 16.4
The security service data section in the SSIE.

The Security Association Sections field of the SSIE contains the information necessary to activate the ATM security functions. This information includes the security service version number, the transport and flow indicator, and the desired security agent scope, followed by the actual security service data (Figure 16.4). The security service data specifies the type of security message exchange protocol used (two-way or three-way; shown in Figure 16.5), the identities of the security agents involved, and the security protocol parameters.

During the UNI connection setup, the SSIE containing the protocol sequence 1–2 is transported as part of the SETUP message, and the response is included in the CONNECT message. SSIE transport at the NNI is analogous. In the three-way security message protocol, the handshake messages are transported as part of the SETUP, CONNECT, and CONNECT ACKNOWLEDGE messages.

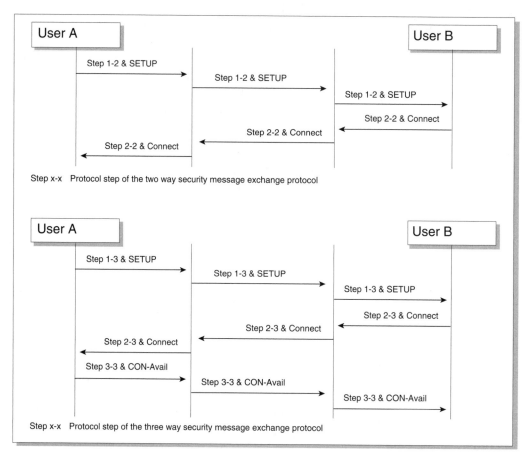

Figure 16.5
Signaling with the two-way and three-way security message exchange protocols.

Part IV

ATM Networks: Analysis and Operation

Chapter 17

ATM SWITCHES

ATM switches and cross-connects are the heart of an ATM network. The uniform size of ATM cells makes immense parallel switching architectures possible, with throughput in the gigabit and even terabit range. An ATM switch's internal data rate is many times faster than that of the connected stations, so that all users' configured bandwidth requirements can be guaranteed.

17.1 ATM Switches: Basic Functions

The two basic functions of an ATM switch are, first, identification and evaluation of each ATM cell's virtual channel and virtual path identifiers (VCIs and VPIs), and second, forwarding of each cell through the switch, from its input port to the output port that will lead the cell to its destination (Figure 17.1). The two basic types of ATM switches are virtual path (VP) switches and virtual channel (VC) switches.

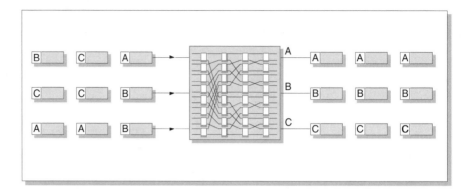

Figure 17.1
Functions of ATM switches.

17.1.1   ATM Virtual Path Switches

ATM virtual paths end at virtual path switches (Figure 17.2). All the virtual channels in the virtual path remain unaffected (the VCI used is not changed), but are forwarded in a new outgoing path. The VPI of the original and new path are generally different for each virtual path connection (the VPI has significance for the local link only, while the VCI has significance for the whole virtual path connection).

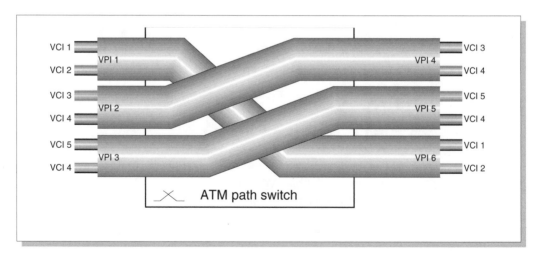

Figure 17.2
ATM virtual path switches.

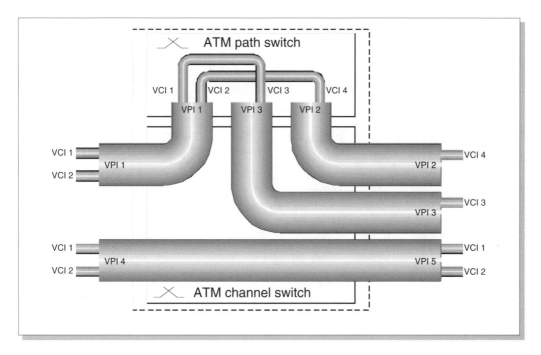

Figure 17.3
ATM virtual channel switches.

17.1.2 ATM Virtual Channel Switches

ATM virtual channel switches terminate both incoming virtual paths (VPs) and incoming virtual channels (VCs) and forward the corresponding streams in new outgoing virtual paths and virtual channels (Figure 17.3). Thus virtual channel switching always entails virtual path switching as well: when the virtual channel is terminated, the virtual path in which it was contained is also terminated. However, virtual channel switches can be used as virtual path switches, forwarding the virtual channels through the switch unchanged. Both the VPI and VCI of the virtual channel connection are, in general, changed by the switch (the VPI-VCI has significance for the local link only).

17.2   ATM Switch Topologies

The heart of every ATM switch is the switching fabric, which performs the actual forwarding of ATM cells within the switch. The switching fabric is responsible for dynamically providing transmission paths from input ports to the appropriate output ports while resolving both internal and output contention. Internal contention occurs when two ATM cells in the same stage of a multistage switching fabric contend for the same output from that stage. The same sort of contention occurring at an output controller—that is, at the output from the switching fabric—is called output contention. See Figure 17.4.

17.2.1   Switching Elements

A switching fabric is made up of small cell-switching units called switching elements (Figure 17.5). Theoretically, one switching element alone performs the function of a switching fabric. In practice, however, a single element generally does not have enough input and output ports to meet the demands placed on ATM switches, which typically have 8, 16, or more input ports. The switching elements themselves are based on a network of connection paths between input and output ports, referred to as the interconnection network. There are two types of interconnection networks for switching elements: matrix networks and time division multiplexing networks. A matrix network connects each input port of a switching element with all of its output ports through a

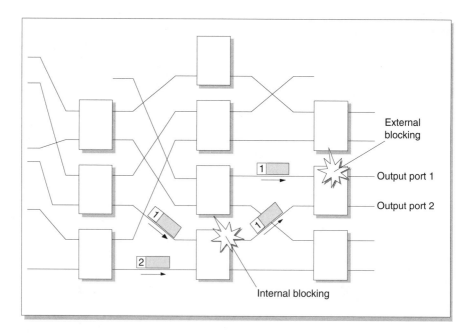

Figure 17.4

Internal and output contention in switching fabrics.

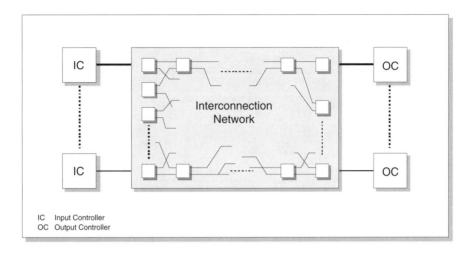

Figure 17.5
Switching element.

network of transmission paths. In time division multiplexing, cells are either transported serially over a common ring or bus structure, and switched to outputs from it as required, or an input controller writes all cells to a common buffer, where they are read by output controllers. This method is also known as central memory switching.

17.2.2   Matrix Switching Elements

A matrix switching element, illustrated in Figure 17.6, transports cells in parallel over a crossbar that connects the input and output ports of the switching element. All cells queued for transport at the input controllers at the switching time are sent simultaneously, driven by a local clock. The period between two switching operations is called the switching cycle, or time slot. If two cells contend for the same output port in the same time slot, blocking can occur. To prevent cell loss in this event, the cells must be buffered at the input and output ports, or at the cross points of the switching paths. One important parameter in this context is the speed-up factor K. This factor is the number of cells that can reach the output buffer in one switching cycle. K is thus the factor by which the internal switching matrix needs to work faster than the port speed. If a given interconnection network has N output controllers and an output buffer capacity of OP_x, then the maximum value for K should be less than or equal to N or OP_x, whichever is lower. If an interconnection network has only eight input ports, then no more than eight cells can arrive simultaneously at one output port ($N = 8$). At a speed-up factor of 8, all eight cells can be written to the output buffer in a single switch cycle. A higher speed-up factor would not result in increased performance. The same is true for output buffer capacity OP_X. If the buffer cannot hold more than eight cells, then a higher speed-up factor would only make it possible for the buffer to overflow in one

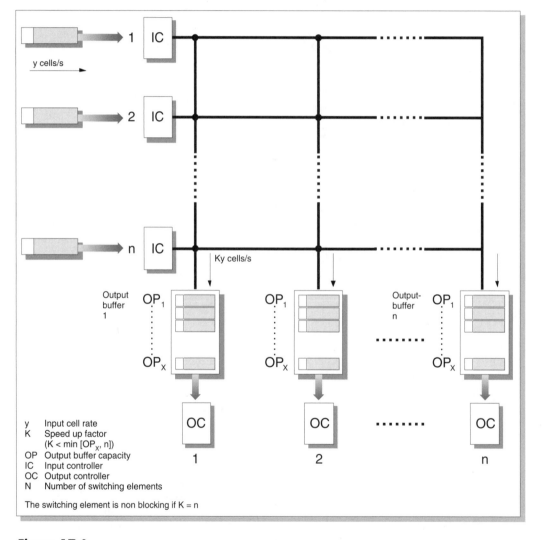

y   Input cell rate
K   Speed up factor
       (K < min [OP_X, n])
OP   Output buffer capacity
IC   Input controller
OC   Output controller
N   Number of switching elements

The switching element is non blocking if K = n

Figure 17.6
Matrix switching element.

switching cycle. If $N = 10$, $K = 10$, and $OP_X = 8$, and if 10 cells arrive at the same destination port, then its buffer would overflow in a single switch cycle even if it had been empty before. Thus an $N \times N$ matrix switching element is non-blocking for randomly distributed loads if the speed-up factor K is equal to N. If K is less than N, then additional buffer is required at the input ports to prevent cell loss.

17.2.3   Time Division Switching Elements

Bus Switching Elements

In bus switching elements, the interconnection network takes the form of a 16- or 32-bit high-speed bus (Figure 17.7). To prevent cell collisions, the throughput of the bus must be at least equal to the total throughput of all input ports. Because the bus speed is many times that of each incoming cell stream, input controllers can forward incoming cells immediately. Not only are the arriving cells at the inputs slow in comparison to the bus, but they need to wait at the output controller to align their bit rate with that of the output port. Thus an output controller may be busy with one cell when the next one arrives. For this reason, bus interconnection networks require output port buffers. With output buffering, their performance is equivalent to that of matrix switching elements.

Ring Switching Elements

Time-division switching elements can also be implemented by means of a ring topology, as shown in Figure 17.8. All input and output controllers are connected to one another in the ring. Compared with bus topology, the ring has the advantage that a single time slot can be used by several input controllers on the ring. Additional overhead is required to control this mechanism, however. Still, this feature can result in an effective load of more than 100% of the ring capacity.

Central Memory Switching Elements

In central memory switching (Figure 17.9), cells are written to a shared memory area by input controllers and read by output controllers. Because all the output port buffers share the same memory area, this technique requires significantly less memory. On the other hand, however, serial–parallel conversion

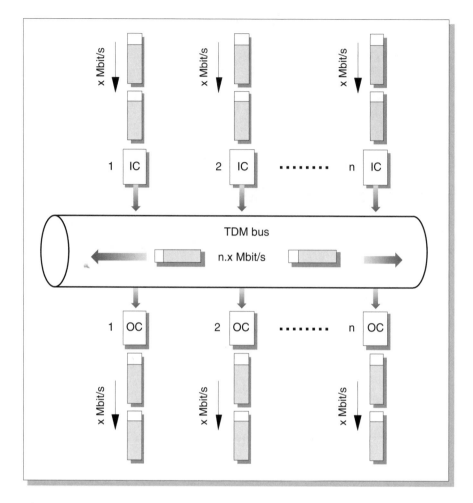

Figure 17.7
Bus switching element.

is required to slow the incoming cell stream, since the internal processing speed of the switching element cannot be faster than the memory chips' read and write operations. The incoming bit stream is usually converted into eight parallel bit streams. At an input port speed of 155 Mbit/s, this yields an internal processing speed of around 20 MHz. Due to their efficient use of memory, central memory switching elements are often used in larger switches with a great number of input and output ports.

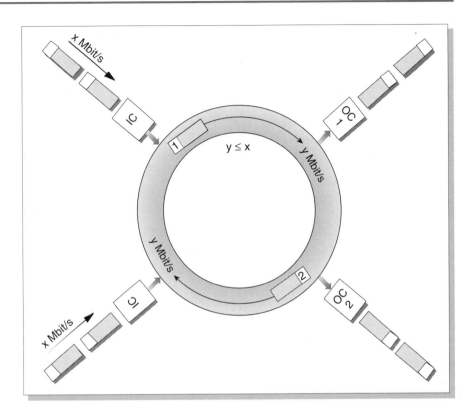

Figure 17.8
Ring switching element.

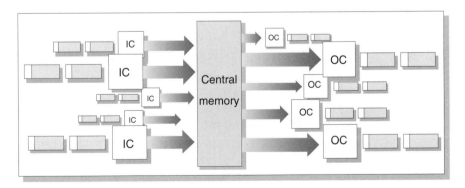

Figure 17.9
Switching element with central memory topology.

17.3   Switching Networks

Switching networks interconnect the individual switching elements to form the actual switching fabric. Because the architecture of the switching network is a critical factor in the performance of a given switching fabric, a great deal of research has been carried out in this field and a number of different topologies developed. The aim of this research is to achieve the highest possible data speeds with the simplest integrated circuits. Figure 17.10 lists the various network topologies.

17.3.1   Shuffle Exchange Network

The shuffle exchange network is a type of single-stage network. In each switching cycle, one cell can be forwarded from each input port to an output port. As shown in Figure 17.11, not all output ports can be reached directly from all input ports. For this reason, an additional feedback mechanism is required to redirect a misrouted cell from an incorrect output to another input port. Thus two or more cycles may be required before a given cell reaches its destination output port. For example, a cell arriving at input 1 with output 3 as its destination is first forwarded to output 2, then fed back to input 2, and then sent to output 3.

17.3.2   Extended Switching Matrix

Like the shuffle-exchange network, the extended switching matrix, illustrated in Figure 17.12, is a single-stage network. Each matrix switching element with N input and N output ports is extended by an additional N "transport inputs" and N "transport outputs," which serve to forward incoming cells to the next switching element in the same row or column, if it is not redirected vertically by the receiving element itself. The advantage of the extended switching matrix is that a given cell risks being blocked only once on its path through the network, namely in that switching element that switches it from a horizontal to a vertical path. Consequently, the cell is buffered no more than once before reaching the appropriate output controller. Single-stage networks are especially suited for the construction of smaller switches, while multistage architectures are used for larger systems. In the extended switching matrix, for example, as the number of input and output ports is doubled, the number of switching elements must be squared. This architecture therefore becomes impractical beyond a maximum of 64 or 128 input and output ports.

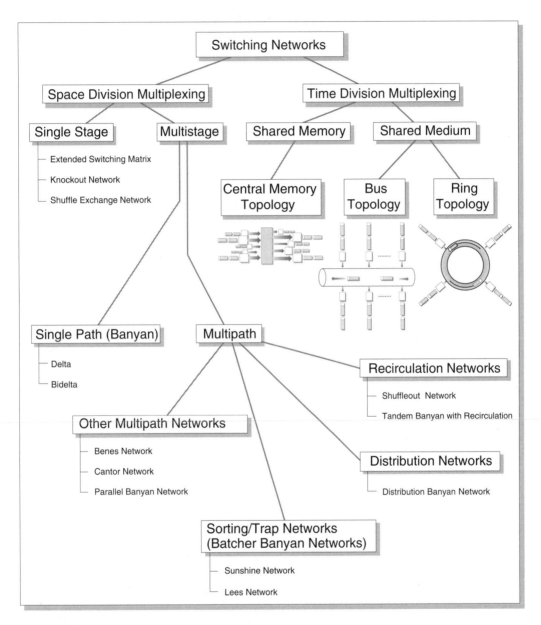

Figure 17.10
Switching networks.

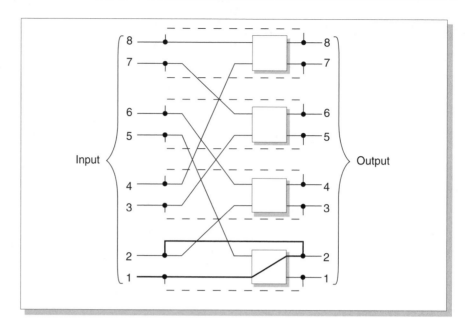

Figure 17.11
Shuffle exchange network.

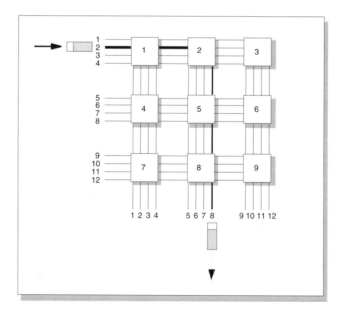

Figure 17.12
Extended switching matrix network.

17.3.3   Banyan Networks

Unlike single-stage networks, multistage networks must make two or more routing decisions to transport a cell from its input to the correct output port. Thus switching is implemented in two or more stages. Cells from different input ports can end up on the same route. In a single-path multistage network (i.e., a Banyan network), there is only one possible path from a given input port to a given output port. Hence route planning is simple. A Banyan network with more than one type of switching element is called an irregular Banyan network; a regular Banyan network uses only one switching element type. The Delta 2 network shown in Figure 17.13 is an example of a Banyan network. Delta networks are made up of $F \times S$ switching elements, and have S^L outputs. The Delta network illustrated in Figure 17.13 has four stages ($S = 4$) and 16 outputs. The parameter L thus equals 2, and this topology is called a Level 2 Delta network.

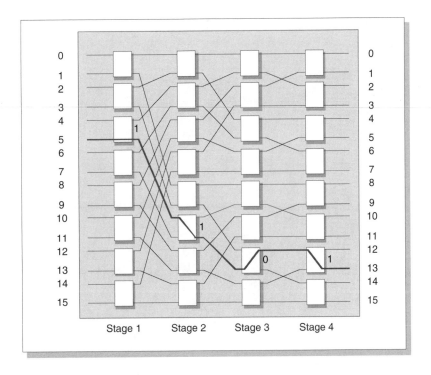

Figure 17.13
Level 2 Delta network.

17.3.4   Benes Networks

A Benes network is a multistage, multipath network, which means there is more than one possible transmission path for each input–output combination. This has the advantage of reducing or even completely eliminating internal contention. (Internal contention occurs during the switching decision from one stage to the next within the switching network. Output contention occurs directly at the output controller of the switching network.) The switching path is determined when the ATM connection is set up, and remains the same for all cells in the connection. A Benes network (Figure 17.14) is formed by adding a second, reversed Level 2 Delta network, without Stage 4, to the Delta network shown in Figure 17.13.

17.3.5   Parallel Banyan Networks

Multipath networks can also be implemented by combining a number of parallel single-path (Banyan) networks (Figure 17.15). All cells belonging to a given connection are forwarded through the same Banyan network. A non-

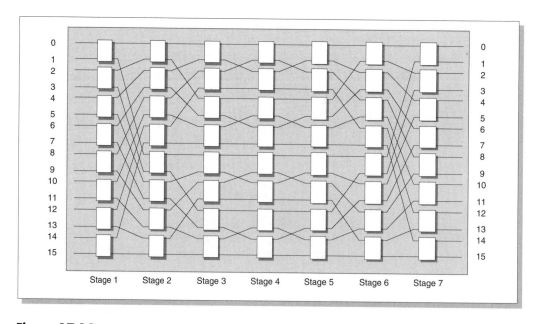

Figure 17.14
Benes network.

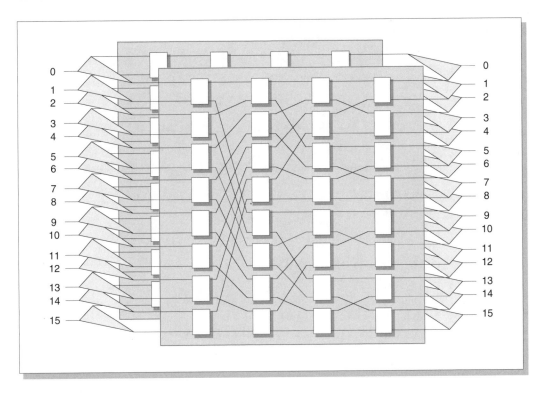

Figure 17.15
Parallel Banyan network.

blocking topology can be created with as few as two parallel Banyan networks. Multipath networks can also be connected in parallel. Cantor networks, for example, are made up of multiple Benes networks in parallel.

17.3.6   Distribution Networks

One way to reduce the probability of internal contention is to combine a switching network with a distribution network (Figure 17.16). In this case, the distribution network has the task of dividing the incoming cell stream as evenly as possible among the inputs of the switching network. The disadvantage of this method is that the order of the cells, or sequence integrity, cannot be maintained. The cells must be put back in the correct order at the outputs of the distribution network.

443

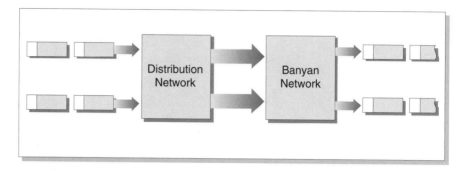

Figure 17.16
Distribution network.

17.3.7   Batcher–Banyan Networks

In Batcher–Banyan networks, a sorting network precedes the switching network. The purpose of this architecture is to prevent two cells with the same destination address from blocking at the output port. If there are multiple cells to be transmitted to a single destination port, the sorting network forwards only one of them to the switching system, while all other cells are redirected to input port queues. This is called input buffering or input queuing. The Sunshine switch design, shown in Figure 17.17, is one example of a Batcher–Banyan network. The batcher sorts cells according to destination addresses, then a trap module selects one of the cells for forwarding and marks the other cells for recirculation. Then a selector assigns priorities to these cells and queues them at the input to the sorting network. Figure 17.17 illustrates the Sunshine switch architecture as an example of a Batcher–Banyan network.

17.3.8   Recirculation Networks

Contention in the switching fabric can be resolved not only by buffering in the switching elements, but also by recirculation networks. If contention occurs between two cells, one of them is forwarded to the desired output, while the other is marked as misrouted and sent to another output. The recirculation network then gives such misrouted cells a second chance to reach their destination. The tandem Banyan network illustrated in Figure 17.18 is an example of the recirculation topology. It consists of k Banyan networks in tandem. The output ports of Banyan networks 1 through $k - 1$ are connected not only to the inputs of the subsequent Banyan network, but also to the output ports of

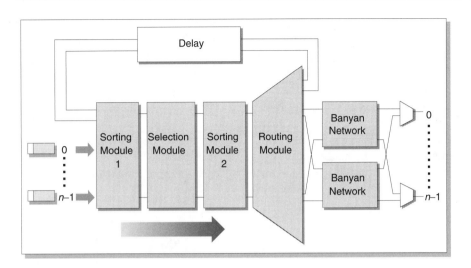

Figure 17.17
Sunshine network.

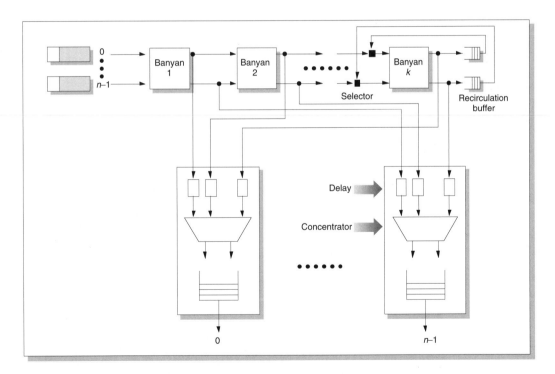

Figure 17.18
Tandem Banyan network.

the entire tandem network. As described above, when contention occurs in a Banyan network, one of the two contending cells continues on its desired path while the other is marked as misrouted and then redirected. Once a cell has been marked as misrouted, it cannot win a contention with any nonmarked cell. Each cell is checked at the output of each Banyan network to see whether it has reached its destination: if so, it is forwarded directly to the switch output port. If the cell exits at an incorrect port due to misrouting in the Banyan network, its marking is cleared and it is forwarded to the next Banyan network, where it can once again attempt to reach the correct destination port. Cells that are misrouted in the last Banyan network are sent through the recirculation buffer back to the input port.

17.4 Cell Routing in Switching Networks

There are two techniques for routing cells within switching networks: self-routing and table-controlled routing.

17.4.1 Self-Routing

In self-routing switching networks, a header that is specific to the switching element type is added to incoming cells. This header contains a code that indicates the switching path. If the switching network is made up of n stages, then the header has n partial fields, which indicate the decision to be made at each node of the switching network (Figure 17.19). The internal processing speed of the switch must be increased proportionately due to added header length. If the self-routing header is 5 bytes long, for example, and the user data stream has a speed of 155 Mbit/s, then an internal processing speed of some 170 Mbit/s must be provided.

17.4.2 Table Routing

Table routing leaves the length of the ATM cells unchanged. Before the cell enters each switching element, its virtual channel or path identifier (VPI/VCI) is translated into a switch-specific value indicating the cell's destination output port for that switching element. The translation values are defined in the connection setup or path selection phase and stored in tables (Figure 17.20). Tests

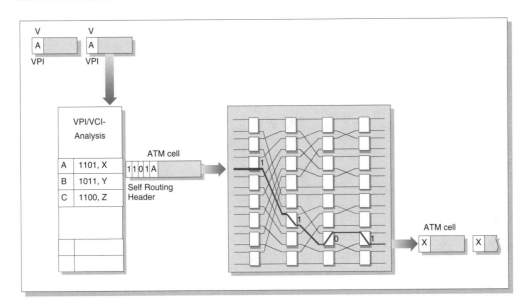

Figure 17.19
Self-routing.

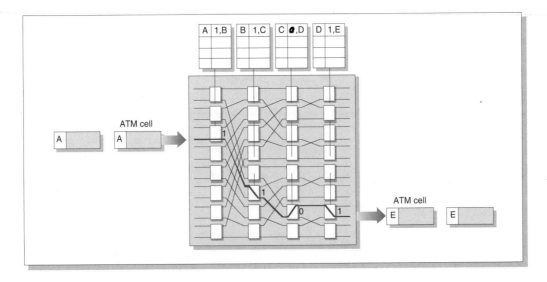

Figure 17.20
Table routing.

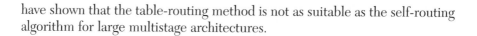

have shown that the table-routing method is not as suitable as the self-routing algorithm for large multistage architectures.

17.5   Selecting a Network Architecture

Which network architecture is best for a given ATM switch depends primarily on the number of input and output ports to be supported, as well as the permissible cell loss rate.

17.5.1   Buffer Type and Size

Buffer capacity has a decisive effect on cell loss probability. A switching element that fulfills the condition $K = N$ with an output buffer capacity of $OP_X = K$, for example, will drop cells if more than $OP_X + T$ cells for the same output port are received within T cycles. Since the buffer size must be finite, OP_X must be large enough that the probability of the occurrence of more than $OP_X + T$ cells within T cycles is less than or equal to the greatest permissible cell loss probability. A comparison of the different types of buffering shows that the central memory method requires by far the least buffer capacity (see Table 17.1). Switching elements with input buffering are also far superior to architectures with output buffering. This is because, although more than one cell can arrive at once in an input buffer, more than one cell at a time can also

Table 17.1   Buffering in ATM Switch Designs

	Switching Element Size 16 x 16*	Switching Element Size 32 x 23*
Central memory	113	199
Input buffering	320	640
Output buffering	896	1824

*Cell storage capacity as such that cell loss probability is less than 10^{-9}.

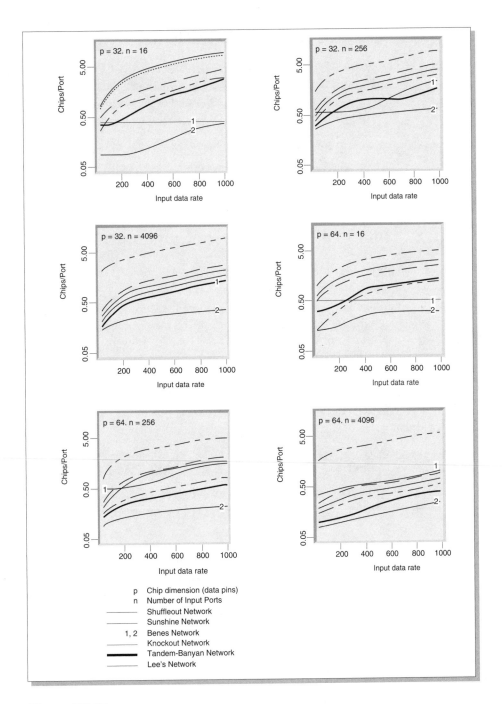

Figure 17.21
Integration density in ATM switch designs.

be forwarded if they do not all use the same route. Output buffers cannot forward more than one cell at a time. On the other hand, systems that use output buffering have much lower cell delay and delay variation than those with input buffering: in input buffering systems, cells blocked at the output port are recirculated to the inputs and must pass through the switching network again. Note that, while larger buffers reduce the probability of cell loss, they increase the cell delay variation (CDV) when the switch is busy. High CDV is thus associated with cell loss, since the buffers are finite.

17.5.2 Integration Density of Switching Architectures

Other important parameters in choosing an ATM switch design are the integration density and the number of chips required to implement the switching fabric. Figure 17.21 gives the results of a study conducted by E.W. Zegura, comparing the number of chips required based on data speeds and number of ports for Knockout, Sunshine, Lee's, Tandem Banyan, Shuffle-Out, and Benes networks. The Benes network architecture is found to require the lowest number of chips of any of the network types examined. The single-stage Knockout topology, on the other hand, is suitable only for small switching fabrics with few input ports and low data rates.

17.6 Performance Parameters for ATM Switches

The performance of ATM switches is defined in terms of three parameters: throughput, average cell delay, and cell loss probability. The goal in switch design is to create the simplest possible switching network topology with a cell throughput rate approaching 1, an average cell delay of only a few switching cycles, and a cell loss rate of 10^{-9} or less.

17.6.1 Cell Throughput r $(0 \leq r \leq 1)$

Cell throughput is the load that the switch can forward, expressed as the probability that a cell exits through an output port on the switch during a given switching cycle (cell slot). The maximum cell throughput rate, r_m, is determined at a load p equal to 1. p is a load of uniform random traffic expressed

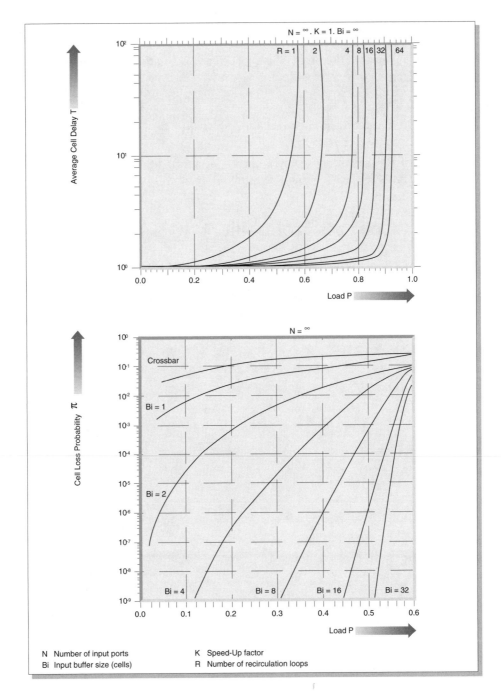

Figure 17.22
Cell loss and cell delay in a Batcher–Banyan switching network

in terms of the probability of a cell arriving at the switch during a given switching cycle ($0 \leq p \leq 1$).

17.6.2   Average Cell Delay T ($T \geq 1$)

The average cell delay is the time in switching cycles (cell slots) that a cell takes to travel through a switch.

17.6.3   Cell Loss Probability p ($0 \leq p \leq 1$)

Cell loss probability is the probability that a cell that has arrived at an input port will be lost during transport through the switch. The example in Figure 17.22 shows the average cell delay and the cell loss probability in a Batcher–Banyan input buffering system.

Chapter 18

TRAFFIC AND CONGESTION CONTROL IN ATM NETWORKS

One attribute that makes ATM stand out is its ability to deliver guaranteed "quality of service" (QoS), end-to-end over an entire network. Work is continuing in the standards bodies to develop methods for delivering QoS via other technologies but so far ATM is the only flexible technology that really achieves this goal. This chapter discusses the subject of ATM quality of service—what it is and why guarantees are possible.

Traffic management, usage control and ATM quality of service (performance) are specified in various places: the ATM Forum's current version of their Traffic Management specification is version 4.1 and is specified in af-tm-0121.000, though it has been amended by two addenda, af-tm-0149.000 (Differentiated UBR) and af-tm-0150.000 (Optional Minimum Desired Cell Rate Indication for UBR); the relevant ITU-T recommendations are I.371 (Traffic Control and Congestion Control in B-ISDN), I.371.1 (Guaranteed Frame Rate ATM Transfer Capability), I.356 (ATM Layer Cell Transfer Performance), and I.357 (Semi-Permanent Connection Availability).

18.1   ATM QoS

For ATM, the degradation of quality of service is measured in terms of the following impairments introduced by the network: cell loss ratio (CLR—cells lost with respect to cells sent), cell delay variation (CDV), and cell transfer delay

(CTD). The impact of these impairments on a particular application depends on the nature of that application. For example, a lost cell will usually destroy a data packet, requiring that a higher layer process resend it, while cell delay variation may not impact it at all; conversely, if a constant bit rate service (e.g., a DS1 or E1 structure) is being carried across an ATM network using Circuit Emulation Service (CES), excessive cell delay variation introduced by the network may delay a cell so long that the carried samples belonging to the service arrive too late to be useful and the late cell might as well have been lost.

Other ATM impairments that can occur include "errored cells" (cells containing one or more bit errors), measured as the "cell error ratio" (CER—cells errored with respect to cells sent) and "misinserted cells," cells originally belonging to another virtual channel that have erroneously arrived in the wrong virtual channel, due, for example, to undetected bit errors in the cell header (very unlikely to happen in practice); misinserted cells are measured as the "cell misinsertion rate" (CMR—cells misinserted with respect to time).

18.2   How ATM QoS is Guaranteed

The major advantage ATM has over some other technologies is that it is "connection oriented." This means that the path over which cells travel is fixed at call set-up time (whether by provisioning, signaling, or label switched protocol). Connectionless packet technologies usually cannot guarantee that a particular path is always followed, although "multiprotocol label switching" (MPLS) methods do deliver this capability within a domain boundary.

So why is connection orientation so important in ATM? Because it is much easier to manage the traffic over such a connection. The answer lies also in the agreement that the user and network make, known as the "traffic contract."

18.3   The Traffic Contract

In order that the network can provide adequate resources to allow it to guarantee the user's QoS requirements, it needs to be told by the user the detailed behavior of the traffic that the user plans to send over the virtual channel. The traffic contract thus established at call setup time provides benefits and responsibilities to each party:

User: I need a guaranteed QoS in terms of CLR and CDV values; in return I promise not to exceed the usage parameter values (bandwidth, burstiness, etc.) I have requested.

Network: I promise to deliver the agreed QoS provided you do not exceed the agreed usage parameters. I will police your usage and, if you break the contract, I will take action, including discarding your cells, in order to protect other users of the network.

or

I do not have the network resources you have requested / I cannot guarantee the QoS you require, so I cannot accept your call. (equivalent to "equipment busy)

18.4   Traffic Parameters

The user traffic is always specified in terms of its PCR (peak cell rate) and, if it is bursty in nature, by its SCR (sustainable cell rate, that is, the long term average rate), and the MBS (maximum burst size, that is, the number of cells in the maximum sized burst) or by the intrinsic burst tolerance (IBT, an alternative way of specifying burst characteristics used by the ITU-T). Note that the PCR of traffic with a constant cell rate (derived from emulation of a constant bit rate service) is the same as that cell rate. This often gives rise to confusion since a constant bit rate service is, in principal, not peaky!

The above parameters could describe the shape of traffic that is carrying data packets. When a packet is being sent, cells carrying that packet may cross the UNI at a constant rate (the PCR), then, after the packet has been sent, there is silence on that virtual channel until the next packet arrives. If, for example, each packet in a multiple packet stream arrived at a rate of 15 cells per second, the packets were 30 cells long (i.e., they take 2 seconds to cross the UNI), and they occurred once every 6 seconds, we would have PCR = 15, MBS = 30, SCR = 5. Note that the PCR may not be the same as the maximum cell rate supported by the link.

It is clear from this example that, if we were really lucky regarding timing, we could interleave three similar packet streams (each described by the same traffic parameters) on three different virtual channels on the same ATM link without exceeding the overall PCR because we provided that extra detail via the SCR and MBS parameters. Had we not had these parameters, we would have had to treat each virtual channel as if it were carrying a constant bit rate (i.e., constant cell rate) service at the PCR and would have wasted lots of link and network bandwidth.

In reality, cell multiplexing between different virtual channels on the same link usually causes cells during a burst to be displaced from their ideal position—they can become bunched, though the average rate during the burst might remain the same. Instantaneously, the PCR may be exceeded (rather contradicts the term "peak," doesn't it?). The network has to tolerate this, provided the excess rate does not occur for too long and is accompanied by a corresponding cell rate that is less than the PCR. An additional parameter is thus required, the cell delay variation tolerance (CDVT), which is usually measured in microseconds.

To summarize:

PCR: peak cell rate (= average cell rate for a CBR service)

SCR: sustainable cell rate—the long-term average cell rate of a bursty traffic profile

MBS: maximum burst size—the maximum number of cells in a burst

CDVT: cell delay variation tolerance—the amount of cell bunching to be tolerated that would take the cell rate above the PCR, typically up to the line rate

IBT: intrinsic burst tolerance—related to MBS, this is to SCR what CDVT is to PCR (this is explained in detail later)

18.5   Policing

The network does not trust the user to keep to the contract unsupervised, so a policing mechanism is implemented on the network side of the user–network interface (UNI), normally in the input port of the first ATM switch or cross-connect at the edge of the ATM network. If the network did not have this policing mechanism, individual users could accidentally or maliciously send excessive traffic, causing congestion and consequent damage (cell loss and cell delay) to the traffic of other users in unforeseeable ways.

Where permanent virtual circuits (PVCs) are concerned, the policing mechanism is supplied with the usage parameters via the network management system; for switched virtual circuits (SVCs), the contract is negotiated and parameters passed via UNI signaling messages and the call setup procedure to the policing mechanism.

Note that the policing mechanism treats each virtual connection at an ATM UNI individually and may police many thousands of virtual connections at an interface. This sounds like an overwhelming job but it is worth remembering that, regardless of the number of virtual connections, only one cell crosses the interface at any given time and that the more virtual connections there are, the lower the average bandwidth of each; most policing mechanisms use context switching methods based upon the VPI-VCI of the current arriving cell to realize a "virtual" policer.

18.5.1 Leaky Buckets

The policing mechanism implements one or more instantiations of the "generic cell rate algorithm" (GCRA), which behaves in a similar way to a leaky bucket. Consider the diagram of a leaky bucket in Figure 18.1. If a drip of water were to enter the bucket every time a cell crossed the UNI (arrived at the policer) and if water were to drip from the hole in the bucket at a constant rate equivalent to the PCR, then, provided the drips caused by the

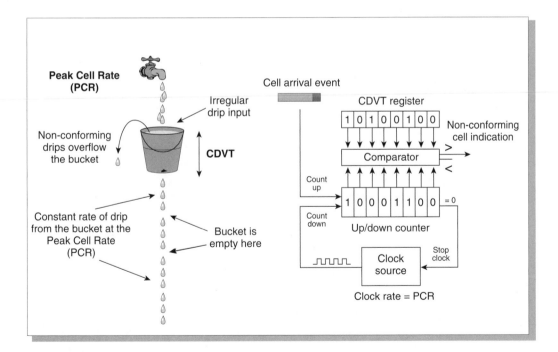

Figure 18.1
Single leaky bucket and equivalent circuit.

arriving cells do not, on average, occur faster than the drips leaking from the bucket, the bucket will not fill up. Clearly, a burst of drips at a rate above the PCR would cause the bucket to fill, but if that burst is matched by a period when the drips occur at a lower rate than the PCR, the bucket would tend to empty. If the burst of drips caused by the arrival of cells occurs at a rate above the PCR for too long, the bucket will overflow. On the other hand, if the bucket empties completely (because cells stop arriving), the drips from the hole in the bucket cease, of course. The depth of the bucket is equivalent to the cell delay variation tolerance (CDVT).

In Figure 18.1, the simple circuit on the right is equivalent to the leaky bucket. The up–down counter is incremented by the arrival of a cell and decremented by the tick from a clock running at the peak cell rate. The counter is not allowed to underflow (the bucket cannot be less than empty in our analogy), ticks from the clock being stopped when the counter is at zero. A comparator compares the counter value to the CDVT value stored in a register; if the counter exceeds the value in this register, the comparator signals that the cell that caused this condition is "nonconforming," a situation equivalent to the bucket overflowing in our analogy.

This single leaky bucket would be the minimum required policing mechanism that would have to be implemented (effectively for each virtual connection) at the UNI. Cells that are declared to be nonconforming to the PCR/CDVT leaky bucket (GCRA) are *always* discarded at the interface.

A single leaky bucket implementation is adequate for policing constant bit rate traffic and could be used even for bursty traffic, although it would be more bandwidth-efficient in this case to implement a dual leaky bucket mechanism to take advantage of the SCR and MBS traffic parameters discussed above, as Figures 18.2 and 18.3 show.

In this case, the second leaky bucket receives identical drips to those arriving at the first bucket; however, this time the hole in the second bucket is smaller so that the drips occur at the (lower) sustainable cell rate (SCR). The depth of the second bucket is equivalent to the "burst tolerance" (BT) plus the CDVT; the burst tolerance is also called the "intrinsic burst tolerance" (IBT) by the ITU-T. Figures 18.4 and 18.5 may help in understanding what is going on. In Figure 18.4, traffic is well behaved—cells are arriving at the PCR, so the top graph of CDVT is flat at 0 (the first bucket remains empty, as all drips entering are leaving at the same rate). The second leaky bucket is slowly filling but, just when it is about to overflow, the burst finishes, so it slowly empties again.

In Figure 18.5 we see two differences. First, there is some CDV on the first burst (note the bunching of the cells at the bottom of the diagram). This causes the first leaky bucket to fill and then empty a couple of times, but the CDVT is not exceeded, so no cell is discarded. The second burst contains too many cells (the MBS is exceeded) so the extra cells that cause this to happen

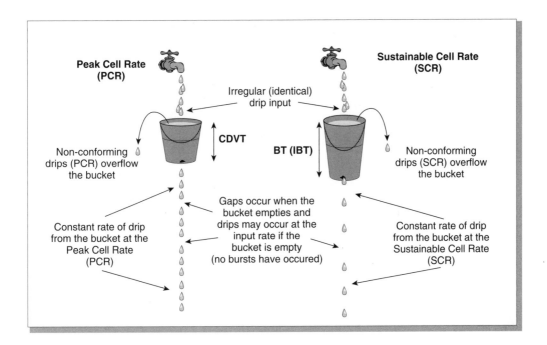

Figure 18.2
Dual leaky buckets.

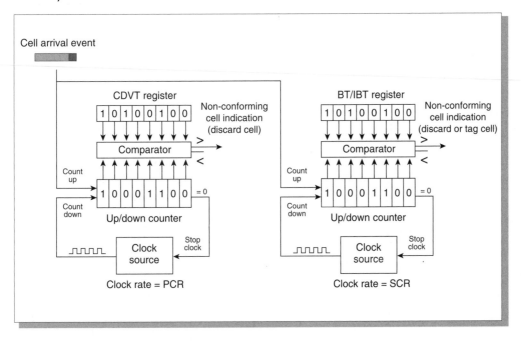

Figure 18.3
Equivalent circuit for dual leaky bucket.

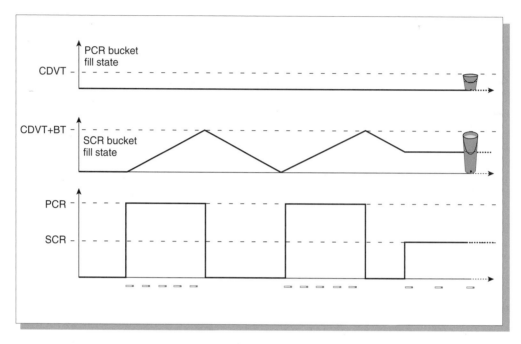

Figure 18.4
Ideal fully confirming traffic.

are nonconforming and they would be discarded or tagged (CLP set to 1) for possible later discard, depending on the contract type (see section 18.6.2).

Figure 18.5 shows graphically the relationship between MSB and the (intrinsic) burst tolerance (BT or IBT). As it is the MBS that is normally provided in signaling messages, the burst tolerance value has to be derived from the PCR, SCR, and MBS, according to the formula, where τ_{SCR} is the burst tolerance:

$$\tau_{IBT} = \lceil (MBS - 1)(T_{SCR} - T_{PCR}) \rceil \text{ seconds}$$

where $\lceil x \rceil$ stands for the first value above x out of the "generic list" of values and where T_{SCR} and T_{PCR} are the time intervals 1/SCR and 1/PCR, respectively. The generic list is a set of values that can be used for either the (intrinsic) burst tolerance τ_{SCR} or the cell delay variation tolerance τ_{PCR} according to the following formula (*SCR* can be substituted for *PCR*):

460

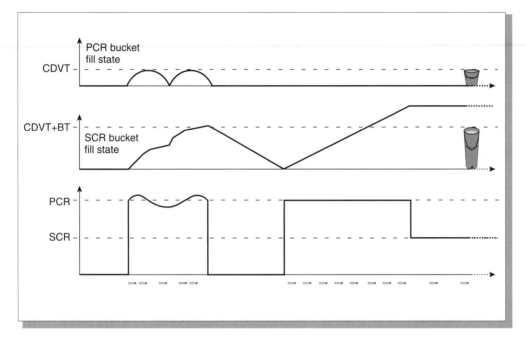

Figure 18.5
Non-ideal, partly non-conforming traffic.

$$\tau_{PCR} = 2^{e_{PCR}-32} \times 2^9 \times \left(1 + \frac{w_{PCR} \cdot 2^5}{2^{10}} \right) \text{seconds}$$

$$0 \le e_{PCR} \le 31$$

$$0 \le w_{PCR} \le 31$$

where e_{PCR} and w_{PCR} are integer values.

Just as the values for CDVT and BT are standardized, so too are the values for PCR and SCR. Another generic list of values can be calculated for cell rates between 1 cell/s to over 4 Gcells/s, using the following formula:

$$\Lambda_{PCR} = 2^{m_{PCR}} \times \left(1 + \frac{k_{PCR}}{512} \right) \text{cells per second}$$

$$0 \le m_{PCR} \le 31$$

$$0 \le k_{PCR} \le 511$$

where Λ_{PCR} is the peak cell rate value and m_{PCR} and k_{PCR} are integer values.

These formulas make it clear that only certain discrete values can be used for the cell delay variation and burst tolerances and for the peak and sustainable cell rates. This standardizes policing.

18.6   Conformance to the Traffic Contract

We have seen how policing can be done, but what, in practice, are the options for policing? The ATM Forum and the ITU-T have defined sets of options for policing for different types of traffic and for the different capabilities of different networks.

It is important to distinguish between the shape of traffic offered to the network and what the network is prepared to tolerate; these may be essentially the same or they may be different. For example, if the user provides bursty traffic that has "perfect" bursts (cells equally spaced in the cell stream at the PCR during the burst then no cells between bursts), the contract is easy to specify and police; furthermore, the user can get the maximum out of the contract, as there is a good match between the parameters supplied and the shape of the traffic. Variable traffic need not have the above "ideal" shape, however, but traffic parameters still have to be supplied even if the traffic is continuously variable. This can give rise to difficulty in specifying ideal parameters and will often result in inefficient use of the network, as more resources may have to be reserved to ensure a sufficiently good QoS.

18.6.1   Constant/Deterministic Bit Rate (VBR/DBR) Service

The simplest kind of traffic is what the ATM Forum calls "constant bit rate" (CBR) traffic and the ITU-T calls "deterministic bit rate" (DBR) traffic. As CBR/DBR traffic results in a constant cell rate, only one GCRA or leaky bucket process is needed to police it, based upon the PCR and the CDVT. All cells in the virtual connection are policed equivalently, so no distinction is made for the cell loss priority. Consequently, the following is used for policing this service:

$$CBR.1 = DBR = GCRA(1/PCR_{0+1}, CDVT_{0+1})$$

Note 1: Conventionally "0" is used to indicate cells of low loss priority, that is, normal priority; "1" is used to indicate cells of high loss priority, that is, low priority; and "0+1" is used to indicate cells of both priorities, that is, all cells in the virtual connection.

Note 2: Conventionally the GCRA expression takes parameters of time; 1/PCR is the minimum "emission interval," the minimum interval between cells occurring at the peak cell rate.

The action that the policing mechanism takes if nonconformance to the above GCRA definition occurs is to delete the cell that caused this; this cell is said to be "nonconforming." Any cell can potentially be nonconforming, only the past history of cell behavior determines which. Once a cell has been declared nonconforming and consequently deleted, the GCRA behaves for the next cell as if the deleted cell had not existed, which means that the next cell is almost bound to conform. If measurements of cell loss were to be made across the network, policing action of this kind would be indistinguishable from cells lost due to congestion in the network. However, because the user traffic violated the traffic contract, the guarantees made by the network as part of the contract do not have to be honored by the network. This gives rise to situations where the user blames the network for impaired QoS when the user is, in fact, to blame.

18.6.2 Variable/Statistical Bit Rate (VBR/SBR) Service

The ATM Forum has defined "variable bit rate" service; the ITU-T has the same service, which it calls "statistical bit rate" service. Three contract modes are defined for VBR/SBR to suit the capability of the network; in all cases, two GCRAs (leaky buckets) are used and in all cases the first GCRA polices the PCR/CDVT for all cells (normal and low priority) of the virtual channel, *always* discarding any cells that do not conform (there are no exceptions to this, despite common misunderstanding to the contrary). The differences lie in how the policing mechanism handles the sustainable cell rate (SCR).

The first and simplest contract is called by the ATM Forum "VBR.1"; the ITU-T calls this "SBR1." In this case, the second GCRA works on all cells of the virtual channel and discards any that do not conform; tagging (changing cell loss priority from "0" to "1") is not allowed:

$$VBR.1 = SBR1 = GCRA(1/PCR_{0+1}, CDVT_{0+1}),$$
$$GCRA(1/SCR_{0+1}, BT_{0+1}), \text{no tagging}$$

The second option is called VBR.2 (SBR2); in this case, the second GCRA polices on normal priority cells only (these cells must, of course, have passed the peak cell rate GCRA); low priority cells are not considered. Tagging is, again, not an option:

$$VBR.2 = SBR2 = GCRA(1/PCR_{0+1}, CDVT_{0+1}),$$
$$GCRA(1/SCR_0, BT_0), \text{no tagging}$$

The third option is like the second option, except that tagging is allowed. What this means is that, instead of discarding nonconforming cells, the policing mechanism changes the priority of the nonconforming (normal priority) cells to low priority (CLP→1). These cells then become candidates for deletion at congested nodes in the network, if congestion occurs, but would probably, on balance, make it through the network successfully:

$$VBR.3 = SBR3 = GCRA(1/PCR_{0+1}, CDVT_{0+1}),$$
$$GCRA(1/SCR_{0+1}, BT_{0+1}), \text{tagging supported}$$

Clearly this option is the most sophisticated and so not all networks can support it.

18.6.3   Unspecified Bit Rate (UBR) Service

Bursty traffic can be treated by the network in several ways. If the user negotiates a "variable bit rate" (VBR) contract with the network, the network guarantees resources for the level of QoS requested.

Alternatively, the user could choose a less expensive option by requesting the ATM Forum's "unspecified bit rate" (UBR) service; the network makes no guarantee about the successful delivery of cells with this service but makes its "best effort"—UBR has, therefore, a lower priority than CBR and VBR services. Note that there is no such thing as "UBR traffic," there is only a "UBR service"—the traffic would look the same whether the network was supplying a UBR or a VBR service. A UBR service would be attractive in a lightly loaded network because it would be tariffed at a lower rate; as the network became busier, the delivered QoS available from a UBR service would get worse until, perhaps, it would become unusable; the user would then be faced with transferring to a VBR service contract, which would guarantee QoS at some extra cost.

This service is only fully specified by the ATM Forum; the ITU-T only touches on it briefly in Recommendation I.371. Two variants exist (UBR.1 and UBR.2) and they differ only upon whether or not tagging is supported; note that where tagging is supported, unlike the VBR services, the network can tag any cell, whether or not it is conforming. The ATM Forum specification is vague about which circumstances tagging would be done.

$$\text{UBR.1} = \text{GCRA}(1/\text{PCR}_{0+1}, \text{CDVT}_{0+1}), \text{ no tagging}$$

$$\text{UBR.2} = \text{GCRA}(1/\text{PCR}_{0+1}, \text{CDVT}_{0+1}), \text{ tagging supported}$$

More recently the ATM Forum introduced two addenda regarding UBR to version 4.1 of the Traffic Management specification: af-tm-0149.000 (Addendum to TM 4.1: Differentiated UBR) and af-tm-0150.000 (Addendum to Traffic Management V4.1 for an Optional Minimum Desired Cell Rate Indication for UBR). The first of these recognizes the increasing use of UBR for use by elastic data networking applications, primarily because it imposes few requirements on the end equipment and enables a higher degree of connectivity than do services that explicitly reserve capacity per connection. It has become increasingly common for technologies that traditionally offered only best effort service, such as Ethernet and IP, to incorporate service differentiation mechanisms. It was desirable that the UBR service category be extended with similar capabilities to optimize their support over ATM. The first addendum introduces the concept of behavior classes; each UBR connection can be optionally associated with a behavior class, which is indicated by a Behavior Class Selector (BCS) parameter.

18.6.4   Available Bit Rate (ABR) Service

The ABR service makes guarantees about the minimum cell rate (MCR) and it also delivers a level of quality of service in terms of cell loss but not in terms of CDV. It operates by making use of spare capacity in the network but it differs from UBR because of its QoS guarantee, which it can make because it has the ability to control the source traffic through an ATM layer flow control feedback process using special "resource management" (RM) cells. This allows the service to adjust the traffic levels to suit the network and to take into account detected network congestion. In this section we give only an overview of ABR, as it is a complex mechanism.

Resource Management (RM) Cells

RM cells are used with both ABR and ABT services. They exist at both the virtual path and virtual channel level and are identified by reserved values of VCI at the virtual path level (i.e., VCI = 6 for any value of VPI), and by the PTI value of 6 (110) at the virtual channel level (any VPI-VCI), in a similar manner to the way OAM cells are identified. Also similar to OAM cells is the CRC-10 error detection contained in the last 10 bits of the RM cells payload. Currently, three different main types of RM cells are standardized by the ITU-T, though only the first of these is used by the ATM Forum, as the ABT service is not specified by that body; these are identified by the Protocol ID, which occupies the first payload byte:

Protocol ID = 1   Available Bit Rate (ABR)

Protocol ID = 2   ATM Block Transfer/ Delayed Transmission (ABT/DT)

Protocol ID = 3   ATM Block Transfer/ Immediate Transmission (ABR/IT)

Table 18.1 shows the cell structure for all current versions of the RM cell.

ABR Flow Control

ABR flow control can be on an end-to-end basis or it can operate over segments of the network. The end-point of an ABR connection is termed either the "source" (S) or "destination" (D), while a switch terminating internal segment end-points is termed a "virtual source" (VS) or "virtual destination" (VD). For flow control operating over the complete network end-to-end, the flow control RM cells run the complete length of the VCC or VPC. When the ABR service is broken into segments, RM cell flows are localized to each segment. So forward RM cells flow from a source or virtual source to a destination or virtual destination, where they are turned around as backward RM cells; the backward RM cells flow from the destination or a virtual destination to the source or a virtual source, where they are removed. For ABR traffic being sent in the opposite direction, everything is reversed, so (virtual) sources and (virtual) destinations are swapped, as are the directions for forward and backward RM cells. Figure 18.6 shows the arrangement for an ABR service flowing from left to right.

The Control Process

The following procedure happens independently from each end of the VPC or VCC. The source starts sending cells at the Allowed Cell Rate (ACR), which should not exceed the Initial Cell Rate (ICR) but should not be less than the

Table 18.1 Resource Management (RM) Cell Structure for ABR, ABT/DT, and ABT/IT RM Cells

Octet	Bit	Field (ABR)	Field (ABT)	Coding
1–5	All		Header	RM-VPC: VPI-VCI = p–6, RM-VCC: VPI-VCI = p–c, PTI = 110 p, c = any legal value
6	All	Protocol ID (ID)	Protocol ID (ID)	1 = ABR, 2 = ABT/DT, 3 = ABT/IT
7	8	Message Type: Direction (DIR)	Message Type: Direction (DIR)	0 = forward RM cell 1 = backward RM cell
7	7	Message Type: BECN Indication (BN)	Message Type: Traffic Management	ABR: 0 = normal cell generated by source 1 = BECN RM cell generated by destination or intermediate switch ABT: 0 = normal cell generated user for BCR negotiation 1 = traffic management cell generated by the network for traffic control
7	6	Message Type: Congestion Indication (CI)	Message Type: Congestion Indication (CI)	ABR: 0 = no congestion 1 = (impending) congestion in forward path ABT: 0 = BCR mod succeeded 1 = BCR mod failed
7	5	Message Type: No-increase (NI)	Message Type: Maintenance (ABT/DT only)	ABR: 0 = allow increase (when CI=0) 1 = no increase (when CI=0) ABT: 0 = normal use 1 = maintenance use
7	4	Message Type: Reserved	Message Type: Req/Ack (ABT/DT only)	ABT: 0 = BCR modification req 1 = BCR modification ack
7	3	Message Type: Reserved	Message Type: Elastic/Rigid (ABT/DT only)	ABT: 0 = elastic 1 = rigid
7	1–2	Message Type: Reserved	Message Type: Reserved	
8–9	All	Explicit Cell Rate (ECR)	Block Cell Rate (BCR_{0+1})	
10–11	All	Current Cell Rate (CCR)	User OAM BCR	
12–13	All	Minimum Cell Rate (MCR)	Reserved	
14–17	All	Queue Length (QL)	Block Size	
18–21	All	Sequence Number (SN)	Sequence Number	
22–51	All	Reserved	Reserved	
52	3–8	Reserved	Reserved	All bits = 0
52	1–2	CRC-10	CRC-10	As OAM cells (see ITU-T I.610)
53	All			

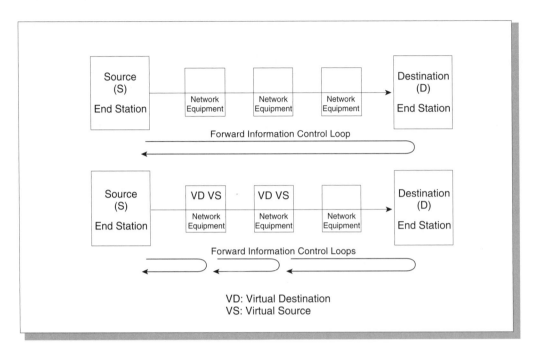

Figure 18.6
End-to-end and segmented ABR control flows.

Minimum Cell Rate (MCR), which may actually be zero. The first cell to be sent from the source is a forward RM cell. Upon receiving this cell, the (virtual) destination notes its content, turns it around, sets the DIR bit to indicate that it is now a backward RM cell, and sends it back toward the source, where its content is again noted and the RM cell is discarded.

At the (virtual) destination, the Explicit Forward Congestion Indication (EFCI) of this forward RM cell (or any other cell) is noted and if it is set, steps are taken to require a reduction in the ACR from the source. This is done through the setting of the Congestion Indication bit in the backward RM cell by the (virtual) destination; the saved EFCI state is then reset. The source, upon receipt of the backward RM cell with the CI bit set, reduces the ACR by at least $ACR°RDF$ (RDF is the Rate Decrease Factor), but to not less than the MCR, which is guaranteed in all events. If the (virtual) destination is itself experiencing congestion, it can reduce the Explicit Cell Rate (ER) value and/or it can set the CI bit or the No Increase (NI) bit in the backward RM cell.

If the source receives a backward RM cell in which the CI and NI bits are reset (= 0), it may increase the ACR by the amount $ACR°RDF$ up to but not exceeding the PCR; however, if the NI bit is set, it must not increase the ACR.

In all events, the ACR cannot be set to a rate greater than the ER that was entered into the backward RM cell by the (virtual) destination.

It can be seen that the ABR mechanism has the ability to raise and lower the cell rate from the source to the (virtual) destination. The mechanism also works between a virtual source and a (virtual) destination. In the middle of the network, cell queuing is necessary to cope with segmented ABR and these queues can be very long indeed, if necessary. Congestion in a network element (switch) can therefore be coped with through dynamic adjustments to the cell rate in the different segments of the end-to-end VPC or VCC.

18.6.5 · ATM Block Transfer (ABT) Service

This service is only currently specified by the ITU-T and is little used so far, if it is used at all. If supported, it would provide the user with the ability to send blocks of cells, delineated by resource management (RM) cells (see Table 18.1), at different peak cell rates known as block cell rates (BCRs), each of which is specified, along with the block size and other parameters, by the leading RM cell of a block; the trailing cell of one block can be the leading cell of the next. Cell blocks are delineated and their BCR specified for each direction independently. A PCR is specified for the connection at setup time and the BCR cannot exceed this. Two types of ABT service are standardized: ABT with delayed transmission (ABT/DT) and ABT with immediate transmission (ABT/IT); the RM cells for each are differentiated by the Protocol ID field (first byte) in the RM cells—the Protocol ID = 2 for ABT/DT and 3 for ABT/IT.

In the case of ABT/DT, the user negotiates the BCR with the network before the burst is sent; this guarantees that sufficient resources exist so that the burst survives intact. With ABT/IT, the burst is sent without advanced negotiation, so it runs the risk of being discarded if network resources are insufficient. In both cases, of course, an ABT RM cell precedes the burst—it is from the ABT/IT RM cell that the network learns what BCR the following burst will have.

18.6.6 Guaranteed Frame Rate (GFR) Service

With the arrival of the current version (4.1) of the ATM Forum's Traffic Management specification (af-tm-0121-000) came the introduction of a new service type, the Guaranteed Frame Rate (GFR) service type; this service is now also standardized by the ITU-T in Recommendation I.371.1 (November

2000). The purpose of the GFR service type is to support non-real-time applications, which are frame based; in this instance, a frame is an AAL-5 CPCS (common part convergence sublayer) PDU. AAL-5 CPCS PDUs are delineated at the ATM layer by the identification of the last cell of the PDU (AUU bit = 1 in the PTI). In the other service types we came across "conforming" and "nonconforming" cells; with GFR we also talk about conforming and nonconforming frames. If a cell is discarded within an AAL-5 PDU, the frame is unusable, so the goals of GFR are to be aware of frames, to attempt to guarantee delivery of undamaged frames (frames where no cells have been lost due to nonconformance of any of the cells comprising the frame), and to discard the remaining cells of damaged frames as part of the policing process, thus saving valuable bandwidth resources. This is really bringing "early frame discard" into the traffic contract procedures.

GFR guarantees a minimum cell rate (MCR_0, expressed in cells per second), where MCR_0 may be zero. The maximum frame size (MFS_{0+1}, expressed in cells) is also specified, along with the maximum burst size (MBS_0, expressed in cells) and the peak cell rate (PCR_{0+1}, expressed in cells per second), which is always greater than the MCR_0. A GFR *cell* is conforming if it conforms to the PCR_{0+1}, if it conforms to the MFS_{0+1}, and if all cells of the frame have the same setting of the CLP bit. A GFR *frame* is conforming if all GFR cells are conforming (as just described) and if the frame conforms to the frame-based generic cell rate algorithm F-GCRA(T, τ), where $T = 1/MCR_0$ and τ (the CDVT) $= \tau_{IBT} + \tau_{MCR}$, where $\tau_{IBT} = (MSB_0 - 1) \times (1/MCR_0 - 1/PCR_{0+1})$ and $\tau_{MCR} =$ the CDVT of MCR_0.

Because all cells within a conforming frame will have the same priority, frames can be said to have normal or low priority too (determined, of course, by the CLP of the cells comprising the frame); low priority frames are candidates for discard in the event of congestion elsewhere. In the event of partial frame discard, network equipment should attempt to deliver the last cell of the partially discarded frame so as to provide frame delineation for the start of the next frame. The ATM network supporting GFR guarantees to deliver all cells of normal priority frames that conform, as defined above, to cope with higher cell rates than MCR_0, if resources permit. Low priority frames or frames comprised of cells of mixed priority are not guaranteed to survive.

Two traffic contracts are specified for guaranteed frame rate: GFR.1 and GFR.2 (GFR1 and GFR2 in ITU-T terminology); they differ with respect to the treatment of the CLP bit based on the F-GCRA (Frame-based Generic Cell Rate Algorithm) test.

GFR.1 = GFR1 = F-GCRA(T, τ), minimum cell rate supported, no tagging

GFR.2 = GFR2 = F-GCRA(T, τ), minimum cell rate supported,
frame tagging supported

Table 18.2 Conformance Requirements for Traffic Contracts

Conformance Definition		PCR Flow	SCR Flow	Tagging Option Active	MCR	CLR On
ATM Forum	ITU-T					
CBR.1	DBR	0 + 1	ns	na	ns	0 + 1
VBR.1	SBR1	0 + 1	0 + 1	na	ns	0 + 1
VBR.2	SBR2	0 + 1	0	No	ns	0
VBR.3	SBR3	0 + 1	0	Yes	ns	0
UBR.1	—	0 + 1	ns	na	ns	U
UBR.2	—	0 + 1	ns	Yes	ns	U
ABR	—	0	ns	na	Yes	0
GFR.1	GFR1	0 + 1	ns	No	Yes	0
GFR.2	GFR2	0 + 1	ns	Yes	Yes	0

18.6.7   Summary of Service Types

Table 18.2 summarizes the conformance definitions for all service types except the two ABT service types; because these are specified in a rather different way, and RM cell conformance is also involved, it makes less sense to include ABT here.

18.7   Network QoS Guarantees

Up until now we have seen how the network protects itself against violations of the contract. However, the network has its side of the bargain to deliver—QoS. Each of the above service types makes its own QoS guarantees (or none).

Before we discuss QoS guarantees, it is necessary to get into more detail about the ATM Forum's VBR traffic type. The ATM Forum distinguishes between "non-real-time" VBR (nrt-VBR) and "real-time" VBR (rt-VBR). The former is used when delay-insensitive data is being serviced and the latter is

Table 18.3 Traffic and QoS Parameters

Attribute	ATM Layer Service Category					
	CBR	**rt-VBR**	**nrt-VBR**	**UBR**	**ABR**	**GFR**
Traffic Parameters						
PCR and CDVT	specified					
SCR, MBS, CDVT	na	specified		na		
MCR	na				specified	na
MCR, MBS, MFS, CDVT	na					specified
QoS Parameters						
Peak-to-Peak CDV	specified		unspecified			
MaxCTD	specified		unspecified			
CLR	specified			unspecified	may be specified	
Congestion Control						
Feedback	unspecified				specified	unspecified
Other Attributes						
BCS	unspecified			optional	unspecified	

used for delay-sensitive traffic (e.g., packetized video). The policing parameters discussed above are independent of this distinction, which is why discussion of it has been delayed until now. Remember that policing exists to protect the network and has nothing to do with the QoS guarantees that the network may be asked to make.

The CBR/DBR service will require guarantees from the network regarding cell loss, CDV, and maximum CTD. For the same reasons, so will rt-VBR. On the other hand, nrt-VBR/SBR will not require guarantees regarding CDV but will require cell loss to be minimized. With the UBR, the network makes no guarantees about either cell loss or CDV. With ABR, cell loss is controlled but there is no way that CDV guarantees could be met because of the flow control mechanisms. Table 18.3 shows the traffic parameters and the associated QoS parameters, indicating which have to be specified for the different categories of service. Where QoS parameters are specified, worst-case values are standardized according to QoS class.

Chapter 19

PERFORMANCE AND OPERATING PARAMETERS OF ATM NETWORKS

The network performance (NP) of ATM networks is substantially dependent on the three lowest layers of the B-ISDN protocol model: the physical layer, the ATM layer, and the AAL layer (see Figure 19.1).

19.1 The Physical Layer

At the inputs to ATM switches, a transition from one physical transmission medium to another necessarily occurs (fiber, connectors, switch port). Transmission errors can arise here due to aging, humidity, dust, or material flaws. Furthermore, the signal quality of the cabling influences the bit error rate in the transmission frame (SDH/SONET, E1, T3, etc.), and consequently the performance of the higher protocol layers.

19.2 The ATM Layer

The ATM layer is independent from the subordinate physical layer on the one hand and from the higher-order application on the other. Thus the communication parameters for ATM cells are a uniform measure for the performance of an ATM network, regardless of the topology and applications used.

19.3 The ATM Adaptation Layer (AAL)

The ATM Adaptation Layer builds on the functions of the ATM layer and allows applications to communicate over the ATM cell stream. It supports various protocol types with different performance characteristics. The efficiency of the AAL protocols in the various operational and load states is critical for the performance of an application transported over an ATM network. In some cases, for example, it can be more important to know the AAL PDU throughput or the AAL PDU loss rate than the corresponding ATM cell parameters, since the AAL PDU figures as a rule are directly proportional to the application data rate.

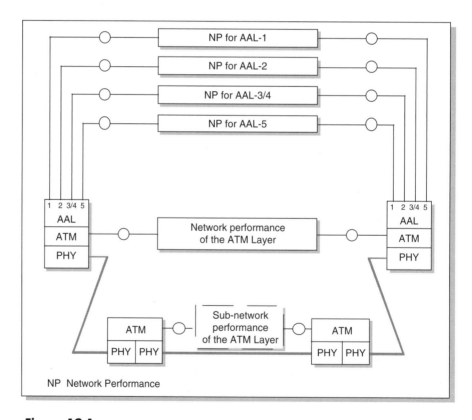

Figure 19.1
Protocol layer model for performance analysis in ATM networks.

19.4   ATM Layer Measurement Points

Before we can specify performance parameters and test methods, we must first have a clear definition of the measurement points (MP) at which the parameters are observed. A measurement point, shown in Figure 19.2, is an interface within the ATM network at which an existing connection can be monitored and cells can be removed from or inserted in the traffic flow. The arrival of ATM cells at a measurement point, or the time at which a cell passes that point, is defined as follows.

A cell has passed a measurement point when the last bit of the ATM cell has left the measurement point. This is also called a cell exit event. Analogously, a cell is considered to have arrived at a measurement point when the first bit of the ATM cell has passed that point. This is called a cell entry event.

Furthermore, two reference events for cell transfer are defined, CRE1 and CRE2, which occur at measurement points MP1 and MP2 (Figure 19.3). In this way, the outcome of a cell transfer between the two measurement points can be designated as the following.

Successful Cell Transfer

A successful transfer has occurred if a CRE2 follows a CRE1 within the time T defined by CRE1, and the contents of the information field of the received cell exactly match the contents of the emitted cell.

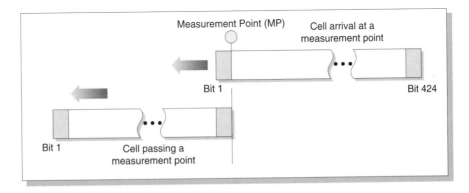

Figure 19.2
Measurement point for ATM layer measurements.

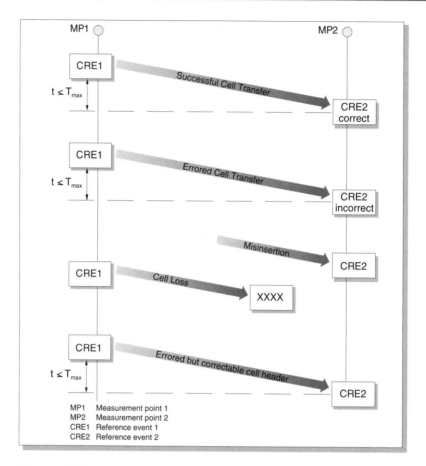

Figure 19.3
Cell transport between ATM layer measurement points.

Errored Cell Transfer

An errored transfer has occurred if a CRE2 follows a CRE1 within the time T defined by CRE1, but the contents of the information field of the received cell are different from the emitted cell, or the cell is received with an invalid header field (assuming HEC delineation has been completed).

Cell Loss

If no CRE2 occurs within the delay T after CRE1, a cell is considered to have been lost.

Misinsertion

If a CRE2 occurs without a prior CRE1, a cell misinsertion has occurred.

Errored but Correctable Cell Header

An errored but correctable cell header occurs if a CRE2 follows a CRE1 within the time T defined by the CRE1, and the header is errored, but can be regenerated by the HEC procedures.

Errored, Noncorrectable Cell Header

An errored and not correctable cell header occurs when a CRE2 follows a CRE1 within the time T defined by CRE1, and the received header contains errors and cannot be regenerated by HEC procedures.

Severely Errored Cell Block (SECB)

If M cells in a block of N cells are errored, lost, or misinserted, this is called a Severely Errored Cell Block (SECB). If no guaranteed cell loss ratio was negotiated, then lost cells with a CLP value of 1 are not included in M. Errored or misinserted cells with CLP = 1 are counted, however. N is chosen so that between 12.5 and 25 cell blocks per second can be counted when the given connection is operated at the peak cell rate. Thus M is $1/32 \times N$. Table 19.1 lists the values of N and M for peak cell rates between 0 and 819,200 cells per second.

19.5 Physical Layer Network Performance Parameters

The network performance parameters for the physical layer are described in the specifications for the individual interfaces. The transmission convergence sublayer, however, is typical for ATM networks. The following performance parameters are therefore defined for this sublayer.

Table 19.1 Values of N and M for Peak Cell Rates

PCR (cells/second)	User Information Rate (Mbit/s)	Block size N (cells)	Threshold M (cells)
$0 < x \leq 3{,}200$	$(0 < y \leq 1.23)$	128	4
$3{,}200 < x \leq 6{,}400$	$(1.23 < y \leq 2.46)$	256	8
$6{,}400 < x \leq 12{,}800$	$(2.46 < y \leq 4.92)$	512	16
$12{,}800 < x \leq 25{,}600$	$(4.92 < y \leq 9.83)$	1,024	32
$25{,}600 < x \leq 51{,}200$	$(9.83 < y \leq 19.66)$	2,048	64
$51{,}200 < x \leq 102{,}400$	$(19.66 < y \leq 39.32)$	4,096	128
$120{,}400 < x \leq 202{,}800$	$(39.32 < y \leq 78.64)$	8,192	256
$202{,}800 < x \leq 409{,}600$	$(78.64 < y \leq 157.29)$	16,384	512
$409{,}600 < x \leq 819{,}200$	$(157.29 < y \leq 314.57)$	32,768	1,024

Corrected Header Ratio

The corrected header ratio is the number of cells with invalid but correctable headers divided by the total number of cells received within the same period. This parameter is mainly influenced by the bit error rate of the transmission path. There is also a small probability that cells with invalid headers may appear as valid cells, and thus lead to incorrect transmissions. The probability of such an event can be calculated from the number of errored headers containing more than two incorrect bits—the HEC checksum of such a header no longer indicates whether it is corrupt—and the ratio of valid header values to the number of all possible header values. Figure 19.4 shows the probability of undetectable errored cell headers as a function of the bit error rate.

Discarded Cell Ratio

The discarded cell ratio equals the number of cells received with errored, non-correctable headers, which are therefore discarded, divided by the total number of cells received (both valid and errored). This quantity is also influenced by the bit error rate of the transmission path.

Loss of Cell Delineation Rate

The loss of cell delineation rate is the number of cell delineation losses over a certain time interval.

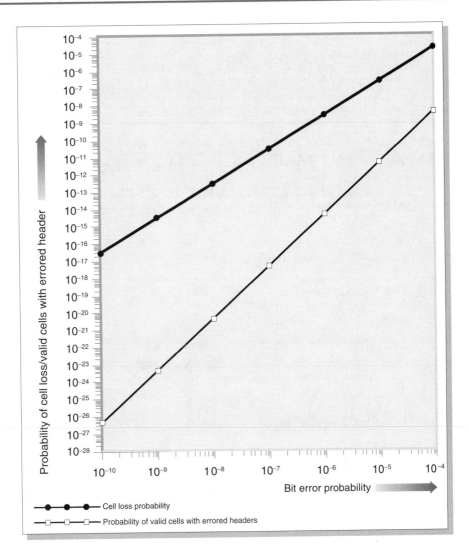

Figure 19.4
Valid cells with errored headers.

Mean Loss of Delineation Duration

The mean loss of delineation duration is defined as the number of missing CRE2 events due to cell delineation loss within a given time interval, divided by the number of CRE2 events expected in that time interval.

Demux Error Ratio

The demux (short for demultiplex) error ratio is the number of all correctly transmitted cells containing an invalid VPI value, divided by the total number of correctly transmitted cells.

19.6 ATM Layer Network Performance Parameters

The performance parameters for the ATM layer are cell error ratio, cell loss ratio, cell misinsertion ratio, and cell transfer delay.

Cell Error Ratio

The cell error ratio is the number of errored cells divided by the total number of transmitted cells, both valid and errored. Invalid cells that are contained in severely errored cell blocks are not counted.

Cell Loss Ratio

The cell loss ratio is the number of cells lost divided by the total number of cells transferred in the same time period. Transferred or lost cells in cell blocks are not counted. There are three different kinds of cell loss ratio measurements:

1. Cell loss ratio for cells with high priority (cell loss priority bit = 0): CLR_0 is defined as $N_l(0) / N_t(0)$, where $N_t(0)$ is the number of cells with $CLP = 0$ and $N_l(0)$ is the number of lost cells plus the number of tagged cells.

2. Cell loss ratio for the entire cell stream: CLR_{0+1} is defined as $N_l(0 + 1) / N_t(0 + 1)$, where $N_t(0 + 1)$ is the number of all cells transmitted and $N_l(0 + 1)$ is the number of lost cells.

3. Cell loss ratio for cells with low priority: CLR_1 is defined as $N_l(1) / N_t(1)$, where $N_t(1)$ is the number of cells with $CLP = 1$ and $N_l(1)$ the number of lost cells.

Cell Misinsertion Ratio

The cell misinsertion ratio is defined as the number of defective cells (i.e., cells containing a wrong VPI/VCI due to noncorrected header errors) transmitted over a time interval.

Cell Transfer Delay (CTD)

The cell transfer delay is defined as the time $t_2 - t_1$ between two corresponding cell transmission/reception events CRE_1 (t_1) and CRE_2 (t_2) (where $t_2 > t_1$). The Mean Cell Transfer Delay is the arithmetic mean of a given number of transfer delay values.

Cell Delay Variation (CDV)

Deviation from the cell transfer delay is called transfer delay variation. Two types of cell transfer delay variations are defined: one-point cell delay variation, which concerns cells arriving at one measurement point, and two-point cell delay variation, which describes the variation in cell delay at measurement point 2 relative to measurement point 1. Both of these are illustrated in Figures 19.5 and 19.6.

One-Point Cell Delay Variation

The one-point cell delay variation (y_k) for cell k at measurement point MP is defined as the difference between the reference arrival time (c_k) of the cell and the actual arrival time (a_k), i.e., $y_k = c_k - a_k$, where the reference arrival time is defined as follows:

$$c_0 = a_0 = 0$$

$$c_{k+1} = c_k + T \qquad \text{if } c_k > a_k$$

$$c_{k+1} = a_k + T \qquad \text{in all other cases}$$

Two-Point Cell Delay Variation

The two-point cell delay variation (v_k) for cell k between MP1 and MP2 is defined as the difference between the actual cell delay (x_k) and the reference delay $(d_{1,2})$ between the two measurements points: $v_k = x_k - d_{1,2}$. The actual

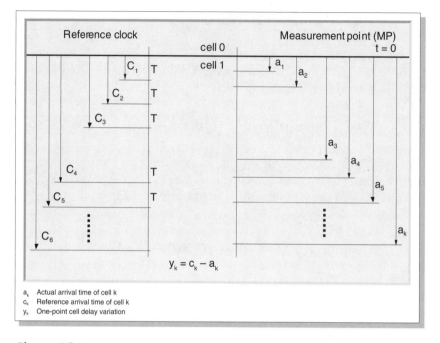

$$y_k = c_k - a_k$$

a_k Actual arrival time of cell k
c_k Reference arrival time of cell k
y_k One-point cell delay variation

Figure 19.5
One-point cell delay variation.

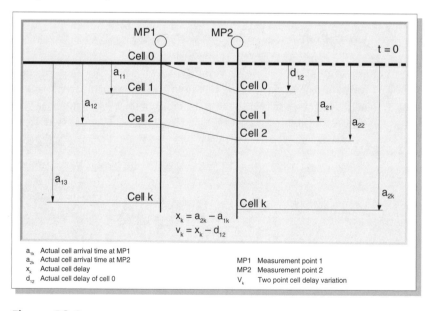

$$x_k = a_{2k} - a_{1k}$$
$$v_k = x_k - d_{12}$$

a_{1k} Actual cell arrival time at MP1
a_{2k} Actual cell arrival time at MP2   MP1   Measurement point 1
x_k Actual cell delay   MP2   Measurement point 2
d_{12} Actual cell delay of cell 0 V_k Two point cell delay variation

Figure 19.6
Two-point cell delay variation.

Table 19.2 ATM Layer Performance Parameters

	Threshold	Default values	QOS Classes			
			Class 1 (Stringent Class)	Class 2 (Tolerant Class)	Class 3 (Bi-Level Class)	U-Class
CTD	Upper limit of the average CTD	None	400 ms	U	U	U
2-Point CDV	Upper limit of the difference between upper and lower 10^{-8} CTD range	None	3 ms	U	U	U
CLR_{0+1}	Upper limit of cell loss rate	None	3×10^{-7}	10^{-5}	U	U
CLR_0	Upper limit of cell loss rate	None	None	None	10^{-5}	U
CER	Upper limit of cell error rate	4×10^{-6}	Default	Default	Default	U
CMR	Upper limit of cell misinsertion rate (CMR)	1/day	Delfault	Delfault	Delfault	U
SECBR	Upper limit of SECB probability	10^{-4}	Delfault	Delfault	Delfault	U

U   not specified or unlimited

cell delay (x_k) is defined as the difference between the actual cell arrival time at MP2 $(a2_k)$ and the actual arrival time at MP1 $(a1_k)$: $x_k = a2_k - a1_k$. The reference cell delay $(d_{1,2})$ between MP1 and MP2 equals the actual cell delay of cell 0 between the two measurement points.

Table 19.2 lists the ATM layer performance parameters for the various QoS classes, which can be attained in ATM wide area networks with the reference diameter of 27,500 km.

Chapter 20

ATM Testing Methods

The methods used to test ATM components and ATM networks are largely dependent on the test environment. There are four basic types of test scenarios:

- Testing in ATM research and development
- Testing in production of ATM components
- Testing during installation and acceptance of ATM networks
- In-service testing in operational ATM networks

In the product development phase, the emphasis is on performance tests, regression tests, conformance tests, and interoperability tests. In performance testing, the various functions of the component are tested at maximum loads, and its behavior at various load levels is recorded. Regression tests ensure that improved designs still fulfill all the functions of their predecessors. In conformance testing, the system is tested against the existing standards. Finally, interoperability tests verify the system's ability to communicate and cooperate with other systems. All of the testing methods applied in the product development phase are out-of-service tests: in other words, they are performed in a laboratory environment, not in a normally operating ATM network environment.

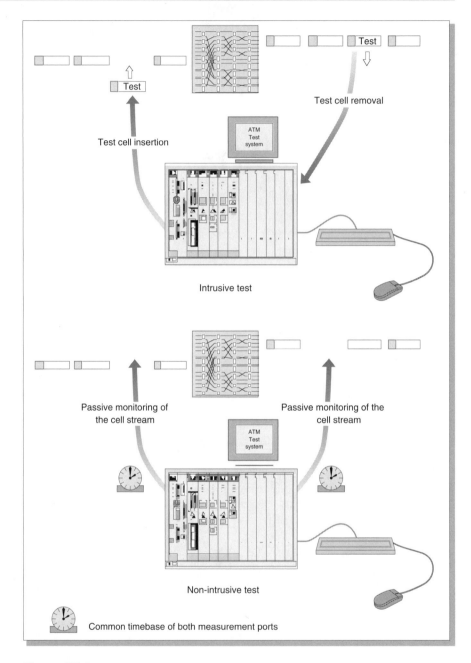

Figure 20.1
Intrusive and nonintrusive testing in ATM networks.

In the production phase, tests are performed to assure the quality of the manufacturing process. Because the production process is under test rather than the system design, the emphasis here is on the lower layers. Typical faults discovered in such testing include assembly errors, bad solder joints, and component defects. In this phase too, all testing is performed out-of-service.

The testing performed in the installation and acceptance phases of an ATM network is based on the assumption that the components are in working order. The correct configuration of the system often proves to be the biggest problem. Because there is no user data traffic on the network in this phase, traffic has to be generated for test purposes. In a later phase, test users are involved as well. Thus both in-service and out-of-service test methods are applied.

Once the ATM network is operational, the testing methods used must not impair user data traffic. Passive monitoring systems are used, as well as network management systems and the various OAM functions of ATM. Tests of this type are also called non-intrusive tests (see Figure 20.1).

20.1 Conformance Testing of ATM Components

Conformance testing is an important specialized field in data communications. Special testing systems are used to test communication terminals and network components for correct behavior in operation. Demonstrable conformance to standards is necessary to ensure interoperability between different manufacturers' systems. The importance of conformance testing for ATM was recognized early on due to the experience gathered on an international scale with communication protocols such as ISDN and X.25. The ATM Forum's testing working group therefore established testing guidelines for the various ATM protocols from the beginning.

20.1.1 ATS (Abstract Test Suite), PICS, and PIXIT

Conformance testing generally begins with the test equipment placing the new system, called the implementation under test (IUT), in a known initial state. Then the test equipment induces a defined protocol event and evaluates the reaction of the IUT. The result of each such test case is recorded with one of three possible results:

- Pass
- Fail
- Inconclusive

The latter result indicates that the conformance testing system cannot assess the IUT's reaction precisely. This can be the case especially in complex protocol processes. The process must then be evaluated by the test operator. The set of all test cases for a given system is called a test suite. Which events are initiated from which initial state for each test case is specified in Abstract Test Suites (ATS). An ATS consists of a number of test purposes or procedures, which are generally specified in tree and tabular combined notation (TTCN). The implementation of an abstract test suite in the form of a program that can be executed by a conformance testing system is called an executable test suite (ETS). Because the various protocol implementations often incorporate only a subset of the many functions included in a protocol specification, the appropriate test purposes for the IUT must be selected from the full test suite before the beginning of a test run. This is done by configuring all parameters specific to the given protocol. The protocol parameters are defined in two specifications, called PICS (Protocol Implementation Conformance Statement) and PIXIT (Protocol Implementation Extra Information for Testing). The PICS describes the IUT's capabilities with respect to the protocol, while the PIXIT contains values for the parameters necessary in communication between the tester and the IUT. In practice, the PICS, PIXIT, and the entire test suite are implemented in the form of an executable program in the conformance testing system. The PICS and PIXIT values can be specified in input dialogs, and the program automatically selects and performs the corresponding test cases. The ATM Forum has specified abstract test suites for UNI 3.0, UNI 3.1, and UNI 4.0 signaling, and for LAN emulation.

20.2   Interoperability Tests

Interoperability tests are performed in order to make sure that two or more systems are able to work together. Unlike conformance testing, interoperability testing focuses not on a standard, but on an operation with respect to another actual implementation. Interoperability tests are thus relative tests, and do not necessarily test the entire scope of an implementation's capabilities, but only those functions that are necessary for interoperability. Because such tests require a great deal of expensive hardware, they are often performed in the context of trade fairs or special test workshops organized by independent testing laboratories or universities. Interoperability test software is also available for a number of protocols. Such software packages generally consist of conformance tests with specific interoperability tests added. Two network components that pass such a test program are very likely to be interoperable.

20.3 ATM Layer Performance Tests

Performance testing is carried out under a variety of load conditions at the ATM layer to determine the classic ATM parameters, Cell Loss Ratio (CLR), Cell Misinsertion Rate (CMR), Cell Error Ratio (CER), Cell Transfer Delay (CTD), Cell Delay Variation (CDV), and the number of non-conforming cells (NCC), or cells transmitted in violation of the traffic contract. The components under test are placed under extreme operating conditions by generating artificial traffic loads before the desired parameters are measured. If the results are not satisfactory, then the design or the configuration is modified until the performance objectives are reached.

The most frequent causes of cell loss are buffer overflows or faults in the physical layer that lead to noncorrectable errors. Cell misinsertion is caused by malfunction of the switching fabric or by multiple bit transmission errors in the header, which can no longer be corrected, as a result of physical layer problems. These errors cause the cell header to be corrupted into another "legal" value (or a "legal" value with a "correctable" single bit error), that is, a header with a VPI-VCI equal to that of the virtual channel into which the cell is therefore misinserted. A high CER usually indicates the occurrence of bit errors in the payload field. (Note that bit errors occurring in the header are reflected in cell loss figures.) In most cases these bit errors are caused by a higher degree of signal jitter than the ATM interface can tolerate. CTD is caused by ordinary electronic switching and signal propagation delays. The cause of delay variations usually lies in the varying states of buffers that the cells must pass through on their way to the destination, and in the effects of cell encapsulation in the physical layer transmission framing. Thus two cells within a single SDH/SONET container/SPE will have a smaller CDV relative to one another than two cells transported in different containers.

Out-of-service measurements are performed using special test cells as defined in ITU-T Recommendation O.191 (see Figure 20.2). These test cells have standard ATM cell headers and can be inserted using any user value of VPI-VCI (VCI > 31). In the test cell payload there is a 32-bit Sequence Number (SN) to permit detection of cell loss and cell misinsertion errors, a 32-bit timestamp (TS), inserted to allow measurement of CTD and CDV, a 32-bit Control Information (CI) field, a 32-bit Data Control Channel (DCC), a Test Cell Payload Type (TCPT) field, and a CRC-16, which can detect the existence of errors anywhere in the payload with a higher probability than that afforded by the ususal CRC-10 used in OAM and RM cells (testing requires such rigor). The Timestamp (TS) field allows CTD and 2-point CDV mea-

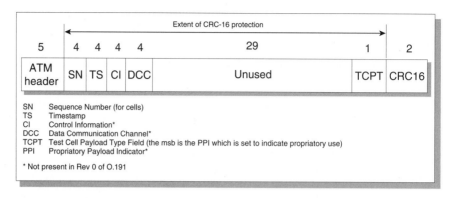

Figure 20.2
Format of the O.191 (Rev 1) test cell for out-of-service testing.

surements at rates up to 2.4 Gbit/s. The least significant bit of the timestamp has a resolution of 10 ns, though equipment designed to test only at lower rate interfaces may increment the timestamp from a higher order bit at a correspondingly lower rate.

In the simplest case, an ATM analyzer with one transmit and one receive port is sufficient to perform these out-of-service measurements, assuming they share a common time-of-day clock, which is easy to implement; for measurements over geographically large distances, two analyzers are required, which have their time-of-day clocks synchronized via, for example, the Global Positioning System (GPS), requiring more sophisticated implementations.

End-to-end quality-of-service testing can be performed bidirectionally with a pair of analyzers, each of which has a transmit and a receive port for handling test cells; two independent test streams are sent, one in each direction. In sophisticated analyzers, the test cell traffic is shaped in terms of PCR, CDVT, SCR, and MBS to conform to the traffic contract negotiated with the network, which is generally different for each direction though the network. Of course, the network should deliver the quality of service that was agreed in the traffic contract and, by operating the test traffic at or marginally below the traffic contract requirements, the end-user can ascertain whether this is so. If the analyzers can be fully synchronized, including time-of-day synchronization, all the standard ATM performance measurements are possible; if time-of-day synchronization is not available, all measurements except cell transfer delay are possible, assuming low relative drift of the analyzer clocks, so the important CLR and CDV measurements can be done. Note that it is important to make these measurements unidirectional; using cell loopback gives false results since (a) the performance of the network in one direction is, in general, different (sometimes dramatically so) to that in the opposite direction;

(b) different traffic contracts are probably operating in each direction; and (c) looped test cell traffic may have suffered sufficient CDV introduced by the network in the forward direction that, when sent back into the network across the UNI at the far end, no longer conforms to the traffic contract for that direction and therefore suffers cell loss, not caused by the poor performance of the network but by legal action by the usage constraint (policing) mechanism.

The purpose of the data communication channel (DCC) is to allow communication between remote analyzers. The advantage of this would be to allow test results from each analyzer to be exchanged so that each analyzer has a picture of the performance in both directions. Currently, the ITU-T has not standardized the communication protocol for this but it has made provision to allow propriatory communication methods to be used over this channel. The Control Information (CI) field has 2 bits in it associated with the DCC field, coded in Table 20.1.

The only other field so far standardized in the Control Information field is the 3-bit Timestamp Synchronization Control (TSC) field, which is coded in Table 20.2.

Following work done by the ATM Forum, the Test Cell Payload Type (TCPT) field had a 1-bit subfield added in the position of the most significant bit, which this is the Propriatory Payload Indicator (PPI) bit; if set, this bit indicates that some of the 29 unused bytes of the test cell are being used for propriatory purposes (propriatory fields should be justified toward the end of the unused field so that new ITU-T standardized fields can follow existing ones); the remaining bits of the TCPT field are used now as a test cell revision number—the current value of this field is 0000001, indication that the test cell conforms to Revision 1 of O.191 (i.e., the second version of the standard). New to this revision is the introduction of the CI, DCC, and PPI fields, Revision 0 having only the SN, TS, TCPT, and CRC-16 fields.

Table 20.1 DCC Control Coding in the Control Information Field

Coding	Meaning
0 0	DCC not present
0 1	Standard DCC present (for further study)
1 0	Propriatory DCC present
1 1	Use for further study

Table 20.2 Time Synchronization Coding in the Control Information Field

Coding	Meaning	Requirement
0 0 0	Full roll-over of the timestamp (after approximately 42 seconds)	Mandatory
0 0 1	10 second timestamp re-synchronization period	Mandatory if the optional timestamp clock synchronization is implemented in the analyzer
0 1 0	1 second timestamp re-synchronization period	Optional
0 1 1	30 second timestamp re-synchronization period	Optional
1 x x	Use for further study	

The ATM Forum in its Performance Testing Specification (af-test-0131.000) has made use of the PPI to indicate a proprietary use of some of the 29 unused bytes—some of these additional features may one day be folded into the O.191 recommendation in a future revision. Specifically, it has extended the use of the test cells from AAL-5 frame testing by adding a Frame Sequence Number and a special test cell format for the end of frame (EOF) required by AAL-5—this test cell is identified by the setting of the AUU bit in the header. Figure 20.3 shows the modified standard test cell and Figure 20.4

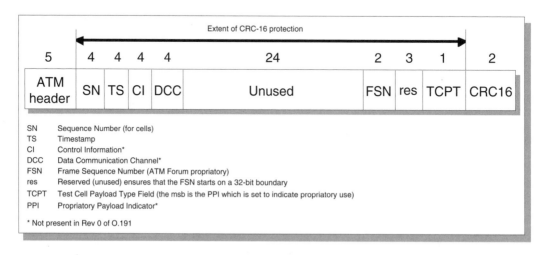

Figure 20.3
The ATM Forum proprietary format of the O.191 test cell.

494

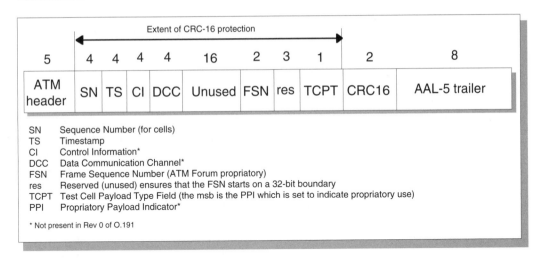

Figure 20.4
The ATM Forum special EOF test cell.

shows the EOF test cell format. Note that the test cells shown are based on the Rev 1 version of O.191, although, at the time af-test-0131.000 was being developed, Rev 0 was current (though under review). Close cooperation between the ATM Forum and Study Group 4 of the ITU-T ensured that the PPI was introduced by the ITU-T, allowing proprietary use of the unused field in this way.

While the Sequence Number (SN) gets incremented every cell by the test cell generator, the Frame Sequence Number (FSN) gets incremented only every AAL-5 frame. This work laid the foundation for AAL level (frame) measurements to be developed for testing ATM.

20.4   In-Service ATM Testing

Dedicated measurement systems used for in-service testing of ATM networks can be either inserted as passive components in the link to be monitored or connected by means of optical couplers. In-service testing also includes the use of ATM's native fault and performance management functions, however.

ATM's integrated fault management mechanisms are contained in the OAM information flows F1 to F5. Flows F1–F3 yield information about the operating state of the SDH/SONET transport structure and other interfaces (though not all flows are used in these), while F4 and F5 contain the corresponding ATM layer data. F4 information concerns ATM virtual path connections (VPCs), F5 the virtual channel connections (VCCs). The fault management function in ATM is based on two types of alarms: the Alarm Indication Signal (AIS) and the Remote Defect Indication (RDI). The alarm indication signal (VP-AIS/VC-AIS) is sent downstream by the channel or path node that detects the fault to all network nodes directly affected. The AIS is transmitted periodically until the fault is corrected. Immediately after the AIS, an RDI signal is sent upstream to the end nodes of the connections affected. These signals are likewise sent periodically until the fault condition is resolved. VP-AIS and VP-RDI messages are always sent in cells with VCI = 3 (for segment F4 flows) or VCI = 4 (for end-to-end F4 flows), while VC-AIS and VC-RDI messages are sent in cells with PT = 100 (for segment F5 flows) and PT = 101 (for end-to-end F5 flows). Two mechanisms are available to detect fault conditions: continuity checks (CC) and loopback tests. Continuity checks continuously monitor the availability of a connection. A system inserts CC cells periodically into the user cell stream. ATM network nodes along the connection path can then check for the presence of these CC cells. If expected CC cells are not received, loss of continuity (LOC) is signaled by means of AIS messages. Loopback cells are used to verify connectivity to specific sections of the ATM network; they are themselves looped back while user traffic continues unaffected (is not looped back).

Network components (such as ATM switches) can periodically insert special OAM cells in the user cell stream for in-service performance monitoring. The measurement parameters contained in the payload of these cells (sequence number, user cell count, timestamp, cell loss counter) can be analyzed to provide information about the operational condition state of the ATM connection. OAM performance management involves two distinct functions, called forward monitoring and backward reporting. If backward reporting is also activated (this is optional), then the network element that terminates and processes the received forward monitoring OAM cells sends OAM performance result information back toward the network element that generated the forward monitoring OAM cells, as well as reporting them to local network management; this is useful if the performance monitoring is being done across network operator boundaries, as one nework operator does not have access to the network management system of other operators (see also "OAM Fault Management" in Chapter 7).

Chapter 21

ATM: STANDARDS AND ORGANIZATIONS

The specifications for ATM and B-ISDN have been developed mainly by two bodies: the ITU-T and the ATM Forum. The ITU-T is the standardization section of the International Telecommunications Union. Due to the complex and slow-moving standardization procedures of the ITU, work on developing standards, particularly in the fast-changing data communications field, is increasingly supported and assisted by industry associations such as the ATM Forum. Other bodies that develop standards for ATM technologies include the Internet Society (ISOC), the American National Standards Institute (ANSI), the European Telecommunications Standards Institute (ETSI), and the Internet Engineering Task Force (IETF).

21.1   ITU (International Telecommunications Union)

The International Telecommunications Union (ITU) was founded in 1932 under the name CCITT (the acronym is derived from the French for International Telegraph and Telephone Consultative Committee). ITU membership is restricted to national telecommunications authorities, and currently includes those of 164 countries.

In 1984 the ITU created the standards for ISDN (Integrated Services Digital Network) with its I series of recommendations. Further recommendations for broadband services, B-ISDN, were added to this series in 1990 as drafts by ITU Study Group XVIII. These standards were adopted in 1991 and have subsequently, in many cases, been revised by what is now Study Group 13. ITU standards can be ordered from the ITU directly either in electronic form (with payment by credit card) through the ITU information server on the World Wide Web *(http://www.itu.int/)* or by postal mail:

International Telecommunications Union
General Secretariat Sales Section
Place des Nations
CH-1211 Geneva 20
Switzerland
Tel.: +41-22-730 5111
Fax: +41-22-730 5194

The most important ITU-T ATM standards are listed below.

I.113	Vocabulary of Terms for Broadband Aspects of ISDN
I.121	Broadband Aspects of ISDN
I.150	B-ISDN ATM Functional Characteristics
I.211	B-ISDN Service Aspects
I.311	B-ISDN General Network Aspects
I.313	B-ISDN Network Requirements
I.321	B-ISDN Protocol Reference Model and Its Application
I.327	B-ISDN Functional Architecture
I.350	General Aspects of Quality-of-Service and Network Performance in Digital Networks, including ISDNs
I.356	B-ISDN ATM Layer Cell Transfer Performance
I.357	B-ISDN Semi-Permanent Connection Availability
I.358	Call Processing Performance for Switched Virtual Channel Connections (VCCs) in a B-ISDN
I.361	B-ISDN ATM Layer Specification
I.362	B-ISDN ATM Adaptation Layer Functional Description

I.363   B-ISDN ATM Adaptation Layer Specification:

    I.363.1   Type 1 AAL

    I.363.2   Type 2 AAL

    I.363.3   Type 3/4 AAL

    I.363.5   Type 5 AAL

I.364   Support of the Broadband Connectionless Data Bearer Service by the B-ISDN

I.365.1   B-ISDN ATM Adaptation Layer Sublayers: Frame Relaying Service-Specific Convergence Sublayer (FR-SSCS)

I.366.1   Segmentation and Reassembly Service-Specific Convergence Sublayer for the AAL Type 2

I.366.2   AAL Type 2 Service-Specific Convergence Sublayer for Narrowband Services

I.370   Congestion Management for the ISDN Frame Relaying Bearer Service

I.371   Traffic Control and Congestion Control in B-ISDN

I.371.1   Guaranteed Frame Rate ATM Transfer Capability

I.372   Frame Relaying Bearer Service Network-to-Network Interface Requirements

I.413   B-ISDN: User–Network Interface

I.432   B-ISDN User–Network Interface—Physical Layer Specification:

    I.432.1   General characteristics

    I.432.2   155 520 kbit/s and 622 080 kbit/s operation

    I.432.3   1544 kbit/s and 2048 kbit/s operation

    I.432.4   51 840 kbit/s operation

    I.432.5   25 600 kbit/s operation

I.555   Frame Relaying Bearer Service Interworking

I.610   B-ISDN Operation and Maintenance Principles and Functions

I.630   ATM Protection Switching

I.761   Inverse Multiplexing for ATM (IMA)—directly references ATM Forum af-phy-0086.001

I.762   ATM over Fractional Physical Links—directly references ATM Forum af-phy-0130-000

F.811   Broadband Connection-Oriented Bearer Service

F.812   Broadband Connectionless Data Bearer Service

Q.2010   Broadband Integrated Services Digital Network Overview— Signaling Capability Set 1, Release 1

Q.2100   B-ISDN Signaling ATM Adaptation Layer (SAAL) Overview Description

Q.2110   B-ISDN ATM Adaptation Layer—Service-Specific Connection-Oriented Protocol (SSCOP)

Q.2120   B-ISDN Meta-Signaling Protocol

Q.2130   B-ISDN Signaling ATM Adaptation Layer—Service-Specific Coordination Function for Support of Signaling at the User–Network Interface (SSFC at UNI)

Q.2140   B-ISDN ATM Adaptation Layer—Service-Specific Coordination Function for Signaling at the Network Node Interface (SSCF at NNI)

Q.2610   Broadband Integrated Services Digital Network (B-ISDN)—Usage of Cause and Location in B-ISDN User Part and DSS 2

Q.2650   Broadband-ISDN, Interworking between Signaling System No. 7—Broadband ISDN User Part (B-ISUP) and Digital Subscriber Signaling System No. 2 (DSS 2)

Q.2660   Broadband Integrated Services Digital Network (B-ISDN)—Interworking between Signaling System No. 7—Broadband ISDN User Part (B-ISUP) and Narrowband ISDN User Part (N-ISUP)

Q.2730   Broadband Integrated Services Digital Network (B-ISDN) Signaling System No. 7 B-ISDN User Part (B-ISUP) Supplementary Services

Q.2761   Broadband Integrated Services Digital Network (B-ISDN) Functional Description of the B-ISDN User Part (B-ISUP) of Signaling System No. 7

Q.2762   Broadband Integrated Services Digital Network (B-ISDN)—General Functions of Messages and Signals of the B-ISDN User Part (B-ISUP) of Signaling System No. 7

Q.2763   Broadband Integrated Services Digital Network (B-ISDN)—Signaling System No. 7 B-ISDN User Part (B-ISUP)—Formats and Codes

Q.2764   Broadband Integrated Services Digital Network (B-ISDN)—Signaling System No. 7 B-ISDN User Part (B-ISUP)—Basic Call Procedures

Q.2931   Broadband Integrated Services Digital Network (B-ISDN)—Digital Subscriber Signaling System No. 2 (DSS 2); User–Network Interface (UNI)—Layer 3 Specification for Basic Call/Connection Control

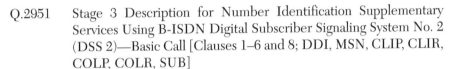

Q.2951   Stage 3 Description for Number Identification Supplementary Services Using B-ISDN Digital Subscriber Signaling System No. 2 (DSS 2)—Basic Call [Clauses 1–6 and 8; DDI, MSN, CLIP, CLIR, COLP, COLR, SUB]

Q.2953.4   TP for DSS2

Q.2957.1   Stage 3 Description for Additional Information Transfer Supplementary Services Using B-ISDN Digital Subscriber Signaling System No. 2 (DSS 2)—Basic Call: Clause 1—User-to-User Signaling (UUS)

Q.2971   Digital Subscriber Signaling System No. 2 (DSS2)—User–Network Interface Layer 3 Specification for Point-to-Multipoint Call/Connection

21.2   ETSI (European Telecommunications Standards Institute)

Since 1980 work has been in progress under the auspices of the European Union to develop applicable standards for telecommunications throughout Europe. These European standards are published by the European Telecommunications Standards Institute, founded in 1988 (*http://www.etsi.org/*).

The European standards are usually based on the corresponding international recommendations, specifically adapted for European requirements. The ETSI working group responsible for B-ISDN and ATM is NA-5 (Network Aspects). The following pertinent documents have been published to date.

B-ISDN

ETS 300 298-1   Broadband Integrated Services Digital Network (ISDN); Asynchronous Transfer Mode (ATM); Basic characteristics and functional specification of ATM; Part 1: B-ISDN ATM functional specification

ETS 300 298-2   Broadband Integrated Services Digital Network (ISDN); Asynchronous Transfer Mode (ATM); Basic characteristics and functional specification of ATM; Part 2: B-ISDN ATM layer specification

I-ETS 300 464   Asynchronous Transfer Mode (ATM); Broadband Integrated Services Digital Network (B-ISDN); ATM layer cell transfer performance for B-ISDN connection types

I-ETS 300 353   Broadband Integrated Services Digital Network (B-ISDN); Asynchronous Transfer Mode (ATM) Adaptation layer (AAL) specification—type 1

ETS 300 349   Broadband Integrated Services Digital Network (B-ISDN); Asynchronous Transfer Mode (ATM) Adaptation layer (AAL) specification—type 3/4

ETS 300 428   Broadband Integrated Services Digital Network (B-ISDN); Asynchronous Transfer Mode (ATM) Adaptation layer (AAL) specification—type 5

ETS 300 354   Broadband Integrated Services Digital Network (B-ISDN); B-ISDN Protocol Reference Model (PRM) ETS 300 301: Broadband Integrated Services Digital Network (B-ISDN); Traffic control and congestion control in B-ISDN

I-ETS 300 404   Broadband Integrated Services Digital Network (B-ISDN); B-ISDN Operation and Maintenance (OAM) principles and functions

ETR 072   Broadband Integrated Services Digital Network (B-ISDN); Connection types and their reference configurations

ETR 073   Broadband Integrated Services Digital Network (B-ISDN); Evolution toward B-ISDN

ETR 089   Broadband Integrated Services Digital Network (B-ISDN); Principles and requirements for signaling and management information transfer

ETR 118   Broadband Integrated Services Digital Network (B-ISDN); Switching, exchange, and cross-connect functions and performance requirements

ATM

ETR 155   Asynchronous Transfer Mode (ATM); Operation Administration and Maintenance (OAM) functions and parameters for assessing performance parameters

CBDS/ATM

ETR 122   Network Aspects (NA); Connectionless Broadband Data Service (CBDS); CBDS over Asynchronous Transfer Mode (ATM)

prETS 300 478 Network Aspects (NA); Connectionless Broadband Data Service (CBDS) over Asynchronous Transfer Mode (ATM); Framework and protocol specification at the User–Network Interface (UNI); Part 1: Specification

prETS 300 479 Network Aspects (NA); Connectionless Broadband Data Service (CBDS) over Asynchronous Transfer Mode (ATM); Framework and protocol specification at the User–Network Interface (UNI); Part 2: Protocol Implementation Conformance Statement (PICS) proforma

Signaling AAL

ETR 117   Broadband Integrated Services Digital Network (B-ISDN); Asynchronous Transfer Mode (ATM) signaling ATM Adaptation layer (AAL) requirements

prETS 300 436-1 Broadband Integrated Services Digital Network (B-ISDN); signaling ATM Adaptation Layer (SAAL); Q.2110 B-ISDN ATM Adaptation Layer—Service-Specific Connection-Oriented Protocol (SSCOP); Part 1: Protocol specification [ITU-T Recommendation Q.2110 (1995), modified]

prETS 300 437-1 Broadband Integrated Services Digital Network (B-ISDN); Signaling ATM Adaptation Layer (SAAL); Service-Specific Coordination Function (SSCF) for support of signaling at the User–Network Interface (UNI); Part 1: Specification of SSCF at UNI [ITU-T Recommendation Q.2130 (1995), modified]

prETS 300 438-1 Broadband Integrated Services Digital Network (B-ISDN); Signaling ATM Adaptation Layer (SAAL); Service-Specific Coordination Function (SSCF) for support of signaling at the Network Node Interface (NNI); Part 1: Specification of SSCF at NNI [ITU-T Recommendation Q.2140 (1995), modified]

SDH

ETS 300 337   Transmission and Multiplexing (TM); Generic frame structures for the transport of various signals (including

Asynchronous Transfer Mode [ATM] cells and Synchronous Digital Hierarchy [SDH] elements) at the CCITT Recommendation G.702 hierarchical rates of 2048 kbit/s, 34,368 kbit/s, and 139,264 kbit/s

21.3   ANSI (American National Standards Institute)

ANSI is the North American standardization body, founded in 1918 (*http://web.ansi.org/*). Its membership currently comprises some 1,300 national and international companies, 30 administrative agencies, and 250 commercial, technical, and consumer associations.

ANSI is comparable with the European ETSI. Its purpose, in addition to the development of national standards, is to adapt international standards to North American conditions.

ANSI
Attention: Customer Service
11 West 42nd St.
New York, NY 10036
USA

21.4   The ATM Forum

The ATM Forum was founded in September 1991, by Cisco Systems, NET/Adaptive, Northern Telecom, and US Sprint. During its time of greatest activity, it had over 700 principle member organizations and has, at time of writing, approaching 170 interoperability agreements (specifications). The purpose of the ATM Forum is to ensure, through close cooperation with official standardization bodies, that suggestions from industry are considered in designing standards, rather than leaving the standardization of ATM up to the ITU-T alone. Furthermore, ATM Forum specifications are intended to serve as industry standards in areas not covered by existing standards. This allows companies to develop products more quickly on the basis of quasi-standards without waiting for the conclusion of ITU-T decision-making processes, which are often slow. One of the first activities of the ATM Forum was the development of UNI 2.0, an extended specification based on the ITU-T UNI standard, adopted in June 1992. The ITU-T had initially defined only SDH-based interfaces for the physical communication layer. UNI 2.0 extended the corresponding recommendations for transporting ATM cells over the existing North American DS3 PDH interface, and defined the 100 Mbit/s TAXI interface for local area ATM networks and the 155 Mbit/s Fiber Channel ATM interface (neither of the latter two interfaces survives today).

The UNI 3.0 and UNI 3.1 specifications followed in 1993 and 1994, introducing ATM signaling specifications for switched virtual circuits (SVCs) for the first time; UNI 4.0 signaling was introduced in 1996 and UNI 4.1 in 2002. Over the same period, a number of stand-alone specifications was introduced to allow ATM to be operated over a wide range of physical interfaces, including the first standard to define local area ATM over twisted-pair cabling. Other important specifications for private ATM networks followed, including PNNI, LANE, and MPOA.

The organization of the ATM Forum comprises the Technical Committee, three marketing committees, and an ATM User Committee (also known as the "Enterprise Network Roundtable," or ENR). The ATM Forum's technical specifications are drafted by the 13 working groups of the Worldwide Technical Committee. Development work takes place in coordination with other standardization bodies, such as the ITU, in order to eliminate discrepancies between existing specifications and to create new standards in areas that are not sufficiently defined.

Working Groups of the Worldwide Technical Committee

ATM–IP Collaboration

Control Signaling

Frame-Based ATM

Network Management

Physical Layer

Residential Broadband

Routing and Addressing

Security

Service Aspects and Applications

Testing

Traffic Management

Voice and Telephony Over ATM

Wireless ATM

The Market Awareness Committees are responsible for coordinating marketing and educational activities that promote the spread of ATM technologies. In addition to organizing events, the committees create presentations and technical documents on all aspects of ATM.

Working Groups of the Asia-Pacific Market Awareness Committee

Education

Interoperability Demo

Marketing Communications

Working Groups of the European Market Awareness Committee

Information and Promotion

Education

Implementation, Market, and Services

Working Groups of the Americas Market Awareness Committee

Education

Interoperability Test and Demo

Marketing Communications

Market Requirements

Residential and Small Business

In 1993, the ATM Forum founded the ATM User Committee. The purpose of this forum is to ensure that the ATM specifications meet the needs that arise in actual practice by maintaining a dialog with ATM users.

Working Groups of the User Committee

European Activities

Marketing Communications

Technical Communications

Worldwide Communications

The ATM Forum makes its decisions by a two-thirds majority of all voting members. As an alternative to full membership, which costs about $5,000 in annual dues, organizations may become auditing members, with dues of about $2,500. Auditing members cannot vote, but receive all documents of the ATM Forum, including drafts and minutes.

ATM Forum Addresses

Worldwide Headquarters
Presedio of San Francisco
Building 572B (surface)
P.O. Box 29920 (mail)
San Francisco, CA
94129-0920 USA
Tel. +1 415 561 6275
Fax. +1 415 561 6120
www.atmforum.com
info@atmforum.com

European Office
Parkshot House
5 Kew Road
Richmond, Surrey TW9 2PR
United Kingdom
Tel. +44(0) 20 8334 8069
Fax +44(0) 20 8334 8880
mccue@atmforum.com

Asia-Pacific Office
Hamamatsucho Suzuki Building 3F
1-2-11, Hamamatsucho, Minato-ku
Tokyo 105-0013, Japan
Tel. +81 3 3438 3694
Fax. +81 3 3438 3698
apinfo@atmforum.com

The ATM Forum publishes a quarterly newsletter called 53 *Bytes,* which can be ordered from the ATM Forum or obtained from the ATM Forum Internet site: *http://www.atmforum.com/atmforum/library/53bytes/current/52title.html.*

ATM Forum specifications in print form can be ordered online at *http://www.atmforum.com/atmforum/store/spec_order.html* or from the ATM Forum offices.

The specifications are available in electronic form free of charge; for listing by name and Working Group, go to: *http://www.atmforum.com/ techspecfs1.html* or for a complete list by number from the ATM Forum's FTP server, *ftp://ftp.atmforum.com/pub/.*

The most important ITU-T ATM standards are listed below.

B-ICI

B-ICI 2.0 Addendum or 2.1	af-bici-0068.000	November 1996

Frame-Based ATM

Frame-based ATM (FATE)	af-fbatm-0139.000	March 2000
Frame-based ATM over SONET/ SDH Transport (FAST)	af-fbatm-0151.000	July 2000

ILMI (Integrated Local Management Interface)

ILMI 4.0	af-ilmi-0065.000	September 1996

Lan Emulation/MPOA

LANE v2.0 LUNI Interface	af-lane-0084.000	July 1997
Multi-Protocol Over ATM Specification v1.1	af-mpoa-0114.000	May 1999

Physical Layer

ATM Physical Medium Dependent Interface Specification for 155 Mb/s over Twisted-Pair Cable	af-phy-0015.000	September 1994
DS1 Physical Layer Specification	af-phy-0016.000	September 1994
E3 UNI	af-phy-0034.000	August 1995
622.08 Mbps Physical Layer	af-phy-0046.000	January 1996
155.52 Mbps Physical Layer Specification for Category 3 UTP	af-phy-0047.000	September 1994
DS3 Physical Layer Interface Specification	af-phy-0054.000	March 1996
E-1 Physical Layer Interface Specification	af-phy-0064.000	September 1996
155 Mbps over Plastic Optical Fiber (POF) 1.1	af-phy-0079.001	January 1999
2.4 Gbps Physical Layer Specification	af-phy-0133.000	October 1999
Inverse Multiplexing for ATM 1.1	af-phy-0086.001	March 1999
ATM on fractional E1/T1	af-phy-0130.000	July 1999

P-NNI

P-NNI V1.0	af-pnni-0055.000	March 1996
PNNI V1.1	af-pnni-0055.002	April 2002
PNNI V1.0 Errata and PICS	af-pnni-0081_000	May 1997
PNNI Augmented Routing (PAR) Version 1.0	af-ra-0104_000	January 1999
PNNI Version 1.0 Security Signaling Addendum	af-cs-0117.000	May 1999
PNNI Addendum for Mobility Extensions Version 1.0	af-ra-0123_000	May 1999
PNNI Addendum for Generic Application Transport v1.0	af-cs-0126_000	July 1999
PNNI SPVC Addendum Version 1.0	af-cs-0127_000	July 1999

Security

ATM Security Specification 1.1	af-sec-0100.002	March 2001

Signaling

UNI Signaling 4.0	af-sig-0061.000	July 1996
UNI Signaling 4.1	af-sig-0061.002	April 2002
Signaling ABR Addendum	af-sig-0076.000	January 1997
UNI Signaling 4.0 Security Addendum	af-cs-0117_000	May 1999
ATM Inter-Network Interface (AINI) Specification	af-cs-0125_000	July 1999
PHY-MAC Identifier Addendum to UNI Signaling 4.0	af-cs-0135_000	November 1999

Testing

PICS Proforma for the DS3 Physical Layer Interface	af-test-0023_000	September 1994
PICS Proforma for the SONET STS-3c Physical Layer Interface	af-test-0024_000	September 1994
PICS Proforma for the 100Mbps Multimode Fiber Physical Layer Interface	af-test-0025_000	September 1994

PICS Proforma for the UNI 3.0 ATM Layer	af-test-0028_000	April 1995
Conformance Abstract Test Suite for the UNI 3.0 ATM Layer of Intermediate Systems	af-test-0030_000	April 1995
Interoperability Abstract Test Suite for the ATM Layer	af-test-0035_000	April 1995
Interoperability Abstract Test Suites for the Physical Layer	af-test-0036_000	April 1995
PICS Proforma for the DS1 Physical Layer Interface	af-test-0037_000	April 1995
Conformance Abstract Test Suite for the UNI 3.0 ATM Layer of End Systems	af-test-0041_000	July 1995
PICS for AAL-5	af-test-0042_000	August 1995
PICS Proforma for the 51.84 Mbps Mid-range Physical Layer Interface	af-test-0044_000	November 1995
Conformance Abstract Test Suite for the UNI 3.1 ATM Layer of Intermediate Systems	af-test-0045_000	November 1995
PICS Proforma for the 25.6 Mbps over Twisted-Pair Cable Physical Layer Interface	af-test-0051_000	March 1996
Conformance Abstract Test Suite for the ATM Adaptation Layer (AAL) Common Part	af-test-0052_000	March 1996
PICS Proforma for the UNI 3.1 ATM Layer	af-test-0059_000	July 1996
Conformance Abstract Test Suite for the UNI 3.0 ATM Layer of End Systems	af-test-0060_000	July 1996
SSCOP Conformance Abstract Test Suite Version 1.1	af-test-0067_001	May 1999
PICS Proforma for the 155 Mbps over Twisted-Pair Cable Physical Medium Dependent Interface.doc	af-test-0070_000	November 1996

PICS Proforma of the DS3 Direct Mapped Physical Layer Interface	af-test-0082_000	May 1997
ATS for UNI 3.1 Signaling for the Network Side	af-test-0090_000	September 1997
ATM Test Access Function (ATAF)	af-test-nm-0094_000	February 1998
PICS Proforma for UNI 3.1 Signaling (User Side)	af-test-cs-0097_000	April 1998
Interoperability Test for PNNI Version 1.0	af-test-csra-0111_000	February 1999
PICS Proforma for UNI 3.1 Signaling (Network Side)	af-test-csra-0118_000	May 1999
ATM Forum Performance Testing Specification	af-test-tm-0131.000	October 1999
Implementation Conformance Statement (ICS) Proforma Style Guide	af-test-0137_000	February 2000
Conformance ATS for PNNI Routing	af-test-0155.000	October 2000
Conformance ATS for PNNI Signaling	af-test-0156.000	October 2000
Conformance ATS for Available Bit Rate (ABR) Source and Destination Behaviors	af-test-tm-0157.000	January 2000
UNI Signaling Performance Test Suite	af-test-0158.000	October 2001
Introduction to ATM Forum Test Specifications, Version 2.0	af-test-0177.000	October 2001

Traffic Management

Traffic Management 4.1	af-tm-0121.000	March 1999
Addendum to TM 4.1— Differentiated UBR	af-tm-0149.000	July 2000
Addendum to Traffic Management V4.1 for an Optional Minimum Desired Cell Rate Indication for UBR	af-tm-0150.000	July 2000

Voice and Multimedia over ATM

Loop Emulation Service Using AAL-2	af-vmoa-0145.000	July 2000

Voice and Telephony over ATM

Circuit Emulation Service Interoperability Specification V2.0	af-vtoa-0078_000	January 1997
Voice and Telephony Over ATM to the Desktop	af-vtoa-0083.000	May 1997
Specifications of (DBCES) Dynamic Bandwidth Utilization —in 64kbps Time Slot Trunking over ATM—using CES	af-vtoa-0085_000	July 1997
ATM Trunking using AAL1 for Narrowband Services V1.0	af-vtoa-0089_000	July 1997
ATM Trunking using AAL2 for Narrowband Services	af-vtoa-0113_000	February 1999
Low Speed Circuit Emulation Service (LSCES)	af-vtoa-0119_000	May 1999
ICS Proforma for ATM Trunking using AAL2 for Narrowband Services	af-vtoa-0120_000	May 1999
Low Speed Circuit Emulation Service (LSCES) Implementation Conformance Statement Proforma	af-vtoa-0132_000	October 1999

User–Network Interface (UNI)

ATM User–Network Interface Specification V2.0	af-uni-0010.000	June 1992
ATM User–Network Interface Specification V3.0	af-uni-0010.001	September 1993
ATM User–Network Interface Specification V3.1	af-uni-0010.002	August 1994

21.5   The Internet Society (ISOC)

As a powerful technology for high-speed wide area and local area data networks, ATM was adopted very early on by operators and organizers of the worldwide Internet for data communication on Internet backbones. This development resulted in the creation of Internet standards to describe the transportation of the Internet Protocol (IP) over ATM. Internet standards are developed by the various organizations grouped under the umbrella of the Internet Society (ISOC). The purpose of ISOC is to coordinate the ongoing international development of the Internet, and to improve and expand existing services. Activities of the ISOC organizations are reported in a quarterly publication, the Internet Society News. ISOC members meet at an annual conference, INET. Current information about the various activities of the ISOC are available from the Internet Society's World Wide Web server (*http://www.isoc.org/*).

Since 1983, the development of technical strategies and guidelines for the Internet has been overseen by the Internet Architecture Board (IAB, *http://www.iab.org/*). Today the IAB is a technical advisory group of the Internet Society. Developmental activities are divided among two main bodies, the Internet Engineering Task Force (IETF) and the Internet Research Task Force (IRTF). The IETF is responsible for short- and medium-term projects, while the IRTF deals with long-term research. Each of these bodies is organized in a number of working groups for specific tasks. Since the 1990s the IETF and IRTF working groups have become increasingly international. One of the IETF's most important tasks is the development of potential Internet standards, published as RFCs (Requests for Comments). These documents bring together ideas and technical details developed in a great number of working groups. There are currently over 80 working groups drafting IETF documents with more than 700 members (*http://www.ietf.org/*). Among the RFCs published to date, which describe the use of ATM with Internet technologies, are:

2684	Multiprotocol Encapsulation over ATM Adaptation Layer 5 (Status: PROPOSED STANDARD)
2226	IP Broadcast over ATM Networks (Status: PROPOSED STANDARD)
2225	Classical IP and ARP over ATM (Status: PROPOSED STANDARD)

2170	Application REQuested IP over ATM (AREQUIPA) (Status: INFORMATIONAL)
2149	Multicast Server Architectures for MARS-based ATM multicasting (Status: INFORMATIONAL)
2107	Ascend Tunnel Management Protocol—ATMP (Status: INFORMATIONAL)
2098	Toshiba's Router Architecture Extensions for ATM: Overview (Status: INFORMATIONAL)
2022	Support for Multicast over UNI 3.0/3.1-based ATM Networks (Status: PROPOSED STANDARD)
1954	Transmission of Flow Labeled IPv4 on ATM Data Links Ipsilon Version 1.0 (Status: INFORMATIONAL)
1946	Native ATM Support for ST2+ (Status: INFORMATIONAL)
1932	IP over ATM: A Framework Document (Status: INFORMATIONAL)
1926	An Experimental Encapsulation of IP Datagrams on Top of ATM (Status: INFORMATIONAL)
1821	Integration of Real-time Services in an IP-ATM Network Architecture (Status: INFORMATIONAL)
1755	ATM Signaling Support for IP over ATM (Status: PROPOSED STANDARD)
1754	IP over ATM Working Group's Recommendations for the ATM Forum's Multiprotocol BOF Version 1 (Status: INFORMATIONAL)
1695	Definitions of Managed Objects for ATM Management Version 8.0 using SMIv2 (Status: PROPOSED STANDARD)
1680	IPng Support for ATM Services (Status: INFORMATIONAL)
1626	Default IP MTU for use over ATM AAL5 (Status: PROPOSED STANDARD)

21.6 The Internet Engineering Task Force (IETF)

The IETF is the organization responsible for standardizing the Internet. These days it focuses mainly on non-ATM technologies and protocols such as Packet over SONET/SDH (PoS) and MPLS (Multi-Protocol Label Switching). In the past, however, it played an important role in adapting ATM for use with the Internet Protocol (IP). In particular, two famous RFCs (Requests for Comment) were developed: RFC 1483 (now replaced by RFC 2684)—Multi-Protocol Encapsulation over ATM Adaptation Layer 5, and RFC 1577 (now replaced by RFC 2225)—Classical IP and ARP over ATM.

INDEX

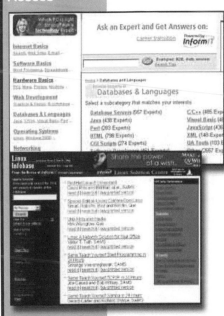

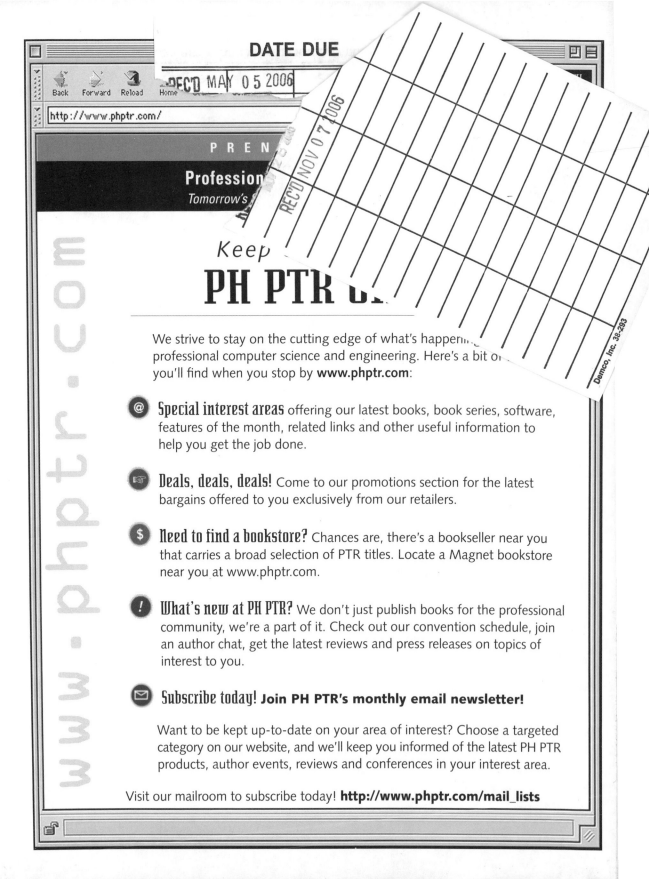